D1559486

AMERICAN FOLK MUSIC AND MUSICIANS SERIES
Edited by Ronald D. Cohen and Ralph Lee Smith

1. *Wasn't That a Time!: Firsthand Accounts of the Folk Music Revival,* edited by Ronald D. Cohen. 1995.
2. *Appalachian Dulcimer Traditions,* by Ralph Lee Smith. 1997.
3. *Ballad of an American: The Autobiography of Earl Robinson,* by Earl Robinson with Eric A. Gordon. 1998.
4. *American Folk Music and Left-Wing Politics,* 1927–1957, by Richard A. Reuss with JoAnne C. Reuss. 2000.
5. *The Unbroken Circle: Tradition and Innovation in the Music of Ry Cooder and Taj Majal,* by Fred Metting. 2000.

American Folk Music and Left-Wing Politics, 1927–1957

Richard A. Reuss with JoAnne C. Reuss

American Folk Music and Musicians Series, No. 4

The Scarecrow Press, Inc.
Lanham, Maryland, and London
2000

285471

SCARECROW PRESS, INC.

Published in the United States of America
by Scarecrow Press, Inc.
4720 Boston Way, Lanham, Maryland 20706
http://www.scarecrowpress.com

4 Pleydell Gardens, Folkestone
Kent CT20 2DN, England

Adapted from Richard Reuss's doctoral dissertation, submitted to Indiana
University in 1971.

British Library Cataloguing in Publication Information Available

Library of Congress Cataloging-in-Publication Data

Reuss, Richard A.
   American folk music and left-wing politics, 1927-1957 / Richard A. Reuss ;
with JoAnne C. Reuss.
      p.   cm. — (American folk music and musicians series ; no. 4)
   ISBN 0-8108-3684-X (cloth : alk. paper)
   1. Folk music—Political aspects—United States.   I. Reuss, JoAnne C.,
1942-   II. Title.   III. American folk music and musicians ; no. 4.

ML3918.F65 R48 2000
781.62'1301599—dc21   00-023240

∞™ The paper used in this publication meets the minimum requirements of
American National Standard for Information Sciences—Permanence of
Paper for Printed Library Materials, ANSI/NISO Z39.48-1992.
Manufactured in the United States of America

Contents

Editor's Foreword

Ralph Lee Smith launched The American Folk Music and Musicians series in 1995 with *Wasn't That A Time!: Firsthand Accounts of the Folk Music Revival*, a compilation of essays drawn from the 1991 Richard Reuss Memorial Folk Music Conference, held at Indiana University. Reuss, a folklorist and music historian, had written extensively concerning folk music, Woody Guthrie, folklore, and so much more, but he had died suddenly in 1986 before witnessing publication of his revised Ph.D. dissertation, *American Folklore and Left-Wing Politics, 1927–1957* (Indiana University, 1971). Reuss's dissertation has been used extensively by countless scholars who have explored the connections between folk music and radical politics, as well as the development of the modern folk music revival (although not always with the necessary attribution). The work of these scholars, however, offers less complexity and perception than the Reuss dissertation. It follows that Reuss should be credited with pioneering the field.

Reuss's extensive publications, often appearing in obscure places, include *A Woody Guthrie Bibliography* (1968) and *Songs of American Labor, Industrialization, and the Urban Work Experience: A Discography* (1983), both monuments to his bibliographic deftness and broad interests. Archie Green, dean of labor folklorists, honored his friend with *Songs about Work: Essays in Occupational Culture for Richard A. Reuss* in 1993. Green's work is yet another fitting testimony to Reuss's scholarly contributions and legacy. Still, Reuss's 1971 dissertation remained his most singular achievement, although as the years passed (while its scope and documentation remained invaluable) it became increasingly outdated as numerous

studies appeared, covering similar topics and themes. Reuss, an in-
defatigable collector, had not only compiled a vast array of primary
written sources (now housed in the Richard A. Reuss collection in the
Indiana University Archives, Bloomington, Indiana), he had also interviewed dozens of individuals who soon passed from the scene.

Perhaps what is more striking is that in dealing with such a particularly
sensitive theme (the role of the Communist Party in musical matters from
the 1920s into the 1950s), Reuss took no partisan stance (always the *objec-
tive* scholar). Considering that the Cold War and accompanying Red Scare
have remained a fixture in American scholarship and politics, with little
consensus and much partisan feuding, Reuss walked a political tightrope
with the skills of a seasoned circus performer.

We are now most fortunate that JoAnne Reuss, Dick's widow, has taken
upon herself the arduous task of revising and updating the original dissertation. While not trained as a historian, she has taught herself the tools
of the trade, in attempting to spruce up the style while simultaneously
adding more recent information and references so that this study remains
current three decades after its initial completion. The editors are proud
to add *American Folk Music and Left-Wing Politics, 1927–1957* to our ever-
growing list of titles that variously explore American folk music, broadly
defined. Dick Reuss's magisterial study is now readily accessible, more
readable, updated with the most recent scholarship, and outfitted with the
proper aids, such as illustrations and an index.

Ronald D. Cohen, Ralph Lee Smith, Ed Kahn
—Series Editors

Preface

American Folk Music and Left-Wing Politics, 1927–1957 has had a long history. Almost thirty years have passed since my husband Richard Reuss did the original research for this book—time enough for hindsight and subsequent scholarship to fill in the factual gaps and for scholars to reconsider the historical record, reconceptualize the author's analyses, and second-guess his sources. Yet the materials and ideas presented in Dick's history of American folk music and left-wing politics are as compelling, insightful, and valid today as when he formulated them.

What scholarly attributes account for such longevity? There are many, of course. In this case, the most important are the uncommon thoroughness with which Dick pursued his research and the intelligence and objectivity he brought to the analysis of sometimes ambiguous information and disparate ideas. A graduate student during the turmoil of the sixties, Dick was not immune to the difficult social questions being posed by so-called campus radicals. But as a student of history and human nature, he was not satisfied with slick responses designed to support a particular political position or answers not grounded in historical reality; and so he spent much of his graduate career relentlessly tracking down obscure sources of information and informants whose memories helped him understand what happened in those heady days of passionate left-wing political activity and union organizing. He conducted dozens of interviews with people who were participants in the events he chronicled and whose recollections had heretofore been neglected. And he did his homework. Asking carefully crafted questions illustrating his command of the history of the period, Dick was able to assure his informants that the information they contributed would be treated with utmost respect and fairness. A master at absorbing and remembering facts and details, Dick came to his interviews prepared to plumb memories and unearth recollections his interviewees thought they had forgotten.

Dick spent summers doing fieldwork in support of his research, immersing himself in the culture of folk music and left-wing activism. One summer he worked at *Sing Out!* magazine organizing the People's Songs collection, a golden opportunity for this young scholar to absorb the ethos of the era through exposure to publications and personalities of the left-wing folk music scene in New York. Like a detective in pursuit of obscure bits of evidence, he traveled all over the country interviewing performers and other participants in left-wing folk music activities, attending concerts, and visiting archives and libraries, from which he compiled an extraordinary collection of ephemeral source materials—broadsides, pamphlets, songbooks, mimeographed meeting handouts, organizations' official records, personal letters, and concert notes. He also logged uncountable hours in close, critical readings of numerous serial publications—newspapers, magazines, broadsides—many of which were short-lived and obscure. From this avalanche of primary source material, he was able to piece together not only the chronology of events presented in this book but, more important, the visions, attitudes, beliefs, purposes, and goals of those who participated in left-wing politics and folk music during the 1930s and 1940s—the singers and writers and organizers and union members whose activities made up such an important part of American cultural history.

American Folk Music and Left-Wing Politics, 1927–1957 began as Dick's doctoral dissertation, submitted to Indiana University in 1971. The University Press at Wayne State University in Detroit, where Dick was an assistant professor, was preparing to publish the work in response to positive reviews by several scholars. But in the 1970s radical dissent still erupted regularly on college campuses, controversy over left-wing politics persisted, and campus leaders had not forgotten the painful legacy of McCarthy witch-hunts. The press, under political pressure, ultimately decided the material was too controversial and so changed its plans. The work remained unpublished through the 1970s, while nevertheless being widely read and cited in academic publications, becoming something of an underground classic. In the mid-1980s, Dick began once again to prepare the manuscript for publication, revising and updating it to reflect subsequent scholarship. His untimely death in 1986 left it once again unfinished and unpublished. Since then, however, the dissertation has remained an important academic work, continually cited by students and scholars to inform studies in folklore and politics. In part inspired by a conference in 1991 at Indiana University on the roots of the folk song revival, organized by Ronald Cohen, renewed interest in publishing Dick's work developed. This book is the result.

American Folk Music and Left-Wing Politics, 1927–1957, entitled to suggest its most prominent themes, concerns an era in U.S. history when large groups of citizens were galvanized by social and economic circumstances to take charge of their lives and livelihoods, to seize control, some say, over how industry paid and treated workers and how politicians responded to their constituencies. Left-wing political activists and labor organizers pursued their goals with missionary zeal—and a strong belief in the power of folk music to spread the word and enlist supporters. Musicians stepped up to play a part in one of the most significant social movements of the twentieth century: left-wing politics and the establishment of labor unions.

The roots of this study go back to Dick's interest in folk music as a young college student in the early 1960s. Queried by one of his undergraduate history professors about why protest songs always seemed to be performed in the folk music idiom, Dick didn't have an answer. But he had an abiding interest in U.S. history, a passion for folk music, and the soul of a detective— he was determined to find an answer. Thus, his interest in politics, social history, and folk music coalesced into a determination to investigate the roots of left-wing interest in folklore and folk music.

In the decades immediately prior to Dick's investigations, academic folklorists had paid scant attention to political/topical folk music. John Greenway published *American Folksongs of Protest,* arguing that protest songs should be categorized as folklore. Most academics disagreed, especially during the 1950s and early 1960s when scholarship was dominated by anticommunist sentiments. Two major studies by David Noebel and R. Serge Denisoff denounced the use of traditional materials for political ends and argued that American topical songs were unduly influenced by communism.

Since the early 1970s, when Dick's dissertation was completed, scholarship on folk music, history, and politics has continued to produce excellent material. Most necessarily overlap in content with this book. But none contradict or supersede Dick's particular approach: a long, encompassing view, assessing the activities of a broad cross section of participants and noting the differences, similarities, and interactions of the many diverse participants. Works by Philip Foner, Michael Denning, and Robbie Lieberman provide excellent historical perspective and detailed descriptions of the sociocultural underpinnings of American politics and protest and labor song traditions. But Dick brings a folklorist's perspective to his analysis. He considers how the use of traditional materials evolved, how perspectives on the value of songs varied from group to group, and what combination of circumstances led to the use of traditional "folk" materials rather than the more ubiquitous popular genres.

Numerous biographies have been produced of most of the well-known players of the period, both musicians and political activists such as Pete Seeger John Lomax, Paul Robeson, and others. They, too, provide a rich source of personal information and historical detail that illuminate the methods and motives of participants in folk music and political events. All touch on some of the same content as *American Folk Music and Left-Wing Politics, 1927–1957* but, of course, focus attention on individuals' lives and how they personally influenced and were affected by historical events.

In describing the evolution of public performances of songs in the folk idiom for radical causes, Dick notes a distinct differentiation between northern, mostly urban, mostly middle-class radicals, whose concerns derived from core values of racial and economic equality for all and frustrations with the excesses of capitalism, and the southern, mostly rural, working-class radicals, whose activism derived more often from immediate hardship due to working conditions, strikes, and other realities. Rural and urban folk song performers and composers exhibited the same complaints about the evils of class distinctions and the excesses of capitalism, but their opinions were based on widely divergent personal experiences.

A particular strength of this book is its emphasis on song texts as illustrative of the passions of the labor organizers and political activists. Many were ephemeral, short-lived, and created for a purpose, but they demonstrate the intensity of the "revolutionary" fervor of the participants in the movement.

Except for some broad observations added by Dick as he prepared the work for publication, I have made little attempt to update the study to take account of recent scholarship or subsequent events in American history. The bibliography and footnotes have been updated to alert the reader to newer editions and recent scholarship. I did not deviate from Dick's original conception, analysis, and arguments. But I did selectively condense some sections, streamline the prose, incorporate many quotations into the text, and delete some lengthy citations from published literature while keeping the references in the footnotes. Overall, I have made every effort to maintain not only the precise meaning of the original manuscript but also the tone and emphasis.

I want to take this opportunity to acknowledge two colleagues whose generous contributions to the project are reflected on every page and without whom I could not have completed the book. Ronald Cohen, professor of history at Indiana University Northwest and author of numerous scholarly publications on folk and topical music, was instrumental in fostering my interest in embarking on the project. In 1991, Cohen organized a conference on the roots of the folk song revival and dedicated the meeting to Dick's memory. The impetus to proceed with preparing Dick's work for publication had its genesis at that conference. In the intervening years, it was Cohen's interest and persistence that prompted my decision to take on the task. He provided significant scholarly assistance and personal support throughout the process, for which he has my enduring gratitude. Early on, one of Dick's college-era friends, the late Jonathan Kwitny, a former journalist and superb writer of numerous books on American current events, provided valuable assistance by allowing me to use, and thereby learn from, his suggested revisions in an early draft.

This study reflects several significant scholarly contributions: Dick's reliance on rich and relatively inaccessible primary source material; his personal access to numerous participants in the events he chronicles; and the intelligence, sensitivity, and objectivity he brought to his interpretation of the information his interviewees offered. Thus, the work stands as a historic milestone in the ongoing scholarship and evolving understanding of one of the most evocative and challenging eras in American history.

On a personal note, the attributes I brought to the task of preparing my husband's work for publication are, first and foremost, an abiding admiration for Dick's keen and fair-minded intellect, which is at the heart of his work; second, an appreciation of what he taught me about human nature and American history, without which I would have been unable to complete this project; and third, my experience and skills as a writer, with which I hope I have managed to bring his work to successful fruition and into the hands of scholars and all other interested readers.

I think perhaps a sketch of Dick's "story" and his personal and scholarly ambitions may offer readers some additional insight into the roots of *American Folk Music and Left-Wing Politics, 1927–1957*.

Richard A. Reuss was born May 24, 1940, the elder of two sons in a middle-class New York family. His father was a banker who commuted daily on the train from suburban Long Island to his office in Manhattan. His mother was a homemaker until the boys were teens, then she attended college and subsequently went to work for the Methodist Church's Office of Missions. Dick's family championed hard work, democratic principles, the importance of helping the less fortunate, and the absolute necessity of treating all people with respect and kindness—indeed, the Golden Rule was the family compass. When as a teenager Dick discovered the Weavers, it is no surprise, then, that the content of their songs resonated so immediately and that he soon became an ardent fan. As a result, a lifelong passion for playing, singing, and studying folk music was born. Dick founded and led a folk-singing group, the Folkmeisters, at Shelter Island, where he was a camper and later employee for most summers in his youth. When he arrived at Ohio Wesleyan University in 1958, he again organized a folk song group, which continued throughout his undergraduate career.

Dick brought to his academic and professional pursuits talents for historical research and writing that seem to have emerged full-blown, even as a youngster. In third grade he edited and wrote articles for a class newsletter, interviewing classmates and reporting on school activities. He gathered "evidence" for his articles by collecting bits of classroom trivia from teachers, students, and even classmates' parents. The art of collecting and organizing was evident even in child's play—he and his brother amassed a collection of well over a hundred stuffed animals, a population that constituted the kingdom of Reussea, with its own history, government, and kinship system. Once baseball consumed his passion as a sandlot athlete, collecting baseball cards was the natural next pastime. From that lifelong hobby, Dick first encountered sports history and later branched out to American history.

So it was that Dick came to his graduate student career well prepared for the task of assembling an astonishing array of primary source materials for his analysis of the left-wing interest in folk music for propaganda purposes. Coupled with his uncompromising belief that fact- and motive-based understandings are the truest underpinning of historical analysis, what his much-admired mentor Archie Green described as "value-free empiricism," Dick approached his work like a hard-boiled detective, unencumbered with axes to grind and eager to uncover the facts, whatever they may be.

Throughout his academic career at Ohio Wesleyan and later at Indiana University, where he earned his Ph.D. in folklore, Dick cultivated and treasured the generous contributions of several mentors. First and foremost was Archie Green, a "fellow traveler" who shared Dick's passion for comprehending the truth about the cultural, political, and aesthetic lives of working-class Americans. Richard Dorson, Dick's doctoral committee chairman, did not share many of Dick's opinions about the functions of left-wing folk music and its place in folk traditions; indeed, Dorson disliked contemporary folk music. But in spite of their differences of opinion, Dorson encouraged his student's work and supported Dick throughout his academic career. His mentor and colleague at Wayne State University, Ellen Stekert, shared with Dick her experience in teaching, her love for folk music, and her contagious enthusiasm for the collection and analysis of urban folk traditions, kindling an interest in urban workers' traditions that underscored the remainder of Dick's academic pursuits. Finally, Dick met David King Dunaway in the mid-1970s, and they quickly established a gratifying and collegial relationship based on their mutual interest in the history of folk music and politics. Through extensive correspondence and phone contacts over the next decade, Dick and David shared ideas, insights, and information, contributing to each other's work through mutual respect and admiration. On Dick's behalf, I offer my profound gratitude for the gifts his colleagues offered to him during his too-short life.

JoAnne C. Reuss

Acknowledgments

Introduction

Unidentified, Alan Lomax, Sonny Terry, Brownie McGhee, Bess Lomax Hawes (l-r)
(courtesy of Bess Lomax Hawes)

In the summer of 1963, popular folk singer Pete Seeger arrived in Los Angeles to perform for a crowd of young concert-goers. Aware of Seeger's long association with radical social causes, a local organization known as the Fire and Police Research Association of Los Angeles, Inc., quickly passed a resolution calling for a congressional investigation of American folk music, and soon its members were busy circulating a pamphlet describing folk song as "an unidentified tool of Communist psychological or cybernetic warfare to ensnare and capture youthful minds."[1]

Barely a month later, the group had their response from Congress—not the investigation they anticipated, but a clever, satirical speech by Kenneth Keating, Republican senator from New York, designed to amuse his colleagues, provoke a response from journalists, and point out "the absurd lengths to which the amateur ferrets of the radical right will go in their quixotic sallies against the Communist menace." Reprinted in the

1

Congressional Record, Keating's speech was entitled "Mine Enemy—The Folk Singer."[2]

"Mr. President," he began, "it will come as a shock to many Senators, but according to a resolution of a certain Los Angeles civic organization the Communists have developed a new secret weapon to ensnare and capture youthful minds in America—folk music."

Keating was aware that the prevailing American attitude toward communism was decidedly antagonistic, so he felt compelled to interrupt himself to assure his colleagues that he was not operating under "any illusions . . . about any possible letup in the intensity and earnestness of the Soviet pursuit toward its ultimate goal of world domination." "Nevertheless," he continued, "I am stunned by the revelation that folk music is part of the Communist arsenal of weapons. . . . I had always had the impression that if anything was thoroughly American in spirit, it was American folk music."

Keating realized

> that folk music tradition is grounded in movements of political, economic and social unrest. . . . I did not expect to find in music which originated among sharecroppers, miners, union organizers, factory workers, cowboys, hill folk, wanderers, and oppressed Negroes, a pattern of tribute and praise to such symbols of orthodoxy as the gold standard, the oil depletion allowance and the standing rules of the U.S. Senate.
>
> To be sure, I was perfectly aware of certain un-American influences in it, like Elizabethan balladry, English Protestant hymns and spirituals, and with respect to jazz and in some cases the Negro spiritual, native African rhythms. But in my naiveté I had never considered these un-American influences to be of a sinister nature, and simply passed them off as part and parcel of the melting-pot tradition, which has contributed so much in the way of variety and interest to the American cultural heritage.

But, Keating continued sarcastically, the Fire and Police Research Association had opened his eyes. He reported that he had assembled evidence of folk music's potential for mischief. As a sample, he produced for the Senate a verse to the quintessential American folk song "Yankee Doodle"—a verse written in 1808 as a protest against the trade embargo President Jefferson had imposed on American business to try to keep the United States out of the Napoleonic wars:

> I've got a vessel at the wharf, w'ell loaded with a cargo,
> And want a few more hands to help and clear the cursed Embargo.
> Yankee doodle, keep it up, Yankee doodle, dandy
> We'll soak our hide in home-made rum if we can't get French brandy.

"It seems perfectly obvious to me," Keating asserted,

that if people went around singing this today, we would be in a pretty fix with our shipping ban against Castro. Before we knew it, we would have rum-running out of Cuba in American bottoms. Already there are signs that the Communists are going beyond folk music in their plot to subvert America . . . Consider for a moment the inroads which have been made into the popular music field by such songs as "The Moon Belongs to Everyone/The Best Things in Life are Free."

Keating continued by converting sarcasm to burlesque, citing "evidence" from American folk and topical song tradition in "support" of the contentions of the Los Angeles Fire and Police Research Association. But in closing, he forsook comedy to express serious concerns:

Vigilante charges such as these can breed the atmosphere of suspicion and confusion, which tends not only to undermine free institutions, but, of equal concern, to divert our energies from tackling the real threats posed by international communism to our liberty and security. With devotion to our freedoms, with trust in the American ideal of cultural diversity, and with, above all, a sense of proportion and discernment in meeting the challenges of our times, I for one have every faith that—in the words of the inspiring song—"we shall overcome."

Keating's speech and plea for tolerance were enthusiastically applauded by the vast majority of commentators—although Georgia's Richard Russell grumbled over his colleague's omission of any mention of "Dixie." But the anticommunist militants, popularly dubbed the "Radical Right," remained eager to keep in the public eye the American communist concern with folk songs and folk singers as purveyors of left-wing propaganda. One, Jere Real, writing for the John Birch Society periodical *American Opinion,* disavowed Keating's casual dismissal of the issue. Real cited dubious evidence in popular magazines and before the House Un-American Activities Committee, implicating nearly every popular folk singer of the past three decades as a conspirator.

Real's tone was one of genuine alarm:

Along with the handclapping, the guitar strumming, the banjo-picking, the shouting and the howling, comes a very subtle but highly effective presentation of standard Communist Party propaganda. Not since the 1930s have so many young people of the United States been so directly, so cleverly, deceived into a widespread parroting of the Communist line.[3]

Another well-known and widely read anticommunist, Herbert Philbrick, a former FBI undercover agent, anticommunist informer, and author of the best-selling memoir *I Led Three Lives,* developed the same theme in an article published in a religious anthology in 1966.[4] The book was called *Your Church—Their Target,* and Philbrick entitled his article "Subverting Youth with Folksinging."

David Noebel, once a young minister in Billy James Hargis's Christian Crusade, observed in a similar vein, "The Communist infiltration into the subversion of American music has been nothing short of phenomenal and in some areas, e.g. folk music, their control is fast approaching the saturation point under the able leadership of Pete Seeger, *Sing Out!,* Folkways Records and Oak Publications, Inc." Noebel went on to spend several years attacking alleged communist folk singers and folk song publishers. During the 1960s, his endeavors included numerous magazine articles (some in *Christian Crusade*); a national speaking tour; a pamphlet entitled *Communism, Hypnotism and the Beatles;* and a 1966 book originally entitled *Rhythm, Riots and Revolution,* which was revised in 1974 and reissued as *The Marxist Minstrels: A Handbook on Communist Subversion of Music.*[5]

Noebel's many writings on the communist plot to spread propaganda using folk music pretend to a certain scholarship, offering copious "documentation" for his assertions. But the questionable quality of his evidence can be gathered from an example noted by Pete Seeger himself. On the cover of the first edition of Noebel's book was printed "Workingmen of all tongues unite—you have nothing to lose but your chains—you have a world to win. Vive la Revolution Sociale.—Pete Seeger." Expressing his amazement in his 1972 collection *The Incompleat Folksinger,* Seeger says, "When did I write or say that? It's just not my style." Noebel cited his source as Seeger's song collection *American Favorite Ballads.* Mystified, Seeger pulled his songbook from the shelf and found an illustration inserted by the publisher to accompany the text and score of the old union song "We Shall Not Be Moved." The picture was a line drawing of an old pre–World War I socialist banner containing the slogan Noebel had attributed to Seeger on the cover of his book! That slogan had derived from a period before Seeger was even born. In 1971, R. Serge Denisoff published an extensive critical examination of the communist movement's involvement with folk music. *Great Day Coming* details the Old Left's discovery and use of folk song materials. Rightists responded by describing the book as a left-wing statement confirming all their major contentions.

Were the anticommunists' fears wholly without merit? Were folk singers and folk music active purveyors of communist propaganda? Were the anticommunist militants and right-wing commentators expressing outrage and spreading warnings about a tempest in a teapot? Was the considerable power that the rightists wielded during the 1950s and early 1960s to ban public performances because of political affiliations and to prevent distribution of left-oriented publications an abrogation of citizens civil rights? The answer is, of course, yes and no, as is usually the case with social movements. Though it is absurd to speak of a "communist takeover" of American folk music, as the blacklisters of the 1950s did, it is also a distortion not to recognize the impact popular left-wing social movements in the past few generations had on the popularization of folk song in the United States.

Rural American folk song tradition, in itself, would be little if any different today had it never been discovered and acclaimed by portions of the communist movement in the 1930s. But the spread of folk music and traditions in urban centers definitely was influenced by the work of singers with a politically radical agenda. Though the Old Left itself fell apart in the 1950s, it managed to pass on its enthusiasm for traditional American music, both as an aesthetic form and as a propaganda medium, to a new generation of political activists. Leaders of civil rights marches, ban-the-bomb parades, and anti–Vietnam War demonstrations fell heir to the earlier Left's coupling of the folk song idiom with protest themes. Though less militantly, their successors in the 1970s and 1980s condemned pollution, strip mining, Watergate, and CIA intervention in Latin America in the same manner.

Mainstream America has become accustomed to the sight of well-known popular folk entertainers appearing on the campaign platforms of Democratic and liberal third-party candidates, from Lyndon Johnson, more certainly to Eugene McCarthy and George McGovern, on to Jesse Jackson and Jerry Brown. Occasionally Republican opponents have been so impressed by the success of these entertainers that they have fought fire with fire, assembling their own folk-styled ensembles. Barry Goldwater supporters in the 1964 presidential election produced a group, the Goldwaters, whose album *Folksongs to Bug the Liberals* (Greenleaf M101-63A) espoused 100 percent Americanism and lampooned the welfare state.

Many performers of traditional, nonpolitical folk songs on college campuses and in city coffeehouses were folk singers who were once a part of the Old Left. It was their performances that sparked the urban folk song revival in the years after World War II. Thus, the communist movement of the 1930s and 1940s did in fact contribute significantly to the popularization of folk music in the United States.

This book presents the growth of American radical political interest in folk traditions, particularly native folk song, as it emerged in the Depression generation and after, focusing on the period from the late 1920s to late 1950s, because that is when the intellectual theories linking folklore to "people's" culture (in the political sense) were developed.

More than anything else, this book analyzes historical events through the filter of a heretofore unspoken proposition—that folk songs and folklore constitute a form of cultural expression alternative to that found in published mass media and aristocratic "fine art," and that because folk tradition represents the creativity of the people, it is intrinsically more satisfying to them than pop culture or high art. All activists in political and social life, Marxists as well as members of the John Birch Society, must grapple with their relationship to the national experience, politically, socially, and philosophically, in their inevitable quest to carve out an identity. It may be that leftists' association with folk song and folklore was a natural outcome of their ongoing efforts to internalize American culture and values. And, to the extent that participants in the communist movement came from recent immigrant stock, absorbing American folk song and folklore is one way to assimilate into American society.

Americans traditionally have been uneasy about the radical impulses generated in their midst from regional, national, industrial, and social experiences. John Adams is said to have remarked that while patriots waged war with Britain for independence, fully a third of the American colonists kept both British and American flags in their attics. Historians have estimated that another third openly supported the Crown. Abolitionists of the pre–Civil War era were viewed by much of the public of their day less as champions of black liberties than as zealots who would go to virtually any lengths, including the disruption of the union, to bring an end to slavery. Greenback farmers and populist agitators provoked anxiety among business interests in the late nineteenth century with their calls for expanded currency and government regulation of railroads; labor organizers well into the twentieth century reaped scorn and bitter hatred in many of the same quarters for their heretical notions concerning the right of American working men to bargain collectively. The discomforting challenges to the nation's traditional axioms of government and morality posed by the New Left of the 1960s, and the accompanying changes wrought in American society, are self-evident.

Body politic perceptions of new political and social doctrines, regardless of their origins, are typically distrusted as foreign, or alien, and are therefore threatening. In the early folklore of many Americans, the alien immigrant, Jew, Catholic, and bomb-throwing anarchist led the parade of sinister bogeyman figures arriving from abroad. Particularly during the McCarthy era of the 1950s, the caricature of the faceless, treacherous Red Agent, slave to the international communist conspiracy, substituted for many earlier stereotypes.

Each succeeding generation and government have had to come to terms with such anxieties according to the dictates of its own times and psychic needs. Since the success of the Bolshevik Revolution in 1917, for example, popular attitudes toward Russia and communism have shifted repeatedly as American–Soviet relations have moved from initial hostility to periods of wary recognition and wartime cooperation, then to cold war, to more recent controversies over human rights, the meaning of détente and glasnost, and, with the collapse of communism, to tentative steps toward economic and political cooperation, even friendship. The process of reassessment of radical impulses and their impact on our lives continues with each new decade.

Throughout the more than half-century since the heyday of the communist movement in the United States during the Depression, controversy over its impact on American life and on folklore and folk songs has persisted. This effect can be seen in microcosm with regard to the treatment of the Old Left's interest in folk music by both scholars and popular writers who have often found it difficult to discuss the topic dispassionately and in any detail. In *American Folksongs of Protest* (1953), published at the height of the McCarthy era, John Greenway devoted one long chapter to then-contemporary labor balladeers Aunt Molly Jackson, Woody Guthrie, and Joe Glazer, but he omitted candid consideration of the impact of communist ideas on the work of Jackson and Guthrie and such earlier labor balladeers as Ella May Wiggins. Even a bland ten-page account of the work of the People's Songs organization in the late 1940s, which Greenway included in his doctoral dissertation (on which his book is based), was dropped entirely.

Oscar Brand, himself a participant in the left-wing folk music scene during the same period, was more candid in his 1962 book *The Ballad Mongers*. But he still glossed over many facts when reviewing the radical portion of the early folk song revival. Apparently, he wished to avoid naming specific individuals in that still-sensitive era and to come to terms with his own actions, having denounced to government investigators his former left-wing folk song milieu.

Less self-consciously, Josh Dunson, son of an Old Left family, acknowledged the left-wing roots behind much of the protest song activity of the early 1960s in *Freedom in the Air: Song Movements of the '60s* (1965). His matter-of-fact presentation is pleasing, but the volume is slim, focusing primarily on contemporary music, with little contextual discussion.

By far the most extensive treatment of the communist movement's involvement with folk music is R. Serge Denisoff's *Great Day Coming: Folk Music and the American Left* (1971). Denisoff reviews the Old Left's discovery and utilization of folk song materials, but from a sociological rather than historical perspective and with a Trotskyist bias, denouncing the Communist Party's influence on American left-wing political activities. Unfortunately, Denisoff uses predominantly secondary materials and communist press articles, rather than personal interviews.

Jerome Rodnitzky's *Minstrels in the Dawn: The Folk-Protest Singer as a Cultural Hero* (1976) is alternately forthright, then hesitant in its commen-

tary on the communist milieu's impact on such early urban protest singers as Woody Guthrie, but highly superficial in its overall attention to and
documentation of the Left's interest in folk song and folklore.[6]

Since the early 1970s, scholarship on folk music and politics has brought
forth an astounding number of excellent publications from the fields of
history and sociology. One exceptionally rich and detailed study by Philip
Foner, *Labor Songs of the Nineteenth Century,* provides invaluable insight
into the labor–protest song tradition that existed prior to the rise of the
twentieth-century communist movement. In his massive study of American culture, *The Cultural Front: The Laboring of American Culture in the Twentieth Century,* Michael Denning describes in impressive detail the sociocultural underpinnings of American politics and society that prevailed in
the 1930s and 1940s, including folklore and folk music traditions that influenced popular entertainment media. Robbie Lieberman, a young
scholar who found in Reuss a guide and mentor while doing research for
her doctoral dissertation, published *"My Song Is My Weapon:" People's
Songs, American Communism, and the Politics of Culture,* in 1989. While there
is much overlap between *American Folk Music and Left-Wing Politics* and
the Denning and Lieberman studies, they are more complementary than
repetitive. Each has its own strengths. Denning's book is broadly conceived and exceedingly rich in detail, but it lacks the folkloristic analysis
that underlies Reuss's presentation of the functions of musical traditions
in formulating participants' political worldview. Lieberman's analysis
focuses particularly on the development of left-wing music activities in
the 1940s, but from a narrower, more historical perspective, omitting the
longer sociopolitical context and the attention to details of song lyrics and
mass media materials.

In 1996, Ronald Cohen and Dave Samuelson released *Songs for Political
Action* (a ten-CD collection), which can be viewed as a companion piece
to this work. It includes a large-format book with an extensive essay on
the development of folk music and left-wing politics, a dazzling collection of photographs of participants in the movement, and detailed information on recording companies and recording sessions. It is a treasure
trove of material illustrating the evolution of traditional and topical songs
that were performed and published in support of political propaganda
and labor rallies. And with the passage of time has come an array of biographies and autobiographies of participants such as Lee Hays, Charles
Seeger, Ruth Crawford Seeger, John Lomax, Will Geer, Earl Robinson,
Woody Guthrie, Aunt Molly Jackson, Paul Robeson, Pete Seeger, Lead
Belly, and Moe Asch, all of which touch on people and events described
in this work. Most notable from the folklore perspective is David King
Dunaway's superb biography of Peter Seeger, *How Can I Keep from Singing,* which takes advantage of the folklorist's sensibility in conducting and

analyzing interviews and interpreting a major participant's complex relationships to the left-wing movement and to his fellow folk singers. A forthcoming book, *Rainbow Quest: Folk Music and American Society, 1940–1970* by Ronald Cohen, also overlaps somewhat with this study, continuing the story of the folk song revival through the turbulent 1960s.

For their part, academic folklorists have mostly ignored or rejected consideration of the folk-styled songs composed by radicals, labor organizers, and "citybillies" of the 1930s as politically suspect and beyond their scholarly purview. The late George Korson, a pioneer industrial folklorist and author of several books on mining lore, consciously excluded from his collections any songs that were "written by an outsider."

"I had to be especially careful," Korson wrote to a colleague, "because in the 1920s and 1930s the Communists were making a determined effort to capture the United Mine Workers of America, and some of the songs were composed by their organizers."[7] To Korson, instead of inspiring discussion of an interesting social and historical phenomenon, the source simply justified tossing out the song.

Some folklorists were so conservative that they refused to acknowledge the popularity of certain folk songs, believing it their duty to thwart what they saw as an attempt by radicals to manipulate folk traditions for political ends. Still more were indifferent or hostile to such songs because of the self-imposed limitations of their field of study; they were interested only in "pure" folk songs, uncontaminated by commercial or political exploitation. They were uninterested in songs of known authorship or recent origin.

When the first academic collection of industrial and protest material appeared in 1953—John Greenway's *American Folksongs of Protest*—Stith Thompson, then dean of folklore studies in the United States, expressed his outrage in the *American Historical Review*:

> Here is a book called *American Folksongs* which contains not a single example of what a competent folklorist would call by that name. Folk songs are songs that are traditional, that are handed down from singer to listener and that are still alive. The songs in this collection are not anonymous and most of them are dead, preserved only in museums. They are not and never were folk songs.[8]

For Thompson, the fact that most of the songs were not traditional was enough to dismiss the collection as irrelevant to folklore studies. He exhibited no curiosity about the context or function of the songs, why they and not others were amenable to the protest genre, or why they sometimes fell out of use. Nor did he bother to distinguish, as Korson had, between compositions created by outsiders and those created by indigenous labor songsmiths. This academic stance gradually shifted, of course, as evidenced by later scholarly works such as Henry Glassie's treatment of folk song creators in *Folksongs and Their Makers* (1971).

A very few professional folklorists of the era, such as Benjamin Botkin, were openly sympathetic to the work (though not necessarily the ideology) of left-wing folk song activists of the Popular Front and People's Songs milieus of the 1930s and 1940s. Others for a time were willing to meet occasionally with representatives of such groups to discuss folk songs.

The high-water mark of such cooperation was at two conferences entitled "Folklore in a Democracy" and "Folklore in the Metropolis," held a year apart at the close of World War II. Scholars and popularizers, radicals and political middle-of-the-roaders gathered to discuss "the place of folklore in the education, the literature, the popular arts in a democracy" and the varieties of New York City folk traditions.[9] With the onset of the cold war and the McCarthy era, however, most of the few academic folklorists who had taken an interest in such topics ceased to maintain any visible communication with left-wing folk song enthusiasts. The urban folk singers were left, instead, to the researches of the House Un-American Activities Committee and the Christian Crusade.

In its 1955 hearing, the House Committee cited two Weavers' songs as communist inspired. One was a rather innocuous look at American history called "Wasn't That a Time," whose first three verses salute victories by the U.S. Army over, in order, King George III, the Confederacy, and Nazi Germany; the fourth and final verse endorses in only the most general terms the ideal of international cooperation:

> Our faith cries out; we have no fear
> We dare to reach our hands to other neighbors far and near
> To friends in every land; isn't this a time
> A time to free the soul of man; isn't this a wonderful time.

The second song cited as communist derived during the House Un-American Activities Committee hearing was "If I Had a Hammer," which by 1963 had been turned into a national hit by the popular group Peter, Paul, and Mary. Later, recorded in Latin rhythm, it rose to the top of popular charts again; millions of high school students danced to it from Juneau to Jacksonville. Yet, only a few years earlier, the House Un-American Activities Committee specifically used the allegedly subversive nature of this song to indict, convict, and sentence to prison its coauthor Pete Seeger.

In part because of such repression against reasonable, free speech, Harry Truman called the House committee "the most un-American thing in America." The committee's actions were extreme and, in retrospect, considered by most to be outside the constitutional scope of American government. Nevertheless, its activities reflected the ongoing uneasiness of most Americans with anything that seemed to sympathize with communist ideology.

Historically, of course, assimilating substantial portions of the ideologies of reformers and revolutionaries has been commonplace in the American experience, accomplished over time and often with little fanfare. Comprehending the diverse social forces and complex factual bases behind once unpopular movements, however, has proven a good deal more troublesome for contemporary commentators. Without the perspective of time and a chance to synthesize information, early accounts of reforms and revolutions written by partisans and critics alike, though often valuable, inevitably are circumscribed by the myopia and passions of the era. Such analyses generally have been left to historians and other scholars who have access to data and hindsight.

A vivid appreciation of the background dynamics of the Depression is of crucial importance in understanding the evolution of the Old Left. Many people whose experiences significantly inform the conclusions of this book expressed anxiety over this. One critic and well-known writer of the 1930s, for example, remarked of an earlier social history of the Left, "It is a book without a heart." In his opinion, the author's analysis caught too little of the intense excitement surrounding the issues under discussion, the air of immediacy hovering over intellectual arguments, the rampant idealism that a new and better society was in the offing.

Truly, the Franklin Roosevelt years were an era of cataclysmic social upheaval. Programs and policies frequently were worked out in the streets rather than in the conference or classrooms. At times the whole country appeared to be a living experimental laboratory. None who lived through those times remained unaffected by them, least of all those who made up the Old Left. For many, it was an age to fight and an era to dream, when, in the words of a participant, Irwin Silber, "We believed that the world was worth saving and that we could help do it with songs."[10]

In the case of the Old Left in the United States, particularly the communist movement, many former proponents are shy to speak frankly. Though decades have passed, participants' openness is still circumscribed by the unusual persecution many radicals of all kinds endured during the political repression of the 1950s. Gradually, however, later examinations began to supplant apologias and polemics of earlier decades: Richard H. Pells's *Radical Visions and American Dreams* (1973) and David Zane Mairowitz's *The Radical Soap Opera* (1974) offer fuller and somewhat less biased accounts of American communist activities. Even more recent treatments benefit from longer hindsight and additional data.[11]

As a matter of fact, the roots of this book trace to the late 1950s when, as an undergraduate folk music aficionado, Richard Reuss was eager to understand and internalize the musical and philosophical sensibilities of Woody Guthrie, Pete Seeger, the Weavers, *Sing Out!* magazine, and the *People's Songs* bulletin. The causes and issues they fought for over the years resonated with the writer's evolving social consciousness, provoking a lifelong interest in folklore and folk music as part of the cultural and political fabric of American life.

NOTES

1. *When Is Folk Music NOT Folk Music?* Pamphlet published by the Fire and Police Research Association (Los Angeles, 1963).

2. *Congressional Record,* 88th Congress, 1st session, vol. 109, Part 13, 18221–23.

3. Jere Real, "Folk Music and Red Tubthumpers," *American Opinion* 7 (December 1964): 19–20.

4. "Subverting Youth with Folksinging," in Kenneth W. Ingwalson, compiler, *Your Church—Their Target: What's Going On in the Protestant Churches"* (Arlington, Va., 1966), 167–77.

5. See, for example, "Suffer Little Children" and "Columbia Records: Home of the Marxist Minstrels" in the February and March 1967 issues of *Christian Crusade,* 7–9 and 18–20, 28 respectively. David Noebel, *Rhythm, Riots and Revolution* (Tulsa: Christian Crusade, 1966), is an outgrowth of ideas first expressed in a pamphlet entitled *Communism, Hypnotism and the Beatles* (Tulsa: Christian Crusade, 1965) by the same author.

6. Several relevant studies have been published since this work was updated by the author: Robbie Lieberman, *"My Song Is My Weapon": People's Songs, American Communism, and the Politics of Culture, 1930–1950* (Urbana: University of Illinois Press, 1989); Joe Klein, *Woody Guthrie: A Life* (New York: Knopf, 1980); David K. Dunaway, *How Can I Keep from Singing: Pete Seeger* (New York: McGraw-Hill, 1981); Robert Cantwell, *When We Were Good: The Folk Revival* (Cambridge, Mass.: Harvard University Press, 1996); Ronald D. Cohen and David Samuelson, *Songs for Political Action: Folk Music, Topical Songs and the American Left, 1926–1953* (Puritan Records, BCD 15720-JL, 1996), with a 212-page large-format book of notes and photographs; see also bibliography for additional related works; Doris Willens, *Lonesome Traveller: The Life of Lee Hays* (New York: Norton, 1988); Shelly Romalis, *Pistol Packin' Mama: Aunt Molly Jackson and the Politics of Folksong* (Urbana: University of Illinois Press, 1999).

7. Letter to Archie Green, May 24, 1958, quoted in Archie Green, *Only a Miner: Studies in Recorded Coal-Mining Songs* (Urbana: University of Illinois Press, 1972), 18.

8. *American Historical Review* 59 (1954): 54.

9. Brief descriptions of the impending conferences, held March 10, 1945, and

May 4, 1946, are in Norman Studer, "Winter Folklore Conference," *New York Folklore Quarterly* 1 (1945): 59–60, and an anonymous "Worth Noting," *New Masses,* May 7, 1946, 24.

10. Irwin Silber, "Introduction," *Reprints from the People's Songs Bulletin, 1946–1949* (New York: Oak, 1961), 4.

11. Michael Denning, *The Cultural Front: The Laboring of American Culture in the Twentieth Century* (New York: Verso, 1996); Ellen Schrecker, *Many Are the Crimes: McCarthyism in America* (Boston: Little, Brown, 1998).

1

Politics and Folklore

Folklorists have a tendency to suppose that the materials of folklore are their own private preserve, to be collected, classified, and analyzed as they see fit. Yet their raw data, by its very nature, is public, and so available to the world at large. Groups that have exploited folklore materials have done so for many reasons—to boost regional pride, to ease the burdens of work, to achieve economic gain, and to influence politics. The con-

Pete Seeger, Butch Hawes, Arthur Stern, Agnes (Sis) Cunningham, Chicago, 1942
(courtesy of Pete Seeger)

15

scious use of folk songs and other traditional lore for political purposes is as old as recorded history. Documented in every type of social organization from the most primitive to our complex and sophisticated society, folklore is used as a cohesive force to maintain and reinforce social institutions, including the structure of government. This is easiest to see in nonliterate societies, where war chants, songs of historical events, genealogies, praise intonations, and ceremonial feasts all contribute to maintaining authority.[1] In Old China, emperors regularly gauged the sentiments of their people from folk songs collected for this purpose.[2] During Reconstruction, the Ku Klux Klan attempted to reassert white supremacy in the South partly by playing on the superstitious fears of unschooled ex-slaves.[3]

But literacy doesn't diminish the political power of folklore. The origins of folklore study are deeply rooted in the political aspirations of the European romantic nationalism movement of the nineteenth century, when politically suppressed peoples collected local folk songs and tales in an effort to preserve and restore an ancient cultural heritage that could serve as an ideological prop in the struggle for national independence. The work of the Grimm brothers of Germany, Elias Lonnrot in Finland, and many other acknowledged pioneers of academic folklore were inspired by and capitalized on such nationalistic fervor.

Governments from across the political spectrum have utilized folklore as a stabilizing, unifying, and sometimes oppressive tool to support ideological positions and maintain power. Those that we recall most vividly are those that seem the least benign: Hitler's social scientists used Germanic folk traditions to glorify the myth of Aryan supremacy and build the legend of the Führer.[4] Stalin reshaped existing Russian folklore to exalt the creativity of the peasantry and link the revolution of 1917 with earlier revolts. Haiti's late dictator, François Duvalier, cowed a superstitious populace with voodoo. Governments of Ireland, India, Egypt, Ghana, and Pakistan have sponsored folklore research with heavy nationalistic overtones and more than a touch of patriotic bias.

By contrast, at least until the 1980s, folklore and folk songs were given relatively little recognition by the U.S. government. Theodore Roosevelt was probably the first American national public official to focus attention on traditional materials. His thumping endorsement of John A. Lomax's *Cowboy Songs* (1910) appeared as a frontispiece and helped the book become a classic.[5]

But it was not until 1928 that the national Archive of American Folk Song was established as a section of the Music Division of the Library of Congress, and then only as a result of private donations. The archive's period of greatest expansion of holdings occurred in the 1930s under John A. Lomax, an enthusiastic field collector and talented administrator with good Washington political connections. Only in 1937 did Congress finally appropriate funds to cover one administrative position for the archive.[6]

By any standard, the New Deal gave folklore its biggest boost to date in support from government. A number of high-ranking officials in the Franklin Roosevelt administration genuinely liked traditional music and found it a pleasant duty, as well as good "down-home" politics to encourage the collection and performance of folk music. President Roosevelt himself was fond of fiddle music and occasionally invited string bands to entertain at his retreat at Warm Springs, Georgia. One such group was waiting at a party to play for him the day he died.[7]

Eleanor Roosevelt, too, was an enthusiast. She attended or sent greetings to a number of regional folk festivals in the 1930s and invited folk singer Josh White to perform at the White House. When the king and queen of England visited the United States in 1939, the Roosevelts, assisted by musicologist Charles Seeger, treated Their Majesties to a well-received, foot-stomping hoedown by a Nashville square dance troupe and a traditional hillbilly band.

Rexford Tugwell, Harold Ickes, Henry Wallace, and many lesser officials in Roosevelt's administration also were known to appreciate indigenous music. Folk music rang out at house parties all over Washington; the field recordings of John Lomax and the guitar playing of his son Alan were heard at many a social evening where politicos gathered.

But the New Deal contributed more than this informal encouragement. The Works Progress Administration (WPA) sponsored folklore fieldwork that even today informs folklore scholars' endeavors. Some fieldworkers sent by the Resettlement Administration were trained to use traditional music to help in the social integration of new communities. Cultural exchange programs, particularly those of the Pan-American Union, frequently relied on folk songs and dances.

Beginning in 1936, the Folklore Studies section of the Federal Writers Project (FWP), later the Joint Committee on Folk Arts, made extensive field recordings of folk songs and supplemented their popular geographic guides with indigenous folklore. Reminiscences and folk narratives from interviews with ex-slaves, collected under the aegis of the FWP, were later excerpted and published as *Lay My Burden Down: A Folk History of Slavery* (1945), by B. A. (Benjamin) Botkin, who succeeded John Lomax as director of the WPA folklore project.[8] A conservative war Congress terminated the WPA in 1942, but before its doors were closed, large field collections of folk materials had been made in twenty-seven states. Resultant publications included a number of regional folklore anthologies and song collections, as well as *Lay My Burden Down*.

While professional folklorists benefited from WPA activities, the New Deal's approach to folklore was decidedly humanitarian rather than academic or political. As Botkin said in 1939, the WPA goal was to "give back to the people what we [collectors] have taken from them and what rightfully belongs to them. . . . The WPA looks upon folklore research not as a private [function], but as a public function and folklore as public, not private property."[9]

For nearly two decades following the Roosevelt era, the U.S. political establishment paid only haphazard attention to folklore and folk songs. The State Department occasionally sponsored foreign tours by American folk singers as part of its cultural exchange series. A few historic American "folk heroes" such as Paul Bunyan and Johnny Appleseed appeared on U.S. postage stamps. More recently, national and state governments, Smithsonian Institution, and state offices of folklife studies have sponsored quite extensive celebrations of folk traditions. Indeed, the U.S. Postal Service issued a four-stamp series commemorating folk singers Woody Guthrie, Huddie (Lead Belly) Ledbetter, Josh White, and Sonny Terry in 1998, and the Smithsonian Institution launched a traveling exhibit of Woody Guthrie memorabilia in 1999.

Even during the folk song revival of the 1960s, although many members of the Kennedy and Johnson administrations were folk song aficionados, precious little official governmental support for folklore was evident. In 1966, the Department of Interior and its then-secretary Stuart Udall honored folk bard Woody Guthrie for his song compositions on behalf of public conservation. An annual two-week folklife festival sponsored by Smithsonian Institute has been held on the Washington Monument mall each summer since 1968, including a summer-long folk culture exhibition during the 1976 bicentennial celebration.

But no significant new federal government institutional support for the study or performance of American folk traditions developed until a seven-year campaign was begun in 1969 by Senators Ralph Yarborough of Texas and J. William Fulbright of Arkansas. Their Senate Bill S. 1591 in the Ninety-first Congress became law in 1976 as the American Folklife Preservation Act, calling for the establishment of the American Folklife Center to "preserve and present American folklife." The Archive of Folk Culture, an extensive repository of American folk music, is part of the center's collection. Because they occupy a place as one section of the Library of Congress, the American Folklife Center and its archive continue to provide a stable, productive focus for the study and dissemination of folklore traditions.

Also in the 1970s, the National Endowment for the Arts (NEA) and the National Endowment for the Humanities (NEH) initiated regular funding of film and sound recordings to capture and preserve folk traditions. In 1982, the NEH Folk Arts Program began honoring distinguished folk artists with annual National Heritage Fellowship awards. And some states, including Maryland, Pennsylvania, Minnesota, and Michigan, hired state folklorists to collect and publicize local traditions. Though these programs have very modest budgets and minimal staffs, taken as a whole they represent official government support for indigenous American folk culture not seen since New Deal days.

Like the federal government, American political groups and reform movements paid little conscious attention to folk materials until the 1930s. One notable exception is, of course, the Industrial Workers of the World (IWW), which had already begun using the folk music idiom to produce rallying songs for union organizing. By the mid-1930s, though, left-wing organizations, influenced by members or supporters of the Communist Party, discovered intrinsic working-class values in folk song and other folklore genres. Without question, this radical interest initially grew out of the discovery that in certain regions the folk song idiom was a convenient musical method for spreading and reinforcing revolutionary ideas, which was what agitation-propaganda, or agit-prop, departments of the communist movement were working hard to accomplish. Once this tactical utility was recognized, and given the rapidly changing social conditions of the decade, the mere utility of folk songs was eclipsed. Participants in the Old Left extended their limited agit-prop interest in traditional music into outright aesthetic appreciation. There naturally followed a further idealization of other aspects of folk culture—tales, games, theater, dances, arts and crafts.

To be sure, the emerging left-oriented activists of the day, like most of the general public in that era and since, frequently were casual in their notions of what precisely constituted folklore. Left-wing folk song enthusiasts seldom cared to make any distinction between being "of the folk" and "for the folk," even when they actually stopped to consider the question, as they sometimes did. Eventually, they invented the term "people's music" to embrace both genres. Something that sounded folksy—a newly composed labor or political song set to a simple, catchy melody and sung by someone who played a banjo or guitar—was just as apt to be labeled "folk" as was a truly traditional mountain ballad or African American work song.

This failure to distinguish actual folk products from contemporary imitations set idealistic folk song enthusiasts at odds with scholars, to the detriment of both. Academic folklorists themselves have habitually quibbled over the fine points of what constitutes folklore, but some basic concepts have persisted in the face of changing fashions. To be traditional in the academic sense, a song, tale, custom, or other traditional product must owe at least part of its existence to informal transmission from person to person, often orally, and usually face to face over a period of time. The time may be months or generations, but it must be sufficient to remove conscious adherence to rote reproduction from a fixed original. In other words, the item must live apart from books, newspapers, phonograph records, tapes, or any other frozen form. And as the song or other traditional item is thus passed on interpersonally, this "folk process" inevitably produces variations, whether regional, ethnic, occupational, or social—much like the children's game of "telephone," in which a phrase repeated many times inevitably winds up significantly changed from its original form and meaning.

Given this definition, "The Star Spangled Banner," despite its long history, is not a folk song because it continues to exist in only one textual and melodic version, and until recently it was performed in only one socially acceptable style. Songs written by Bob Dylan and the Beatles likewise would not be classified as folk songs by folklorists, since they don't exhibit changes by the community; their performance life and poetic and musical structures as yet are bound up with media dissemination, which freezes their shape and format even as it endlessly reproduces them.

On the other hand, many urban children's street songs, military barracks obscenities, and college and occupational parodies (even of Beatles' songs) are traditional even though they may have a history of only a few months. The academic term *folk song* properly applies to many rural Carolina love songs, sea chanteys, a few early composed hillbilly pieces ("The Death of Floyd Collins"), Mississippi Delta blues, and ballads on nearly every conceivable subject. Whatever their authorship, these folk songs come in numerous versions and owe much of their existence to oral circulation. Many folklorists define folklore and folk song not by origins, content, style, or aesthetic preference but as the end result of a particular type of communication process.

UTILITY OF PROPAGANDA SONGS

The "discovery" by members of some communist and other left-wing groups in the 1930s of folk song as a convenient propaganda tool was hardly original. As John Greenway, Philip Foner, David Dunaway, and others have documented,[10] Americans have always enlisted songs of persuasion on behalf of political and social causes. The colonists bedeviled Britain and lauded each other in broadsides. Their descendants wrangled over slavery in hymns and marched off in half a dozen wars to propaganda rationales in four/four time. Social reformers of the nineteenth and early twentieth centuries took their stand at Armageddon and battled in song for the Lord, the eight-hour day, populism, temperance, and women's suffrage.

One remarkable singing group, the Hutchinson family of New Milford, New Hampshire, toured the country for thirty-five years (1841–1876), performing topical compositions in the name of numerous causes, such as temperance and the abolition of slavery. The labor movement from earliest times has voiced its complaints and solidarity in song. Most political campaigns from John Adams's to George Bush's have featured partisan music as well as flatulent oratory.

"Give me the making of the songs of a nation," wrote the political philosopher Andrew Fletcher in 1703, "and I care not who makes its laws."[11] Legend has it that General Robert E. Lee, hearing union soldiers at Appomattox singing "Rally 'Round the Flag, Boys," commented, "If we had had that song, we'd have won the war." Ironically, the same song was a staple of the Weavers when they were tossed out of work in the 1950s on charges of abandoning American patriotism in favor of radical left-wing sympathies.

It is no accident that folk song (rather than folk tale, legend, or proverb) was the first traditional genre discovered by the Left to have propaganda value. Adding music to words espousing a cause creates a charged atmosphere of militancy and solidarity that is difficult to duplicate by speechmaking alone. Other means of performance, like theater and dance, were also employed early on for propaganda purposes, being equally evocative as music. But they were not as easy to master and perform as songs accompanied by simple instruments and so were less widespread as propaganda tools.[12]

The political utility of songs of persuasion as rallying, reinforcing, and indoctrinating devices among American protest groups has spawned much impressionistic and explanatory commentary from observers throughout the years. R. Serge Denisoff, writing in the *Journal of American Folklore* in 1966, offers an analysis of six possible functions for protest songs (besides entertainment):

1. To solicit outside support and sympathy for a cause.
2. To reinforce the values held by those already active in a movement.
3. To promote cohesion and high morale within the protest organization.
4. To recruit new members for the organization.
5. To propose specific actions to solve real or imagined social problems.
6. To identify conflict or discontent in a society, usually in emotional terms.

Additional functions were later suggested by another scholar:

1. Marking the boundaries between the protest group and the outside world.
2. Counteracting despair when hoped-for change fails to materialize.[13]

Propaganda songs generally fall into one of two categories: the magnetic and the rhetorical. Magnetic songs attempt to woo the outside listener to the movement or ideology or to promote solidarity among those already converted:

> Are you poor, forlorn and hungry,
> Are there lots of things you lack?
> Is your life made up of misery?
> Then dump the bosses off your back.

Or:

> Oh, you can't scare me, I'm sticking to the Union
> I'm sticking to the Union, I'm sticking to the Union
> Oh, you can't scare me, I'm sticking to the Union
> I'm sticking to the Union till the day I die.

> UNION MAID
> Words and Music by Woody Guthrie
> TRO -©- Copyright 1961 (Renewed) 1963 (Renewed)
> Ludlow Music, Inc., New York, NY
> Used by Permission

The rhetorical song merely identifies and describes a real or presumed social crisis without offering an explicit solution in terms of action or dogma:

> The farmer is the man, the farmer is the man
> Lives off of credit till the fall
> Then they take him by the hand and they lead him from the land
> And the middleman's the one who gets it all.

To suggest that a song has propaganda value or that it serves an agit-prop purpose does not imply something sinister or conspiratorial about those who sing it. Any group that believes sincerely in a cause—whether independence from England, abolition of slavery, promotion of labor unions, or Christianity, for that matter—is likely to use music to disseminate and promote its beliefs, because it works. That groups of people with similar social and political philosophies will gather to share the music for rallying purposes as well as aesthetic appreciation is to be expected.

The truly sinister notion—the one the House Un-American Activities Committee and Fire and Police Research Association of Los Angeles, Inc., tried to suggest—is that somehow the appeal of such songs is malevolent, secret, and designed to snare the unwitting into supporting things they would not knowingly support. For example, Woody Guthrie's song

"Union Maid" certainly fits the agit-prop category. But its sentiments would be unlikely to deceive anyone. Like "We Shall Overcome," or "If I Had a Hammer," or "God Bless America," "Union Maid" espouses a political agenda but an open and obvious one.

Without a doubt, propaganda songs vary in content, quality, and durability. Although a good tune certainly helps, the words in each case are paramount. A melody will function as long as it carries the lyrics without obscuring their content or contradicting their mood. For mass singing, tunes must be familiar to most participants or at least simple enough to be learned after one or two repetitions. That is why propaganda songs often resort to parody. With a few notable exceptions—"La Marseillaise" and "The Internationale," for example—a new melody is seldom found among the better-known songs of any mass movement.

In the United States, the staple tune stock underlying most agit-prop lyrics derives from hymns, patriotic airs, sentimental popular tunes, as well as folk songs. Rural communities have tended to use a greater proportion of folk songs for topical and propaganda purposes than have urban groups, but only because of familiarity and not conscious intent.

Thus, the notion, developed in the communist movement, that the folk song idiom has exceptional aesthetic value as well as pragmatic utility is striking and unusual. It can be explained only by special ideological and historical circumstances rooted in the 1930s.

NOTES

1. See William R. Bascom, "Four Functions of Folklore," *Journal of American Folklore* 67 (1954): 344, 346–47.

2. Betty Wang, "Folk Songs as Regulators of Politics" in *The Study of Folklore*, ed. Alan Dundes (Upper Saddle River, N.J.: Prentice Hall, 1965), 308–13.

3. See Gladys-Marie Fry, *Night Riders in Black Folk History* (Knoxville: University of Tennessee Press, 1975).

4. See, for example, Christa Kamenetsky, "Folklore as a Political Tool in Nazi Germany," *Journal of American Folklore* 85 (1972): 221–35.

5. For a photographic reproduction of Roosevelt's letter, see the revised edition, *Cowboy Songs and Other Frontier Ballads* (New York, 1938), 1x–x. See also Nolan Porterfield, *Last Cavalier: The Life and Times of John A. Lomax, 1867–1948* (Urbana: University of Illinois Press, 1996).

6. Rae Korson, "The Archive of Folk Song in the Library of Congress," *The Folklore and Folk Music Archivist* 2, no. 1 (Spring 1959), and 2, no. 2 (Summer 1959). See also D. K. Wilgus, *Anglo-American Folksong Scholarship since 1898* (New Brunswick, N.J.: Rutgers University Press, 1959), 186–88.

7. A photo of Franklin Roosevelt surrounded by country musicians at Warm Springs, Georgia, is reprinted in the liner notes to *Songs of the Depression*, sung

by the New Lost City Ramblers (Folkways 5264). The group waiting to play for the president the day he died is mentioned in Bernard Asbell, *When FDR Died* (New York, 1961), 74–75.

8. Nolan Porterfield, *Last Cavalier: The Life and Times of John A. Lomax, 1867–1948* (Urbana: University of Illinois Press, 1996).

9. B. A. Botkin, "WPA and Folklore Research: 'Bread and Song,'" *Southern Folklore Quarterly* 3, no. 1 (March 1939): 13. See also Norman R. Yetman, "The Background of the Slave Narrative Collection," *American Quarterly* 19 (1967): 534–53.

10. John Greenway, *American Folksongs of Protest* (Philadelphia: Temple University Press, 1953); Philip Foner, *American Labor Songs of the Nineteenth Century* (Urbana: University of Illinois Press, 1975); David K. Dunaway, "Music and Politics in the United States," *Folk Music Journal* 5, no. 3 (1987): 268–94. Others include *Idaho Lore* (Caxton, 1939); John Harrington Cox, *Traditional Ballads Mainly from West Virginia* (Washington, D.C.: Smithsonian Institution Press, 1939); and Roger L. Welsch, *A Treasury of Nebraska Pioneer Folklore* (Lincoln: University of Nebraska Press, 1966).

11. The quote is from *Conversation Concerning a Right Regulation of Government for the Common Good of Mankind*, cited in John Bartlett, *Familiar Quotations*, 13th ed. (Boston: Little, Brown, 1955), 290b.

12. See Gene Bluestein, *The Voice of the Folk: Folklore and American Literary Theory* (Amherst: University of Massachusetts Press, 1972), and Ellen Graff, *Stepping Left: Dance and Politics, New York City, 1928–1942* (Durham, N.C.: Duke University Press, 1997).

13. R. Serge Denisoff, "Songs of Persuasion: A Sociological Analysis of Urban Propaganda Songs," *Journal of American Folklore* 79 (1966): 581–89.

2

Early Marxism and Folklore

The significance of propaganda song itself was understood from the beginning by all varieties of Marxists. Friedrich Engels wrote of their importance in a letter to Hermann Schlueter, a socialist contemporary, in 1885, though he chafed at the caliber of poetry in the lyrics.[1] Socialist songs were sung in the streets of the Paris Commune in 1871. By the turn of the twentieth century, workers' choral groups were singing across Europe and even in the United States.

Folksay Group Meeting, New York City—Irwin Silber, Beena Licht
(courtesy of Irwin Silber)

Toward the end of the nineteenth century, the director of a workers' chorus in Lille, France, Pierre Degeyter, composed the music for "The Internationale," which became one of the most widely recognized theme songs of the socialist movement for half a century. With its stirring, even melodramatic, opening lines, "Arise, you pris'ners of starvation! Arise, you wretched of the earth!" set to a compelling marching anthem, "The Internationale" has ignited the passions of several generations of rebellious protesters. It yielded the title for one of the most important Marxist works of the latter half of the twentieth century, *The Wretched of the Earth* by Frantz Fanon, an Algerian revolutionary and social theorist. Fanon's book influenced the decision of many African and some Asian leaders to choose Marxist models for their countries' first postcolonial governments.

Song collections devoted to socialism and the cause of the proletariat soon made their appearance, among the earliest in English being *Chants of Labour* (London, 1888), edited by Edward Carpenter.[2] Lenin in exile sought contact with the proletariat by occasionally venturing out to the cafés and theaters of suburban Paris to listen to revolutionary songs. As the Bolsheviks moved toward national power, *Pravda* printed "The Internationale" in its first issue. In its sixth issue, March 11, 1917, there appeared an article in bold type entitled "Revolutionary Songs," saying, "We call [to] the attention of the comrades, that it is desirable to organize collective singing and rehearsals of choral performances of revolutionary songs."

By the early twentieth century, in the United States and Europe, anarchists, socialists, Wobblies, communists, and later Trotskyists all developed their own stock of revolutionary lyrics, though certain standards were common to the international socialist movement as a whole. The latter included such songs as "The Internationale" and "The Red Flag" and were derived primarily from European rather than American sources. Many early radical composers were influenced by Christian socialist thought, so songs of the American Left often contained a distinct religious strain in both text and melody.

Chicago was the publishing center for most revolutionary music prior to 1920. The best-known publications were *Socialist Songs with Music* (1901) and *I.W.W. Songs* (1909), better known as "The Little Red Songbook"; both went through numerous editions.

Of all the early American Marxist groups, the Industrial Workers of the World—the Wobblies—are most remembered for their effective use of propaganda music.[3] They wrote almost all their own songs, which were grounded firmly in real labor experiences in contrast to the verse of other radical groups before 1930. The Wobblies took great pride in their singing and sometimes reprinted favorable comment from outsiders in their own publications. One such comment came from journalist Ray Stannard Baker following a 1912 IWW strike in Lawrence, Massachusetts:

> The movement in Lawrence was strongly a singing movement. It is the first strike I ever saw which sang! I shall not soon forget the curious lift, the strange sudden fire of the mingled nationalities, at the strike meetings when they broke into the universal language of song. And not only at the meetings did they sing but at the soup houses and in the streets.[4]

Wobbly bards Joe Hill, Ralph Chaplin, and others won international reputations as labor poets for their militant verse. Joe Hill did have the inspiration to use well-known popular tunes of the day, so that his compositions could be picked up and used easily. Yet neither the IWW composers nor any of their contemporaries in other socialist movements thought in terms of emphasizing folk song as a propaganda medium or as an aesthetic base for a new workers' music culture. The communists would develop these premises, but only much later. Until the 1930s, Marxist theory, communist and noncommunist alike, contained little commentary on traditional song or any other forms of folklore.

EARLY EUROPEAN MARXISM ON FOLKLORE

Little, really, is known of the views of Karl Marx, Georgi Plekhanov, Vladimir Lenin, and their radical contemporaries concerning folklore traditions. What evidence exists must be reconstructed from passing references and anecdotal reminiscences of friends. When tracing one's academic pedigree to the Marxist classics became fashionable in communist circles, Soviet folklorists could do little more than cite obscure quotes from the works of the pantheon of Marxist heroes. The folklorists V. I. Chicherov in the 1930s and Y. M. Sokolov in the 1960s each presented examples of anecdotes indicating that Marx, Friedrich Engels, and Lenin were appreciative of the value of Russian oral tradition.[5]

Reading Chicherov and Sokolov, one learns, for example, that Marx and Engels both were acquainted with German folklore. Marx enjoyed folk songs and, according to Sokolov, is even alleged to have been an able teller of folk tales. Engels, on looking over some editions of folk tales, once wrote, "These folk books, with their ancient speech, with their misprints and poor engravings, possess for me an exceptional poetic charm. They carry me away from our over-tense time, with its contemporary conditions, 'confusion and delicate interrelationships,' into another world, which is much closer to nature." A friend once heard Lenin express admiration for Russian oral materials and allude to the value of tales, epics, proverbs, and other popular lore as "important for the study of popular psychology of our days." But turning such obscure musings into a Marxist theory of folklore requires a leap of imagination.

Marxist literature prior to the Bolshevik Revolution examined folklore and other cultural products from a historic evolutionary perspective with stress on concurrent labor conditions, class structure, and social position. In 1896, Karl Bucher, a German Marxist economist , wrote the tract *Arbeit und Rhythmus* (work and rhythms), in which he dealt with folk song but hardly exalted it: "While in the first stages of their development labor, music and poetry were usually blended, labor was the predominant element, the others being only of secondary importance."[6] When anthropologist Paul Lafargue (1842–1911) wrote a study of wedding songs in various cultures, his Marxist orientation led him to underscore the position of women in the family structure of traditional societies.

Marx, in fact, once observed that as an art form, the classic epic was "possible only at a comparatively low stage of artistic development," reflecting an attitude consistent with the theory of cultural evolution coming into vogue in his day. Marx believed that folklore was aesthetic in its essence and rooted in the primeval world of mankind, and that as society advances, oral traditions like epics, tales, songs, and myths give way to conscious art and mass media. "Is an Achilles possible in the era of gunpowder and lead?" he asked. "Or an Iliad alongside of the printing press?"[7]

One looks in vain for similar or contradictory statements on traditional materials in the writings of other major socialist thinkers before the Bolshevik Revolution, suggesting that prior to 1917, Marxist folkloristics remained grounded in the social Darwinian ethos. Nevertheless, the roots for the idea of using folk songs as propaganda tools can be seen as a logical outgrowth of Marxist insistence that all art was a potential weapon in the class struggle. Plekhanov's *Art and Society*, for example, contended that "art for art's sake" was a hopeless bourgeois illusion. "Pure art has never existed," he wrote. "He who devotes himself to 'pure art' does not thereby become independent of the biological, historical and social conditions that determine his esthetic tastes, he simply shuts his eyes more or less consciously to those conditions."[8] "The rightful task of the artist," Plekhanov asserted, "was to ally himself with the progressive forces of his age."

Lenin saw things similarly. He rejected abstract expression. "Art belongs to the people," he said. "It should be understood and loved by [them]. . . . [W]e must always have before our eyes the workers and the peasants."[9] But in his writing on art, Lenin never singled out folk tradition for even the merest mention.

During the Bolshevik Revolution, folklore was used widely in an agit-prop context. But it was used because of tactical considerations, not ideological dogma. Russia in 1917 was a land in which most people were peasants, steeped in tradition. Rural, agrarian peasant societies still constituted the great majority of the population. Illiteracy was still the rule rather than the exception. Most workers in urban areas were scarcely a generation removed from the farm. When formal education and mass media are lacking people cling naturally to the songs, tales, maxims, and customs of their ancestors. Propaganda couched in the popular vernacular and set in the context of familiar oral traditions is able to circumvent illiteracy in rural areas. Thus, Isaac Deutscher, in his biography of Leon Trotsky, describes a number of tracts written especially for the peasantry by Trotsky. "In these proclamations," Deutscher writes:

> Trotsky had before his eyes a primitive, illiterate mass of farm labourers, such as he could remember from his father's farm, a crowd in which a few individuals might be able to read his words aloud to the rest. He framed his appeal in the simplest terms and in the rhythm of a Slavonic folk rhapsody, with characteristic refrains and evocations. The words and the rhythm were as if designed for recital by a semi-agitator, semibard in a village. . . . He described how the workers had marched "peacefully and calmly" to the Tsar's palace [in 1905] with the Tsar's pictures, icons, and church banners:

"What did the Tsar do? How did he answer the toilers of St. Petersburg?
"Hearken, hearken peasants. . . .
"This is the way the Tsar talked with his people. . . .
"All the troops of Petersburg were raised to their feet. . . .
"Thus the Russian Tsar girded himself for the talk with his subjects. . . .
"Hearken, hearken peasants!
"Let every word engrave itself on your hearts. . . .
"All the streets and squares, where the peaceful workers were to march, were occupied by troops.
'Let us through to the Tsar!', the workers begged. . . .
"And then it happened!
"The guns went off with a thunder. . . .
"The snow reddened with workers' blood. . . .
"Tell all and sundry in what way the Tsar has dealt with the toilers of St. Petersburg!"

> Thus in plain words, without weakening for a moment his grasp on the muzhik's imagination, [Trotsky] explained the ends his Party was pursuing and the means it would employ; and he translated the alien term "revolution" into the peasants' idiom: "Peasants, let this fire burst all over Russia at one and the same time, and no force will put it out. Such a nation-wide fire is called revolution.[10]

The cadence and stylized expression of Trotsky's writings clearly suggests his familiarity with the East European, especially Russian, epic song form.

Invoking old tales and historical songs also had a legitimizing value for the Bolsheviks, linking their revolution to the traditions of earlier revolts against czarist tyranny associated with Stenka Razin, Emelyan Pugachev, and the Cossacks. Aleksander Pushkin, Nikolai Gogol, Leo Tolstoy, and other great nineteenth-century Russian writers used folklore in their work, underscoring the spiritual and physical abuses of the old regime. Moreover, many songs, legends, tales, and customs of the Russian people owed their existence to periods when outside powers controlled portions of what became the Soviet state; much of this lore grew out of popular resistance to foreign domination, and using it allowed the Bolsheviks to tap into these nationalistic feelings as they assumed power.

When the Bolsheviks seized national control, they withdrew Russia from World War I and signed a humiliating treaty with Germany at Brest-Litovsk. Foreign enemies encamped on Russian soil during the ensuing civil war, trying to bring down Lenin's government. Setting new words to old songs of resistance was one method of rallying popular support to the Red banner. One newly revised Siberian partisan song quoted by Sokolov said:

> Comrades, forward
> The Siberian partisan
> Is not afraid of the Japanese cannon,
> For the power of the Soviets we will fight
> The power of the workers and the peasants.

The Soviet revolutionaries certainly used traditional materials for political ends. But it would be a mistake to think that this resulted from the work of some highly organized central propaganda ministry in Moscow or Petrograd. Sokolov, seeking some evidence that folklore was integral to the Marxist plan, acknowledges that "[t]he song creation of the masses of workmen and peasants at first developed in an altogether spontaneous way" as "the heroic moods at the time of the civil war sought expression for themselves."[11]

Nor should it be inferred that folklore supplanted other art forms as propaganda tools. Where folklore was serviceable for the Leninist cause, it was used; where it was not, or where other means of communication were more advantageous, it was dispensed with or ignored.

Folklore, indeed, had its drawbacks as a propaganda vehicle, which contributed to the Bolsheviks' ambivalent attitude toward popular traditions in the early years. Leninist ideology demanded a militant class consciousness, rigid personal discipline of one's thoughts and actions, and the rejection of sentimental nostalgia about the past in favor of socio-political alternatives designed to bolster the modern proletariat. Some peasant lore reflected popular resistance to the oppression of earlier periods and in other instances could be updated. Yet as a whole, Russian folklore exhibited no striking revolutionary zeal. In keeping with oral tradition generally, it in fact was basically conservative and often contradictory in its portrayal of the past. Frequently it served to reinforce old mores, values, and customs that the Bolsheviks were seeking to destroy.

The basic Soviet dilemma in using popular traditions either as propaganda or as the basis of a new proletarian culture is illustrated by the intellectual controversy surrounding the death of Sergei Esenin, the Russian poet. Born of peasant origins and a bohemian by temperament, Esenin was regarded by many as among the most talented literary artists to ally himself with the Bolsheviks. His poems were based principally on firsthand observation and often set in taverns, marketplaces, or other lower-class meeting sites. They portrayed the earthy life, sentimentality, crudeness, and sporadic revelry of those who came there.

In December 1925, Esenin committed suicide. Trotsky, already in the midst of his final power struggle with Stalin, delivered a eulogy that was published in *Pravda*:

> Yessenin's [Esenin's] roots are deeply national, and his nationalism, as everything in him, is real and genuine. . . . The peasant background, purified and refracted through his creative art, is very strong. . . . But the strength of this peasant background constitutes the real weakness of Yessenin's [Esenin's] personality; he was uprooted from the old without striking root in the new.

Esenin, Trotsky noted, "was not aloof from the Revolution. He was simply not akin to it. Yessenin [Esenin] is intimate, tender, lyrical; the Revolution is public, epic and catastrophic. That is why the brief life of the poet ended in tragedy."[12]

Stalin's rejoinder came through his then-trusted ally, Nicolai Bukharin, who made clear that the Soviet state saw no tolerable virtue in Esenin's poetry. The poet, he said, represented the most ideologically backward areas of Russia and its national character, that which was rooted in the decadent spirit of the past. "Is Yessenin [Esenin] talented? Of course he is," Bukharin conceded. But he went on to make clear that his talent had been a weapon for ill, not good: "Yessenin [Esenin] as a whole is [a] disgusting, vulgarly painted and powdered Russian obscenity." He followed these strong words by noting that Esenin's poetry

is saturated with alcoholic tears and therefore still more vile. A monstrous mixture of "male dogs," ikons, "glaring candles," birches, the moon, bitches, gods, necrophilia, a lot of drunken tears, and "tragic," drunken hiccoughs; religion and hooliganism, "love" for animals and a barbarous attitude toward men and especially women, impotent longings for "wide" open spaces (while sitting within the four narrow walls of a common cabaret), decadence raised to the height of a principle, and so on—all this, under the cloak of a wild "quasi-folk" nationalism constitutes Yessenin.[13]

The ferocity of this polemic says all there is to say about the skepticism of the regime toward the heritage bequeathed from the "Old Russia" of Tolstoy, Fyodor Dostoyevsky, Sergei Esenin (sometimes spelled Yessenin), and the czars. Folk traditions and peasant culture contained much romanticism, barbarism, dissipation, and superstition, which the Soviets saw as their duty to eliminate in order to construct a modern state.

So it is not surprising that as they consolidated national power, the Bolsheviks did not incorporate folklore as a major element of their philosophical and cultural frame of reference. The traditions of the past were useful on occasion, aesthetically pleasing as well. But too infrequently did they transmit the necessary Spartan discipline and correct ideology to suit the Bolsheviks. Fifteen years would pass and profound changes occur on the national and international scenes before the Soviet Union would elevate folklore to the pinnacle of ideological respectability.

EARLY AMERICAN MARXISM ON FOLKLORE

In the United States, the writings of Eugene V. Debs, Victor Berger, Daniel DeLeon, Big Bill Haywood, Emma Goldman, and other native radicals devoted little attention to traditional materials and their real or potential function in society. A search of much of the daily press and song literature of the socialists, IWW, early communists, and other splinter groups yields scarcely half a dozen references to folk song and other forms of oral tradition.[14] In the anarchist writings, there is nothing. Given the voluminous socialist output, relatively few referenced folk music. A few songbooks linked with the agrarian uprising appeared in the 1890s, and a songbook labeled *Socialist Songs with Music* was published in about 1901.[15]

As for the IWW, ironically more of the group's creations entered folklore tradition than came from it. The IWW left more genuine folklore in its wake than any other labor group in the American history.[16] And although the Wobblies disdained armchair theorizing and preferred direct action, from the vortex of the class struggle, they produced their own brand of intellectuals, men rough in manners who toiled with their hands as much as with their pens but who also read widely and argued violently about literature, philosophy, and art.

"During its heyday, the Wobbly movement was violently distrustful of intellectuals," said Alan Calmer, writing in *New Masses* in 1934.

> But this does not mean that it sneered at all intellectual endeavor. Contrary to most beliefs, the "official" attitude of the I.W.W. toward culture was by no means a negative one. It displayed a high regard for any kind of literary or artistic expression—when such work praised the manual worker, or sniped at anybody hostile to the working-class.[17]

In fact, in 1915, a pseudonymous "J.E." published an article in the I.W.W. newspaper *Solidarity* drawing a parallel between the functions of Wobbly songs in contemporary American society and the ballads and broadsides sung by the minstrels to the common people. J.E.'s observations were inspired by a much-discussed literary work, *The Development of the English Novel*, by Wilbur L. Cross, a Yale professor (and later governor of Connecticut).[18] Cross argued that the form of the realistic novel grew out of the humorous musical commentaries of British street minstrels, whose broadside songs and ballads poked fun at the intrigues and frailties of the British aristocracy and clergy. The *Solidarity* article suggested that in similar fashion Wobbly songs exposed the pretensions and frauds of capitalist society. "The result," J.E. said, "may not be a new literary form, but a new class expression within the old forms, and the beginning of the new thoughts and new ideals necessary to the beginning of a new society."[19]

Much the same idea was advanced a few years later by the anonymous writer of the notes to a piece of Wobbly sheet music, "The Advancing Proletaire," published in Chicago:

> Each epoch in the world's history gives forth its own art expression. We are told that the day of the folk song is past, that in a complex civilization such as we have in America, no true folk song can be produced; that America never has had true folk song of a distinct racial type because of the many nationalities composing our population.

"As our civilization becomes more complex," the notes say, "our art must express that complexity." Such commentary is not indicative of cultural nihilism. The notes continue: "The proletariat working in the modern industries constitutes the majority of the people. Shall not the activities of these groups influence the art of their time as they become more and more conscious of their social status?"[20]

An important distinction is being made by these two anonymous Wobbly commentators, J.E. and the writer of the notes to "The Advancing

Proletaire." Folk songs, they point out, are rooted in ancient times, when society was rural and relatively noncomplex. The music of the proletariat, on the other hand, is the product of the latest stage of modern urbanization, technological innovation, and social evolution toward socialism. There are no hints of the linkage to come between traditional music and the culture of the proletariat.

But two other IWW references to folk song do make such a link. Soon after J.E.'s article appeared in 1915, Elizabeth Gurley Flynn visited the young Swedish immigrant laborer–turned–Wobbly songwriter Joe Hill in prison and wrote in *Solidarity*, "Joe writes songs that sing, that lilt and laugh and sparkle, that kindle the fires of revolt in the most crushed spirit and quicken the desire for fuller life in the most humble slave. . . . He has crystallized the organization's [IWW] spirit into imperishable forms, songs of the people—folk songs."[21] Joe Hill immortalized Flynn as the "Rebel Girl" in his song of the same name.

Flynn could hardly have been aware of it, but she had caught a glimpse of the future position of the communist movement, which consciously tied traditional folk songs and propaganda music composed mostly in folk-style into one collective genre, "people's songs," the true music of the working masses.

And in 1918, International Song Publishers, the IWW's Chicago outlet, dropped a similar, if less eloquent, hint of what was to come. The notes accompanying the publication of "The Funeral Song of a Russian Revolutionist" say, "We have chosen as our first offering the translation of a Russian song as a tribute to the nation which has produced some of the most beautiful folk songs of the world, and as a wreath to lay upon the tomb of the thousands of Russians who have died for the cause of freedom."

Taken together, these references to folk song constitute no more in the way of a Marxist theory of folklore than similar passing remarks do in the socialist literature of Europe. On both continents, the tendency was to view folk traditions as interesting and often pleasing outgrowths of early stages in the cultural evolution of humankind.

Folklore and folk songs generally were not a significant part of American intellectual consciousness in the early 1900s. The few interested scholars thought the United States had no folklore of significance. Yet by the time the American communist movement established itself as a going concern in the 1920s, academic studies of indigenous folk traditions had begun to appear at a rapid rate. An American society caught up in the agonizing and uncertain transition from rural to urban culture sought out its roots. Stories of John Henry, Paul Bunyan, and other folk and fake heroes of the people were widely circulated in the mass media.[22]

Henry Ford, whose automobile sales did as much as anything to destroy the rustic past in the United States, garnered much publicity for his hobby of importing old-time fiddlers and folk dancers to Dearborn, Michigan.[23] Carl Sandburg brought out his best-selling folk song collection, *The American Songbag*, in 1927—the same year John Jacob Niles gave the first formal folk song recital to a college audience at Princeton University.[24] It thus is not too surprising that references to folk traditions in American communist literature began to appear more frequently during this period.

The first known comments by native communists on folklore appeared in 1927 in the *Daily Worker* and *New Masses*. Both referred in reviews to Em Jo Basshe's play *Earth*, as a "folk drama." Basshe, a young radical of Russian Jewish parentage, focused on an isolated post–Civil War Negro community in the South, which vacillated between Christianity and voodoo in an unsuccessful attempt to ward off its poverty and misery. Although *Earth* was not truly a traditional play, nor was it performed by a folk group, such fine academic distinctions were never to bother the Left. What was important is that the play bore the label "folk drama" in the communist press and that it provoked speculation on the relationship of folk materials to proletarian culture, precisely the problem that had to be resolved with regard to folk song a few years later.

Harbor Allen, better known for his proletarian plays in the 1930s under the pseudonym Paul Peters, asked the right questions in his review for the *Daily Worker* but gave no answers: "Is this proletarian drama?" he asked. "Is 'Earth' good for workers because it deals with simple people, because it isn't cluttered with intellectual patter, because it goes out in the fields and huts and mountain tops, into a community of people, a mass?" Allen further asks, "Well, what is proletarian drama? Does it include folk drama? Nobody knows. No American has written one."[25]

Ten days after his review, Allen returned to the subject in a *Daily Worker* article entitled "What Is a Proletarian Play?" He groped his way toward a somewhat more positive statement:

> When communism has triumphed, will come pedantic plays, like the old miracle plays, narrow, propagandistic. Who is to say they will lack art value? It will be a different sort of value, that's all; a folk art, the art of the ballads, of early paintings, of the songs of the people. And still later there will be a renaissance. A Communist Shakespeare will arise, an individual, yet one of the people . . . that will be Communism's Golden Age.[26]

But still this view was not representative of the attitudes of the movement. Allen's editor felt compelled to include an editorial note disclaiming responsibility for Allen's views. And *New Masses*, another periodical committed to the communist movement, actually panned the play *Earth*, editorializing that because it concerned "a mode of life that is alien to us and a problem that does not touch us," it shouldn't have been produced.[27]

In this same period, though, the communist press for the first time took notice of several folk song collections. In November 1927, the *Daily Worker* reviewed George Korson's *Songs and Ballads of the Anthracite Miners*, suggesting that it illustrated the theory of the materialistic interpretation of history. "All people, without exception, during a certain stage of culture develop sagas and epics, and during another and later stage take to producing ballads," wrote the *Worker*'s reviewer Vern Smith. While his review was mostly favorable, Smith complained that Korson did not sharply distinguish between the "old, true ballad, based on the everyday work . . . strictly local in tone" and the "more sophisticated successor[s] of the folk ballad, the class war songs now sung by striking workers . . . universal, and class wide in their appeals" and that too few of the latter kind of song were included in the collection.[28]

Writing in the *New Masses*, Ed Falkowski, a young miner from Pennsylvania, was much more hostile, but not for any political reasons. Falkowski argued that Korson hadn't "been there"—hadn't caught the true feeling of those who had actually worked in the coal pits. His review consisted primarily of an extraordinarily graphic resume of mining life, lyrical and Whitmanesque in its description, which all but stated that its author could better capture the soul of the anthracite miners in prose than Korson could in his book of songs. Falkowski, however, said nothing whatever theoretical about ballads, folk songs, and the class struggle.[29] The *Daily Worker* also critiqued Sandburg's *American Songbag* in January 1928 and Charles J. Finger's *Frontier Ballads* in April. Neither review had anything substantive to say about the role of folk music in the communist movement.[30]

In sum, the American communist movement in its first decade (1919–1928) established no firm position, favorable or otherwise, on folklore. In this it differed not at all from other radical groups of the time, or earlier. One scarcely would suspect that in less than ten years folk songs and other lore of the people would occupy an exalted position in American communist cultural circles. This startling reversal occurred as a byproduct of ideological and historical circumstances that reshaped the international communist movement but that were rooted even more in the intellectual climate stimulated by the Great Depression in the United States.

NOTES

1. Karl Marx and Friedrich Engels, *Literature and Art: Selections from Their Writings* (New York: International, 1947), 113–14.

2. A negative review of this songbook appeared in the British *Saturday Review*, 66 (August 18,1888): 211–13.

3. The IWW is still active today, centered in Chicago with a few small local chapters. A well-known member is Bruce Philips, known as U. Utah Philips, storyteller extraordinaire, who still performs today on the folk club circuit.

4. "The Revolutionary Strike." *The American Magazine* (May 1912): 4, reprinted in *Solidarity* 3, no. 3, 4.

5. Y. M. Sokolov, *Russian Folklore*, English-language reprint edition (Hatboro, Pa.: Folklore Institute, 1966), 28–39. See V. I. Chicherov, "Karl Marx and Friedrich Engels on Folklore," *Soviet Folklore* 4–5 (1936), for a more detailed list of citations of the words of these men on folklore.

6. Quoted in George V. Plekhanov, *Art and Society* (New York: Critics Group, 1936), 9.

7. Sokolov, *Russian Folklore*, 30–31.

8. Plekhanov, *Art and Society*, 93; italicized in the original.

9. V. I. Lenin, *On Culture and Cultural Revolution* (Moscow: Progress Publishers, 1966), 237–38.

10. Isaac Deutscher, *The Prophet Armed* (New York: Vintage, 1965), 122–23. The cadence of Trotsky's writing suggests his intimate familiarity with the East European, especially Russian, epic song form like that discussed by Albert Lord in *The Singer of Tales* (Cambridge: Cambridge University Press, 1960). For brief general remarks on the Bolshevik use of folklore, see R. Serge Denisoff, "The Proletarian Renascence: The Folkness of the Ideological Folk," *Journal of American Folklore* 82 (1969): 53.

11. Sokolov, *Russian Folklore*, 615.

12. Reprinted as "The Death of a Poet" in *New Masses* (June 1926): 18, 30.

13. Quoted by Joseph Freeman, "Poetry and Common Sense," *New Masses* (May 1927): 9.

14. I obviously have been unable to read all the early socialist literature, though I have tried to scan the relevant statements on culture of the more prominent leaders of each Marxist group. In part, I have been guided by quotations and leads provided by secondary sources such as Egbert and Person's *Socialism and American Life*. I have, however, read the IWW and communist press in minute detail. A recent publication covers the topic in detail: *Mass Culture in Soviet Russia: Tales, Poems, Songs, Movies, Plays and Folklore, 1917–1953*, ed. James von Geldern and Richard Stites (Bloomington: Indiana University Press, 1995).

15. A copy of this collection has not been located, but to judge by another publication that reprints part of the contents, socialist lyrics are set to a number of well-known traditional tunes but more often to popular melodies. The few unadulterated "folk songs" included are really "folksy" songs of the "Old Oaken Bucket" and "Suwanee River" variety. See also Leopold Vincent, comp., *The Alliance and Labor Songster* (1891); Ronald Cohen and Dave Samuelson, *Songs for Political Action: Folk Music, Topical Songs and the American Left, 1926–1953* (Puritan Records, BCD 15720-JL, 1996), with a 212-page large-format book of notes; Philip Foner, *American Labor Songs of the Nineteenth Century* (Urbana: University of Illinois, 1975); Archie Green, *Wobblies, Pile Butts, and Other Heroes: Laborlore*

Explorations (Urbana: University of Illinois Press, 1993); and David K. Dunaway,
"Music and Politics in the United States," *Folk Music Journal* 5, no. 3 (1987): 268–
94.

16. Much Wobbly lore, though not all of it folkloristic, is contained in Joyce
Kornbluh, ed., *Rebel Voices: An I.W.W. Anthology* (Ann Arbor: University of Michigan Press, 1964).

17. Alan Calmer, "The Wobbly in American Literature," *New Masses* (September 18, 1934), 21.

18. New York, 1899, and in numerous editions thereafter, sixteen of which had
appeared by the time of J.E.'s review. The comments in the *Solidarity* article are
based on Cross's remarks in chapter 1. The terms *ballads* and *broadsides* are not
actually used by J.E., although the concepts they represent are.

19. J.E., "The English Novel and I.W.W. Songs," *Solidarity* (February 13, 1915),
4. Jas. J. Ettor, an important Wobbly organizer, is listed on the paper's masthead,
but there is no direct proof that he wrote this article.

20. International Song Publishers, 204 N. Clark St. (Chicago: n.d.—probably
1918).

21. "A Visit to Joe Hill," *Solidarity* (May 22, 1915), 1.

22. For a discussion of these and other heroes, see Richard M. Dorson, *American Folklore* (Chicago: University of Chicago Press, 1975), 214–26, and "The Career
of 'John Henry,'" *Western Folklore* 24 (1965): 155–63. Paul Bunyan is given an able
book-length scholarly assessment in Daniel G. Hoffman, *Paul Bunyan, Last of the
Frontier Demigods* (East Lansing: Michigan State University Press, 1999).

23. William E. Leuchtenberg, *The Perils of Prosperity: 1914–32*, 2d ed. (Chicago:
University of Chicago Press, 1993), 229; Allan Nevins and Frank Ernest Hill, *Ford*,
3 vols. (New York: Scribner, 1957), 491–93.

24. Carl Sandburg, *The American Songbag* (New York: Harcourt, Brace, 1927).
John A. Lomax and others had given recitals of traditional songs to classes and
specialized folklore groups prior to this time. Niles's performance, however, was
the prototype for later "folk song revival" concert performances.

25. Harbor Allen, "A Black Folk Drama," *Daily Worker* (March 13, 1927), 4. In
discussing *Earth* as folk drama, communist reviewers apparently were following
the lead of various literary playwrights of this period who wrote of rural societies and accordingly labeled their efforts "folk drama." See, for example, the dramatic productions included in Frederick H. Koch, ed., *Carolina Folk-Plays* (New
York: Holt, 1941).

26. Allen, *Daily Worker* (March 23, 1927), 6.

27. Bernard Smith, review of *Earth, New Masses* (March 1927): 23.

28. Vern Smith, "Folk Ballads and Fighting Songs," *Daily Worker* (November
10, 1927), 4.

29. Ed Falkowski, review of *Songs and Ballads of the Anthracite Miners, New
Masses* (February 1928): 28–30.

30. "Folk-Lore Collected," *Daily Worker* (January 13, 1928), 6; Walt Carmon,
"Songs from Sea, Field and Camp," *Daily Worker* (April 30, 1928), 5.

3

The Communist Search for a
Proletarian Music Culture

In July 1928, Nicolai Bukharin ascended the podium to address the Sixth World Congress of the Communist International, meeting in Moscow.[1] It had been three years since Bukharin spoke for Stalin against Trotsky in the contretemps over the death of poet Serge Esenin (Yessenin). It had been two years since Stalin selected Bukharin to head the International. And it was still ten years *before* Stalin would have Bukharin tried for treason and executed.

Pete Seeger, circa: 1942 (courtesy of Pete Seeger)

What Bukharin had to say that day in Moscow plunged the world communist movement into its so-called "Third Period," wherein it was postulated that the collapse of world capitalism was imminent and that intensification of the class struggle in all areas was necessary to hasten the final overthrow of the bourgeoisie and the establishment of the rule of the proletariat.

The Third Period ideology that Bukharin promulgated had stern implications for American communists' attitudes toward culture. All artistic expression was to be politicized. The function of art was to be confined to the agit-prop context—"art as a weapon." Aesthetic questions weren't even to be discussed. Artists and bureaucrats were expected to root out any bourgeois influence in workers' cultural media.

One immediate byproduct was a sharp drop in the coverage of music, dance, and nonpolitical books in the communist press—a process that was not to be reversed until the Third Period began to crumble well into 1933. Simultaneously, however, rejecting all bourgeois taint in the development of workers' culture required a definition of exactly what constituted proletarian literature, art, music, and drama in the first place. Artists in every field were faced with defining the new communist alternative culture as it applied to their own discipline and instituting concrete programs of activity reflecting their definitions. The American communist movement's unsuccessful search during the Third Period for a unique but broadly based native proletarian music resulted in the "discovery" of folklore as "people's" culture.

THE WORKER'S MUSIC LEAGUE

The American communist movement began in 1919 when the radical wing of the Socialist Party split from the main body to form two independent revolutionary organizations, the Communist Party and the Communist Labor Party. These were united in 1923, but not before factional quarrels and harassment by the federal government during the Red Scare following World War I decimated both groups and posed a dire threat to their very existence.[2] Consolidating its leadership, and merely staying alive, preoccupied the movement's attention during its first decade, leaving no time to devote to such peripheral activity as discussing music theory. Relatively little singing of any kind was done, even in an agit-prop context. On those few occasions when revolutionary songs were needed, old standards inherited from the IWW and international socialist repertoire sufficed. In time the repertoire was supplemented by a number of early European communist songs. Eventually, Russian and German experiences with workers' music became models for American attempts to create a proletarian music.

Revolutionary choruses were an exception to this relative indifference to music among American communists during the 1920s. In the United States, these choruses were located entirely within the immigrant language groups, mostly East European, which made up the majority of the movement's early membership. In Europe, workers' music organizations had been a staple of left-wing cultural activity for decades and were transplanted by immigrants to the United States beginning around 1900. Nearly every language group in the communist movement developed its own chorus, orchestra, or other musical unit, and some developed several.

Perhaps the best known was the Jewish Freiheit Gesang Ferein, loosely translated as the "Freedom Singers' Society." Formed in 1923 and directed for most of its early existence by Jacob Schaefer, the Freiheit achieved a standard of excellence and a measure of acclaim unusual for American revolutionary choruses.[3] But in other respects, its members and activities were fairly typical: first-generation immigrants, many of them factory workers and sweatshop laborers, gathered evenings for long rehearsals of workers' songs and homeland choral music, supervised by a dedicated but poorly paid conductor. Recitals were given periodically, aimed at community audiences or left-affiliated labor organizations.

Ethnic musical groups weren't professional in caliber, nor did they attract much public attention outside the immigrant language groups. But they occupied a position of central importance in the cultural life of the early communist movement and so influenced the direction of the movement's musical activity for a considerable period. For the same reason, though, it is apparent that the continuous popularity of the choruses was as much a product of the social functions they served as of their political expression .

The chorus was "one of the most popular mediums for reaching the masses. The capitalist class, through the churches and the so-called people's choruses use this medium for lulling the workers. The revolutionary movement uses it for rousing the workers against [their] oppressors," the *Daily Worker* said in 1934.[4] Contrary to this assertion, workers' choruses were not common in the United States outside the immigrant language groups, nor did their repertoires hold any great attraction for other American laborers. For one thing, much of the communist revolutionary choral music was technically difficult to perform without rehearsal, thereby limiting its use in an agit-prop context. More important, nearly all of it was sung in a foreign language, at least at first. No English-language chorus was even started within the communist movement until 1933.

Political lyrics usually were bombastic, European oriented, and highly doctrinaire, such as "Varshavianka," which translates as:

Whirlwinds of danger are raging around us,
O'erwhelming forces of darkness assail,
Still in the fight, see advancing before us
Red Flag of liberty that yet shall prevail.
Then forward you workers, freedom awaits you
O'er all the world, on the land and the sea.
On with the fight for the cause of humanity,
March, march you toilers and the world shall be free.[5]

Other songs of the international Communist movement, such as "Oh, Tortured and Broken," "Bankers and Bosses," and "Song of the Red Air Fleet," expressed revolutionary sentiments in similarly florid language. During the Third Period, sloganeering in music became even more shrill and tendentious. One agit-prop song written by the Hungarian composer F. Szabo was translated in the *Daily Worker* as:

End, end, end their rule
Wipe out the bloody hangman . . .
Workers, let us remember
Sacco, Vanzetti, Scottsboro case.[6]

To American-born workers of the 1920s, such lyrics sounded both anachronistic and alien—not apt to arouse the desired militancy in the proletarian masses. In spite of the popularity of the revolutionary choruses and the efforts of communist bureaucrats, the early American communist movement was not a singing movement.

"Our comrades can't sing," one plaintive letter to the *Daily Worker* in 1927 reported. "They sing half bad the Internationale and the English Boatman song, further they are deaf and dumb. The Freiheit Gesang Ferein does valuable work," the writer conceded, "but we have so many comrades who do not happen to be born Jews and they simply do not understand Yiddish." Arguing for the use of English, the writer cautioned, "It is hard for a movement to grow if it cannot express itself in song. Let the Workers School teach one more subject—teaching of the revolutionary songs."[7]

Four years later, Mike Gold, a communist columnist ever on the lookout for signs of the dawning proletarian culture, wrote in the *New Masses* that the many singing societies like the Freiheit Chorus, with its three hundred members, "sings the most complicated chorals." Complained Gold, "there are no new workers' songs and music being written in this country."[8] And two years later, in 1933, he was still lamenting, "Why don't American workers sing? The Wobblies knew how, but we have still to develop a Communist Joe Hill."[9]

Beginning in 1925, the party leadership had sought to Americanize the movement by directing the main thrust of its organizing activity toward native-born workers. Foreign-language federations, which had existed as political entities since their creation in the Socialist Party in the early 1900s, were officially dissolved. When the rabidly ideological Third Period arrived in 1928, the American communist movement, now stabilized and Stalinized, girded itself for the projected death struggle with capitalist society. The stock market collapse in late 1929 and the onset of the Great Depression legitimized for many this extreme perception of socioeconomic trends. The drastic impact of the Depression broadened communism's appeal to the urban middle class, especially to intellectuals and artists.

The early 1930s thus witnessed a steady influx of bourgeois artists into the movement. There followed a spate of left-wing cultural organizations devoted to furthering "proletarian art," among them the John Reed Clubs for writers and the New Theatre League for actors. Such groups were charged with producing culture that was both realistic (as opposed to abstract) in form and agit-prop in character. In essence, the task of communist artists was not only to portray the continuing revolutionary struggle for the movement's adherents but also to awaken class-conscious feelings in the uncommitted masses. Music certainly was to be a part of all this. But the initial production of songs was sporadic and slim, provided by a few individuals.

V. J. Jerome, Mike Gold, and other communist writers composed or translated a limited number of militant radical lyrics which others set to music. The New York John Reed Club elected a Music Committee in May 1931, whose announced goals were the "creation of songs expressing and projecting the class struggle" and "aiding workers in the creation of such songs [on their own]."[10]

Comrade Harry Alan Potamkin compiled a Pioneer Song Book of parodies and original compositions for youth, published posthumously in 1933. The *Daily Worker* praised it for having caught the "sound of children's voices" in such lyrics as:

> The kids are having a peach of a time, parlez vous,
> The kids are having a peach of a time
> Kicking the cops from the picket line,
> Hinky dinky, parlez vous.[11]

On June 14, 1931, some Communist Party members established the Workers Music League, both to consolidate such song activity and, for the first time, to try to formulate a systematic theoretical approach to proletarian music. The League began functioning that fall and soon had some eighteen or more affiliated organizations located in Boston, Philadelphia, and Chicago, but especially New York.[12] In the main, they still consisted of the revolutionary choral and orchestral units of the foreign-language groups. As part of the League, however, they now had ideological leadership, provided by the Workers Musicians Club in New York—which was renamed the Pierre Degeyter Club, after the composer of the "Internationale" who had died in 1932. The Degeyter Club was a catch-all for otherwise unaffiliated radical musicians. There were divisions for composers, performing artists, and publishers. The most significant of these was the Composers Collective, which developed the most important theoretical statements on music in the American communist movement.

THE COMPOSERS COLLECTIVE

Founded in February 1932, the Composers Collective was a left-wing musician's workshop, producing and performing new and old revolutionary compositions, and formulating detailed guidelines for the creation of proletarian music. Its members numbered some two dozen composers and critics, who had been formally schooled in the standard bourgeois conservatories, including Harvard, Julliard, and Columbia. Many had already written and published important musical work.

They were some of the best young talents in American music—referred to at least once as "the counterculture of the Philharmonic."[13] Among the active participants were ethnomusicologist Charles Seeger (Pete's father); Freiheit Chorus leader Jacob Schaefer; songwriter Marc Blitzstein; and composers Henry Cowell, Wallingford Riegger, George Antheil, Lan Adomian, Elie Siegmeister, Max Margulis, Herbert Haufrecht, and, on the periphery, such luminaries as Aaron Copland.[14] There was still enough stigma attached to membership that some, such as Seeger and Siegmeister, used pseudonyms. From orchestral rehearsals in full formal dress to Greenwich Village in leather jackets they would go, changing names as often as they changed clothes. As Alan Lomax comments, "These were passionate people, you must understand: dedicated to their music, and to their political ideals."[15]

Many of the significant observations that came out of the group's work appeared in the writings of "Carl Sands" and "L. E. Swift"—pseudonyms for, respectively, Charles Seeger and Elie Siegmeister. Most of the Collective's members were not bona fide communists but, as in other fields of cultural activity, had gravitated into the movement's intellectual orbit as a result of the economic and social upheaval of the Depression.

Still, the party paid the rent on the room where the Collective met and maintained a voice within its discussions through a member who acted as a liaison. In the beginning, Collective participants also attended weekly classes in Marxism-Leninism.[16] In view of the political orientation of the group, therefore, it is not surprising that many of its generalizations were often burdened with the heavy ideological cliches of the Third Period. Yet some statements, most often those by Elie Siegmeister, probed previously unexplored relationships between the composer and society with sensitivity and refinement. Siegmeister's most elaborate statement was a sixty-page booklet, *Music and Society* (New York: Critics Group Press, 1938), but his shorter articles and reviews in the left-wing press are also relatively free of the worst Third Period clichés.

Initially, the Collective conceived of music as an extension of the "art is a weapon" theory. "Music is propaganda—always propaganda—and of the most powerful sort," wrote Carl Sands, the Collective's leading spokesperson. Later, he added, "The special task of the Workers Music League is the development of music as a weapon in the class struggle."[17] Such statements in themselves suggest little more than an amateurish application of Marxist agit-prop sloganeering to a previously unpoliticized area of the arts. But as the Collective's elaboration of this notion unfolded in numerous articles by various members in the pages of the *Daily Worker* from 1933 to 1935, they proved a striking cultural manifestation of the political ideology of the Third Period.[18]

Following Stalin's mandate, workers' music was to be "national in form, revolutionary in content," militant in terms of both texts and tunes. Decadent bourgeois influences were to be exorcised as much as possible, although the Collective conceded that all traces of the corrupt musical past could not be eliminated overnight. Ideally, proletarian music was to be created in so unique a form that it would be impossible to imitate and hence remain forever associated with the working masses.

Just how such an original music was to be fashioned, however, was never satisfactorily spelled out. The Collective fumed when Nazi songsmiths in Europe set fascist lyrics to militant German communist and socialist songs, which they believed should be immune from parody. Still, the Collective's writings were mostly optimistic, reporting that progress was being made toward a unique music of the masses. On one occasion, for instance, Charles Seeger, describing an Elie Siegmeister composition alternating four/four and five/eight meter, noted that it was apt to cause technical performance difficulties for most bourgeois singing groups, but "workers' choruses that have tried it do not have any trouble."[19] The transparency of such arguments was evident to many in the Collective even as they were being expounded. Yet members continued to propagandize in this vein for three years in the hope, as one of them recalled, that with the triumph of socialism, greater security and status would accrue to working-class musicians. Once this happened, faulty theories might be refined or eliminated at leisure.

Lacking significant American models for what was envisaged as the new proletarian music, the Collective took as guidance the songs of Hanns Eisler, a composer whose work in the left-wing sector of pre-Hitler Germany won widespread acclaim throughout the international communist movement. Eisler was born in Leipzig in 1898 but spent his early life in Austria. Following World War I, he became a music pupil of the immensely successful Arnold Schoenberg, for whom he retained a profound respect in spite of Eisler's subsequent rejection of bourgeois culture. Moving to Berlin in the mid-1920s, he soon was devoting most of his time to creating music with a communist agenda.[20]

Eisler proved as gifted in this capacity as he was in composing complicated scores using twelve-tone scales. Such songs as "Comintern" and "In Praise of Learning" became exceedingly popular in European political cabarets and radical street demonstrations during the late 1920s and early 1930s. Though he was thoroughly doctrinaire in his statements on proletarian music, Eisler nonetheless viewed himself as an artist rather than a politico. He allowed his membership in the German Communist Party to lapse soon after he secured it in 1926 but continued to contribute his musical services to the revolutionary cause for many years. High on the Nazi liquidation list, he fled Germany in 1933 after Hitler's ascension to power. His first visit to the United States was a triumphal procession as far as the American communist movement was concerned. He was escorted about by no less a personage than Earl Browder, the party's longtime leader. Later he undertook a two-month cross-country tour, demonstrating his music for radical cultural and worker organizations. The Workers Music League feted him lavishly on several occasions, and the Composers Collective received him enthusiastically.

This laudatory response to Eisler's visit was understandable. He was a product of the best European tradition of classical music, in which the Collective's members were also steeped. He symbolized the growing cultural resistance to the rising tide of fascism. And, perhaps most important, his political compositions were indisputably successful—in some cases they were actually being sung by workers. In sum, his influence on the course of American radical music through the mid-1930s was considerable.[21]

Yet in emulating the songs of Eisler and other contemporary European revolutionary composers, the Composers Collective overlooked the fact that such musical expression had few real roots in American culture. Everyone simply assumed that once the workers were exposed to the agit-prop clichés of the Third Period and had their meaning explained, they would welcome the militant ideology expressed in radical song lyrics and the martial spirit of proletarian tunes. But such was not the case. Both the sloganeering and music that the Composers Collective and the Workers Music League created proved too far removed from the mainstream of the American experience to take firm hold among the masses. Sample stanzas from songs in their repertoire, reflecting the tone of much of the music being created at the time, shows why:

> We are the builders, we build the future
> The future world is in our hands.
> We swing our hammers, we use our weapons
> Against our foes in many lands. . . .
> And we, the workers, who are the builders,
> We fight, we do not fear to die.
> "All power and freedom unto the workers!"
> Is our defiant battle cry.

> * * *

> From Atlantic to Pacific
> Sounds the warning; WORKERS, BEWARE!
> Guns are trained on the Soviet Union.
> Proletarians, prepare!

> * * *

> Workers, farmers, Negro and white,
> The lynching bosses we must fight.
> Close your fists and raise them high,
> Labor Defense is our battle cry.
> The Scottsboro boys shall not die,
> Scottsboro boys shall not die,
> Workers led by I.L.D.
> Will set them free, set them free.[22]

Most other lyrics were equally grim. Sometimes the tunes were nearly as bad, because, at least initially, the Composers Collective's search for a "unique" workers' music led it to experiment with dissonant melody lines and irregular meters. Unlike Eisler's songs, quite a few of its "mass" compositions were unsingable in agit-prop situations without prior rehearsal.

Even Charles Seeger, as Carl Sands, produced lyrics like these:

> We are fighting with a host of foes, we do not fear guns or cannon.
> Fascist promises cannot fool us; we will fight them to a finish.
> Comrade, victory is leading you; to the battle gladly marching.
> Mount the Barricades; Mount the Barricades; for the workers' cause
> Carry on the fight for freedom.

Dunaway reports that the melody for Sands's composition was in "a Russian-sounding F-minor, and featuring intervals of fourths against a darkened and dissonant piano accompaniment marked: 'relentlessly.'"[23]

During most of the Third Period, the only relief from such tedious musical production was the series of "workers' rounds" composed by Seeger and Siegmeister. These usually substituted verbal satire for polemics and had light, catchy melodies instead of the ponderous tunes the composers were creating. The lyrics for two such examples were as follows:

> Poor Mister Morgan cannot pay his income tax;
> Pity poor Morgan, he cannot pay.
> He's dead broke, he hasn't got a cent. ("Poor Mister Morgan")

> * * *

> Oh joy upon this earth to live and see the day
> When Rockefeller senior shall up to me and say:
> "Comrade, can you spare a dime?"[24] ("Not If, But When")

While no great importance was attached to these rounds at the time, they were significant nonetheless since they contained the first humor to penetrate American radical music since the days of the IWW. They represented a small break from the rigid forms of European proletarian music. In addition, the publicity surrounding publication of these rounds in *The Workers Song Book No. 1* casually noted that the round was an old form of folk music useful for "introducing part-singing to newly-formed workers' choruses." This marked one of the few times during these years that folksongs received any favorable mention from the orthodox leadership of the communist music movement.

With the onset of the Third Period in late 1928, traditional music and other lore had ceased to be of intellectual interest to most radicals on the Left. The immigrant-language choruses did perform some folk material from Europe, but this was not considered politically or culturally significant until much later. Before 1935, folk songs were mentioned only in the rare instance they contained revolutionary lyrics that coincided with strike or protest activity. In general, Third Period ideologues took a dim view of folk music.

Eisler, for example, scorned traditional songs, calling folk music "a badge of servitude from pre-revolutionary times."[25] In the late 1940s, long after folk music had become a staple of left-wing culture, Eisler still publicly berated Alan Lomax for foisting those "damn songs" on the working class.[26] The original attitude of the Composers Collective was fundamentally hostile as well. Leader Henry Cowell was quoted in the *Daily Worker* as saying: "One of the great faults in the field of workers music has been that of combining revolutionary lyrics with traditional music—music which can by no means be termed revolutionary."[27] In 1934, Charles Seeger—whose fifteen-year-old son would become arguably the most effective proponent of folk songs in the twentieth century—patiently spelled out in the *Daily Worker* why the Collective distrusted traditional music: "Not all folk-tunes are suitable to the revolutionary movement," he wrote. "Many of them are complacent, melancholy, defeatist— originally intended to make slaves endure their lot—pretty, but not the stuff for a militant proletariat to feed upon." He praised the movement for distancing itself from traditional music. "Already the best mass songs begin to sound less like melancholy folk-songs, dreary hymn tunes, silly patriotic propaganda and sentimental anesthetics from Broadway," he complained. He did concede that

> [f]olk-music that shows clearly a spirit of resentment toward oppression or vigorous resistance is valuable. There is still some room for occasional paro-dies of old songs such as "Pie in the Sky" and "Soup," but not for many of them. The revolutionary movement will have its own music. We shall keep as much as we like of the old, but build better upon it.[28]

CHARLES SEEGER

Charles Seeger, who died in 1979 at the age of ninety-two, enjoyed a comfortable early life that seemed unlikely to lead him to membership in the left-wing movements of his day. The development of his left-wing sensibilities is an interesting example of how the movement became attractive to intellectuals. Though he was born in Mexico City, Seeger came from a long New England tradition of Unitarianism. He was influenced by his mother's close adherence to Protestant morality and by an ancestral sense of *noblesse oblige*. He grew up in financial circumstances that alternated between average and quite well off, depending on turns in his father's business. He recalled during an interview that his only glimpse of poverty in childhood came at age nine when he inadvertently stumbled on the dwelling of the Seegers' gardener, who lived on the Seeger estate in Staten Island, New York.

When the family moved back to Mexico as Seeger turned thirteen, he began to study violin and guitar and acquainted himself with Mexican folk and popular song. At seventeen he entered Harvard to study music composition, much to the disappointment of his father, who wanted him to become a businessman. But Seeger's musical aptitude was clear—he was graduated magna cum laude and went to Germany to study music for three years. During that time he had an opportunity to conduct at the Cologne Opera. At age twenty-four he returned to the United States and soon accepted a full professorship at the University of California, Berkeley, the youngest full professor in the university's history.

Important critics were hailing Seeger as among the most promising of young composers in America. His courses concentrated on the technical aspects of Western fine art music; folk music was dismissed in a lecture or two as an expression of the art forms of a dying past, and popular music was ignored. While at Berkeley, though, Seeger's outlook on society and his own career changed, as he began to read widely in the literature of the humanities and social sciences that he'd missed during his undergraduate education. Recalling his introduction to the great philosophers like Friedrich Hegel, Immanuel Kant, Sigmund Freud, Alfred Kroeber, and Karl Marx, he noted the great difficulty he'd experienced trying to comprehend Marx.

Berkeley also offered exposure to some socialists and reformers. One, Carlton Parker, later an influential sociologist, took Seeger through the California central valley, exhibiting the deplorable conditions among migratory workers. That trip opened Seeger's eyes to the discrepancies between the comforts of his own life and the agonies suffered by workers not far from his doorstep. He was profoundly affected. Seeger began listening to—and sometimes debating—anarchists, socialists and Wobblies, from Emma Goldman to Bertrand Russell. In time, Russell became Seeger's spiritual mentor.

Once Seeger was invited to address the Radical Club of San Francisco on Wagner's role in the 1848 socialist revolt in Germany—after which a Wobbly sympathizer blasted him as a "lily-livered professor who didn't know anything about life" and could only theorize about it from a university armchair. Seeger replied, "You're right. I'm just leaving." After that, Seeger just got friendlier with the Wobblies, attending their meetings, saving their literature, treasuring their songs, and sometimes addressing their gatherings, though he never joined them formally. In December 1916, he addressed a large audience at Harvard on "The Value of Music," saying:

> I can compose music for $5,000 a year. But there has just been published a Congressional survey of living standards. A very large percentage of people in this country are living on substandard wages. It bothers me to think that my salary represents the difference between starvation and minimum living standards for people and a comfortable life for me.

The dilemma troubled him deeply. "I [gave] up composition because I couldn't approve of the music I liked, and I couldn't like the music that I approved, and I couldn't make either one of them connect in any way with the social situation I found."

In 1919, Seeger was fired from his professorship at Berkeley because of the pacifist sentiments he had been uttering since the U.S. entry into World

War I. Lacking funds to fight his dismissal in the courts and finding himself unable to compose, he was emotionally exhausted. He retired to his father's home in New York—with his wife and children (including two-year-old Pete) to recover his health and think things over. Two years later, Seeger packed his family and possessions into a trailer and headed South on a tour intended to bring "good music to the music-less people of America." Aiming for Florida, they never got past North Carolina, where the local folk at first took them to be internal revenue agents bent on raiding local whiskey stills. They and the town eventually made friends, but the cultural gap remained large. The Seegers played piano and violin and listened to a lot of traditional fiddling, and they developed with their new friends a mutual admiration of virtuosity in instrumental technique but little appreciation of style.

Faced with this musical standoff, and unskilled at raising money from the wealthy to pay for his efforts at educating the poor, Seeger abandoned his venture in the spring of 1921, returning with his family to New York to resume his professional music life, devoid of politics or overt social commitment.[29]

Then came the Great Depression. Though he was never threatened with financial ruin, Seeger was shaken by economic dislocation and saw the strain of the crisis on the morale and lives of many contemporaries. His philosophical education at Berkeley and experiences of real-life social ills instilled in him a call to personal action, and in the winter of 1932 he joined the new Composers Collective. His writing ranged from the hackneyed clichés and fiery slogans of the propagandist to the dispassionate but committed concern of the professional scholar. With Sidney Finkelstein, who came on the scene later, Seeger remains one of two American Marxist musical theoreticians of consequence.[30]

Charles Seeger wrote for the *Daily Worker* as well as for scholarly journals such as the *Encyclopedia of the Social Sciences*. Always, he was wrestling with the dilemma he saw posed by his social concerns and his musical interests. "I was strictly partisan in the former as I could be, and as strictly scholarly as I could be in the latter," he wrote in a 1971 letter. He has said several times that he occasionally wrote propagandistic pronouncements of music that his own academic knowledge would have led him to dispute in other contexts. Both at the time and later, he acknowledged the duality of this intellectual existence. "As to the double life," he wrote me, "I had always been conscious of that from early childhood on. When I ran into Freud, I was delighted to find I was not the only person in the world that knew it."

In the 1930s, he viewed his political actions as a tactical or strategic necessity, not as a moral issue. He reasoned that the prime need of musicians, like everyone else, was the reorganization of society along socialist lines so that all workers, including cultural, might obtain a better life for themselves. Intellectual discrepancies over music theory could be ironed out after that happened, he believed. We will return to Seeger later, when he and others in the movement elevated their opinions of folk music. But it's worth noting here that even in his letter of 1971, he wrote:

> Folklore and folk music are only temporary bypaths for me, and I sometimes rile up a bit when I am referred to as a student of folk music. . . . I make this sole and last appeal *not* to represent me as a student of folk music except as a necessary fulfillment of the ordinary task of the musicologist as I see it, namely the study of *all* the music of a culture, a geographical area, or the whole world.

There was obvious disagreement within the leftist movement about the virtues of folk music. In 1932, the Workers Music League published the *Red Song Book,* which included half a dozen Appalachian and other strike songs based on folk and popular tunes. Among them were "Miners' Song," "On the Picket Line," "Poor Miner's Farewell" by Aunt Molly Jackson, "I.L.D. Song" by Ella May Wiggins, "Soup Song" by Maurice Sugar (printed anonymously), and "Miner's Flux." But the Workers Music League's own house organ, *The Worker Musician,* panned the *Red Song Book,* complaining of the "immaturity" and "arrested development" of the Kentucky mining songs, and attributing the songs' poor musical quality to the "exploitation of the coal barons."[31]

The Composers Collective published its own compositions in the two-volume *Workers Song Book* in 1934 and 1935. Underscoring the skepticism with which the Collective viewed traditional song is the absence of any folk song parodies or words and music in the traditional style, except for the humorous workers' rounds by Siegmeister and Seeger and, in the second volume, two Negro protest songs collected by Lawrence Gellert. But the songbook also includes a pseudospiritual, with lyrics by *Daily Worker* editor V. J. Jerome, that seem blindly patronizing toward African Americans:

> Daddy is a Communist
> Locked up in de pen;
> Didn' rob nor didn' steal
> Led de workin' men
> Wisht ah had a sea of milk
> Make you strong an' soun';
> Daddy's waitin' till you come,
> Break dat prison down![32]

Further evidence of the Composers Collective's failure to understand the folk idiom is illustrated in its inability to comprehend the songs and musical style of Aunt Molly Jackson. This Kentucky mountain woman, ballad maker, and blacklisted militant organizer for the radical National Miners Union, attended two or three meetings of the Collective around 1933 during which members debated how to construct a good proletarian song. She rose and sang some of her own strike compositions, which were set to traditional melodies and couched in the language of rural Appalachia. It was a perfect, and perfectly natural, fusion of music with social struggle, in a medium comfortable to her constituents. It went right over the Collective's collective heads. In a 1967 interview, Charles Seeger recalled that Aunt Molly's songs left the group more bewildered than inspired and that members of the Collective then showed her their own work, which likewise made no meaningful impression on Aunt Molly.[33] She sat quietly in the back from then on, never asked to sing again. Seeger took her back to her little apartment and said, "Molly, they didn't understand you. But I know some young people who will want to learn your songs." His son was one.[34]

In December 1934, the Composers Collective's members met to discuss emerging American and Soviet communist theories of socialist realism. New ideas suggested that proletarian songs be constructed in simplistic folk song–like style to make them more meaningful to workers. The *Daily Worker* reported that Henry Cowell, a leader in the group, flatly rejected such notions. Sticking to the old, orthodox call for a "unique" music culture for the masses, Cowell contended instead that "technical innovations must be steadily and slowly introduced into workers' music, and that workers appreciate it."[35]

But events were occurring in both the international and domestic communist movements that would render this statement one of the last of its kind. Soon, the esoteric and unrealistic Third Period precepts of the Workers Music League would be relegated to the scrap heap of left-wing cultural history. New musical orientations were arising that would place workers' songs firmly in the American experience and redirect communist music activity toward folk songs.

NOTES

1. The beginnings of the Third Period and the Sixth World Congress are traced by Theodore Draper in *American Communism and Soviet Russia* (New York: Viking, 1960), chap. 14.

2. See Theodore Draper, *The Roots of American Communism* (New York: Viking, 1957), and Robert K. Murray, *Red Scare: A Study in National Hysteria, 1919–1920* (New York: McGraw-Hill, 1955) for detailed coverage of the early American communist movement and its struggle for existence. More recent works include

Maurice Isserman, *Which Side Were You On? The American Communist Party during the Second World War* (Middletown, Conn.: Wesleyan University Press, 1982); Harvey Klehr and John Earl Haynes, *The American Communist Movement: Storming Heaven Itself* (New York: Twayne, 1992); Harvey Klehr, *The Heyday of American Communism: The Depression Decade* (New York: Basic Books, 1984); Harvey Klehr, John E. Haynes, and Jyrill M. Anderson, *The Soviet World of American Communism* (New Haven, Conn.: Yale University Press, 1998); Fraser M. Ottanelli, *The Communist Party of the United States: From the Depression to World War II* (New Brunswick, N.J.: Rutgers University Press, 1991); Irving Howe and Lewis Coser, *The American Communist Party: A Critical History,* 2d ed. (New York: Da Capo, 1974).

3. Information on the Freiheit Gesang Ferein can be found in David Shapiro, "Schaefer's 'Twelve' and the Freiheit Singing Society," *Daily Worker* (May 27, 1927), 6, and also in Carl Sands (a.k.a. Charles Seeger), "The Freiheit Gesang Ferein," *Daily Worker* (March 22, 1935), 5. Data on Schaefer himself may be found in the obituary "J. Schaefer, Noted Music Leader, Dead," *Daily Worker* (December 2, 1936), 5.

4. Robert Kent, "Singing for the 'Daily,'" *Daily Worker* (January 17, 1934), 5.

5. As printed in the *Red Song Book* (New York, 1932), 15.

6. "Lenin Meetings Hear New Songs and Fine Pageant," *Daily Worker* (January 23, 1933), 2.

7. David Berkingoff, "Why Not Sing" ("Letters From Our Readers" column), *Daily Worker* (October 11, 1927), 4.

8. "Toward an American Revolutionary Culture," *New Masses* (July 1931): 13.

9. "What a World," *Daily Worker* (October 19, 1933), 5.

10. "Workers Music" ("Workers Art" column), *New Masses* (May 1931): 13.

11. "Fighting Songs for Workers' Children" (review), *Daily Worker* (August 12, 1933), 5.

12. "History of the Workers Music League," *The Worker Musician* 1, no. 1 (December 1932): 7; Charles Seeger, "On Proletarian Music," *Modern Music* 11 (March–April 1934): 124. The League did not begin functioning until the fall of 1931, and several articles date its formation at this time rather than in the spring; see "Workers Music League," *New Masses* (October 1931): 31.

13. David K. Dunaway, "Unsung Songs of Protest: The Composers Collective of New York," *New York Folklore* 5, nos. 1–2 (Summer 1979): 2.

14. See Ann M. Pescatello, *Charles Seeger: A Life in American Music* (Pittsburgh: University of Pittsburgh Press, 1992), and Eric Gordon, *Mark the Music: The Life and Work of Marc Blitzstein* (New York: St. Martin's, 1989).

15. Dunaway, "Unsung Songs of Protest."

16. "Pierre Degeyter Club" in the *1933 First American Workers Music Olympiad* program, New York, 3.

17. C.S. [Carl Sands], "The Concert of the Pierre Degeyter Club Orchestra," *Daily Worker* (January 2, 1934), 5; "Workers Audience Applauds Gold's Poem Set to Music," *Daily Worker* (June 26, 1934), 5.

18. See especially C.S. [Carl Sands], "A Program for Proletarian Composers," *Daily Worker* (January 16, 1934), 5, and Sands's four-part series on proletarian music (March 1934), 5–8; also Seeger, "On Proletarian Music."

19. Seeger, "On Proletarian Music," 125.

20. For details on Eisler, see Eric Bentley's introduction to his *Songs of Bertolt Brecht and Hanns Eisler* (New York: Oak, 1966), and "The Songs of Hanns Eisler," *Sing Out!* 14, no. 6 (January 1965): 34–37; in the contemporary communist press of the 1930s, see "Famous Composer of 'Comintern' to Tour America," *Daily Worker* (February 9, 1935), 9, and Ashley Pettis, "Eisler, Maker of Red Songs," *New Masses* (February 26, 1935), 18–19.

21. Much of this discussion of Eisler is based on material gleaned in interviews with Mordecai Bauman, Max Margulis, Elie Siegmeister, Charles Seeger, and Earl Browder. See the sources list in the bibliography for specific dates. For Eisler's political affiliations, see Robert K. Carr, *The House Committee on Un-American Activities, 1945–1950* (Ithaca, N.Y.: Cornell University Press, 1952), 43.

22. Texts are from the *Red Song Book,* 14, 22, and the *Workers Song Book No. 1* (New York: Workers Music League, 1934), 5, respectively.

23. David Dunaway, "Unsung Songs of Protest," 4.

24. *Workers Song Book No. 1,* 10, and *Workers Song Book No. 2* (New York: Workers Music League, 1935), 48, respectively.

25. David K. Dunaway, *How Can I Keep from Singing: Pete Seeger* (New York: McGraw-Hill, 1981), 40.

26. Charles Seeger interview, November 3, 1967.

27. "Cowell Performs Own Compositions in Piano Recital," *Daily Worker* (November 21, 1933), 5.

28. "Workers Audience Applauds Gold's Poem Set to Music" and "A Program for Proletarian Composers."

29. See Ann M. Pescatello, *Charles Seeger: A Life in American Music* (Pittsburgh: University of Pittsburgh Press, 1992); Judith Tick, *Ruth Crawford Seeger: A Composer's Search for American Music* (New York: Oxford University Press, 1997).

30. Pete Seeger, "Charles Seeger: A Man of Music," *Sing Out!* (May 1979): 18–19.

31. Nathan Nevins, "Red Song Book," *Worker Musician,* 8.

32. Quoted in David King Dunaway, "Unsung Songs of Protest," 10.

33. Charles Seeger interview, June 7, 1967. See also Shelly Ramalis, *Pistol Packin' Mama: Aunt Molly Jackson and the Politics of Folksong* (Urbana: University of Illinois Press, 1999).

34. Communication with Pete Seeger, December 1998.

35. A. B., "Symposium and Concert at John Reed Club," *Daily Worker* (December 20, 1934), 5.

4

The Growth of Communist Interest in Folklore

The American communist movement's rapidly developing admiration for folk culture was neither dictated from nor controlled by Moscow. But there was certainly a correlation. The American movement shifted from negative to positive in its attitudes toward traditional song and art around the same time the leaders of the Soviet Union did, and for some of the same reasons.

Lee Hays, Burl Ives, Cisco Houston, Woody Guthrie (l-r)

Soviet state control of musical expression in Russia was not accomplished overnight. The Bolsheviks nationalized all music publishing houses as soon as they seized power, but they still had to wage a fifteen-year struggle before achieving control over the ideology, form, and direction of contemporary Russian musical activity. Even up through the mid-1920s, communist and nonpolitical music organizations flourished side by side. One Moscow periodical entitled *Musical Culture* made its debut in 1924 under the slogan "Music is music, not ideology."[1] Gradually, however, the Soviet-oriented musicians' groups gained the upper hand. In the same year, 1924, the Russian Association of Proletarian Musicians (RAPM) was founded and served thereafter as the state's chief official music society until the government dissolved it in 1932. According to Nicholas Slonimsky:

> The Association minced no words about its mandate to promulgate Third Period ideology among Soviet musicians. Its third and last statement of intentions, posited in 1929, proclaimed: "The ultimate aim of the RAPM is extension of the hegemony of the proletariat in the music field," it proclaimed in 1929. It set three tasks for itself; the ponderous language of the proclamation suggests the dogmatic mood of the times:
>
> a) Extension of the proletarian Communist influence to the musical masses, re-education and reorganization of these masses in order to direct their work and creative talents towards Socialist upbuilding.
>
> b) Creation of Marxist musicology and Marxist musical criticism, critical absorption of the musical culture of the past and of contemporary musical literature from the viewpoint of the proletariat.
>
> c) Demonstration of proletarian musical creative productions and creation of necessary conditions for complete development and growth of proletarian music.[2]

Rigid government control of artistic forms may seem incomprehensible to Americans in the early twenty-first century. But an appreciation for historical context is critical to understanding the communist movement of the 1930s. Freedom of expression was still a concept more alien than familiar in most parts of the world. Monarchies were just starting to exit as the prevailing form of government and had often punished creative expression that offended the royal court. Early communist policy was distinguished more by the clumsy, untempered way it was articulated and carried out than by the basic notion that politicians wanted to control mass communication. The proletarian musicians' association was an instrument of the Soviet government to systematically exercise such control.

But when it came to folklore, the association was just as ambivalent as were the early Bolshevik organizations. There were many flattering references to Russian folksong tradition but also corresponding complaints.

The czarist-era composers who were still working in the 1920s were criticized for using traditional motifs and melodies in their compositions. They were accused of being unnecessarily romantic and nonrevolutionary and were sometimes made to confess the error of their ways. In March 1926, the Political Bureau of the Department of Education of the Soviet Union actually instructed musicians "not to follow the folklore pattern in composition of choral works designed for mass singing."[3]

Such vague dogma was an invisible tightrope on which musicians were supposed to dance without falling, guided by the proletarian musicians' association. RAPM divided the music of the past into two classes: that produced by the "toilers, the exploited, and the oppressed classes (the so called folk music)" and that created by the bourgeoisie ("virtually the entire bulk of written 'cultured' music").[4] Even with this distinction, folk music evoked ambivalent responses. On the one hand, the association called it "the most valuable possession" of the downtrodden masses; yet at the same time it was suspect for its "contamination" with patriotic, religious, and other capitalist themes.[5] In practice, traditional music was seldom incorporated into RAPM's Third Period proletarian cultural ethos.

By 1932, the winds of change swept through the Soviet world of arts and letters as the Third Period began to give way to the era of the Popular Front, and proletarian art theories gradually were replaced by the doctrine of "socialist realism." The RAPM and other similar cultural organizations were disbanded in 1932, partly because it was recognized that their sectarian dogma was stifling artistic expression at all levels, but more because the bureaucrats in charge of these units were beginning to function independently of national government control.

Disbanding the RAPM did not allay concerns that folk music was counterrevolutionary. In June 1933, Soviet cultural official Lev Lebedinsky delivered the government's view to the Second International Music Conference of the International Union of Revolutionary Music, criticizing the lack of class-conscious spirit in traditional peasant music: "the peasantry have created music of great value, but now only of an historical character;" Lebedinsky chided contemptuously, adding:

> These old peasant folk songs were created by an individualist-peasant consciousness, enslaved and made impotent by nature and economics. Intonation, language, means of musical expression and instruments of old folk music are absolutely incapable of expressing the emotional world of the proletariat, the class standing at the helm of history.[6]

With the First All-Union Congress of Soviet Writers in the late summer of 1934, the final curtain fell on the traditional Third Period dogma. At that meeting, Andrei Zhdanov and Maxim Gorky formally promulgated the new doctrine of "socialist realism."

Socialist realism at bottom was and is a political theory; as is usually the case with political theories, its literary and aesthetic applications are in many ways contradictory and ambiguous. The fundamental philosophy of socialist realism is that art is a reflection of reality, and therefore it ought to be historical and concrete (in other words, realistic) in its representation of reality. This is especially important during phases of "revolutionary" development. As historian Donald Drew Egbert describes, "by definition it [art] must be socially useful, socially dynamic, and educational; consequently . . . it can be produced only by socially-minded artists, each of whom is participating in the daily activities and emotions of the community as a whole."[7]

To the communist world, this definition signified that art should seek to uplift the masses, affirm their aspirations, and guide their thoughts in class-conscious or "progressive" directions. For art to be socially useful implied that artists must attempt to communicate with the people through mediums understandable to them. That approach eliminated, for example, formalism in literature, futurism in poetry, and abstractions in painting; these forms of art expression were considered introverted and not readily comprehensible to the masses. In cultural terms, the "realistic" representation of life through art was the only way to serve the needs of society. Socialist realism also encouraged glorification of past revolutionary struggles and the explication of their triumphs and travails throughout the world. Its orientation was both regional and cross-cultural; as the 1930s progressed, the new doctrine was used both to bolster Soviet nationalist spirit and to serve as a theoretical underpinning of a united cultural front against world fascism.

So composers stopped searching for a "unique" proletarian music in esoteric corridors of classical music expression. Instead, the new emphasis on socialist realism fostered a return to familiar lyric and melodic forms more acceptable to the masses. And this led to an official communist upgrading of folklore as a positive creative force in the life of the people. In time, this attitude would lead to the popularization and intellectual use of folk songs and traditional melodies of the people on a scale unimaginable in the previous decade.

Hitherto, folk traditions had been regarded as an important cultural product of the masses but too corrupt or nonmilitant in themselves to be of use to the proletariat. Now it was emphasized that songs, legends, and other lore offered a realistic reflection of the people's historical and social experiences and that folk art portrayed the people's genuine feelings for reality. Folklore provided emotional solace for the folk and helped ease their burdens of toil and misery. Frequently, if not always, it recounted the democratic aspirations and revolutionary traditions of the past and present, lending a sense of hope and communal spirit. Since popular traditions were produced by the lower classes, not the bourgeoisie, then surely they were suffused with a class-consciousness. Folk traditions were seen as the collective cultural expression of the masses themselves—as opposed to the formulations of intellectuals, artists, and bureaucrats who spoke of and for the people but without real knowledge of their lives.

Moreover, folklore seemed to satisfy both the extrovert and introvert worldviews of socialist realism, the communists' desire to be both nationalistic and internationalistic. Egbert explains:

> On the one hand, folk art can be regarded as having international implications because it is considered to possess the germinating power out of which all great art everywhere arises . . . its content, like that of homely proverbs, is much the same regardless of national boundaries. Yet folk art . . . can also be considered national in spirit in that it expresses the traditions of some specific nationality or region.[8]

Hence both international and national cultural unity could be demonstrated through folk art in the face of the spreading threat of fascism throughout the globe. In addition, although folklore was an expression of the collective cultural and aesthetic experiences of the people, it found artistic release through the words, music, and visual creativity of gifted individuals imbued with the spirit and understanding of the larger group's ways and worldview.

So the content and form of folklore, taken as a whole, seemed particularly well suited to represent the ideals of socialist realism. Furthermore, the fear that this prerevolutionary lore had been contaminated by capitalism diminished dramatically, as Stalin himself began to collaborate with bourgeois countries to combat fascism. The USSR cultural intelligentsia was free thereafter to extol folk art without excessive hedging on what previously were considered its drawbacks. Traditions voicing national or regional patriotism were no longer shunned but in many cases encouraged. Sad songs, laments, and other nonpolitical material were recognized as reflecting hard times and real life even if they were not as militant as was previously thought desirable. Indeed, as the years wore on, so much emphasis was placed on what were deemed folklore's "progressive" features that it obscured the innately conservative, sometimes even reactionary (in political terms), tendencies of oral and social tradition.

THE SOVIET WRITERS CONGRESS OF 1934

The rise of folklore to official prominence in the Soviet Union was obviously a gradual and incremental process, responsive to both domestic and international political developments. Certainly the economic and cultural autonomy granted to national minority groups by Stalin in the 1920s helped pave the way for the political acceptance of folk art a decade later. The drive for collective security against fascist tyranny was another prime factor, as was the promulgation of the doctrine of socialist realism. But two landmark events in the mid-1930s pinpoint the arrival of folklore as a tour de force in the aesthetic ideology of the state. One was the series of speeches by Maxim Gorky at the First All-Union Congress of Soviet Writers in the late summer of 1934. Gorky, the most prominent Russian author alive at the time, had been selected by Stalin's government to head the newly formed Union of Soviet Writers, which replaced the disbanded proletarian literature organizations. Gorky was sympathetic to the revolution and had been a friend of Lenin's, though over the years criticized the excesses of both.

In his chief address to the 1934 Congress, Gorky attempted to chart the future course of Soviet writers under socialist realism. In doing so, he drew heavily on the literature and folk traditions of the past. Reminiscent of earlier thinking, notably Bucher's *Arbeit und Rhythmus,* he asserted that folklore owed its artistic strength to its functions—people's attempts to lighten their labors and increase productivity.

Near the end of his address, he interrupted his remarks to point out the presence at the Congress of the distinguished traditional singer Suleyman Stalsky. "Cherish the people who are able to create such pearls of poetry as Suleyman produces," he urged his audience of writers.

> The beginning of the art of words is in folklore. Collect your folklore, make a study of it, work it over. It will yield a great deal of material both to you and to us, the poets and prose writers of the Soviet Union. The better we come to know the past, the more easily, the more deeply and joyfully we shall understand the great significance of the present which we are creating.[9]

Other delegates, particularly those from national minorities and the more remote provinces, also touched on folklore in their addresses. Looking back at the Congress, Y. M. Sokolov, a later Soviet folklore scholar, wrote, "Public sanction was given to the idea of folklore, oral poetry, as one of the inalienable parts of the contemporary literary movement . . . [that] folklore is just as much a part of contemporary social life, of the structure of the new socialist society, as is artistic written literature."[10]

Following the Writers' Congress, folklore became a favorite topic of discussion in the Soviet press. Folklore clubs were founded in many factories, and on collective farms, teachers, workers, and farmers collected traditional materials, some of which eventually proved valuable to scholars. At official functions, traditional singers, narrators, and artists received lavish honors and publicity. Some actually were granted financial stipends by the government. Academic folklore activity also increased markedly.

FOLKLORE AND SOVIET POLITICS

While the Writers' Congress was clearly pivotal, another bellwether event dramatically underscored the heightened political importance of traditional materials in the Soviet Union. Late in 1936, the communist newspaper *Pravda* turned what might have been a minor squabble over the origins of epic folk songs into a national debate over the value of folklore. The controversy arose when the government's Committee on Matters of Art ordered one of the Moscow theaters to cease production of Denjan Bednyj's play *The Knights*. The committee charged that the drama misrepresented the nation's history and epic tradition through its desultory portrait of certain epic folk songs, known as *byliny,* and, further, that the play suggested that *byliny* were created by singers in the courts of the medieval nobility and only much later did the poems seep down to the masses— which also happened to be the view of many Soviet folklorists. (The scholars' outlook in turn derived from the more general *gesunkenes kulturgut* theories of Hans Naumann, the German scholar, and others that were temporarily in vogue throughout academic folklore quarters in Europe during the 1920s.)

Beginning on November 15, *Pravda, Izvestia,* and various literary and teaching publications joined the controversy. In prominent articles they supported the closing of the play, insisting that Russian epic poetry reflected the heroic qualities of the Soviet people and was created by the people rather than the upper classes. Actually, the state's insistence on the popular origins of folk traditions was largely valid. What was socially significant was the intensity of the public controversy the episode generated.

Delinquent academicians promptly recanted previous writings adjudged to be erroneous. Even such noted scholars as the brothers Sokolov, N. P. Andreyev, A. M. Astakhova, and M. K. Azadovsky proclaimed adherence to the new party theories of folklore. Subsequently, a rewritten version of *The Knights* was allowed to reopen on the Moscow stage.[11]

To grasp the real meaning of the controversy, one can read between the lines of what folklorist Y. M. Sokolov wrote about it later: "Soviet folkloristics began to be impressed more deeply with those tasks with which science is faced in our time, tasks set for it by the Party and the government." These tasks, he said, were "to collaborate in the fostering of Soviet patriotism" and, as well, in "the fostering of genuine internationalism, based upon respect for the national culture of every fraternal nation." Such respect for the culture, he noted, meant "the revelation of that vast significance which the creations of workingmen have had in the development of world culture; [and] for those ideational and artistic heights attained by the creative work of the people at the present time in the USSR."[12] The manner in which the whole affair was handled indicates the Soviet government's determination to control the use and interpretation of the lore of the people.

The Russian Association of Proletarian Musicians had little or no direct influence on its American counterparts; in fact, the RAPM was nearly out of business before the Workers Music League and Composers Collective got started in the fall–winter of 1931–32. Even though the American groups were mostly oblivious to the forces in motion that soon would outmode their narrow and doctrinaire approach to music, they generally maintained the same hostility toward folksong that was ideologically chic throughout the international communist movement.

Plenty of other revolutionary music, however, was independently popular in left-wing circles in many countries. Between 1932 and 1935, the Communist International in Moscow attempted to coordinate and consolidate the performance and discussion of such music. To this end, the International Music Buro was organized in Moscow in February 1932 under the aegis of the International Union of Revolutionary Theatres, then the principal agit-prop cultural unit of the international communist movement.[13] Within two years, the Buro claimed affiliates in France, England, Japan, Czechoslovakia, Alsace-Lorraine, Belgium, and the United States and contacts with music organizations in nine other countries. The Workers Music League (WML), founded a few months earlier than the Buro itself, was incorporated into its structure as the American Section. But the Buro's ties with the WML proved stronger on paper than in fact. The League did at least pay lip service in the beginning to Moscow's coordinating efforts. It sent Jacob Schaefer, conductor of the Freiheit Gesang Ferein, as its delegate to Moscow's First International Music Conference in November 1932. Schaefer and Lan Adomian were among three League representatives on the Buro's staff. The German representative who joined them there was Hanns Eisler, the composer who had earlier achieved such influence over international left-wing music, including that in the United States.

A Workers Music Olympiad was held in the City College of New York Auditorium in May 1933, timed to coincide with a similar music festival held in Moscow. The Buro's *International Collection of Revolutionary Songs* (Moscow, 1934) contained Russian, German, and English texts of thirteen proletarian songs from eight countries. The collection was extolled at length in a two-part review essay by Carl Sands (Charles Seeger) in the *Daily Worker,* especially for its militant introduction outlining Third Period music ideology.[14] The WML also participated in various international song and choral work contests sponsored by the Buro.[15]

But still there is scant evidence of much positive response to the Buro's ideological directives. The Buro's parent group in Moscow issued a twenty-five-page marching order to its affiliates in other countries in June 1934, just before the landmark All-Union Congress of Soviet Writers where Gorky restored folk music to respectability. An uncatalogued collection in the Library of Congress contains what appears to be a translation, just as it must have been received by members of the Workers Music League. It was cleverly entitled "Theses on Organizational Principles in the Revolutionary Movement in the Theatre, Cinema, Music, Dance and Song." Moscow wanted its cultural affiliates to enforce "discipline" in artistic expression wherever possible. "The bourgeoisie," it said, "was using all means in order to win over the farm population and to isolate it from the revolutionary proletariat." To counteract these efforts, the Buro wanted its sections to stress themes of antifascist cooperation and socialist realism and to pay special attention to work "in the village, on the farms, among small peasants and peasant workers." The document was intended to address the work of many cultural organizations in a variety of countries and doesn't seem particularly addressed to the American scene. The Workers Music League is mentioned only once in passing, and revolutionary music activity in the United States is mentioned hardly at all. Nor is there evidence that any American readers marched as directed.

To the contrary, by 1934–35, the influence of the International Music Buro had begun to wane in many quarters of the American left-wing music scene. Members of the Composers Collective, in particular, started to chafe at party dogma and to break with many of the rigid assumptions of the past regarding workers' music. This process of reassessment resulted in part from an accumulated series of conflicts with bureaucrats and dogmatists in the Pierre Degeyter Club and party spokespeople about the WML. Though the collective continued to be tolerant of outside political criticism throughout its existence, some of the doctrinaire haggling that took place bordered on the absurd. Elie Siegmeister, for example, was once told that he knew nothing about creating proletarian mass songs because his composition about the Scottsboro case ended on a downbeat, whereas workers' music *always* ended on an upbeat! Lawrence Gellert, an important collector of African American music and a visitor at the collective's meetings on the infrequent occasions when he returned from the South, was called to task for his use of the term *nigger* in his articles and song texts, even though he only used the word in the course of direct quotation, usually of the speech and verse of southern blacks themselves. Gellert argued back without conceding the point. Under pressure, Charles Seeger reluctantly added a few lines espousing Marxist music theory to an otherwise nonpolitical essay entitled "Preface to an All Linguistic Treatment of Music." The addition distorted the meaning of his concluding remarks, but ironically, the passage got cut for length and never reached print. Such incidents were comic in some instances but highly irritating and unsettling in many more.

AMERICAN RESPONSE TO SOVIET INTEREST IN FOLKLORE

Well before Gorky started removing the stigma from folk music (in communist eyes, at least) in his talk to the Writers' Congress in 1934, the American collective had begun changing its own position on the subject. Charles Seeger, Elie Siegmeister, and others had developed their individual sensibilities about folk arts as they pursued their own private research and began saying as much in print. In January 1934, the *Daily Worker* ran a long, serious article praising folk music even while acknowledging that most of it wasn't political. George Maynard wrote in "Music Appreciation among Workers," "Since time began the masses of the people have been the truest creators of music." He cited "aboriginal, Australian, and African tribes, Central Asiatic nomads, Negroes and Hillbillies in America, for having created music forms and contents of the highest value."

Having thus contradicted previous Marxist writings about art improving with science, Maynard went on to dispense with the idea that art was valuable only as a political instrument and that folk music had been corrupted by selfish, capitalist emotions ("an individualist-peasant consciousness, enslaved and made impotent by nature and economics, the Party had lately described folk tradition"). He observed approvingly, "Love, fear, worship and bondage have been some of the themes which give birth to folk music," adding, "[T]he theme of revolt has been rarer, but strong and compelling when it appeared."[16]

Two weeks later, Lan Adomian proposed broadening the repertoires of workers' choruses to include "Negro songs of protest, work songs, railroad songs, [and] cowboy and hill songs," explaining, "These would be a colorful addition to our repertoire. Such an approach would carry us a long way toward rooting our work in the tradition of American music. It would give the lie to those who insist that our music is nothing but an importation from the outside."[17]

Over the next two years, the collective undertook an independent review of the international communist movement's theoretical premises about proletarian music. This reassessment was stimulated, survivors have acknowledged, by the members' realization that their song efforts were not having the desired impact on the masses. So the collective set out to modify its mostly esoteric and unrealistic approach to workers' music. At first, changes were relatively minor. For instance, simple expediency in the crisis atmosphere of strikes dictated that familiar melodies and ear-catching lyrics be use to rally support for the local cause and to propagandize the uncommitted native proletariat. Yet, while recognizing this intellectually, the collective continued to compose songs with complicated tunes and alien terminology. And it continued to equate the singing masses with the Freiheit Gesang Ferein or the *Daily Worker* Chorus.

But there was at least a sense of something wrong. For example, Siegmeister, as "L. E. Swift," complained of the inferiority of proletarian song texts, characterizing them as "stilted, un-American, old fashioned, difficult to sing [and] politically vague."[18] He suggested that simplicity, directness, fairly regular verse patterns, and rhyme would do much to make mass songs palatable to the workers to whom they were intended to appeal.

Charles Seeger repeatedly said much the same thing. As "Carl Sands," he asked in the *Daily Worker* why choral groups such as the Freiheit Gesang Ferein limited their repertoires to the language of the foreign-born members—and immediately answered himself that they shouldn't.[19] When Aaron Copland won the 1934 May Day song contest by composing music to Alfred Hayes's poem "Into the Streets May First," Seeger queried Copland in a public forum whether Copland thought his complicated melody would ever popularize Hayes's lyrics among musically untrained workers. Copland somewhat ruefully admitted that he supposed not.[20]

On yet another occasion, Seeger pointedly asked songwriter Earl Robinson whether it was really necessary to smother an essentially simple melody line in a welter of dissonant harmonies and chord changes.[21] The lesson was not lost on Robinson, who emerged in the late 1930s as perhaps the most successful composer of mass music of the American Left, of which "I Dreamed I Saw Joe Hill Last Night" is a stunning example.

Although the Composers Collective never formally disassociated itself from the communist music scene, in 1935 it did take steps to liberate itself from the worst of these bureaucratic strictures. For one, it began bimonthly publication of a semi-independent journal, *Music Vanguard,* edited by Max Margulis, Amnon Balber, and Charles Seeger. The magazine lasted only two issues, but during its brief existence, it won plaudits in many quarters for its handsome format and "superior musical journalism." There were feature articles and critiques on workers' music by Henry Cowell, Charles Seeger, Hanns Eisler, Lawrence Gellert, Elie Siegmeister, and others. Although the content was very much oriented to the current communist cultural and political outlook, the magazine amply lived up to its subtitle "A Critical Review." Margulis recalls that the founders wanted to make *Music Vanguard* more than just "another house organ," and they succeeded.[22] In many respects, it was the most sophisticated music journal ever published in the left-wing movement.

In a more formal move to foster greater intellectual independence, the Composers Collective withdrew from the Pierre Degeyter Club and functioned from 1935 on as a separate entity. The secession was prompted by a combination of grievances consisting of repeated irritation at bureaucratic interference, personality conflicts within the Degeyter Club, and the feeling by many members that they were doing more than their share of the club's work. By 1937, when the collective published its last songbook, half of the contents were labor-radical songs set to familiar tunes.

Some in the collective began to dissent directly, not just coincidentally, from positions taken by communist music critics in the Soviet Union, though they did not often express such opinions in print. Doctrinaire theoretical articles, such as Sergei Tchemodanov's "The Origin of Music," published in 1935 in the *New Masses,*[23] were derided as pedantic and unrealistic. (Building on ideas advanced by Bucher in *Arbeit und Rhythmus* and Plekhanov in *Art and Society,* Tchemodanov's tome boiled down to the thesis that music has no independent aesthetic existence but always contains a conscious or unconscious concept of utility.)

In 1936, members of the collective were shocked when the Soviet music bureaucracy suddenly attacked Dmitri Shostakovich's highly regarded opera *Lady Macbeth of Mzensk.* Though Shostakovich had already shown signs of becoming the twentieth-century musical giant he is now recognized as being, the Soviet authorities in 1936 determined that his opera was "a muddle instead of music" and was insufficiently grounded in the new concept of socialist realism to be acceptable to the state.[24]

Far more important, however, was the Composers Collective's ideological break with Hanns Eisler, its chief mentor in the creation of proletarian song. In the summer of 1936, Eisler published a pamphlet entitled *The Crisis in Music,* which duly propounded much of the orthodox "music is a weapon of the working class" theory in vogue during the Third Period. Not long before, his essay would have been received with the highest praise, but now Max Margulis, successor to Charles Seeger as the *Daily Worker*'s principal music critic, wrote a sharply pointed analysis: "Its point of view is that which dominated the early stages of literary criticism." By discussing music almost exclusively in political and social terms, Margulis concludes that Eisler apparently believed the functions of music should be (1) to enlighten the conscience of the working class and (2) to influence practical action. According to Eisler, he went on, present-day music aims to "effect a state of psychic stupefaction or anarchic excitation in the listener."

The limitations underlying this point of view are as deliberate as they are apparent. To require of music practical, direct effects only, is to wish to "escape" from music. Music that is directly a "weapon in the class struggle" is indispensable, but music as an art must do more than educate, and influence practical actions. Certainly, the variety and complexity of Marxist knowledge and experience demands an art as varied and complex. Eisler realizes this, if his large choral works are any testimony.

That was the closest anyone came to a personal attack on Eisler. But it was enough to foster a philosophical split. Margulis called for "an organic criticism" and urged an end to mechanical division between Marxist interpretation and aesthetic judgment. "The crisis in music is a fact," he insisted. "The great, political audiences wish not only 'music for definite purposes' but a musical art."[25]

Many in the Composers Collective expressed their agreement with Margulis, not only demonstrating their disenchantment with the old party line but in a way putting the shoe on the other foot. Where previously most Marxist critics from Plekhanov to Eisler had asserted that to engage in a music aesthetic beyond the purely functional was to attempt to "escape" from reality, Margulis now argued that the very reverse was true. Margulis did not say that music should be viewed solely as an art without practical utility, but he strongly asserted that rejecting pure art in music was truly the escape from reality.

While these communist-associated musicians were clearly marching to their own tune, not Moscow's, the whole communist movement in the United States was trying to Americanize its appeal. The party now sought to attract the broad middle class to its ranks along with the lower-class "proletariat." Nearly all phases of radical life—including terminology, dress, and social deportment—were revised to conform more closely to the routine existence of the average citizen.

Earl Browder, titular head of the Communist Party of the United States of America (CPUSA) during its most successful years, 1935–45, coined the slogan "Communism Is Twentieth-Century Americanism," and Marx, Lenin, and Stalin soon were joined by Thomas Jefferson, Abraham Lincoln, and Franklin D. Roosevelt in the American movement's pantheon of heroes. The Third Period dissolved into a popular-front alignment designed to bring cooperation with more moderately left-of-center groups in the struggle against fascism. In the process it became possible, even desirable, for party members and fellow travelers to share more extensively in the greater cultural activity of the nation. One result was that an interest in native traditions and folklore was no longer considered a sign of bourgeois decadence.

Popular folklore interest was on the rise, concurrent with but indepen-dent of developments in the communist movement. The nationalist spirit generated by the Depression, coupled with New Deal efforts to provide employment for displaced workers in the arts, resulted in widespread interest in the collection and preservation of artifacts from the American past. The Lomaxes and George Pullen Jackson published best-selling col-lections of folksongs. The Works Progress Administration channeled tax money into folklore projects. Artists such as Thomas Hart Benton deco-rated the walls of public buildings with scenes depicting traditional life in the United States. And the Roosevelts and other important figures in the administration paid tribute to popular lore. The national interest in the American folk heritage, begun in the 1920s as a search for cultural roots, reached full flower. By the mid-1930s, folk songs and folk life were much closer to the public consciousness than at any time in the past. They were no longer the sole possession of scholars, the avant-garde, much less the folk.

Thus, the reawakening of radical interest in traditional music and folk-ways in the United States in the mid-1930s was part of a larger popular acclaim with which it interacted and mingled freely. This new domestic admiration for the spontaneous creativity of the people was paralleled elsewhere internationally, especially in the Soviet Union. The emphasis on socialist realism in art after 1934 in the Soviet Union inevitably led com-munist movements in other countries toward a more positive outlook on traditional cultures and lore. But this revived interest in folklore was flour-ishing in the U.S.-supported Pan-American Union, and other institutions around the globe, not just the Communist International. Folklore, as a universal artistic expression of all peoples, provided a cultural basis for unity and goodwill among antifascist nations everywhere.

MARGARET LARKIN AND MIKE GOLD

If anything, the Composers Collective was relatively slow and lukewarm in its espousal of traditional song, even for strictly propaganda purposes. Actually, it never fully endorsed the idiom in any sort of official statement. But as the American communist Left gradually developed interest in in-digenous folk materials, movement activists from outside the collective recalled to public attention the militant songs and moving folk verse to be found in American traditional music. The main prophets of this mes-sage were Margaret Larkin and Mike Gold.

Through the depths of the Third Period, there had been one lone voice at all prominent in the movement advocating folksong for use by prole-tarian music organizations. Margaret Larkin believed that the songs created by rural workers deserved emulation by urban radical musicians. She grew up in New Mexico and as a young adult developed a considerable interest in the cowboy, Mexican, and Indian subcultures of the Southwest. About 1921, while attending the University of Kansas, she met Carl Sandburg, whose renditions of American folk songs deeply impressed her. Her own tastes soon ranged from British ballads to cowboy laments to Spanish American love songs to bawdy lyrics. In 1931, she published some of the songs she heard in the West in *Singing Cowboy* (1931), which is still viewed by scholars as an important collection.

Larkin moved to New York in the mid-1920s and gravitated to left-wing circles, becoming active in proletarian drama groups. For some years she entertained at small radical social gatherings from a mixed songbag of cowboy tunes, folk-styled protest songs, and topical compositions of her own. The left-wing immigrant groups and others she sang for regarded her as pleasing entertainment but attached no special importance to her material. Recalls a friend, Paul Peters, "While most people were moved and impressed by Margaret and her style of singing, her strange stillness before and after singing, her strange power over her listeners while she sang, nobody thought this material had any particular musical value."[26]

At first, Larkin apparently made no philosophical connection among folk songs, protest songs, and her own topical songs, even as she mixed them in her program to vary her performances. But by the early 1930s, the bond between them was clear to her. As a journalist and publicist, her assignments took her to the union struggles in Passaic, New Jersey, Gastonia, North Carolina, and, indirectly, Harlan, Kentucky. There she heard firsthand the strike songs and rural protest creations of native-born workers. Larkin befriended prolific textile labor leader and songwriter Ella May Wiggins in the weeks before the balladeer's death at the height of the Gastonia strike in 1929. She was chiefly responsible for the subsequent perpetuation of Wiggins's fame in left-wing circles as a labor ballad maker, by writing articles about her in the radical press and singing Wiggins's songs.

Larkin also promoted Aunt Molly Jackson, labor leader and songwriter for the mine workers, and incorporated several of her songs into her repertoire. When the Workers Music League house organ panned some of these songs in 1932 for their alleged "immaturity" and "arrested development," Larkin fired back in the *New Masses,* defending the songs as "a direct and vigorous expression of large numbers of American workers."[27]

This was perhaps the boldest statement supporting folk song tradition in topical labor music to appear in an important communist cultural publication since Elizabeth Gurley Flynn wrote about Joe Hill's songs in *Solidarity* in 1915. But Margaret Larkin was essentially an outsider, and her associations with musicians in the Workers Music League were casual at best. It was left to others, principally Mike Gold, to develop and sustain a belief in the value of indigenous folk music to a point where it profoundly influenced the course of song activity in left-wing circles.

Michael Gold, a self-appointed critic of cultural affairs in the communist movement for half a century, was a dynamic and controversial personality who stirred strong admiration or antipathy in those who came in contact with him. Raised in the tenements of New York's Lower East Side, he became a radical in 1914, and from then until his death in 1967 devoted most of his energy to filling newspaper and magazine columns with discourses on nearly every phase of art and its place in society. Gold's unorthodox ideas often horrified Communist Party leaders. Many intellectuals regarded him as a romantic visionary or a fool. Yet his popularity with rank and file sympathizers was enormous, and his journalism was among the most widely read in the movement.

Gold hated the capitalist system with a ferocious intensity. On its witting or unwitting supporters he unleashed some of the most vitriolic attacks in the annals of communist literature. At the same time, he was sincerely devoted to the great masses of American men and women laborers and translated his affection into warm, often humorous, accounts of their struggles and triumphs (notably in his moving and influential autobiography, *Jews without Money* [1930]). All his life, he retained a passionate love for genuine working-class culture, which he professed to see proliferating at almost every turn in the road.[28]

In particular, Gold was attracted to working-class songs. His own family tradition of Yiddish folk music was supplemented in the teens by IWW parodies and the popular airs of the Mexican Revolution, with which he became acquainted during a two-year stay south of the border at the time of World War I.[29] Gold was so fond of Lawrence Gellert's collection of African American songs that he provided the title "Negro Songs of Protest." His fondness for "people's music" included many forms of native and world folk music. And his interest remained undiminished to the end; in a characteristic gesture as he lay dying in the hospital in 1967, he asked his visitor, his old friend Pete Seeger, to serenade him with "Guantanamera," a beautiful melody set to words by the nineteenth-century Cuban revolutionary poet José Martí.

Given Gold's background and passionate love for "songs of the people," it is not surprising that he was among the most forceful of the 1930s communists to hammer at the notion that folk songs were songs of the working people, reflecting their hopes, aspirations, and frustrations, and ought to be appreciated more in proletarian music quarters. Gold was friendly with members of the Composers Collective, but he became impatient with their esoteric approach to mass music.

In the *Daily Worker* in 1934, he quoted a union member complaining that the tunes of the songs were unsingably complicated and clashed with the upbeat spirit of the words. "I think a new content often demands a new form," Gold wrote, "but when the new form gets so far ahead of all of us that we can't understand its content, it is time to write letters to the press." "Reaching the masses," he added, "is as much a test of Communist art today as any other test."[30] By contrast, Gold pumped constantly for a singing radical movement based on indigenous folk and folklike compositions that would both appeal to, and have its roots in, the working class. He extolled Joe Hill and the Wobblies of two decades before who had successfully created such music. "The nearest thing we've had to Joe Hill's kind of folk balladry" he observed, "has been from such southern mountaineer Communists as Aunt Molly Jackson and the martyred textile weaver, Ella May Wiggins." But he saw a growing number of similar songs among militant workers, and declared optimistically that "a new balladry is being created under our noses, actually the only authentic folk music of this period."[31]

Gold was understandably jubilant when he learned of Ray and Lida Auville and received a copy of their small, partly folk-styled collection of radical songs. The Auvilles were southern mountaineers with a traditional folk song repertory who had settled in Cleveland. In the early thirties, they had moved from socialism to the Communist Party in their ideology and thereafter devoted their limited songwriting ability to the left-wing cause. Mixing Third Period political ideology with traditional and popular music forms, they accompanied themselves on guitar and other instruments associated with folk songs, becoming prototypes for the "People's Songsters" of a decade later. The John Reed Club of Cleveland discovered and publicized the couple in 1934, which brought them to the attention of the communist movement in general. Their *Songs of the American Worker,* published the same year, contained twelve compositions on the order of the following:

> Just a boy without work, I decided
> Along with some pals of mine
> To answer the call of our country
> And with the Home Guards to sign.
> We thrilled to the tho't of a uniform
> And "the Army makes men" we were told;
> So I went to my father to tell him,
> Before I made ready to go.
> He stood with his face to the window
> And listened to every word,
> Then after a moment of silence,

These were the words that I heard:
"I have worked all my life as a miner,
My hands are all gnarled and worn;
If you give your strength to the bosses,
I'd rather you'd never been born.
The miners must strike from starvation,
I'll be on the old picket line;
The Home Guards will be called to break us,
If you're with them you're no son of mine." ("The Miner's Son")

* * *

Oh, the Ghost of the Depression's sticking 'round this town!
Just see those hungry mobs a-hanging 'round;
There's mis'ry on the face of people every place,
It's the nearest thing to hell that can be found. ("The Ghost of the Depression")

Gold waxed enthusiastic about these songs and acclaimed the Auvilles as the latest in the line of true working-class folk bards: "Note how timely the themes are, how specific," he exclaimed.

> Note the style, which has the true ring of American balladry. The lines might not be approved by an esthetic grammarian, but no intellectual poet could even hope to imitate them. One has this folk-feeling or one hasn't. Joe Hill had it, and the Auvilles have it.[32]

In retrospect, the discussion in the communist press of the Auville collection marks the single most identifiable watershed in the American Left's acceptance of traditional songs and lyrics composed in the folk idiom. Members of the Composers Collective reviewed *Songs of the American Worker* in cautiously favorable terms.[33] The mere appearance of these more singable topical creations was applauded, yet reviewers Charles Seeger and Elie Siegmeister (using their pseudonyms) both found much that was banal and artificial in the texts and melodies. Seeger particularly lamented the low musical quality of the tunes. "For every step forward in the verse, one takes a step backward in the music," he wrote. "That one is unaware of it makes it all the more dangerous."

Months later, in January 1936, Mike Gold replied in defense of the Auville songs and, in so doing, launched a devastating attack on the proletarian music theories of the collective as epitomized by Seeger's review:

> Ray Auville fiddles; no, he doesn't play the violin, he fiddles with gusto and native style, as rousingly as any old moustached veteran of the Great Smokies in Tennessee. . . .

It is the real thing, folk song in the making, workers' music coming right out of the soul. . . .

Really, Comrade Sands [Seeger], I think you have missed the point. It is sectarian and utopian to use Arnold Schoenberg or Stravinsky as a yardstick by which to measure working class music.

What songs do the masses of America now sing? They sing "Old Black Joe" and the semijazz things concocted by Tin Pan Alley. In the South they sing the old ballads. This is the reality; and to leap from that into Schoenberg seems to me a desertion of the masses.

Not to see what a step forward it is to find two native musicians of the American people turning to revolutionary themes, converting the tradition to working class uses, is to be blind to progress. . . .

It may shock you, but I think the Composers Collective has something to learn from Ray and Lida Auville, as well as to give to them. They write catchy tunes that many American workers can sing and like, and the words of their songs make the revolution as intimate and simple as "Old Black Joe."[34]

One can see in this passage the style of writing that brought Gold his reputation in some circles for being anti-intellectual and a hack critic for the party. But his argument contained much merit. Gold scored some telling points on Seeger and the collective, especially since they represented many of the most sophisticated musicians in the country and had, in all their years of work, failed to produce music that would capture widespread attention for the political ideals of the movement. Gold's comments did not go unnoticed. That same day an Auville composition was printed in the *Daily Worker* alongside Gold's column, with the admonition that every *Worker*'s bookshop in the country should carry the Auvilles' songbook.

Much had been happening on the Left in the several months between Seeger's reviews and Gold's critique to create a hospitable climate for Gold's position. The Popular Front—in which party members were urged to forsake purity in favor of cooperation with other antifascist groups—had finally become a political reality in the summer of 1935, after nearly two years' agitation by the communists. Radicals who had opposed Roosevelt and the New Deal in previous years had begun to swing behind the administration and wholeheartedly backed many of the social and economic relief programs, including the public sector job creation of the Works Progress Administration and other federal agencies. In response to widespread public interest, many WPA jobs involved collecting traditional materials.

In keeping with the national, as well as international, flowering of popular interest in folk traditions, artists in all fields of the American communist movement began to call attention to the aesthetic qualities and social implications of the various forms of grassroots people's expression. The publication of *Proletarian Literature in the United States* (New York: International, 1936) marked the first time that folk-styled protest lyrics (written by Aunt Molly Jackson and others) had been featured in an important radical volume on culture. In announcing a Latin American Folk Festival at New York's Town Hall, the *Workers Music League Bulletin* waxed eloquent over both the traditional authenticity and "most burning social desires" carried within the songs and dances.[35]

Will Geer, a principal actor in *Let Freedom Ring!*—a "folk" play about southern textile workers—began performing western sketches and homemade topical ballads composed in folk style for radical audiences. In November 1935, his successful attempt to rally the striking weavers at Paterson, New Jersey, by singing labor lyrics in the folk idiom was the subject of a long feature article in the *Daily Worker*.[36]

In sum, Gold's polemic against the Composers Collective on behalf of native folk song tradition was the crest of a wave building for some time, rather than a startling initiator of a new trend. A month after it appeared, the *Daily Worker* announced that the Workers Music League was dissolving of its own accord. This followed nearly a year of political disputes within the League. At the same time, the *Worker* reported that another, more broadly based, popular-front music society was being created in the League's place.[37] It may be significant that the new organization, originally to be called the United Music League, was upon its actual inception the American Music League (AML). And it is most certainly significant that one of its principal objectives, in addition to establishing a musical front against fascism, was "to collect, study and popularize American folk music and its traditions."[38]

Concurrently, the Composers Collective lingered on for a time under the aegis of the newly formed American Music League, but most of its original members drifted away into other activities. Of its principal early participants, only Elie Siegmeister, Marc Blitzstein, and Earl Robinson continued to play important roles in the left-wing music scene.

Thus, by early 1936 the groundwork had been laid for the American communist movement's subsequent ideological and social commitment to folk songs and traditional "people's" culture. The varied work of such later groups as the Almanac Singers, People's Songs, and People's Artists sprang from the void created by the clumsy gropings of radical musicians for a "unique" class music for the proletariat in the early 1930s. The delay in developing such a music was at least in part occasioned by the inability of the Composers Collective and Workers Music League to translate theory into practical results. A viable left-wing music expression, rooted in the past and present experiences of the American people, was stunted for years, even though during the same period the communist movement was making creative advances in other areas of the arts.

Siegmeister himself lamented, "[T]he comparative backwardness of proletarian music in this country as compared with the corresponding development of proletarian literature, theater, dance [and] art." Writing in the *Daily Worker* late in 1935, he conceded that despite the longstanding mandate of his own collective, "a clear Marxist critique of the whole function of music in, and its dependence on, the successive developments of bourgeois society has not yet been worked out or popularized among American musicians."[39]

Ironically, when communist musical activity entered its dynamic phase in the late 1930s and through much of the 1940s, based, as it turned out, on native folk song tradition, the fires in other spheres of proletarian culture (art, theater, and literature) had by then ebbed considerably. Meanwhile, in other parts of the movement, American communists were uncovering indigenous folk traditions as they sought to organize workers in rural areas of the country. At first, organizers noted folk materials with only mild curiosity. But soon, once a strong class-conscious character was imputed to the traditional songs, a few embraced them with considerable enthusiasm. Eventually, urban radicals seized on these songs and their creators—discovered in the field during the 1930s—as the basis for their own proletarian "folk" culture.

NOTES

1. Nicholas Slonimsky, *Music since 1900* (New York: Schirmer, 1937), 242.

2. Slonimsky, *Music since 1900*, 554.

3. Slonimsky, *Music since 1900*, 273.

4. "The Ideological Platform of the Russian Association of Proletarian Musicians" in Slonimsky, *Music since 1900*, 549.

5. Slonimsky, *Music since 1900*, 273.

6. "The Crisis of Bourgeoisie Music and the Creative Problems [of] the International Revolutionary Movement," typed manuscript in the Music Division of the Library of Congress (uncatalogued), 13.

7. For discussion of the dissolution of the proletarian culture organizations, see Donald Drew Egbert, "Socialism and American Art" in *Socialism and American Life* (Princeton, N.J.: Princeton University Press, 1952), 687–89, 695.

8. Egbert, "Socialism and American Art," 701.

9. Y. M. Sokolov, *Russian Folklore*, English-language reprint edition (Hatboro, Pa.: Folklore Associates, 1966), 24–25. See also the *New Masses* abridgment of Gorky's remarks in "Proletarian Literature Today" (October 2, 1934), 29–33.

10. Sokolov, *Russian Folklore*, 26.

11. The discussion of Soviet criticism of the *byliny* is drawn from the account in Sokolov, *Russian Folklore*, 149–50, and Felix J. Oinas, "Folklore Activities in

Russia" in *Folklore Research Around the World,* ed. Richard M. Dorson (Bloomington: Indiana University Press, 1961), 81.

12. Sokolov, *Russian Folklore,* 150.

13. "The International Music Buro," in the *1934 Second American Workers Music Olympiad* program, [2].

14. "The International Collection of Revolutionary Songs" and "Stirring Songs of Struggle in International Collection," *Daily Worker* (January 31 and February 1, 1934), 5.

15. See "Gold's Poem, Set to Music, to be Sung at Concert Sunday Night," *Daily Worker* (March 3, 1934), 7; "International Music Buro, USSR, Announces Choral Work Contest," *Daily Worker* (July 23, 1934), 5; "Competition in Honor of Thaelman," *Daily Worker* (March 9, 1935), 7.

16. George Maynard, "Music Appreciation among Workers," *Daily Worker* (January 13, 1934), 5.

17. "What Songs Should Workers' Choruses Sing?" *Daily Worker* (February 7, 1934), 5.

18. Letter printed in Michael Gold, "Battle Song of the Poor Millionaires" ("Change the World" column), *Daily Worker* (June 4, 1934), 5.

19. Carl Sands, "The Freiheit Gesang Ferein," *Daily Worker* (March 22, 1935), 5.

20. Interview with Charles Seeger, June 8, 1967.

21. Interview with Earl Robinson, December, 1967.

22. Interview with Max Margulis, March 12, 1968.

23. Sergei Tchemodanov, "The Origin of Music," *New Masses* (April 2, 1935), 30–31.

24. Sidney Finkelstein, *Composer and Nation* (New York: International, 1960), 285–86, gives a succinct summary of the controversy in Russia surrounding the opera.

25. Max Margulis, "The Crisis in Music," *Daily Worker* (July 25, 1936), 7.

26. Paul Peters, "About Margaret Larkin," manuscript communication to the writer, August 28, 1968, 1. For other material on Margaret Larkin, I am indebted to Katherine Larkin, Albert Maltz, Austa C. Hutchcraft, Liston Oak, Evelyn Stewart, and Grace Granich.

27. Margaret Larkin, "Revolutionary Music," *New Masses* (February, 1933), 27.

28. For a detailed sketch of Mike Gold's early career, see Daniel Aaron, *Writers on the Left* (New York: Avon, 1965), 102–08 and *passim.* Michael Brewster Folsom, "Mike Gold's Battle to Change the World," *National Guardian* (June 3, 1967), 10, is an excellent obituary résumé of Gold's life.

29. Letter from Mrs. Grace Granich (Gold's sister-in-law) to the writer, May 27, 1969. Michael Brewster Folsom and Lawrence Gellert also provided useful material on Gold.

30. "The Steam Hammer" ("Change the World" column), *Daily Worker* (June 11, 1934), 5.

31. "Change the World," *Daily Worker* (April 21, 1934), 7, and "Change the World" (November 22, 1934), 5.

32. "Change the World," *Daily Worker* (November 22, 1934), 5.

33. Carl Sands, "Songs by Auvilles Mark Step Ahead in Workers' Music," *Daily*

Worker (January 15, 1935), 5; L. E. Swift, "The Auvilles' Songs," *New Masses* (February 5, 1935), 28.

34. "Change the World," *Daily Worker* (January 2, 1936), 5.

35. "Latin American Folk Festival," *Workers Music League Bulletin* (n.d. [ca. June 1935]), 5.

36. An ad announcing Geer's western sketches and songs as part of a "New Theatre Night" appears in the *New Masses* (October 8, 1935), 28; Al Hayes, "Paterson Strikers Get a Ballad," *Daily Worker* (November 26, 1935), 5.

37. H. E. [Hanns Eisler?], "A New Music League," *Daily Worker* (February 10, 1936), 7.

38. *Unison* 1, no. 1 (May, 1936), 1; see also M. M. [Max Margulis], "Festival of Music League to Open Here Tomorrow," *Daily Worker* (May 16, 1936), 7.

39. "The Return of Hanns Eisler," *Daily Worker* (October 2, 1935), 5.

5

Communist Encounters with American Unions

All through the Third Period, American communist intellectuals in the Workers Music League and the Composers Collective paid only scant, and usually skeptical, attention to folklore traditions, a reflection of their firm commitment to the militant proletarian ideology. During this time, though, local organizers were encountering living folk traditions in the field. Idealists from the urban North ventured out to try to inoculate the rural working-class groups with their own passion for the class

Woody Guthrie, Fred Hellerman, others unidentified (l-r)
(courtesy of Jackie Gibson Alper)

struggle. In many cases, they witnessed local sympathizers adapt folk traditions to the cause. These contacts between working culture and radical
political organizers were sporadic at first and were reported only inciden-
tally in the left-wing press. But in the end, they proved to be a major factor in bringing folklore into prominence as a cultural prop of the American
communist movement. And the interaction was two-way. The ideology
and agit-prop slogans of northern radicals were traded for and tempered
by a local worldview. As folklorist Archie Green has pointed out, the
northern organizers "were teaching 'Solidarity Forever' in West Virginia
in 1931, [and] in return moved 'The Death of Mother Jones' into urban
circles."[1]

Most of the encounters between radical urban organizers and Anglo-
American folk traditions occurred in rural areas surrounding the textile
and coal industries. These industries were concentrated especially in the
South where folk communities were common. Conditions for the workers were particularly abysmal, making them a fertile ground for radical
proselytizing. In communities where oral traditions were strong, it was
natural for local converts to Marxism to want to blend class-conscious
sentiments with native folk art—to spread the message in forms, notably
songs, that were particularly suited to the culture. Organizers who otherwise had little concept of folklore, and even less interest, soon observed
that indigenous creations were a lot more effective in recruiting and agitating the local populace than were doctrinaire slogans and pamphlets
written by urban party leaders. Still, party leaders lived in a world of their
own. With few exceptions, they and other urban intellectuals failed to
appreciate the potential effectiveness of strike, labor, and protest expressions of the folk. They directed their occasional attention toward radical
political content, not the traditional forms of protest typically created by
workers.

Gradually interest in such songs increased. Less doctrinaire members
of the movement, such as Mike Gold, began hailing them as native "proletarian" music that had been lacking in the American communist movement. The lyrics were apt to be rough, unpolished, and uncomplicated by
sophisticated political dogma. But they contained an inherent vigor, ro-
bust quality, and familiar vernacular that made them effective propaganda
tools in the areas where they were created. The lyrics might be banal and
the tunes sentimental, but they were a lot less stilted than the old revolutionary songs produced during the early days of the communist movement. Certainly they had greater appeal to native-born workers.

Folk tunes had the advantage of being familiar and singable, in large
part because they were often repetitive in structure. Occasionally, as in
"We Shall Not Be Moved" and similarly constructed songs, the substitution of a single line or word was enough to prolong the singing indefi-

nitely. (In the later People's Songs vernacular, these were called "zipper songs.") Though radicals were apt to admit it only infrequently, these local agit-prop songs often caught the essence of folk poetry. They reflected both the virtues and limitations of American folk song tradition. Eventually, repeated encounters with living folk cultures in the United States helped reshape urban, left-wing music.

TEXTILE INDUSTRY LAMENTS

The U.S. Communist Party had expressed interest in the textile industry as far back as 1925, when it passed a resolution urging the unionization of mill workers. A year later, the Passaic, New Jersey, textile strike became the first labor struggle of any kind to be directed entirely by communists, though in the end the American Federation of Labor (AFL) was invited to assume leadership for tactical reasons. The strike failed, but the party got a lot of favorable publicity for its efforts on behalf of the indisputably underpaid workers.

Then, however, came the disastrous Third Period. Beginning in 1928, communists suspended all cooperation with the AFL and began forming their own duplicate unions, known as "dual unions." Soon, these were affiliated with a new organization called the Trade Union Unity League (TUUL). For five years, the TUUL described itself as a rival counterpart to the "bourgeois" labor structure. Many of its organizers and local sympathizers acted heroically in the field. But at the bureaucratic level, the TUUL was run by short-sighted planners who manipulated the organization more for their own purposes than for the welfare of the workers. Finally, in 1935, the movement recognized that the dual union idea was a fiasco and abandoned it.[2] In the meantime, however, an unintended but important byproduct had been created: Mill hands and miners in the heartlands of Appalachia had exposed their classic American heritage to admiring left-wing organizers from the cities, who had heretofore been unaware of workers' rough but effective creativity.

After an unsuccessful communist-led textile strike in New Bedford, Massachusetts, in 1928, party organizers turned their attention to the mill hands of the South. In the spring and summer of 1929, a wave of strikes swept through the textile mills in the Piedmont region of Virginia, Tennessee, and the Carolinas. Most were conducted by the AFL or local unionists, but the most important one at Gastonia, North Carolina, was promoted by the communist-sponsored National Textile Workers Union (NTWU).

Gastonia was the most important textile center in the South. A 1927 survey of the area counted nearly ten million spindles operating in over

570 mills.[3] Conditions for the workers who ran them were deplorable: the work week was sixty-six hours; two 10 percent wage cuts had been instituted in less than a year; and speedup and stretch-out demands on top of long hours, low pay, and poor food exhausted the strength of employees. On April 1, five local workers were fired for union activity. The NTWU had not been prepared for a strike, but demands for action by the aroused nonunion mill hands forced the union to declare a walk-out. For five months the strikers held out amid ever increasing hysteria, marked by innumerable acts of vigilante terrorism. Police Chief O. F. Aderholt was slain in an exchange of gunfire; union leaders were jailed and later tried on trumped-up charges. In the end, the struggle was lost, but Gastonia became the focus of international attention.

The communist press covered the strike intensely, reporting in detail on the lives of the textile workers in the area. Inevitably it chanced upon vernacular poems created in the heat of the struggle and printed them for northern readers. The first such verse appeared in the *New Masses* in August 1929—a parody, written by an eleven-year old boy, of the sentimental folk song "May I Sleep in Your Barn Tonight, Mister?" The boy, Odell Corey, was charitably described as the "poet laureate" of the strike. The song, which contains references to Fred Beal, the NTWU strike leader, and Manville Jenckes, owner of Gastonia's largest mill, went as follows:

> May I sleep in your tent tonight, Beal?
> For its cold lying out on the ground,
> And the cold North wind whistles upon us,
> And we have no place to lie down.
> Manville Jenckes had done us dirty,
> And he set us out on the ground.
> We are sorry we didn't join you
> When the rest went out and joined.[4]

Whether this song really was as popular among Gastonia textile workers as the *New Masses* alleged is impossible to determine. However, a somewhat better composition by the same author was printed in *The Nation* a few months later in a article about the strike by Margaret Larkin, the collector of southwest cowboy songs who moved east to be a journalist. The song she chose of young Corey's was a parody of the popular folk song "Casey Jones." It began:

> Come all you scabs if you want to hear
> The story of a cruel millionaire.
> Manville Jenckes was the millionaire's name;
> He bought the law with his money and frame [frame-up]
> But he can't buy the union with his money and fame.[5]

But the parodies of Odell Corey were dwarfed in cultural importance by the work of Ella May Wiggins. At age twenty-nine, Wiggins had borne nine children, four of whom died of the whooping cough complicated by poor nourishment and lack of funds to buy medicine. The impressionable Larkin saw her as a fine traditional singer, whose repertoire included such native folk songs as "Little Mary Fagan," "Lord Lovel," and "Sweet William."[6]

Wiggins rose to prominence through her work for the NTWU. Tired of trying to support her children and crippled husband on nine dollars a week as a spinner in one of the Gastonia mills, Wiggins joined the fight with fervor. During the strike, she addressed public gatherings, helped organize union activities, and composed new songs about the struggle. She scribbled her compositions on the backs of leaflets and handbills and sang them for her fellow-workers. Her best-known creations were "Chief Aderholt," "Come and Join the I.L.D.," and "The Mill Mother's Lament." According to various accounts, these were widely popular among the Gastonia mill hands. "Chief Aderholt" was typical of the rest in its folk vernacular and union sentiments:

> Come all of you good people and listen to what I tell
> The story of Chief Aderholt, the man you all knew well.
> It was on one Friday evening, the seventh day of June,
> He went down to the union ground and met his fatal doom. . . .
> We're going to have a union all over the South,
> Where we can wear good clothes and live in a better house;
> Now we must stand together and to the boss reply
> We'll never, no, we'll never let our leaders die.[7]

On September 14, with tension at its height between strikers and mill operators, Wiggins was shot and killed as she rode in a truck with other union workers to an NTWU rally. (In spite of many claims to the contrary, there is no evidence to show that she was the prime target of the vigilante bullets on this occasion.)[8] At the funeral, mourners sang her plaintive "Mill Mother's Lament" as she was lowered into the ground:

> We leave our homes in the morning,
> We kiss our children goodbye;
> While we slave for the bosses
> Our children scream and cry.
> And when we draw our money
> Our grocery bills to pay,
> Not a cent to spend for clothing,
> Not a cent to lay away. . . .
> But understand, all workers,

> Our union they do fear;
> Let's stand together, workers,
> And have a union here.[9]

Wiggins's death immediately transformed her into a martyr-heroine of the labor movement. Her work was celebrated and her name honored in left-wing circles everywhere. Years later, her strike ballads were remembered as outstanding contributions to the cause of the Gastonia textile workers. "Mill Mother's Lament" was reprinted in John Greenway's classic 1953 collection, *American Folksongs of Protest*. Yet it is interesting to note that of nearly forty articles about Wiggins in the communist press following her murder, only three mentioned the songs she wrote for the mill hands, which is some indication of the leadership's musical myopia in 1929 under Third Period ideology.[10]

Struggles in other textile communities brought more folk-protest lyrics to the ears of radical reporters. One important source of these radical labor organizers was an organization called the Brookwood Labor School, based in Katonah, New York. Brookwood had an independent socialist orientation, but some members shuttled between it and the Communist Party. Brookwood organizers seemed especially sensitive to the value of the Anglo-American folk tradition they were encountering. Eventually, they transmitted several labor adaptations of old spirituals back to urban centers, where in time their popularity become nearly as great as it was in the southern labor movement. But the Brookwood organizers also helped spread these songs in the South, as they traveled from one strike site to another.

For example, the song "We Are Building a Strong Union," to the tune of the old spiritual "We Are Climbing Jacob's Ladder," was a product of the 1929 Marion, North Carolina, strike:

> We are building a strong union,
> We are building a strong union,
> We are building a strong union,
> Workers in the mill![11]

Novelist Grace Lumpkin heard the thirteen-stanza song, "Southern Cotton Mill Rhyme," at an NTWU hall in Charlotte, North Carolina. She brought it north, and in May 1930, it was published in *New Masses*. Seemingly set to the tune of "The Butcha Boy," a ballad of a forsaken girl, it had been composed many years earlier by an anonymous mill weaver in Buffalo, South Carolina. Originally, it concluded with the following lyrics:

> Just let them wear their watches fine,
> And rings and golden chains.

But when the day of Judgment comes
They'll have to shed those purty things.

In April 1929, however, striking union workers in Charlotte changed the third line to "But when the great Revolution comes."[12]

The textile workers' campaigns had a profound impact on many left-wing writers, much as the civil rights and anti–Vietnam War movements would have in a later era. A whole spate of proletarian novels and plays appeared in the early 1930s fictionalizing the struggles of the mill hands at Gastonia and elsewhere. Among them were Mary Heaton Vorse's *Strike! A Novel of Gastonia* (1930); Grace Lumpkin's *To Make My Bread* (1932), dramatized in 1935 as the Albert Bein production *Let Freedom Ring;* Tom Tippett's *Mill Shadows* (1932); and Fielding Burke's *Call Home the Heart* (1932), as well as *A Stone Came Rolling* (1935). In addition, historical and journalistic accounts of the textile strikes were published, such as Tippett's *When Southern Labor Stirs* (1931), and somewhat later Liston Pope's *Mill Hands and Preachers* (1942). All these works referred to the folk-styled compositions of the local people about labor conditions in the mills and union activities during the strikes.

CLASS WAR AND SONGS IN THE COALFIELDS

Conditions in the coalfields of the eastern United States were, if anything, worse than in the textile centers. The coal industry was none too stable in the 1920s, and the onset of the Depression quickly knocked the bottom out of what prosperity remained in the mining business. As the 1930s began, production slumped and unemployment skyrocketed. The market price for a ton of coal dropped from $5.22 in 1929 to $4.17 in 1932. Hemmed in by accelerating capital investment and depreciation costs, and played off against one another by steel, rail, and utility corporations, the coal operators engaged in savage cutthroat competition.

Companies passed on falling prices in coal to employees through wage cuts that in many cases reduced whole mining communities to the brink of starvation. In the first four years of the 1930s, coal prices fell 20 percent and wages declined 26 percent, from sixty-eight to fifty cents an hour.[13] Mine owners put pitmen on a tonnage rather than hourly wage, then installed crooked weighing procedures, cutting the workers' income still further. The effects of such warfare on the miners were devastating, taking a fearsome toll in health, spirit, and lives. Stores owned by the coal operators—"the company store" popularized in the song "Sixteen Tons"—charged exorbitant prices for food and other necessities when the miners could buy them nowhere else; there was more bitterness than humor in the lyric "St. Peter, don't you call me 'cause I can't go, I owe my soul to the company store."

Adding to this dismal economic picture as the Depression deepened was the woeful state of unionism in the coalfields. Mine owners viewed any form of labor organizing in their industry as a further threat to their already ailing business operations. By the late 1920s, their implacable opposition to union activity had all but eliminated the remaining labor structure from earlier years. When organizing attempts were resumed in the early thirties, matters were complicated even more by the dual-union rivalry between the AFL's United Mine Workers and the TUUL's communist-led National Miners Union (NMU). In truth, it was a wretched time for the coal operators and a far worse one for their employees. But, as one historian of the era remarked, "The troubles in coal were singing troubles."[14] The miners, like the textile workers, had a long history of recounting their onerous work and meager living conditions in ballads and songs. Their compositions needed no new themes. The old complaints persisted. Only the circumstances were new. And it was in the context of these new circumstances that communist organizers began penetrating the coal fields. Once radical organizers committed themselves to agitation in the coal fields of Kentucky, West Virginia, Pennsylvania, and Ohio, it was only a matter of time before they stumbled on the hard-bitten folk poetry of the mining communities and enlisted it in their cause.

The most memorable contacts with folk tradition were made in and around Harlan County, Kentucky, scene of some of the most violent class warfare in the history of the United States. By the spring of 1931, cutbacks in wages and employment in the coal industry had pushed miners past the breaking point. "We starve while we work; we might as well strike while we starve" was a common expression. A brief walk-out led by the AFL's United Mine Workers collapsed amid charges, partly justified, that the UMW "sold out" its local membership. Communist organizers for the rival National Miners Union soon moved in to fill the leadership vacuum. Few of the mine workers understood Marxist theory or the proletarian ideology of the Third Period. But they understood that their situation was desperate and that someone was trying to help them. The mine workers welcomed the organizers warmly.

The coal operators struck back with a vengeance. Beginning in the summer of 1931, the operators organized a reign of terror to end "foreign intrusion" in the region. Many workers were killed, and still others injured or made homeless. Miners' property was destroyed, and civil liberties became a farce as "Bloody Harlan" lived up to its name in the ensuing months. One verse from the single most famous song to emerge from this struggle summed up the situation in a few classic lines. They refer specifically to John Henry Blair, a mine owner who also served as Harlan County sheriff:

> They say in Harlan County,
> There are no neutrals there.
> You'll either be a union man
> Or a thug for J. H. Blair.

The chorus asked:

> Which side are you on?
> Which side are you on?

By early 1932, the NMU had been smashed, its leaders jailed, killed, or forced into hiding. All labor activity in the coal camps ceased. Only much later, under CIO auspices, did a rejuvenated United Mine Workers organization finally succeed in unionizing the miners of the area.

Like the textile industry campaigns, the coal strikes of this period were covered extensively in the radical press. Particular attention was focused on the Kentucky conflicts in late 1931 when the novelist Theodore Dreiser led a committee of distinguished northern writers, including Sherwood Anderson and John Dos Passos, to the Harlan area to investigate and publicize local mining conditions.[15] More than fifty representatives of the coal camp communities and the NMU testified at the Dreiser hearings, extracts of which were published as *Harlan Miners Speak* (1932). Aunt Molly Jackson, midwife, ballad singer, coal miner's daughter, sister, wife, and militant unionist, was questioned by the committee. So was Jim Garland, her stepbrother and a songwriter and NMU organizer. On November 7, at the Glendon Baptist Church in Arjay, Kentucky, Aunt Molly answered questions on infant mortality and malnutrition in her capacity as a midwife. But to dramatize the pitiful conditions in the coal camps, she sang her own composition "Ragged Hungry Blues":

> I'm sad and weary, I got those hungry ragged blues; .
> I'm sad and weary, I got those hungry ragged blues;
> Not a penny in my pocket to buy one thing I need to use.
> I woke up this morning with the worst blues I ever had in my life;
> I woke up this morning with the worst blues I ever had in my life;
> Not a bite to cook for breakfast; poor coal miner's wife. . . .
> This mining town I live in is a dead and lonely place;
> This mining town I live in is a dead and lonely place;
> Where pity and starvation are pictured on every face.[16]

The song received a big ovation from the writers and miners in attendance. But more significant was the considerable mention it attracted in the communist press. Little more than two years had passed since Ella May Wiggins's singing in the textile strike was roundly ignored. Now, Aunt Molly and her song were mentioned at least seven times in the *Daily Worker* in the weeks following her performance; the *Worker* even printed the song lyrics on one occasion.

Aunt Molly Jackson and Jim Garland followed the Dreiser Committee north in December 1931 and spent the winter helping publicize the Kentucky miners' plight. They sang and spoke to groups of left-wing intellectuals and workers in New York, Cleveland, and elsewhere. They also collected money and goods that they sent back to the coal families in desperate need of relief. In the process, many more urban radicals were exposed to indigenous American folk traditions.

Aunt Molly Jackson and her stepbrother were descendants of many generations of mountain people, steeped in the idiomatic expression, aesthetic values, and folkways of Appalachia.[17] Now, thanks to the crisis of the strike, their music and speech combined the terse language of the folk with the class-conscious slogans of northern organizers. The result was a body of powerful and militant statements on the ruthless union struggles, at once sounding both old and new:

> I am a union woman,
> As brave as I can be;
> I do not like the bosses,
> And the bosses don't like me.
> Join the NMU, Come join the NMU.
> I was raised in old Kentucky,
> In Kentucky borned and bred;
> And when I joined the union
> They called me a Rooshian Red. . . .
> The bosses ride big fine horses,
> While we walk in the mud,
> Their banner is the dollar sign,
> And ours is striped with blood. ("I Am a Union Woman")

When asked at the Dreiser hearings whether her husband was a member of the NMU, Jackson replied, "My husband is a member of the National Miners' Union, and I am, too, and I have never stopped, brother, since I know of this work of the NMU. It think it is one of the greatest things that has ever come into this world."

When Harry Simms, a nineteen-year-old organizer for the Young Communist League, was killed by vigilantes in February 1932, Aunt Molly Jackson wrote "The Ballad of Harry Simms," which recounted, in part:

> Harry Simms was killed on Brush Creek
> In nineteen thirty-two

> He organized the Y.C.L.,
> Also the N.M.U.
> He gave his life in struggle,
> That was all that he could do.
> He died to save the union,
> Also for me and you.
> Comrades, we must vow today,
> This one thing we must do,
> [We] must organize all the miners
> In the dear old N.M.U.
> And get a million volunteers
> Into the Y.C.L.
> And sink this rotten system
> In the deepest pits of Hell.[18]

Eventually, both Aunt Molly Jackson and Jim Garland settled in New York. The threat of violent reprisal from the coal operators' vigilante squads was real enough to drive them from Kentucky, and their families had been blacklisted from mining work there anyway. Their importance as spokespersons for the miners waned in time, as the coalfield struggles receded from public attention. But in left-wing circles, Aunt Molly remained a symbol of the militant folk until her death in 1961.[19] Shortly thereafter, her half-sister, Sarah Ogan Gunning, was "discovered" by latter-day folk music fans and scholars; she enjoyed a brief career as a performer and informant for folklorists' field studies.

Folk-styled songs from other singers in the miners' conflict impressed urban radical audiences as well. The one that became the most famous, "Which Side Are You On," by Florence Reese, wife of another local NMU organizer, did not reach the urban audience until the late thirties. But an adaptation of a Holiness hymn, written by an anonymous miner in the Harlan conflict, was printed in the *Daily Worker* as "It Just Suits Me":

> Come along, boys, and
> I'll tell you what I'll do:
> I'll sign you up in the NMU,
> And it just suits me.[20]

Sometimes the urban listeners could not distinguish what was "of the folk" from what was not. For example, Vernon Dalhart, a hillbilly music star in the 1920s, wrote and recorded a sentimental dirge called "A Miner's Prayer." In Washington, Pennsylvania, the song came to the attention of Myra Page, a veteran writer for the *Daily Worker*, when a miner sang it and some other hard-times songs and strike ballads in the course of a hunger march demonstration. "Nobody knows who wrote the words or music," she misinformed her readers in 1931. "They are real folk-work-songs, similar in their plaintive melodies and origins to the ballads which the southern mountaineers and Poor Whites sing." Accompanying her article were the words:

> I keep listening for the whistles in the morning,
> But mines are still, no noise [is] in the air.
> And the children wake up crying in the morning,
> For the cupboard is so empty and so bare.
> And their little feet are so cold they stumble,
> And I have to pin the rags upon their back.
> And our home is broken down and very humble,
> While the winter winds are blowing through each crack.
> Oh, it's hard to hear the hungry children crying,
> While I've got two hands that want to do their share.
> Oh, you rich men in the city, won't you have a little pity,
> And just listen to a miner's prayer.

Page readily admitted the miners' love for these mournful dirges. But she also predicted that the same workers soon would create new songs more militant in tone, on the grounds that "they have learned to give up expecting 'the rich men in the city' to 'have a little pity.'"[21]

Just as they had in the textile strikes, organizers from the Brookwood Labor School in Katonah, New York, worked the coalfields and were especially sensitive to the music they heard. Probably the best-known song the Brookwood organizers brought north was "We Shall Not Be Moved," first sung in 1931 by members of the West Virginia Miners' Union. The song derived from a hymn inspired by a verse in the book of Jeremiah: "Blessed is the man that trusteth in the Lord for he shall be as a tree planted by the waters." The hymn lyrics are as follows:

> Jesus is my saviour, I shall not be moved
> Jesus is my saviour, I shall not be moved
> Just like a tree that's planted by the water,
> I shall not be moved.

In the miners' hands, it became:

> The union is behind us, we shall not be moved,
> The union is behind us, we shall not be moved
> Just like a tree that's planted by the water,
> We shall not be moved.[22]

Over the years, "We Shall Not Be Moved" has become familiar to several generations while being used to support a whole panoply of social causes. A lesser-known but still widely circulated favorite, "We Are Building a Strong Union," was borrowed from the textile workers. The miners just changed the last line from "workers in the mills" to "workers in the mines." Other folk-styled labor songs brought north by Brookwood organizers included "The Death of Mother Jones" and "The West Virginia Hills," but these never caught on in communist circles.

THE NEGROS SING THEIR PROTEST

One other thing the Brookwood organizers and other northern unionists noticed about the striking mill and mine workers: they were white. As bad a deal as the poor whites had, African Americans were even worse off. This was still the South of total segregation and lynchings. The radicals who ventured south to work with the workers to get a fairer shake from employers ran into another important American musical tradition, with its roots in Africa. Spirituals and jazz had been popular in northern urban areas for decades. But communists initially disparaged such music as being insufficiently militant and corrupted by bourgeois influences. This political bigotry even extended to Paul Robeson, the great African American athlete, singer, and actor who eventually became a hero to the Left. Robeson saw his career derailed for his outspokenly antiestablishment views during the McCarthy period. As late as 1935, however, Robeson was condemned by the *Daily Worker* for singing his artistically stylized arrangements of black spirituals. The paper called them "white men's music"![23]

In their "pure" form, African American religious songs and work chants sometimes met with approval in radical circles—they could be seen as the complaint of an oppressed people about their lot. Em Jo Basshe incorporated traditional spirituals into his left-wing play *Earth* as far back as 1926. Four years later, Philip Schatz wrote a feature article for the *New Masses* entitled "Songs of the Negro Worker," which included fragmentary texts of "Take This Hammer" and "John Henry," among others.[24] Richard Frank asserted in the same magazine in 1934 that these black songs represented "the most sublime folk-music, with the possible exception of the Russian, of any people on earth."[25]

But what really interested the communist movement were the protest lyrics being created by blacks in the early 1930s. These compositions were deeply rooted in African American folk song patterns, but the words were adapted from the slogans of urban radicals and reflected class-conscious sentiments far more overtly than most traditional black songs. "[T]he ideology of the international working-class movement is beginning to be expressed in Native Negro music," Frank wrote in the *New Masses*. And when communist organizers worked in black communities, usually some evidence existed to back this up. For example, at a Birmingham, Alabama, antilynching conference in 1933, a local Negro woman recast the old spiritual "My Mother's Got a Stone That Was Hewn Out of the Mountain" into a widely acclaimed militant labor anthem:

> We got a stone that was hewn out of history,
> That was hewn out of history,
> Come a-rollin' thru Dixie,
> Come a-rollin' thru Dixie,
> A tearin' down the kingdom of the boss.[26]

Subsequent verses simply introduced variations in the first line:

> Don't you want that stone that was hewn out of history . . .
> The I.L.D. is the stone . . .
> The bosses hate the stone . . .
> The workers need the stone.

In Charlotte, North Carolina, "In That Great Gettin'-Up Mornin'" became "In That Great Revolutionary Mornin'," and in several areas of the South, blacks, like whites, were reported improvising radical lyrics to "We Shall Not Be Moved."[27]

Because so many more blacks were illiterate, music was that much more important as a means of introducing them to political ideas. "Leaflets cannot appeal to them," Richard Frank instructed readers of *New Masses* in 1934. "Among the Negroes, it will be to a great extent through mass singing that recruiting will be done, for masses of Negro workers are held at illiteracy." Perhaps revealing that his own education was a bit bound by stereotypes, he declared that "singing is their great form of artistic expression. In order to win the Negro people most effectively, the revolutionary movement will have to make use of this instrument."[28]

Thus, on picket lines in Chicago during the mid-1930s, rural blacks newly arrived from the South could be heard singing:

> Gimme that new Communist spirit,
> Gimme that new Communist spirit,
> Gimme that new Communist spirit,
> It's good enough for me.
> It was good for Comrade Lenin,
> It was good for Comrade Lenin,
> It was good for Comrade Lenin,
> And it's good enough for me.[29]

Another spiritual, "St. John the Revelator," was converted from

> Tell me, whose that a-writing?
> St. John is a-writing.
> And what's he writing?
> He's writing the Revelation,
> And signed it with the golden seal.

to

> Tell me, whose that a-writing?
> Karl Marx is a-writing.
> And what's he writing?
> He's writing a manifesto,
> And signed it with the Communist seal.[30]

It is doubtful, of course, that many of the poorly schooled African Americans who sang such songs really understood the Marxist dialectics and proletarian ideology implicit in the lyrics. But they were certainly aware of the grievances they had suffered at the hands of the dominant white social and economic system. So, while the musical adaptation of radical slogans might seem superficial, the underlying protest it affirmed was pure conviction. The modification of communist terminology in the agit-prop songs of the 1930s was comparable to the skimming of Protestant religious cant during slavery to create spirituals and gospel hymns, many of which also voiced objections to the status quo, but out of necessity in subtler language. Though choral singing was not the only art form African Americans pursued, it certainly was a natural part of their musical heritage. Ear-catching harmonies came spontaneously, and the enthusiasm with which these black sympathizers sang their militant lyrics made a profound impression on left-wing organizers.

Yet during the early 1930s, relatively few urban radicals were exposed directly to black folk music. Mention of its "new" revolutionary qualities was confined principally to the discussion surrounding Lawrence Gellert's "Negro Songs of Protest." The son of a Hungarian immigrant, Gellert as a teenager was adopted as something of a junior mascot by the band of Greenwich Village radicals who edited the old *Masses*. For a time he held odd jobs as a reporter, undertaker's secretary, and actor, but when his health broke in the early 1920s, he moved to the warmer climes and assumed the editorship of a small newspaper in the resort town of Tryon, North Carolina.[31] There he discovered chain gang songs and other African American folk-protest lyrics, which attracted his attention because of his own growing left-wing sympathies.

Gellert forwarded some songs to his brother Hugo, then art editor for the *New Masses;* Hugo was quite excited by it and urged him to gather more. For years thereafter, Gellert scoured the black communities of the southeastern United States in search of protest songs. Often he was aided by whites who mistook his efforts for an attempt to garner new spirituals. Beginning in 1930, he published a series of articles in the *New Masses* entitled "Negro Songs of Protest," detailing his findings and including numerous lyrics but few tunes. In 1934, three of these articles were woven together as one essay in Nancy Cunard's mammoth anthology *Negro,* and two years later twenty-four texts with music were issued as *Negro Songs of Protest;* a second volume, *Me and My Captain,* appeared in 1939.[32]

The songs Gellert collected were all protest oriented. Despite what some of his southern neighbors thought, he had no interest in and didn't try to locate any other kind. The lyrics he was interested in typically contrasted the plight of the African American—often a chain gang worker—with the secure existence of his white oppressor or in other ways commented on the subordinate status of the black person in the South:

> I went to 'Tlanta,
> Nebber bin dere afo'.
> White folks eat de apple,
> Nigger wait fo' co' . . .
> I went to Hebben,
> Nebber bin dere afo'.
> White folk sit in Lawd's place,
> Chase nigger down below.
> Catch dat Southern, grab dat train,
> Won' come back no mo'. ("I Went To 'Tlanta")

* * *

> Wake up, boys, spit on de rock,
> Ain' quite day but it's fo' o'clock.
> Ah wouldn't call you, but jes' has to,
> Ah don' wan' you but de white man do. ("Wake Up, Boys")

In some cases, recitations of grievances were mingled with clear threats of reprisals or calls for overt resistance:

> Sistren and brethren,
> Stop foolin' with pray,
> When black face is lifted,
> Lawd turnin' 'way . . .
> We're buryin' a brudder
> Dey kill fo' de crime

Tryin' to keep
What was his all de time . . .
Stand on yo' feet,
Club gripp'd 'tween yo' hands;
Spill their blood, too,
Show 'em yours is a man's.[33]

For urban radicals familiar with Negro folk music principally in the contexts of minstrel buffoonery and mournful spirituals performed by soothing chorales, such militant fare was electrifying indeed. In time, some folk song scholars tried to cast doubt on the authenticity of Gellert's material because the genre was not well documented and because he included creations not strictly in oral tradition. Yet at the time of initial publication, few questioned their genuine quality. They had a considerable impact in communist music circles from the start. As early as 1934, one or two of the revolutionary choruses added selections from Gellert's collection to their repertoires—though usually with European-style art music arrangements that all but obscured their African American origins. "I Went to 'Tlanta" and "Sistren and Brethren" were among the first indigenous American "folk" creations to appear in a communist song anthology, *Workers Song Book No. 2*, published in 1935.

Remarking over the increased size and other improvements over *Book No. 1*, the forward to *Book No. 2* asserted, "Particularly noteworthy in the present collection [is] . . . the publication for the first time of two original Negro songs of protest revealing the rising discontent and militancy of the oppressed Negro people." When the Gellert collection appeared as a book in 1936, the songs enjoyed a tremendous vogue among human rights supporters. Gellert himself asserted that the songs he collected contributed in important ways to the Communist Party's belief in the revolutionary ardor of southern blacks and its active agitation for self-determination of the "suppressed nation" of Negroes living in the Blackbelt of Georgia, Alabama, Mississippi, and Louisiana.[34]

Gellert also assisted in securing material for *Negro* (1934), edited by Nancy Cunard, the rebellious and disowned heiress of the British steamship line family. For forty years, until her death in 1965, Cunard led a wandering and often bohemian existence as a poet, newspaperwoman, and crusader for radical causes, though her political commitments seemed more emotional than intellectual.[35] She came to the United States in 1931 to collect material for her militant volume, which was published in London by Wishart entirely at her own expense.

Negro is one of the most important documents on African American culture ever printed, and it deserved to be far better known by scholars and the general public than it was. On its more than 800 oversize pages are 385 illustrations and more than 220 articles written by some 150 contributors, white and black. These range from novelists and poets such as Theodore Dreiser, Ezra Pound, Langston Hughes, and Sterling Brown, to communist leaders such as Earl Browder and James Ford, and to African writers who later became heads of state, notably Johnstone (Jomo) Kenyatta. The book covers politics, art, religion, economics, literature, and many other aspects of African American life. Some thirty articles deal with the folklore and anthropology of black communities around the world, authored by such distinguished academicians as Melville J. Herskovits, George Herzog, Guy B. Johnson, and Zora Neale Hurston. Their contributions are devoid of all political commentary, but other portions of the book, especially Cunard's introduction and editorial remarks, are heavily pro-communist.

The book's relative obscurity was due in part to its large size and price—$13.50 in paperback even at the Depression's rock bottom. But the fact that it became an expensive collectors' item within a very few years was due also to a warehouse fire touched off by German bombing during the Blitz that destroyed all but a few hundred copies. Thus, while the anthology documented the growing interest in African American folk song and folklore among human rights advocates and other left-wing partisans, its impact on the American radical movement itself was not very great.

SOUTHERN LABOR SCHOOLS

The radical organizers responsible for the early communist contacts with rural folk traditions, both white and African American, were essentially in the position of onlookers. The militant strike and protest songs that were created around the framework of old ballads, mountain hymns, and spirituals were almost entirely the inspiration and product of the "folk" themselves, not the labor organizers and journalists who carried them north. Soon, however, Marxist organizers took a more active hand in shaping a native working-class music based on local traditional expression. These organizers had more education, sophistication, travel experience, and Marxist background than their predecessors. They were far more worldly than the rural proletariat they addressed. Their activity was channeled primarily through the labor schools and grassroots unionizing efforts scattered throughout the South—notably the Brookwood movement, Kentucky Workers Alliance, Southern School for Workers, Red Dust Players, Southern Tenant Farmers Union, Highlander Folk School, and Commonwealth Labor College. The Brookwood movement discovered the use of the folk song idiom in its West Virginia organizing. Under leaders like Tom

Tippett and Walter Seacrist, collecting songs was supplemented by the original creation and dissemination of folk-styled labor songs.[36]

Similarly active was the Kentucky Workers Alliance (KWA), a local division of the national Workers Alliance of America, a union founded primarily to represent state WPA workers and the unemployed. With the help of Don West, a Georgia-born poet and communist organizer in several Eastern Seaboard states during the 1930s, the Kentucky Workers Alliance stimulated the production and singing of labor and topical songs by local workers based on their own folk music traditions.[37] Its *Songs for Southern Workers*, published in 1937, was modeled along the utilitarian lines of the famous IWW "Little Red Songbook," and in the KWA domain it was nearly as popular. Except for a few radical standards such as "The Internationale" and "Solidarity Forever," almost all of the songs were recent folk-derivative compositions. They were printed as texts and marked, broadside style, "to be sung to the tune of" well-known traditional pieces, both sacred and secular. West's daughter, Hedy, absorbed traditional and protest songs she learned from her father and people around him and took them north. With this musical heritage, she became a recording artist and concert entertainer during the urban folk music boom of the 1960s, and she continued to perform into the 1990s.

Another of the left-wing labor movement's educational centers in the South was the Southern School for Workers, a few miles outside Asheville, North Carolina, an area vibrant with traditional music. The Southern School for Workers also issued songbooks—mimeographed, not printed—and stressed the use of folk-based materials for local agit-prop purposes. Its principal collection was *Songs of the Southern School for Workers*, published in Asheville in 1940. By this time, national interest in traditional music was widespread. Students and staff of the school developed a keen appreciation for the intrinsic merits of native American folk songs, not just their usefulness as propaganda tools. Many went into the field to collect traditional lyrics and tunes and sometimes attended the annual Asheville Folk Festival, organized by Bascom Lamar Lunsford. Particularly notable was the work of Bill Wolff, a young organizer, former writer for the John Reed Club, and cultural worker for the International Ladies Garment Workers Union, whose folk song activity was described in the national press.[38]

In Oklahoma, a troupe of nine professional actors, calling themselves the Red Dust Players, toured the state performing politically charged dramatic productions for oil workers and tenant farmers that relied heavily on the vernacular idiom of southern workers to get their message across. Agnes "Sis" Cunningham, the Red Dust Players' principal songwriter, recalled, "We sang of and acted out all of the things closest to sharecroppers' hearts, from their long-range hunger to own their own land to their immediate needs such as medical care, glasses, and false teeth."[39] The Players were repeatedly thwarted by anticommunists. Following a raid on a bookstore in Oklahoma City, Communist Party leaders were arrested, jailed, and tried. The career of the Red Dust Players lasted only seven months (late 1939 to early 1940), its demise the result of relentless conservative harassment.

Sis Cunningham soon became a member of the Almanac Singers with Pete Seeger and her fellow Oklahoman, Woody Guthrie. With her husband, Gordon Friesen, in 1962 she founded *Broadside* magazine. From the 1960s through the 1980s, the Cunningham-Freisen New York City apartment served as a breeding ground for such creative talents as Bob Dylan, Tom Paxton, Phil Ochs, Janis Ian, and scores of other topical songwriters who relied on the folk idiom.

Meanwhile, in the Arkansas region, the Southern Tenant Farmers Union, founded in 1934, functioned as a rural labor adjunct to the Socialist Party under Norman Thomas. Among its principal spokespeople were two African American preachers who were outstanding adapters of folk songs and hymns for union purposes: A. B. Brookins and John Handcox. Brookins, though he was an effective song leader in the union, did not become well known among the urban radical song movement. But Handcox is still remembered today for his vibrant, moving compositions "Raggedy, Raggedy Are We" and "There Are Mean Things Happening in This Land," as well as helping create the labor classic "Roll the Union On."[40]

Among all these active groups, Commonwealth Labor College and the Highlander Folk School had by far the greatest impact on the northern radical movement's slowly awakening interest in the use of folk materials, both for propaganda and eventually for aesthetic enjoyment. The Commonwealth Labor College was an offshoot of the utopian socialist New Llano cooperative colony of Leesville, Louisiana, established on April 2, 1923. The college had begun its union and education activities in 1925 in the area around Mena, Arkansas. Because of its Arkansas location, Commonwealth College often shared song material with the Southern Tenant Farmers Union. Like its parent, the New Llano cooperative, Commonwealth maintained a fully communal lifestyle. By the early 1930s it adopted a pro-communist political outlook, and shaped its worldview to fit the proletarian ideology of the Third Period. At first, students came mainly from northern urban centers to receive instruction in history, economics, political theory, labor problems, culture, and the practical arts from a Marxist viewpoint.

There was plenty of singing. But in the early days it usually took the form of denouncing cliched "Bankers and Bosses" songs, drawing from the proletariat-oriented English Chartist movement and "The Internationale," rather than any American-based workers' lyrics. Sis Cunningham, who attended the college from 1931 to 1933, remembers being taught that the revolution to topple the capitalist system in the United States would happen any day. She recalls that students and staff rarely tried to mingle with people living in the region and showed little interest in their folk songs. But she persisted in her efforts to identify local traditions and engage neighbors, compiling a songbook and leading the singing.[41]

> Kids would come into the [school] to exchange a bucket of blueberries for canned goods. I remember one saying, "do you think anybody here wants to buy a song-ballad?" So every once in a while there was some talk about there being some songs in the neighborhood, but nobody was particularly interested to go out and get them.[42]

In the mid-1930s, however, all this began to change. And with the arrival in September 1937 of the Reverend Claude Williams as director of the college, radical changes began. Presbyterian minister Williams was nicknamed "The Red Preacher" by his local enemies. Raised in Tennessee, Williams began his ministerial career as a religious fundamentalist but progressed theologically to preach a combination of Marxist humanism and social gospel philosophy.[43] More than anything else, he believed in striving to better the lot of the downtrodden rural folk he served in several states. To this end, he strongly favored practical results over abstruse political theory. Accordingly, at Commonwealth he actively encouraged school members to communicate with people in the surrounding community in terms they could understand and accept. He brought to song leading a thorough familiarity with scores of old hymns, spirituals, and folk liturgies of the rural southern churches. He took a leading hand in local union organizing activities, frequently converting the liturgical song repertoire into labor songs to support the organizing efforts.

One of his many pupils was Lee Hays, who subsequently went on to fame as a singer and songwriter with the Almanac Singers, People's Songs, and the Weavers. It was Hays, writing in the *People's Songs* bulletin, who gave "The Red Preacher" the new nickname of "The Singing Preacher." Hays grew up in Georgia and Arkansas in a family so politically conservative that he recalls being whipped for reading the works of the atheist Robert Ingersoll.[44] He matured to an itinerant career—preacher, schoolteacher, and librarian, among other occupations—before drifting into the labor movement as a Christian Socialist in the early 1930s.

Hays was briefly the secretary of the Arkansas Socialist Party. By the late 1930s, he had moved left into the communist milieu. During his three-year stay at Commonwealth College (1936–1939), he served on the school's staff in various capacities, including dramatics instructor. Like Claude Williams, he had a fine voice, a commanding stage presence, a talent for leading singing, and exceptional ability as a songwriter. Musically he was steeped in the rich Methodist and Baptist hymnody and white and African American folk song traditions of the rural South. But his education and intellect gave his later creative work an urbane sophistication much different from his family's aesthetic sensibilities.

Through their shrewd, often instinctive use of native folklore traditions, Williams, Hays, and others at Commonwealth College were able to interest local people in the school's activities and extend its reach in the community. Hays recounted in a later article that farmers and rural townspeople disliked urban proletarian art works. Plays such as *Waiting for Lefty* were considered "in the worst possible taste," he said.[45] But these same people flocked to the college grounds on weekends when the college presented the blind Ozark folk singer Emma Dusenberry performing her traditional ballads and songs or when it held square dances. At other times, the community was exposed to more direct agit-prop work for the union cause. Students and staff composed labor lyrics based on native speech patterns, old hymns, and folk melodies. So-called "chapbooks" containing union, folk, and topical verse were distributed. And traditional songs and motifs were incorporated into the school's class-conscious dramatic shows, which were often performed "on the road" in nearby communities and even neighboring states.

At the same time, Commonwealth College publicized itself in radical circles in the North, trying to lure additional funds and students by capitalizing on the growing left-wing interest in folk music. One *New Masses* advertisement of the late 1930s seemed aimed at combining politics and recreation. The ad cited "hiking, swimming, folk songs and dances, fishing, [and] tennis," in addition to its Marxist studies program as inducements for prospective vacationers.[46]

Williams and Hays left the school in late 1939—a year before the college was forced by reactionary authorities to close its doors. But by that time, a large body of union and other topical material based on indigenous folk traditions had been created by its members and used with notable success in organizing efforts in the region. The impact of all this music on the recruiting efforts of the communist movement of the 1930s was greater than any of the other Southern labor schools and folk-based regional agit-prop groups, with the possible exception of the Highlander Folk School of Monteagle, Tennessee.

Before he went to Commonwealth College, Lee Hays had learned song leading at Highlander Folk School.[47] Don West, who had stimulated southern workers to sing of their plight through his work with the Kentucky Workers Alliance, founded the Highlander Folk School in November 1932, along with Myles Horton and Dr. John Thompson, all three one-time preachers. For three decades, Highlander provided education and leadership training for workers trying to cope with the many economic and social problems of the South. In time it gained considerable support from the entire labor movement, including both the AFL and CIO. Forced to close its doors in 1961 through the efforts of local right-wing leaders opposed to its support of civil rights, Highlander reopened in 1962 as the Highlander Research and Education Center, and it still prospers today.[48] Myles Horton, Highlander director and principal figure behind the school for much of its history, began his career in the Cumberland mountains as a Presbyterian minister. He went to Denmark to study cooperative communities, returning home to try out what he had learned. In 1935, he married Zilphia Johnson, a young Arkansas music student who had participated in cultural activities in the New York left-wing community and was strongly influenced by the work of the Reverend Claude Williams. From her marriage to Myles Horton in 1935 to her death in 1956, Zilphia Horton was the Highlander Folk School's music director. She collected more than 1,300 labor, topical, and folk songs from a variety of union, left-wing, and traditional groups and helped disseminate many of them through the eleven different songbooks put out by the school over the years.

The best known of her discoveries was "We Shall Overcome," collected from striking Food and Tobacco Workers in 1946, who sang it as a version of a well-known African American gospel song "I'll Be All Right." Horton revised the lyrics and tune a bit and taught it to Pete Seeger, who published it in *People's Songs* bulletin as "We Will Overcome." It took until the next generation of protesters began looking for songs to support the budding civil rights movement for the song to find its audience. But once it did, it's simple, compelling message and easy-to-learn melody made it eminently transferable among enthusiastic movement organizers in the South. Before long, "We Shall Overcome" became the anthem of the civil rights movement.[49]

Zilphia Horton, who died in 1956, had a fine voice and an inspirational manner, helping make her a great teacher of songs. Through her work and that of many Highlander pupils, and other southern labor groups like the Kentucky Workers Alliance and Commonwealth College, the principle of foraging in the folk idiom to harvest new union and topical songs became standard practice for the northern urban radical culture beginning in the early 1940s.

THE LABOR MOVEMENT'S AGIT-PROP USE
OF RURAL FOLK TRADITIONS

Contrary to the accusations of the McCarthyite Red baiters, the link between folk song and the politics of radical change was practical and aesthetic, not part of any conspiracy. The distinguishing feature of southern labor's agit-prop use of rural folk traditions in contrast to the North's was familiarity with the material; city unionization drives used other musical forms more successfully for sociopolitical purposes. Southern organizers acted out of very practical considerations, in deciding to use folk songs and traditional verbal patterns to capture the attention of the workers. In the rural South, folk music was the music of the people in the truest sense. The popular songs and church hymns of most urban centers, especially in the North, were unfamiliar in these areas. The art music of the European and American aristocracy—the kind the northern radicals originally turned to for agit-prop purposes—was very likely totally unknown .

Like the Wobblies before them, the radical labor leaders in the South in the 1930s who seized on the folk idiom in an attempt to further their own social and political ends were simply using the most generally accessible song material available to the local population. True, the types of musical idioms varied; the IWW worked with popular songs and urban evangelistic hymns, while the southern organizers relied on spirituals and folk songs. Yet the agit-prop principle was the same. In the rush to acclaim the tradition-based aesthetic of the rural proletariat in the 1930s, the fact that Aunt Molly Jackson and Ella May Wiggins were also conscious parodists in a league with Joe Hill and the Wobbly bards is often overlooked.[50] Moreover, it is clear that sophisticated city dwellers such as Margaret Larkin, who brought southern songs to the attention of northerners, had more than politics in mind. She, as well as later propagators with southern radical roots, like Don West's daughter Hedy, clearly liked the folk idiom from an artistic perspective.

It is important to keep in mind that many of the most effective organizers in the South were successful because they grew up in the region. They were familiar with its values, folkways, and culture and had been steeped as a matter of course in local idiomatic speech and song patterns. Though their commitment to Marxism varied by degrees, they shared an awareness that southern workers would be well served to develop a collective identity and aesthetic expression within the framework of their own sociopolitical experiences and traditions. Some bitterly resented the outside interference and bureaucratic meddling of labor agitators from the North who often were unfamiliar with local conditions and more obsessed with proper adherence to dogma than practical results.

They sometimes lashed out at the stereotyped prejudices of urban radicals about the rural people of the South. In one instance, a *New Masses* cartoon depicted William Randolph Hearst and a chorus of antiproletarian slanderers with the caption "Hearst's Hill Billy Crooners." Don West responded with an angry letter:

> Such usage of this term [Hill Billy] is a slur and a insult to a broad mass of white workers and poor farmers, especially in the South. . . . This term . . . is one applied to the mountain people—poor white workers and farmers who are among the most oppressed of the South. . . . My whole background is that of the mountaineer, "hill billy," "white trash." I know my folks would resent such a hook-up in the use of the term as [the] NEW MASSES used [it]. While it is not an exact analogy, you can easily see what effect it would have on the Negro people to say "Hearst 'nigger' Spiritualists." You can also see how incorrect this would be.[51]

West's warning to "be much more careful in the use of such anti–working class terms in the future" apparently was taken to heart. From then on, the communist press tended to avoid use of the term *"hillbilly."*

The heavy dialectic cant of European Marxism also bothered southern organizers who wanted to present union and class issues in the local vernacular. Many of the most effective of these workers were also preachers, past or present, and thus particularly suited oratorically—and sometimes musically—to blend their political and labor sentiments with traditional folk expression. Where topical lyrics were easily superimposed over a traditional framework through the change of a mere word or line, as in "We Shall Not Be Moved" or "Give Me That Old Time Religion," their audiences were not far behind them. In fact, union meetings in the South were often suffused with a religious quality, and it wasn't unusual for meeting formats to wander back and forth repeatedly between songs and spoken texts, a phenomenon skillfully capitalized on by the more adept labor organizers.

In many areas, churches and religious meeting halls were the only buildings large enough to hold union gatherings. Meetings called ostensibly for the purpose of discussing union activities might begin with the singing of several hymns.[52] At the proper point, perhaps after a few words of introduction by the preacher/labor leader, "Roll the Chariot On" would be changed to "Roll the Union On." The "devil" would be changed to "boss" in the stanza beginning "If the *boss* gets in the way, we're gonna roll right over him." The congregation would pick up the new thrust of the lyrics, add other similar lines ("if the sheriff gets in the way," etc.), and then conclude its singing to hear another speaker. Speakers' remarks often were couched in biblical rhetoric and imagery and in turn would be punctuated

with hearty calls of "amen," "that's right, Brother," and "praise the Lord."
More singing, oratory, and union planning would follow in turn. If local
vigilantes or antilabor law enforcement authorities appeared, song leaders and preachers smoothly guided the meeting back into a routine religious assembly. The church cant would be resumed until the danger—
often very real—was over.

To be sure, some fundamentalist audiences objected to mixing political and religious sentiments in this fashion. Lee Hays wrote in *New Masses*
of hearing an African American congregation in Cotton Plant, Arkansas,
singing an old hymn, "Let the Will of the Lord Be Done":

> Let the will (let the will—)
> Let the will (let the will—)
> Let the will of the Lord be done.

Hays recalled:

> I began to think, "Here's a good union song. Let's see—let the will of the
> union—let the will of the people"—Just then, the song leader interrupted
> [with] "Now, wait a minute. Don't you go changin' that song. It's all right
> just like it stands. 'Let the will of the Lord be done'—that says just exactly
> what we want to say. What do you think the Lord's will is, anyhow? It's
> freedom! You leave that song alone!"

Hays and the song leader worked out a compromise:

> Organize! (Organize—)
> Organize! (Organize—)
> Let the will of the Lord be done.

And then Hays zippered in verse after verse:

> Freedom again;
> On the farm;
> In the fields; etc.[53]

In the South, among both blacks and whites, traditional music and other
folk arts were integrated into other kinds of daily activity as a cultural
totality. Therefore, fusing progressive political sentiments with the folk
idiom to create a dynamic agit-prop, working-class form of expression
were much more successful than in northern urban centers where traditional singing and folk speech patterns had been obliterated, or nearly so,
through the passage of time. Ethnic and workers' choruses did continue
to flourish, but they functioned more as social-cultural gathering oppor-

tunities, and their repertoires consisted mostly of immigrant songs or American popular music. Attempts to superimpose the traditions of the rural American heartlands on a city-oriented labor movement therefore at best had only a limited success and a certain artificiality. It's true that Will Geer was acclaimed by Patterson, New Jersey, weavers in 1935 for creating entertaining strike ballads based on local labor conditions.[54] And the Almanac Singers or People's Songsters of a later era won cheers from union members for their folk-based organizing material. But the applause from these northern audiences had more to do with performance presentation and the timeliness of the subject matter than with the use of the folk song idiom, compared to the genuine appreciation of the songs found in southern audiences.

In truth, the most effective agit-prop verse produced in the northern labor movement during these same years was cast in an essentially popular vein. Such songs as "Picket on the Picket Line," "Oh, Mister Sloan," and "There Was a Rich Man Who Lived in Detroitium"[55] emphasized humor, cleverness, and "cute" lyrics for the most part. They frequently had a jingle-like quality different from the folk-derived union music of the South, which was by comparison unpretentious and straightforward, manifesting a gut militancy absent in the majority of urban labor songs created in the 1930s.

There were exceptions, principally the songs of Maurice Sugar and the combined efforts of Alfred Hayes and Earl Robinson. Sugar was a Detroit lawyer with socialist convictions who during the Depression years often was criticized for defending union leaders and communist officials.[56] But Sugar contributed more to the labor movement than just legal talent. He also composed protest songs that became popular with rank-and-file workers. Among the most widely sung was "The Soup Song," written in 1931 to the tune of "My Bonnie." Decrying the pittance offered to struggling toilers in the era of high unemployment, the song verses describe a series of down-and-out situations, followed by a chorus in which "Bring back, bring back, bring back my Bonnie to me" was changed to "Soo-oup, soo-uop, they bring us a bowl of soo-oo-oup."

Another Sugar success was "Sit Down," a rousing call to action roared out by strikers in many General Motors plants during the sit-down struggles of 1937:

> When they tie the can to a union man,
> Sit down! Sit down!
> When they give him the sack, they'll take him back,
> Sit down! Sit down!
> Sit down, just take a seat,
> Sit down, and rest your feet,

Sit down you've got 'em beat.
Sit down! Sit down![57]

In the summer of 1936, a radical poet and dramatist named Alfred Hayes collaborated with the composer Earl Robinson—who had started with the organized communist movement in the Composers Collective—to write two of the most memorable agit-prop songs of the decade: "Joe Hill" and "Abe Lincoln." The first ("I Dreamed I Saw Joe Hill Last Night") was introduced casually during a "Joe Hill" evening at Camp Unity, a left-wing upstate New York resort where Hayes and Robinson were employed for the season.[58] It was quickly taken up by the entire labor-radical movement, and more than three decades later it was still being sung at countless informal gatherings, not to mention being one of Joan Baez's concert mainstays.

"Abe Lincoln" also had a substantial initial impact, though its durability was limited—partly because it was harder to sing than "Joe Hill." The other reason is especially ironic: its chorus is jarringly revolutionary, containing some of the most militant rhetoric produced in song of the period, though the words of the chorus were quoted directly from Lincoln's speech:

> This country, with its institutions,
> Belongs to the people who inhabit it;
> This country, with its Constitution,
> Belongs to us who live in it.
> "Whenever they shall grow weary
> Of the existing government,
> They can exercise their constitutional right of amending it,
> Or the revolutionary right to dismember or overthrow it."[59]

Obviously, to accommodate these words, the melody of "Abe Lincoln" had to be a bit contrived. But except for that, the songs of Sugar, Robinson, and Alfred Hayes possessed a folklike simplicity and directness in their lyrics and music. They were, though, atypical of northern labor music of the time. Strike parodies and jingles remained more popular and influential with politically oriented urban audiences.

So, too, were the agit-prop songs couched in the Broadway show idiom. These were numerous, often combined with topical material into revues and plays. The best known were *Pins and Needles,* a production of the International Ladies Garment Workers Union; *The Cradle Will Rock* by Marc Blitzstein (formerly of the Composers Collective); various productions of the American Student Union; and cabaret numbers of the Theater Arts Committee (TAC).

For the most part, their form and content are suggested by such titles as "Sing Me a Song of Social Significance," "Not Cricket to Picket," and "You Can't Live on Love." They seldom strayed toward the folk idiom or traditional motifs. One exception was "Ballad for Americans," a cantata by John LaTouche and Earl Robinson, which was given its first wide hearing by Paul Robeson on CBS's *Pursuit of Happiness*." "Ballad for Americans" blended sentimental patriotism with pro-working-class politics. It was so broad in its appeal that it was performed at the Republican Party National Convention in July 1940.[60]

The folk idiom also provided the inspiration for the Theater Arts Committee's spoof on trail ditties—a Brooklyn cowboy song, it was called—"The Horse with a Union Label (Old Paint)." It began:

> My daddy was a cowboy, and
> I follow in his footsteps
>   Riding the range.
> My chaps are wide, my shirt is red,
> I'll wear my Stetson till I'm dead,
> I keep my boots on the table.
> I brand my cows and turn 'em free,
> But the brand ain't what it used to be
> 'Cause now I ride a horse
>   With a union label.
> Old Paint, Old Paint,
> A prouder horse there ain't,
> 'Cause my Old Paint
> Is a horse with a union label.[61]

Thus, folk music occupied a compartmentalized and often secondary position in the urban communist movement, quite unlike its integrated totality with the rest of working-class life in the South. The northern movement did, after 1935, put rural traditional music on a pedestal as the "people's" culture, but the format at a typical labor or political rally in the North during the 1940s continued to differ sharply from similar meetings held in the southern labor movement This was true even when the Almanac Singers or other left-wing folk singers performed. A roll call of members or a general welcoming speech would be followed by a series of reports or lesser speakers. Then would come, perhaps, a major address, then discussion, or a vote on issues up for decision. Sometimes there would be a collection, and only then the announcement "Now we'll take a break [or conclude] and have some entertainment by the Almanac Singers." While the ensuing performance invariably had a strong agit-prop character, it nevertheless remained first and foremost entertainment, segregated from what went before or came after in the minds of most listeners.

This format was never characteristic of labor union gatherings or move-ment meetings in the South. Unlike their colleagues in the South, most northern union officials saw no further practical application of folk songs and other traditional genres. This was true of communist leaders and northern rank-and-file union activists as well, notwithstanding all the talk about the value of folk song by radicals in the late 1930s and thereafter. Even as late as 1934, Richard Frank instructed in the *New Masses:*

> Outside of the revolutionary movement there is today nothing culturally valid. Hence, from now on artists and students of folk-lore, for the sake merely of their art o[r] science, if for nothing else, if they would attain vi-tality, must enter the revolutionary movement. Only there can one be in touch with the people, with the society of the future.[62]

Nevertheless, during the 1930s, left-wing organizers and reporters acted as catalytic agents, introducing urban communists and rural folk culture to one another. The interaction, it should be remembered, was a two-way affair, for northern radicals exchanged their ideology and agit-prop slo-gans in return for the local worldview, folk song, and sometimes sympa-thetic personnel from traditional communities. There was a group of po-litically conscious folk singers centered around Alan Lomax for whom folklore did have the importance and symbolic representation held by the rural peoples of the South. This group tried to develop a similar working-class cultural totality in the North based on rural folk idioms and content. However quixotic their mission, it was not without accomplishment.

NOTES

1. Archie Green, "The Death of Mother Jones," *Labor History* 1, no. 1 (Winter 1960): 68-80. Also, see *Songs of the American Worker,* published by the John Reed Club of Cleveland, Ohio, 1934.
2. For an account of communist dual-union activities during the Third Period, see Irving Howe and Lewis Coser, *The American Communist Party: A Critical History,* 2d ed. (New York: Da Capo, 1974), chap. 6.
3. Irving Bernstein, *The Lean Years* (Baltimore: Penguin, 1966), 20. For general coverage of the textile strikes in the Piedmont, see 1–43.
4. "Gastonia Strike Songs," *New Masses* (August 1929): 14.
5. Printed in Margaret Larkin, "Ella May's Songs," *The Nation* (October 9, 1929), 383.
6. Margaret Larkin, "The Story of Ella May," *New Masses* (November 1929): 2.
7. Larkin, "Ella May's Songs," 382.
8. The accounts of Larkin, cited in prior notes, and others printed in the radical press at the time of Wiggins's death stress the random nature of the shots

into the truck, which was packed with people. Lurid headlines in the *Daily Worker* sometimes suggested the snipers were out to kill Wiggins specifically. It is true that on other occasions she was subjected to harassment, and once her well was poisoned, but there still is no concrete evidence for her planned murder at the time she was shot.

9. John Greenway, *American Folksongs of Protest* (New York: Barnes, 1960), 251–52.

10. These are Bill Dunne, "Armed Workers Bear Ella May to Her Grave," *Daily Worker* (September 18, 1929), 1; Jessie Lloyd, "Ella May, Murdered, Lives in Her Songs of Class Strife," *Daily Worker* (September 20, 1929), 1, 3; and Larkin, "The Story of Ella May."

11. Edith Fowke and Joe Glazer, eds., *Songs of Work and Freedom* (Chicago, 1960), 72–73, provides the text and details on the song's origin.

12. See Grace Lumpkin, "A Southern Cotton Mill Rhyme," *New Masses* (May 1930): 8, and her follow-up letter to the editor in the same publication: June 1930: 22.

13. Bernstein, *The Lean Years,* 360.

14. Bernstein, *The Lean Years,* 358.

15. For Dreiser's role in the hearings, see W. A. Swanberg, *Dreiser* (New York: Scribner, 1965), 383–87.

16. Greenway, *American Folksongs of Protest,* 267–68.

17. Shelly Romalis, *Pistol Packin' Mama: Aunt Molly Jackson and the Politics of Folksong* (Urbana: University of Illinois Press 1999). For a résumé of Aunt Molly Jackson's traditional background and repertoire, see Alan Lomax, "Aunt Molly Jackson: An Appreciation," *Kentucky Folklore Record* 7 (1961): 131–32. See also Julia S. Ardery, ed., *Welcome the Traveler Home: Jim Garland's Story of the Kentucky Mountains* (Lexington: University of Kentucky Press, 1983).

18. "I Am a Union Woman" from *Hard Hitting Songs for Hard-Hit People,* ed. Alan Lomax, Woody Guthrie, and Pete Seeger (New York: Oak, 1967), 142–43; the quotation of Aunt Molly Jackson from Swanberg, *Dreiser,* 385–86; excerpt from "The Murder of Harry Simms" in *Hard Hitting Songs,* 171.

19. See also Jim Garland, *Welcome the Traveler Home,* ed. Julia Ardery (Lexington: University of Kentucky Press, 1983).

20. "Kentucky Miner's Song," *Daily Worker* (April 2, 1932), 4.

21. Myra Page, "Miner's Ballad Song," *Daily Worker* (July 11, 1931), 4.

22. Fowke and Glazer, *Songs of Work and Freedom,* 38.

23. M.M. [Max Margulis], "Paul Robeson Concert," *Daily Worker* (October 25, 1935), 5.

24. Philip Schatz, "Songs of the Negro Worker," *New Masses* (May 1930): 6–8. This article drew heavily on an unauthorized use of Lawrence Gellert's material that was then being considered for publication by *New Masses.*

25. Richard Frank," Negro Revolutionary Music," *New Masses* (May 1934): 29.

26. "New Defense Song Gains Wide Popularity in South," *Daily Worker* (November 7, 1933) 5

27. Frank, "Negro Revolutionary Music," 29.

28. Frank, "Negro Revolutionary Music," 30.

29. Harold Lasswell and Dorothy Blumenstock, *World Revolutionary Propaganda* (New York: Knopf, 1939), 89.

30. Lyrics recalled by Waldemar Hille and Bill Wolff in separate interviews on July 21 and 23, 1967, respectively.

31. Material on Gellert is drawn from "Songs of Protest," *Time* (June 13, 1936), 51, and a series of interviews with Gellert (see the bibliography's sources list). See also Bruce Harrah-Conforth, "Laughing Just to Keep from Crying: Afro-American Folksong & the Field Recordings of Lawrence Gellert," unpublished master's thesis, Indiana University, Bloomington, 1984.

32. Gellert's articles in *New Masses* (November 1930): 10–11; (January 1931): 16–17; (April 1931): 6–8; (May 1932): 22; and (May 1933): 15–16. A few other songs were printed later in the same magazine and elsewhere. See especially "Four Negro Songs of Protest" in *Music Vanguard* 1, no. 2 (Summer 1935): 68–70.

33. Texts are reprinted from *Workers Song Book No. 2*, 22–26, and Lawrence Gellert, *Negro Songs of Protest* (New York: American Music League, 1936), 30–31.

34. Interview with Lawrence Gellert, May 7, 1968. For a detailed discussion of the "suppressed nation" theory regarding blacks held by the Communist Party, see Wilson Record, *The Negro and the Communist Party*, 3d ed. (Westport, Conn.: Greenwood, 1980). See also Harry Haywood, *Negro Liberation* (Chicago: Liberator, 1976), and *Black Bolshevik: Autobiography of an African American Communist* (Chicago: Liberator, 1978); Earl O. Hutchinson, *Blacks and Reds: Race and Class in Conflict 1919–1990* (East Lansing: Michigan State University Press, 1995); Henry Williams, *Black Response to the American Left, 1917–1929* (Princeton, N.J.: Princeton University Press, 1973); Philip S. Foner and Herbert Shapiro, eds., *American Communism and Black Americans: A Documentary History, 1930–1934* (Philadelphia: Chilton, 1991).

35. A volume of reminiscences by friends of Nancy Cunard, containing much biographical data and sketches of her personality, was compiled and edited by Hugh Ford, *Nancy Cunard: Brave Poet, Indomitable Rebel, 1896–1965* (Philadelphia: Temple University Press, 1968).

36. For a description of the activities of these Brookwooders, see Archie Green, "The Death of Mother Jones," *Labor History* 1, no. 1 (Winter 1960): 68–80.

37. West provides a useful autobiographical sketch of himself in "Georgia Wants Me—Dead or Alive," *New Masses* (June 26, 1934), 15–16.

38. A sketch of Wolff is provided in "American People's Artists: Story of William Wolff," *People's World* (October 4, 1946), 5.

39. Agnes Cunningham, "The Red Dust Players," *People's Songs* bulletin 3, no. 8 (September 1948): 4–5. See also Ellen Schrecker, *Many Are the Crimes: McCarthyism in America* (Boston: Little, Brown, 1998) for a review of the early development of HUAC activity in some states.

40. Printed in *Hard Hitting Songs for Hard-Hit People*, 260, 265, 268.

41. Interview with Agnes "Sis" Cunningham, September 7, 1965. See also Agnes "Sis" Cunningham and Gordon Friesen, *Red Dust and Broadsides: A Joint Autobiography*, ed. Ronald D. Cohen (Amherst: University of Massachusetts Press, 1999).

42. Josh Dunson, *Freedom in the Air: Song Movements of the '60s* (New York: International, 1965), 25.

43. Williams's career is traced by Cedric Belfrage in *A Faith to Free the People* (New York: Dryden, 1944), also published as *Let My People Go* and *South of God*. See also Lee Hays, "The Singing Preacher," *People's Songs* bulletin 3, nos. 1 and 2 (February and March 1948): 11, 13.

44. Interview with Lee Hays, August 16, 1965. See also Doris Willens, *Lonesome Traveler: The Life of Lee Hays* (New York: Norton, 1988).

45. Monthly column (no title), *People's Songs* bulletin 2, no. 3 (April 1947): 11.

46. Lee Hays, ""Vacation at Commonwealth College," *New Masses* (June 6, 1939), 29.

47. Lee Hays, "How I *Fell* into Songleading," *People's Songs* bulletin 1, no. 12 (January 1947): 11.

48. Information on the Highlander Folk School is taken from Anne Braden, "Highlander Folk School—The End and the Beginning," *Sing Out!* 12, no. 1 (February–March, 1962): 30–31; Lillian Barnard Bilkes, "Experiment at Highlander," *Direction* 1, no. 2 (October 1939): 10–11; and Dunson, *Freedom in the Air*, 27–30. See also John Glen, *Highlander, No Ordinary School*, 2d ed. (Knoxville: University of Tennessee Press, 1996).

49. For a generally accurate résumé of the song's history, see Robert Shelton, "Rights Song Has Own History of Integration," *New York Times* (July 23, 1963), and Pete Seeger, *Where Have All the Flowers Gone: A Singer's Stories, Songs, Seeds, Robberies*, ed. Peter Blook (Bethlehem, Pa.: Sing Out!, 1993), 32–35.

50. "Fighting Songs of the Unemployed," *Daily Worker*, Section II (September 2, 1939).

51. "We Stand Corrected" (letter to the editor), *New Masses* (May 21, 1935), 23.

52. This sketch is based on conversations with Hays and others.

53. Lee Hays, "Let the Will . . . ," *New Masses* (August 1, 1939), 15.

54. Al Hayes, "Paterson Strikers Get a Ballad," *Daily Worker* (November 26, 1935), 5.

55. Printed in *Hard Hitting Songs for Hard-Hit People*, 243–44, 254.

56. A good sketch of Sugar is provided by Bill Porterfield in "Found: Labor's Fiery Warrior, Maurice Sugar," *Detroit Free Press Sunday Magazine* (July 23, 1967), 20–22, 24.

57. The texts for this and "The Soup Song" are printed in *Hard Hitting Songs for Hard-Hit People*, 243–44, respectively. Several of Sugar's songs were printed in the *Daily Worker* between July 1936 and July 1938.

58. Interview with Earl Robinson, December 1967. See also Earl Robinson *Ballad of an American: The Autobiography of Earl Robinson*, with Eric A. Gordon (Lanham, Md.: Rowman & Littlefield, 1997). For a review of the history of this song, see Richard A. Reuss, "The Ballad of 'Joe Hill' Revisited," *Western Folklore* 22 (July 1967): 187–88.

59. The text is taken from *The People's Song Book* (New York, 1948), 50–51.

60. A sketch of the early history of and popular response to "The Ballad for Americans" may be obtained from the advertisement for the album of the same

name in *New Masses* (May 7, 1940), 32; and Hugh J. Riddell, "In the True Spirit of the '4th,'" *Daily Worker* (July 4, 1940), 7. Also see Earl Robinson's obituary tribute to John LaTouche, "Balladier for Americans," *The Nation* (August 25, 1956), 161.

61. Text from *The People's Song Book,* 82–83.

62. Frank, "Negro Revolutionary Music," 30.

6

Communist "Folk" Culture and the Popular Front

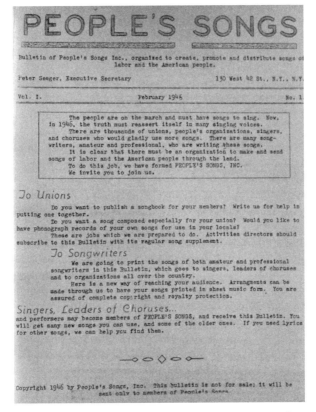

Reproduction of People's Songs inaugural issue of the Bulletin

I n the mid-1930s era of social instability, the threat of fascism preoccupied the minds of political leaders—revolutionary and nonrevolutionary alike—throughout Europe, the Soviet Union, and the United
States. Eager to establish friendly relations with as many allies as possible,
the Communist International called for a new policy: pursue a worldwide
"collective security" by embracing democracy to defeat fascism. Georgi
Dmitroff, in his address to the Seventh World Congress of the Comintern
in Moscow in 1935, officially proclaimed the communists' dedication to
fighting fascism by abandoning the comparatively isolationist position of
the Third Period.[1] Directly reactive to the rapid spread of Nazi and fascist political strength, the Popular Front ushered in a retreat from the more
rigid formulations of the proletarian revolutionary line and embraced
bourgeois culture and politics, encouraging new coalitions between the
communist movement and other liberal and progressive organizations.
Within a couple of years, American communists who had been so critical
of Roosevelt's domestic and foreign policies were championing democratic
New Deal programs and endorsing Roosevelt's approach of collective
security against Nazi and fascist aggressors. Howe and Coser point out
that "it was the first approach the CP had found that enabled it to gain a
measure of acceptance, respectability, and power within ordinary American life."[2] Later observers concur and further suggest that, in retrospect,
it is clear that the Popular Front was the beginning of a profound shift in
political, cultural, and social worldview in the United States.[3]

    This new Popular Front worldview had widespread implications for
developing left-wing ideology, particularly in the sphere of radical aesthetic expression. The changeover to Popular Front ideology took place
gradually over many months. During the transition, workers' art exhibited an unmistakable shift in emphasis from the creations of the vanguard
proletariat to native "people's" traditional materials, a shift that also reflected variability in the degree of social consciousness. This brought about
the corresponding full flowering of the American communist movement's
interest in folk traditions.

    Between 1936 and 1941, folk songs in particular enjoyed increasing
popularity in left-wing circles, driven by two principal sociocultural traditions. One was the workers' chorus tradition, by now having adopted
a more native repertoire and language but performing in a style still firmly
rooted in the formal European classical music heritage. The other was a
developing cadre of folk music performers who were acutely concerned
with the specifics of native American singing styles and the social and
aesthetic cultures that produced them. Toward the end of the Popular
Front era, the solo and small group performers loosely coalesced into what
may be termed the "Alan Lomax school" of musicians. Both of these
musical groups remained actively performing and linked to the commu-

nist movement until 1956, when the Lomax group foundered on the rocks of disillusionment and disarray in response to the Khrushchev Report and the Soviet suppression of the Hungarian Revolt. By the early 1940s, the preeminence of the radical choruses in communist activity was waning, being supplanted by the folk-based traditions of "people's music" mid-wifed by Alan Lomax and his protégés. Ironically, by the time the Lomax folk song tradition emerged as a clearly visible and dynamic entity, the Popular Front milieu that had spawned it was a thing of the past. But so fully did they replace the classical fine art tradition in communist propaganda activities and achieve widespread familiarity in the wider left-wing audience, they left a mark on the American musical scene that would remain long after the Old Left itself had become moribund.

THE AMERICAN MUSIC LEAGUE

Like its predecessor, the Workers Music League, the American Music League was made up of revolutionary choruses, bands, and orchestras affiliated with left-wing social and fraternal groups, whose members were mostly first or second-generation immigrants. Elie Siegmeister, Lan Adomian, Marc Blitzstein, and Jacob Schaefer (who died in 1936) continued on as AML leaders. Hanns Eisler's musical influences, if not his pedantic theoretical expositions, remained pronounced in League circles until the AML's demise toward the end of the 1930s. Mordecai Bauman, for a time the AML president, was the best known of the few soloists of the chorus movement from the WML days.[4] Bauman remained the preeminent concert artist of the radical stage during the Popular Front era, eventually supplanted by Paul Robeson. The Composers Collective, Downtown Music School, and other adjunct groups continued their activities under the aegis of the new organization, and the League periodically featured concerts of formal art music that drew large crowds.

By 1937, the chorus movement, the backbone of the AML, had instituted significant changes in keeping with the spirit of the Popular Front. Performances were more often in English and featured native American music—labor songs, revolutionary songs, and folk songs.[5] The Daily Worker Chorus changed its name to the Manhattan Chorus in an effort to expand its partisan base, and spawned several similar English-language singing groups. Their repertoires relied as much on home-produced music—traditional, radical, and classical—as on translations from other languages. The AML platform reflected the nativist principles of the Popular Front. Its six cardinal points underscored the League's desire to broaden its appeal among all segments of the "progressive American music public:

1. to organise amateur musical activities on a mass scale;
2. to create a closer understanding and collaboration between professional and amateur musicians;
3. to give concerts at popular prices;
4. to support American music and to bring its composer closer to its audience;
5. to publish and popularize American folk music, and
6. to work for the defense of musical culture against the dangers of fascism, censorship, and war.[6]

The League's sporadically distributed newsletter, *Unison,* and its music publications, notably those of Lawrence Gellert's "Negro Songs of Protest," further exhorted these principles.

At the same time, the AML tried without much success to widen its base of activities to include communist music organizations. Its affiliate, the American Music Alliance, boasted many respectable liberal musicians. But support from the emerging Congress of Industrial Organizations, initially the Committee for Industrial Organizing (CIO), never materialized, nor did much interest develop in mainstream music organizations. Moreover, with the coming of the Popular Front, communists everywhere gave up their attempts to direct ideological leadership openly in cultural organizations. "Art is a weapon" lost its power as an agit-prop message. Popular Front music programs in which the AML participated, as in other areas of the arts, were less well directed and more ambiguous about ends to be achieved. In the last years of the 1930s, as the perspectives of left-wing musicians harmonized more and more with the ideas of New Deal liberals, they directed their energies increasingly into the activities of the Federal Theatre Project and similar "respectable" agencies, abandoning the American Music League.[7]

By decade's end, the AML was stagnating, its influence on the American music scene significantly diminished. But in its heydey, the League and its affiliates affected music developments on the Left in three important ways. They were responsible for popularizing the earliest songs associated with the Loyalist cause of the Spanish Civil War. They introduced singing with audience participation, an essentially "entertainment" context outside of the picket line, street rally, or march milieu. And they helped make indigenous folk songs a staple of latter-day left-wing culture by introducing previously uninterested members of the communist movement to the "Alan Lomax" folk singers and their music.

Musically speaking, the Spanish Civil War is best remembered for its simple but eloquent partisan sentiments set to old Spanish folk melodies and fiery flamenco tunes on the order of "Viva La Quince Brigada," "Los Cuatros Generales," and "Si Me Quieres Escribir."[8] These were so often sung by folk singers at Spanish Refugee Benefits, left-wing "cause" parties, and hootenannies *after* the close of the struggle that many today think of the conflict's songs solely in a folk song–revival context, an impression furthered by the release in 1943 of the influential album *Songs of the Lincoln Battalion,* recorded for Asch-Stinson Records by Pete Seeger, Tom Glazer, and Baldwin and Bess Hawes. Some historians of the Popular Front's music legacy—Oscar Brand and R. Serge Denisoff, for example—have overemphasized the importance of the Loyalist songs as a stimulus for general radical interest in folk music. Brand even goes so far as to state that the Iberian war "caused the left wing to swallow the folk music world almost whole."[9]

In reality the songs heard so frequently at Loyalist rallies during the years of the Spanish war were generated almost entirely from within the non-folk-oriented revolutionary chorus tradition. The chorus music, which had dominated the left-wing movement for decades, simply took its place in communist street corner meetings, and Popular Front cultural benefits as well as at Loyalist rallies. The first topical compositions about the Spanish conflict appeared in quantity in 1937 and were as much a product of home poets as those serving in Spain.

They included such songs as "Spain Marches," "No Pasaran," and "We Shall Pass" ("Marching Song of the International Brigades"). None showed any degree of "folk consciousness" either in lyrics or music except for the few penned by Ray Auville, the southern mountaineer-turned-Red, which were not widely publicized.[10] In the long run, however, the antifascist songs produced or arranged during the 1930s by Hanns Eisler and fellow German left-wing musicians had greater impact, such as "Song of the United Front," "Peatbog Soldiers," "Frieheit," and "Hans Beimler." For the most part they were written in German and in some cases antedated or did not mention the Spanish conflict, yet during the years of the Franco rebellion, they invariably were sung in the name of the Loyalist cause. Such songs were the real crux of the Spanish Civil War music popularized within the American Left prior to 1940 and were typified by the spirited and enormously successful album *Six Songs for Democracy,* released by Eric Bernay, featuring the singing of Ernst Busch and veterans of the Thaelmann Battalion (Eleventh International Brigade). Thereafter, the folk-rooted songs of the Spanish conflict came to the fore (a few such as "Viva La Quince Brigada" were already known) and gradually supplanted the chorus-oriented marching songs in the repertoire of "people's music." It is true, as Denisoff remarks, that "the emotional impact of the Spanish Civil War songs . . . contribute[d] greatly to the [left-wing folk] Renascence of the early 1940s and indeed after the war," but such a statement indicates neither that this result was an unplanned-for byproduct of circumstances nor that the Spanish war music originally popularized in the

American communist movement was prompted primarily by the workers chorus tradition rather than the budding folk song interest of many individuals on the Left.

Musical performance techniques such as mass singing and audience participation similarly have their roots in the presentations of the American Music League and the revolutionary choral groups in the middle and late 1930s. It had been customary as far back as the early public performances of the Workers Music League to combine performing choruses in a finale of songs and invite the audience to join the singing. Following the shift in repertoire to more familiar and singable airs that occurred with the onset of the Popular Front, the emphasis on mass participation increased dramatically. At nearly every major communist rally, performers made special efforts to provoke audience singing of patriotic and labor songs. Earl Browder, then the party's unchallenged leader, years later proudly recalled the stirring renditions of "The Star Spangled Banner" and other national songs performed by packed crowds for communist speakers at such venues as Madison Square Garden.[11] On one such occasion, the *Daily Worker* heralded, "20,000 Voices in Mass Chorus at CP Convention," referring to the anticipated size of the audience, which was to be led by a combined five-hundred-voice chorus composed of various radical singing groups.[12] The AML, American Music Alliance, and other left-wing music organizations devoted much of their time to encouraging all forms of musical activity among the "people," and, indeed, throughout the movement the rank and file were lifting their voices more and more often in song.

In the historical context of the late 1930s, the evolving use of audience participation in revolutionary chorus events was a logical and practical extension of the spirit and philosophy of the Popular Front, which dictated that progressive groups should join collectively under the umbrella of antifascism. Propaganda music has always been used to rally intragroup support when outside forces threaten. Faced with the emergence of fascism, what would seem more fitting than to encourage mass singing, which, consciously or unconsciously, served as a device to promote group unity and solidarity, while also reflecting the movement's changing sociopolitical worldview. If an individual himself could not fight in Spain or march on the picket line in front of "Little Steel," he still could sit comfortably in a seat at a Garden rally or stand in a crowded room at a "cause" party, singing songs implicitly or explicitly linking himself to his "side" of the issues of the day. He could feel a part of the antifascist or "people's" struggle. By then, establishing collective security had become as much a musical ideal as a political goal of the Popular Front.

Perhaps the most significant contribution of the AML and the revolutionary choruses was to popularize American folk music among those segments of the communist movement that were uninterested in the songs and musical style of the "Lomax" singers, like Pete Seeger and Woody Guthrie. Classically oriented musicians, and also first-generation immigrants, often found folk music styles alien, whether the folk song were really or just approximately indigenous. And they dismissed the casual musicianship of folk music's city practitioners as too unsophisticated for their ears. They were understandably more comfortable with the artistic, complex choral arrangements of labor anthems and folk songs that were deeply rooted in both the art and folk music traditions of Europe. When the left-wing emphasis on American music became pronounced in such circles, it was natural for them to disregard the original folk performance styles and transpose native texts and tunes to more formal choral settings. This was the strategy employed by the IWW-sponsored American People's Chorus, conducted initially by Earl Robinson, and the politically independent American Ballad Singers directed by Elie Siegmeister. Their repertoires consisted almost entirely of American "working-class" music arranged in fine-art style. Both of these choruses were widely publicized by the Left. The American People's Chorus received a far greater hearing from the general American public than any other chorus produced by the progressive movement of the Depression generation, in part because of its nonpartisan character.[13]

Since it was based predominantly on the old foreign-language workers' chorus groups, the AML similarly encouraged a formal art style for the American folk songs in its repertoire. The organization sponsored numerous concerts emphasizing traditional music and other "songs of the people" in both Old World and native varieties. It helped commemorate the lore of the masses at every opportunity, from left-wing ethnic group folk festivals, to presentation on the use of folk themes in fine art music. Yet while it contributed substantially to the "folk ethos" of the communist movement during the late 1930s, its overall impact in the long run proved far less than that of the new group of folk singers centering around Alan Lomax, who emerged on the Left scene at the start of the 1940s.

ALAN LOMAX AND THE NEW URBAN RADICAL FOLK SINGERS

It is not uncommon for a historical period, social trend, or intellectual development to derive its name from that of a key individual located at the vortex of the given milieu—the Victorian Age, Jacksonian Democracy, McCarthyism, and social Darwinism, for example. The individuals who lend their names to such catchphrases are often the products of their times, rather than the causes of significant social change. Yet their personalities and actions inevitably had a profound impact on their own and subsequent generations. Thus, in a symbolic sense, the association of a historical period with an individual is accurate, for the person so singled out crystallizes in microcosm the key forces and trends of his or her era. With this in mind, it is not inappropriate to call the ardent activist folk singers of the Popular Front era the "Lomax singers."

Alan Lomax, more than any other scholar or performer of the 1930s, shaped the popular outlook on folk song, particularly in left-wing circles. His collections of indigenous American music and his recordings of heretofore obscure traditional musicians influenced an entire generation of urban folk singers long after the Old Left had collapsed. The "Lomax singers," who came from both rural and urban roots, were those who were guided by his scholarship, inspired by his political spirit, and educated in his ideological worldview. Lomax himself shied away from center stage, leaving the limelight to his protégés. Indeed, he appeared only here and there at critical junctures, with a suggestion, an idea, a song, or a proposal, before retiring once again into the background. And yet he managed to be practically everywhere. He had acquired a broad knowledge of the Anglo- and African American folk song corpus at an early age. This helped him wangle strategic positions at the Library of Congress and the Office of War Information. With his limitless enthusiasm for spreading the gospel of folk songs as the true "music of the people" and his natural political savvy, Lomax was able to develop far-reaching social and political connections. During the New Deal and Popular Front eras, Lomax indeed stood at the center of the evolving radical approach to native folk song style and content.

Alan Lomax, born in Austin, Texas, January 31, 1915, the son of John A. and Bess Brown Lomax, graduated from Choate prep school at fifteen. He displayed an active, inquiring mind even at that early age. His father sang him a few cowboy ballads in his youth but more often read Shakespeare aloud, instilling in his son a love of learning and an appreciation of culture. Lomax spent his freshman college year at the University of Texas (1930–31) but transferred to Harvard the following year, in part to study with his father's long-standing friend, George Lyman Kittredge, dean of Shakespeare and ballad studies and the elder Lomax's mentor at Harvard a generation before. By this time, Alan's explorations in philosophy had brought him first to Nietzsche, then to a widening variety of radical thinkers. While at Harvard his growing left-wing awareness was transformed from intellectual speculation into student activism. The details are obscure, but apparently a combination of low grades, financial worries, and political difficulties with the administration, his father, or both led Alan to leave Cambridge and join Lomax Senior on folk song–collecting expeditions. When he finally returned to college, it was once more at the University of Texas where he was graduated summa cum laude in 1936.

Years later, various popular magazine and newspaper articles reported that Lomax experienced a "conversion" to American folk music during his first field trip with his father, during which he heard the moving singing of an African American woman washing clothes.[14] Factual or not, the truth was that Alan had been following his father's interest in folk song collecting closely for some months prior to leaving Harvard. Just before Christmas in 1932, he wrote to his father:

> For your own good and happiness I believe that your ballad collecting and distributing per the lecture platform is the best way to earn money. With your uncanny ability to make friends with anything and anybody and your quiet, friendly way with folk less prosperous in life, and your own intense enjoyment of people and what they've got to say it seems to me that you are made before you start in ballad-collecting. You know more about th[at] part of folk-lore than anyone else. Mr. [J. Frank] Dobie has created a popular demand for it. Why don't you supply it?[15]

In an even more prescient letter written in April of the following year, he advised his father to "spend your years in folk-song work," and then stated with regard to his own future:

> I think now that . . . I should like to look at the folk-songs of the country along with you and do some research in that field from the point of view of sociology and anthropology. You and I are peculiarly well fitted for a partnership in this task, it seems to me. You have the practical experience in the field and an instinct for what is genuine and what [is] not. That experience I believe I can soon begin to supplement by making correlations between the ideas in the songs and their social implications. Why not, for instance, study the relations between the content of the Kentucky mountain songs and the mores popular in that district, the geographical isolation of the folk, the way the carryover of the attitude in the English ballads has affected the ideology of the mountaineers. Why not do the same for the negroes in different parts of the country. You and I and Mr. [Robert Winslow] Gordon, who knows his origins ought to be able to do some very valuable work in that field.[16]

Once in the field, his political consciousness sensitized him to the manner in which the lower classes voiced their complaints "as much as they dared" through folk songs. At that time, he suspected that the folk idiom might prove useful in helping to stimulate sociopolitical change in urban centers, but he could not foresee how complex the process would turn out to be.[17]

In subsequent years, Alan assisted John Lomax in editing *American Folk Songs and Ballads* (1934) and *Negro Folk Songs As Sung By Lead Belly* (1936), pursued graduate work at Harvard and Columbia, and spent his honeymoon in Haiti collecting the traditions of that island. By 1937, his reputation as a scholar and collector was sufficiently established for him to be hired as the director of the Archive of American Folk Song in the Library of Congress at an annual salary of $1,620.[18]

In Washington, Lomax took advantage of frequent informal contacts with Charles Seeger, who was at that time employed by the WPA Federal Music Project, to broaden his musical perspectives. Seeger willingly shared his knowledge of the history and theory of music, enabling Alan to comprehend native folk song in the wider context of global ethnomusicology.[19] He also quickly established a network of contacts from every political, social, and commercial walk of life, many of whom later would provide him with essential services as he attempted to place specific songs, singers, or programs before the public. By now he was a "fanatic"—as he admitted later—in his commitment to get the "American sound to the American people."[20] Egotistical, brilliant, impatient with the snail's pace of plodding bureaucrats and reactionary politicians, his proselytizing in behalf of folk songs and his radical social views constantly had his superiors in the Library of Congress on edge and ultimately led to the loss of his directorship of the folk song archives.

One by one, Lomax encountered singers of American folk songs, some with traditional roots, others of "citybilly" origin, whom he encouraged as performers in the urban milieu: Josh White, Burl Ives, Woody Guthrie, Pete Seeger, Lead Belly, Jelly Roll Morton, the Golden Gate Quartet, and others. He helped get them bookings and an occasional record contract, devoting much of his personal time to overseeing their careers. Functioning as mentor and friend, he shepherded them around "sophisticated" Washington and New York society, teaching them songs, socializing with them, and serving as their intellectual guide. To this role he brought extensive knowledge of American folk song, gleaned from fieldwork and his experience at the Archive of Folk Song, and his unflagging commitment to left-wing ideology. Reflecting on this period in Woody Guthrie's life, his biographer Joe Klein notes that Lomax was "an idealist, inordinately protective of the music he loved, scornful of those who attempted to dilute or fancify it, and utterly contemptuous of the music executives who peddled garbage and refused to acknowledge the treasures in his storehouse."[21] He was the perfect mentor to provide "his" singers with a cultural framework and sociopolitical rationale for their musical activities. For singers whose political sensibilities and styles were dictated by rural roots and little exposure to urban intellectual exchanges, such as Josh

White and Woody Guthrie, Lomax's influence broadened their world-views considerably.

Lomax featured many of his protégés regularly on his widely acclaimed CBS *School of the Air* broadcasts (1938–40), and later WNYC's *Back Where I Come From* (1940). He had a substantial role in writing and producing his show and so took advantage of the opportunity to book performers. By the early 1940s, the urban folk singers he had encouraged and who shared his worldview were ready to make a substantial imprint on American music life, on the left-wing cultural scene, as well as on the national stage.

The Lomax singers came to the radical urban scene of the late 1930s and early 1940s from every walk of life, social background, and musical orientation. Some, like Aunt Molly Jackson and her stepbrother Jim Garland, indeed had their roots in the rural "folk" currently idealized by the communist movement. Discovered by the Dreiser Committee in 1931, they were among the first traditional singers to perform in the urban left-wing setting. Lead Belly, who had been imprisoned in a Louisiana penitentiary several years earlier when he came to the attention of the Lomaxes, joined Jackson and Garland in performing at urban left-wing events in 1936. Burl Ives left his rural Illinois upbringing and a boring college lecture on *Beowulf* to hobo about the country singing folk songs for his keep. In the late 1930s, he came to New York where he studied music and began entertaining at left-wing "cause" parties, drawing on his repertoire of traditional ballads and lyrics. Josh White was born in North Carolina and took to the road at an early age to become a street singer in the blues tradition of Blind Lemon Jefferson. Indeed, he earned his living as a teenager leading blind street singers on their daily rounds. He recorded numerous religious and secular songs on commercial "race" labels under a variety of pseudonyms before reaching stardom in the early 1940s as a cabaret and matinee idol, performing folk and topical songs in a formalized but earthy style. Woody Guthrie spent his early years in the Southwest, had a limited but successful career as a hillbilly entertainer on a Los Angeles radio station, then encountered communists and other leftists. He had already composed his own socially conscious song commentaries on the dust bowl and other life experiences. At first billed by radicals as the people's Will Rogers and later as the incarnation of Steinbeck's Okies in *The Grapes of Wrath,* Guthrie wrote a whimsical Rogers-styled daily column in the California *People's World* for six months before migrating to New York in February 1940, where he resumed writing, this time for the *Daily Worker.* The previous year, Lee Hays emigrated North, forsaking his rural Arkansas environment, gospel-rooted traditional music background, and Commonwealth Labor College experiences for the urban left-wing milieu of Philadelphia and New York. Better educated and more intellectual than his fellow performers, Hays's radical commitment also differed from most of theirs in that it antedated his move away from his early folk environment.[22]

City-bred musicians, who by one means or another came to value folk songs as the "people's art," joined these traditional singers in demonstrating the effectiveness of traditional music in a "progressive" setting. Chief among them was Charles Seeger's son Peter, whose "conversion" to traditional music came in 1936 while attending the Asheville, North Carolina, folk festival with his father.[23] Seeger's political awareness began as a teenager, stimulated in large part by conversations with his father and also by contacts with the social conscience of family friends and schoolmates, reinforcing in him his own family tradition of personal involvement in human concerns. Sympathetic to the communist movement since his student days at Harvard, he subsequently served as Lomax's assistant in the Archive of American Folk Song during the winter of 1939–40, and from June to December 1946, he supplemented his book learning and record-listening sessions at the Library of Congress hitchhiking to rural folk communities in Montana, Alabama, and Florida. Partly at Lomax's suggestion, Seeger mastered the five-string banjo, later his musical trademark, then all but unknown to urban audiences interested in folk songs.

Others with similar middle-class backgrounds and tastes in traditional music were Gilbert Ray "Cisco" Houston, Will Geer the actor, Bill Wolff, and the members of the American Square Dance Group. Houston left his moderately comfortable California origins for a life of music, acting, itinerant wandering as a workaday laborer, and progressive sympathies. During his travels he learned many folk and hillbilly songs, and made a few popular music recordings in the 1930s. At the end of the decade, Houston met Woody Guthrie, afterward his lifelong friend and singing companion, and was often to be found sharing his traditional repertoire at gatherings frequented by the Lomax singers. Geer sang cowboy songs at left-wing functions as far back as 1935, but he subsequently became better known in radical folk song circles as a master of ceremonies and a public relations booster and friend to various contemporary performers of folk songs to whom he often gave material assistance, notably Burl Ives and Woody Guthrie. Klein notes that Geer organized what has been called the first "folk revival" get-together at the Forrest Theater in New York in 1940, featuring many of the Lomax singers. Billed as a "Grapes of Wrath" fund-raiser, the event was a benefit for migrant workers. Bill Wolff grew up in New York and attended the University of Illinois in the early thirties before moving into labor-radical activities as an actor, writer, and union organizer. Primarily a newspaper commentator, collector, and songwriter rather than a singer, he proved a prime mover in the left-wing folk music scenes of Chicago and, later, Los Angeles.

The American Square Dance Group was founded in 1939 as a splinter organization of another dance society and grew in size until it numbered nearly a hundred members just before and after World War II. Devoted to the study and performance of indigenous folk song and dance, it was directed for its entire fifteen-year existence by Margot Mayo, herself a descendant of a rural southern family with roots deep in the traditional music heritage. While the ASDG's activity was nonpolitical in terms of content, many young radicals did belong to the organization, and the group itself occasionally performed at left-wing cultural affairs.[24]

More self-consciously stylized was the singing of Richard Dyer-Bennet and the Golden Gate Quartet and the compositions of Earl Robinson. Dyer-Bennet was born in England, moved with his family to the United States in 1924, and acquired a left-wing social commitment while attending the University of California at Berkeley in the mid-1930s.[25] Classically trained with a highly polished voice, he embarked on a successful career as a concert artist performing folk and art songs following his initial debut at New York's Village Vanguard nightclub in 1942. The gospel music of the Golden Gate Quartet, four African American men from Norfolk, Virginia, was not nearly as eclectic as Dyer-Bennet's songs, but was certainly popular as progressive entertainment in the prewar years. The music of Earl Robinson was even more unusual. Robinson was a formally trained composer schooled in the European classic tradition and a fringe member of the Workers Music League in the early 1930s. During that time, the WML was experimenting with esoteric forms of modern music expression in an effort to find a new and original "proletarian" song idiom. By 1936, however, Robinson turned to composing music in technically noncomplex forms that were strongly influenced by the content and structure of American folk music. Well-known works for which he composed the music are "Joe Hill," "Abe Lincoln," and "The Ballad for Americans." Classically trained colleagues decried Robinson's creations as superficial and musically naïve, but his music proved extremely popular with the "masses" of urban progressives of the Popular Front era and indeed characterized the extent to which the folk ethos permeated the fine arts during the 1930s. Robinson was the only formally schooled musician of the early Workers Music League period to fully throw in his lot with the Lomax folk singers at the close of the thirties decade.[26]

Both in content and style, the Lomax performers differed in many important respects from the workers choruses which also sang folk songs in left-wing circles in these years. The contents of the Lomax performers' songs were rooted deeply in the American soil, chiefly the white and black traditional music of the southern United States, while that of the choruses drew proportionately much more heavily on European folk song themes. The Lomax artists' performance styles, if not strictly imitative of that of one or another of the rural "folk" groups of the American nation in every case, at least approximated the sound of native traditional singers more closely than it did the formal art music settings of the AML choruses. Solo and small-group singing were the rule rather than large ensembles; guitar, banjo, or other instruments associated with American folk music replaced piano or orchestral accompaniment; and vocal flexibility was substituted for the stiff song arrangements of the workers choral units.

More important than technical differences in content and style was the aesthetic raisons d'être of the two singing milieus. The buoyant nationalist tone of the New Deal and antifascist spirit of the Popular Front were the environmental cradle of the Lomax tradition, just as the austere "proletarian" worldview of the preceding Third Period, the Popular Front's ecological opposite, was the appropriate setting for the comparatively formal and rigid revolutionary choral music with its accompanying doctrinaire political sentiments. The practitioners of the new urban folk singing school drew their strength and dynamism primarily from the national sociocultural milieu rather than the international political scene; they perceived folk music largely in nativist terms, Jeffersonian and egalitarian to the core. As Lomax said later, "the big theme of American folk song . . . [was] stated by Burns, 'A man's a man for a' that,' and even more powerfully in the Negro ballad, 'John Henry,' 'A man ain't nothin' but a man.'"[27] Patriotism and radical dogma went hand in hand in the traditional and folk-styled lyrics sung by the Lomax singers, much as did Browder's concurrent slogan "Communism Is Twentieth-Century Americanism" or the performance of the national anthem at party rallies.

In sum, while individual attitudes and outlooks varied within the Lomax tradition, folk music was regarded as considerably more than entertainment with a "progressive" flavor or as a new agit-prop strategy. It was both class oriented and indigenous in origin; therefore, it was the true "people's" music of the United States, the rightful heritage of American workers. As such, it represented a democratic worldview with which the Lomax singers could identify simultaneously as citizens and political radicals; in some cases, like that of the Almanac Singers, it also provided a central focal point around which to create a new personal lifestyle. Folk songs thus were at the center of ideology for the Lomax performers, who promoted them with all the missionary zeal of a new religious sect. "We believed the world was worth saving and that we could do it with songs," Irwin Silber wrote later, in the best single statement characterizing the Lomax tradition.[28]

The idealism and dedicated fervor with which the Lomax singers went about propagating folk songs and the folk idiom were matched only by their naiveté. American city dwellers by and large were attuned far more to Bing Crosby, Benny Goodman, or Roy Acuff than to Burl Ives, much less any folk singer with a less mellow voice. Labor unions outside of the radical fringe of the CIO proved to have little interest in music of any kind in spite of John L. Lewis's often quoted *obiter dictum* "A Singing Army Is a Winning Army!"; "We offered them our lily-white bodies," Lomax ruefully recalled later, "but they weren't interested."[29] That folk traditions, musical or otherwise, often reflected politically and socially conservative values was not seriously discussed; "To the extent that we considered [that]," Irwin Silber remarked afterward, "we [said] that [it] was a temporary aberration . . . that whatever the people expressed was almost by definition democratic and progressive."[30]

Nevertheless, in time the impact of the Lomax performers proved enormous, molding the musical tastes of both the Old Left in its later years and significant segments of the popular folk song revival that developed in the late 1950s and early 1960s. More than any other group in the communist movement, the Lomax singers recognized and tried to implement folk songs as the logical and practical basis for the viable workers' music culture that had been sought in theoretical terms for years. They failed to create that culture along class lines but succeeded ultimately in laying the groundwork for the popularization of traditional music on a scale hitherto unknown in American society and the interweaving of folk songs and the folk idiom into the entire fabric of American music and cultural life. As such, their contribution cannot be underestimated.

The Lomax singers arrived on the left-wing stage singly and largely unheralded. Only in retrospect is it clear that together they constituted a performance and ideological tradition, for their musical styles, song repertoires, political philosophies, lifestyles, and personalities varied considerably, and not all were strong in their intellectual commitment to the communist movement. If one were to choose a single date marking their first collective surfacing as a visible entity, the logical choice would be March 3, 1940. On that occasion, Aunt Molly Jackson, Woody Guthrie, Lead Belly, Burl Ives, Pete Seeger, the Golden Gate Quartet, the American Square Dance Group, Will Geer, and Alan and Bess Lomax appeared at a "Grapes of Wrath" evening of folk songs in New York for the benefit of the John Steinbeck Committee for California farm workers. The program consisted of a mixture of traditional songs and folk-styled topical pieces that were typically characteristic of the majority of left-wing folk songs and nonpartisan folk song revival hootenannies for many years afterward: "Boll Weevil," "Let's Join the CIO," "Columbus Stockade

Blues," "Joe Hill," and "Study War No More."[31] By this time, however, the idealization and popularization of all forms of the folk arts in the communist movement already was approaching full tide.

THE FLOWERING OF "FOLK" INTEREST ON THE LEFT

The communist movement's acceptance of the folk arts as the cornerstone of "people's" culture began as an esoteric intellectual ideal based in sociopolitical ideology and was firmly established by 1936. As the popular acceptance of the concept snowballed, it was only a matter of time before people's culture was converted to an important emotional value. Things "folk" became equated with "good," and "nonfolk" with "bad," or at least "secondary" or "also-ran." The best writers, composers, artists, and poets were those who made use of traditional themes and images in their work. Writing in the *Daily Worker,* Mike Gold expressed his enthusiasm for the value of folklore: "Even today I find time to read fairy tales, folk stories, legends. They reveal better than any other literature, the permanent soul of mankind." Evoking the relationship between oral tradition and literary masterpieces, he explained, "When a master like Thomas Mann takes some legend like the Joseph story in the Bible and reinterprets it, he is able to evolve an epic. For truly understood, these legends are the spiritual autobiography of the people."[32] A *Daily Worker* dance critic commented on a modern interpretation of folk themes in American life: "[The performance] may mark a turning point away from an increasing complexity and abstractness which has marred . . . Modern dance, toward an increased simplicity and directness of statement. The folk themes are more than a novelty. They are an invigorating influence."[33] And numerous radical critics and music lovers attempted to generalize about their intellectual and emotional commitment to traditional song in words like those of Waldemar Hille:

> I am interested particularly in American folk music because I am an American. . . . [T]he folk song makes articulate the exploitation of the American workers . . . and tells the truth of American history, the inner feelings and meanings, which have only too frequently been distorted by unsympathetic historians.

Hille went on to insist, "It therefore becomes a social duty for those of us who know these songs to let their existence and use be known and to demonstrate their social value and meaning wherever possible."[34]

And these are not isolated voices. Evidence of the growing interest in folk materials is amply demonstrated by attention in the radical press. In one twelve-month period, December 1938 to December 1939, the *Daily Worker* featured a dozen major articles and numerous shorter pieces on such topics as cowboy songs, calypso music, Paul Bunyan, the WPA Folklore Project, W. C. Handy's lectures on Negro blues, Martha Graham's use of native folk themes in her modern dance, the superiority of folk songs to "pop" tunes, Paul Robeson's appearance in the play *John Henry,* reviews of half a dozen academic and popular folklore books, and announcements and critiques of various folk song concerts. Generally speaking, considerable space was devoted to regional and ethnic folk festivals, American outlaw heroes, children's rhymes, traditional square dances, folktales, and proverbial sayings. Much of the discussion, to be sure, was amateurish in quality and more the product of wishful thinking than fact, as when one reviewer remarked of one of Jean Thomas's informants in *Ballad Makin' in the Mountains of Kentucky:* "He has probably never heard of Marx or Lenin, but there can be no doubt where his roots lay, as he sings 'Union men should have a say in what they receive each hour/Factories cannot operate without the labor power.'"[35] Yet in spite of many not infrequent propagandistic absurdities and journalistic clichés, much good material was placed before the left-wing public, and the enthusiasm with which it was presented and received partially compensated for its naive handling.[36]

More sophisticated left-wing publications also regularly covered folklore topics, usually exhibiting more critical thought and creative writing. These tended to concentrate less on the pop culture of concerts and singers and more on folk culture reflected in books and recorded music. *New Masses,* for instance, reviewed many books and some records pertaining to folklore, both academic and popular, during the Popular Front years. These included such diverse works as Zora Neale Hurston's *Mules and Men,* the first scholarly non–folk song volume reviewed in the radical press; Dorothy Scarborough's *A Songcatcher in the Southern Mountains,* Gene Fowler's book depicting Javanese folklore; George Korson's *Minstrels of the Mine Patch;* Robert Winslow Gordon's collected series of articles on American folklore originally published in the *New York Times;* J. Rosamund Johnson's *Rolling Along in Song,* a successor to his popular *Book of American Negro Spirituals;* and others.[37] *Direction,* a short-lived "progressive" magazine that appeared at the end of the thirties, featured several essays on folklore topics during its two-year life span, among them sketches of the Negro badman-hero Stackalee, the blind Ozark ballad singer Emma Dusenberry, the Piney Woods folk of New Jersey as described by folklorist Herbert Halpert, and a regular music column written by Elie Siegmeister that frequently discussed folk songs as part of its music coverage.[38]

Even poetry criticism in the pages of *New Masses* and other left-wing publications frequently alluded to the esoteric nature of most fine-art verse, and the corresponding need for poetry with a folklike simplicity that would actually appeal to the masses. "Is it too much to ask that *some* communist poetry be written for workers and worker-audiences?" one southern union leader demanded. "[T]o hell with cleverness for its own sake—these unimpressive attempts to build new forms."[39] As early as 1930 a reader had written to *New Masses,* "Workers are more stirred to revolt by something lyrical, even romantic. What group of poems has been read and repeated more widely by class-conscious workers or has played a more helpful part in agitation than the I.W.W. song book?" The writer was not shy about his opinion that "accessible" poetry is more effective than "crude free verse." "I've read often enough to class conscious proletarian audiences to know that a poem with rhyme and rhythm, emotional appeal and drama, gets across a vast deal better than . . . the kind of free verse you prefer to publish."[40]

But the same cry was being leveled eight years later by others, such as *New Masses* writer Robert Forsythe: "When the workers ask plaintively for poetry they can recite aloud, they are yearning for poetry that can be sung . . . and if I have a complaint against our poets it is that not one of them has done what Joe Hill did in the days of the Wobblies."[41] It was against the backdrop of this running series of objections that Robert Morse Lovett remarked of the contributors to *Proletarian Literature in the United States* (1935), "Genevieve Taggard, Isidor Schneider, Alfred Kreymborg, [and] Kenneth Fearing are genuine poets, but one may feel sure that Aunt Molly Jackson, Ella May Wiggins and Don West are nearer the hearts of the workers."[42] Others, though by no means all, were ready to agree. The Executive Committee of a radical poetry group wrote to *New Masses,* "We have felt that a good work-song or a spiritual was, strictly speaking, more intellectual than something which is an imitative compound of MacLeish, Eliot, Hopkins, with an elusive dash of Marx."[43] A few additional critics called on Mike Gold, the arch-expounder of a truly "proletarian" workers' poetry, to "rise up and slay these demons for us, for his is a sensible voice crying in what appears to be a wilderness of ivory towers."[44]

That the role and function of folklore materials was shifting in the thirties from esoteric interesting diversion to a fundamental part of left-wing ideology is dramatically revealed in a telescoped summary of four writers' congresses sponsored by the League of American Writers in New York in alternate years beginning in 1935. At these events the increasing tempo and correspondingly decreasing intellectualization of the radical interest in folklore during the prewar period is most clearly evident These gatherings brought together noted antifascist and "progressive" writers from all parts of the Popular Front spectrum, but from the beginning were dominated by the Communist Party and its literary spokespeople.[45]

At the first congress in 1935, there was no direct discussion whatever about folklore. Kenneth Burke's paper on "Revolutionary Symbolism in America" dealt with concepts that folklorists might accept as within the purview of their field, but neither Burke nor the Third Period–oriented party hard-liners who attacked his theses couched their arguments in folkloristic terms.[46] However, by the time the second Writers' Congress was held in 1937, there was considerably less concern with revolution and much more debate about the nature of contemporary American society. There still was little discussion of folklore per se, but Benjamin A. Botkin did engender some controversy in response to his paper entitled "Regionalism and Culture" in which he argued for a socially conscious regional literature based on the words and descriptions of the life of the rural "folk":

> This contemporary and realistic regional literature can perform several valuable functions for both society and literature. It can give first-hand data on the people and on their living and working conditions. It can help make the masses articulate by letting them tell their own story, in their own words. And it does not simply provide source material—it can create new forms, styles, and modes of literature by drawing upon place, work, and folk for motifs, images, symbols, slogans, and idioms.[47]

Botkin's conclusions were praised by some and damned by others, but the arguments pro and con were voiced in comparatively abstract and theoretical terms. Many left-wing intellectuals remained unaware or unconvinced that traditional materials had much relevance to the creation of a modern, urban-oriented class literature, and as yet there were few examples of folk and folk-based aesthetic expression produced by or known to radicals which could be cited as illustrations.

By the time the third Writers' Congress met in 1939, the "folk" ethos had become a well-established part of the Popular Front cultural milieu. The potential value of folklore to the cause of the workers was no longer a contested ideological issue. Rather than considering what place rural and labor traditions might have in the new urban "people's" culture, the congress instead sought to document the myriad forms of traditional materials already a part of the national scene and to ascertain more fully how they might be utilized on behalf of the masses. With the popularization of folk themes reaching crescendo proportions on the Left, all or part of at least two sessions at the 1939 congress were devoted to these matters. Botkin chaired one panel on the subject of "The Uses of American Folk Literature," the participants including Hyde Partnow, a folklore collector employed by the Federal Writers Project, Alan Lomax, Earl Robinson, Aunt Molly Jackson, and Victor Campbell ("Forty Fathoms"), a sailor who composed topical sea songs in traditional style. A second discussion concerning the Negro in American literature featured, among others, Lawrence Gellert and the well-known anthropologist Melville J. Herskovits. Gellert's remarks centered on the "Negro Songs of Protest" he had collected; those by Herskovits on white America's stereotyped views of blacks as "cultureless" people, which he soon expounded in *The Myth of the Negro Past* (1941).[48]

The final Writers' Congress in 1941 may be said to have evolved into a folk song revival atmosphere—a hootenanny, actually. Burl Ives, the Almanac Singers, Earl Robinson, Lead Belly, Tony Kraber, Josh White, and the American Ballad Singers participated in a three-hour composite session devoted to poetry, songwriting, and folk singing. Reports on what ensued are difficult to come by since the proceedings were never published, but apparently musical performance took precedence over theoretical discussion. At least some of the poets felt their dignity and verse were diminished by the presence of the musicians.[49] In spite of this event, though, the hootenanny environment was more typical of the left-wing folk song scene of the 1940s than an integral part of the Popular Front milieu.

Phonograph recordings of the prewar years also reflect the growing popularity of folk songs in the communist movement. Beginning in the late 1930s, a series of small record companies owned or financed by radicals started to issue albums of traditional music or urban interpretations of folk songs, and the number of releases gradually increased. The first was Timely Records, founded in 1935 by Leo Waldman, an insurance man with left-wing sympathies. Timely's first albums consisted of familiar classical music selections and Eislerian revolutionary songs, but the label later produced a collection of native American ballads sung by Earl Robinson. Timely also pressed recordings of Lawrence Gellert's "Negro Songs of Protest," but they were never released because of some unresolved legal barriers. In September 1939, the Stinson record company, owned by Robert Harris Sr. began the sale of large quantities of Russian folk music to radical outlets in the United States. Stinson originally had an arrangement with the USSR's New York World's Fair Pavilion, an earlier distributor, but this was abruptly canceled when the USSR signed the Nazi–Soviet nonaggression pact.[50] During the next decade, Stinson also was responsible for many early and important commercial recordings of American folk songs and singers. The Keynote label under the proprietorship of Eric Bernay, onetime *New Masses* treasurer, started production in 1940 with *Six Songs for Democracy*, about the Spanish Civil War, and followed in the next five years with albums by the Almanac Singers, Paul Robeson, Earl Robinson, and other native singers of folk songs, along with a potpourri of traditional European and antifascist music.[51]

Far more important in the long run, however, were the series of companies owned and operated by Moses Asch, son of Sholem Asch, the well-regarded Jewish novelist. Asch was born in Poland in 1905, educated in Germany during the early 1920s, and worked for several American radio manufacturers and stores before launching his own record label bearing the Asch name in 1939.[52] Living in several different European countries prior to his emigration with his parents to the United States, Asch was exposed to a variety of languages and styles of cultural expression. More than any other individual of his generation, Asch committed himself to documenting the music and culture of the world's people at a time when the traditional sounds of any group, native or foreign, scarcely existed anywhere on commercial records.[53] Over the years a stream of albums numbering into the thousands were issued by the Asch, Disc, and later Folkways companies under Asch's management, often in the face of economic constraints. Among them were some of the first and finest recordings of Burl Ives, Lead Belly, Woody Guthrie, Pete Seeger, and other scions of the fledgling folk song revival, and many topical, blues, jazz, ethnic, and classical releases. Asch's sales, like those of his left-wing competitors, were small during the prewar period, but the market for folk music recordings steadily expanded—although not fast enough in some cases to prevent various of his and similar companies from going out of business.[54]

While folklore was seldom if ever mentioned formally at any political meeting or rally of the general communist movement during the late 1930s, folk songs, dances, and other traditional arts frequently were in evidence on such occasions. The fact that entertainment was regularly scheduled for many communist political meetings and rallies in itself was a revolutionary departure from the usual meeting practices during the preceding Third Period. The AML choral groups, later the Lomax folk singers, appeared on many platforms with the party's leadership, now and then including Earl Browder himself. A characteristic example was the mass celebration in 1937 of the seventy-fifth birthday of communist heroine Ella Reeve "Mother" Bloor. At the rally were performances of folk dancing and interpretive modern dances of traditional themes, mass singing led by the American Music League, and finally the unison presentation of the "Mother Bloor Song" set to the old cowboy ballad "When the Work's All Done This Fall":

> Come all you loyal comrades,
> Both men and women, too,
> Come sing about a woman
> So dear to me and you.
> Oh, kings will be forgotten,
> Their names be known no more,

But the workers never will forget
Our fighting Mother Bloor.[55]

In later years, folk artists were so common at left-wing political gatherings that an antiparty joke told of two comrades planning a meeting, one admonishing the other, "You bring the Negro, I'll bring the folk singer."[56]

Actually, the Popular Front focused significant attention on African American traditional music as interest in folklore continued to develop during the late 1930s. Unlike during the Third Period, when "Negro" music was viewed as nonrevolutionary, now spirituals were upgraded from their previously suspect status as "sorrow songs" and described anew in terms of their protest character.[57] The performances of Paul Robeson, the Hall Johnson Choir, Juanita Hall, and other black concert artists were covered extensively in the radical press. Lawrence Gellert's "Negro Songs of Protest" now became widely popular in "progressive" cultural circles; seven were interpreted in modern dance form by Helen Tamiris in the very successful production "How Long Brethren," and others were performed regularly by left-wing choruses. "Negro Songs of Protest" and Gellert received frequent publicity in the communist news media. *New Masses* devoted considerable space to blues recordings in the late 1930s, which were reviewed expertly by John Hammond, initially under the pseudonym Henry Johnson. *New Masses* was in fact the Left's intellectual center for the discussion and appreciation of black music. It sponsored the famous and widely acclaimed "Spirituals to Swing" concert at Carnegie Hall in December 1938 and again the following year, which featured a wide range of African American music, from traditional spirituals and blues to jazz and the swing bands of Count Basie and Benny Goodman.[58]

Jazz is a somewhat different story. *New Masses* routinely supported jazz as good "progressive" music and as a folk-derived art form. For many years, though, European and American communists disagreed on the value of jazz. In the earliest phase of the party's history, jazz often was dismissed out of hand as bourgeois and decadent, and though it won limited acceptance from some radicals, in part because of its folk origins, others continued to criticize jazz as a product of capitalism. Scholars Donald Drew Egbert and Stow Persons, editors of *Socialism and American Life,* summarized the Left's ambivalence:

> In those periods when jazz has been in favor in Russia, or else when the Party line in the United States has especially sought to foster "Self-Determination in the Black Belt," the American Communist Party has usually upheld jazz either as a Negro "folk" art, or as a product of a minority downtrodden under "capitalism."

Explaining the difference between the roots versus the commercialization of jazz, the writers state:

> During the 1930s . . . the Party line in this country usually made a distinction between those aspects of jazz regarded as Negro folk music, and therefore considered good, and the more "commercial" varieties of jazz, which were looked upon as "capitalistic," and therefore bad.[59]

But with the onset of the Popular Front, jazz enthusiasts in the ranks of the movement became far more numerous. The left-wing cabarets such as the Cafe Society Uptown and Downtown in New York, and the radical press, including the *Daily Worker* and *New Masses,* regularly featured jazz artists and music. Yet throughout the thirties many communists still vehemently dissented from the popular acclaim for the idiom. "I like jazz," Mike Gold wrote:

> but I do not consider it real music. There is occasionally found in jazz a residue of some genuine emotion that suggests true music, but this residue is always something carried over from some older and uncommercial tradition—the Negro spirituals and the blues, mainly.[60]

Harrison George, an antijazz polemicist, repeatedly attacked the medium for its prostitution of folk song themes and considered "hot jazz . . . the musical expression of capitalism's decadence."[61] By the mid-1940s, after World War II, vocal opposition to jazz in the communist movement had all but disappeared. Journals and scholars continued to debate the proper left-wing interpretation of jazz and its history throughout the Popular Front years and afterward, usually confirming its essential aesthetic integrity as an art form. But whether praised or criticized, jazz invariably was also considered in the context of its relationship to folk music and culture.[62]

Still, jazz, like the rest of folklore or folk-derived tradition, was viewed from a fine-arts perspective by most urban radicals. The communist movement, just like the rest of the contemporary American public, found it difficult to conceive of the presentation of folk materials in any other context. It was one thing to applaud the people's lore, creativity, and native style abstractly, but quite another to appreciate and intelligently comprehend actual folk performances. For in reality, the raw texts and tones of folk music and many of its performers were too "crude," too chaotic, and very often too undisciplined—politically and artistically—to be readily acceptable to the majority of left-wingers in the 1930s. It is not surprising, therefore, that the few activists within the urban communist movement with genuine rural roots were valued more as folk symbols than for their musical presentations. Aunt Molly Jackson, for instance, was revered as a militant example of the Kentucky proletariat, admired for her ability to blend class sentiments with old mountain tunes, yet few radicals other than some of the Lomax singers really enjoyed the harsh, tense sound of her voice, or the modal or minor-key tunes of many of her songs. In spite of later occasional publicity in the left-wing press, she seldom was asked to perform at progressive functions once the Dreiser hearings and the Harlan County coal struggles of the early thirties receded from public attention.

Lead Belly proved to be a far more popular entertainer than Aunt Molly Jackson. But in the beginning many found it difficult to cope with the realities of his traditional background. Earl Robinson relates a typical incident: "I remember bringing Huddie to a progressive summer camp for a weekend in 1936, shortly after I met him. I was so interested and excited by him and his work that I perhaps failed to screen his songs as well as I could have." The result was disastrous:

> After an evening of "Frankie and Albert," "DeKalb Blues," "Ella Speed," songs of bad women and gun-toting Negro gamblers, . . . where the protest could barely be understood through his dialect, the camp was in an uproar. Argument [flared about] whether to censure him, or me, or both.

The solution was to provide the listeners with some background on Lead Belly. "By the next morning . . . . when he sang his 'Bourgeois Blues' and a song he had composed about the Scottsboro Boys, the air was considerably changed."[63]

Woody Guthrie, even more than Lead Belly, proved a disquieting paradox to the radical Left. In addition to being an able performer in his prime years, Guthrie was more intellectual than either Aunt Molly Jackson or Lead Belly and far more capable of articulating the specifics of communist ideology in his folk-styled songs and prose. When he first appeared on the folk music scene, many left-wingers were ecstatic, and hailed him as the folk Will Rogers and the people's John Steinbeck.[64] "Sing it Woody, sing it!" *People's World* columnist Mike Quin once wrote enthusiastically. "Karl Marx wrote it and Lincoln said it and Lenin did it. You sing it, Woody. And we'll all laugh together yet."[65] Ironically, it was the more sophisticated, urban aspects of Guthrie's lifestyle that precluded his acceptance by political left-wingers who were at heart very socially conservative. Irwin Silber reflected in later years, "Like most revolutionaries, Woody was, at best, only partially understood by the revolutionary movements of his time." Noting the criticisms of Guthrie's unwillingness to be bound by social mores, Silber observed:

The puritanical, nearsighted left . . . didn't quite know what to make of this strange bemused poet who drank and bummed and chased after women and spoke in syllables dreadful strange. They loved his songs and they sang "Union Maid" or "So Long" or "Roll on Columbia" or "Pastures of Plenty" . . . on picket lines and at parties, summer camps and demonstrations. But they never really accepted the man himself—and many thought that as a singer, he was a pretty good songwriter, and they'd just as soon hear Pete Seeger sing the same songs.[66]

Thus, while the "folk" and their traditions were idealized widely by radicals in the prewar years, the reality of specific performers, their talents, widely divergent performance styles and lifestyles were confusing and harder to accept. Musically speaking, left activists preferred the smoother voices and polished performance styles of Burl Ives and Josh White, which were aesthetically more pleasing to urban audiences familiar with fine art performances. The concertized song arrangements and formal evening clothes of Richard Dyer-Bennet and the American Ballad Singers, and the folk-inspired art music of Earl Robinson, such as "Ballad for Americans" and "The Lonesome Train," were preferable as entertainment at left-wing functions.

The same held true for other forms of folk expression. Professional editing and "art" arrangements of the people's traditions often supplanted the actual lore from which it derived. Literary transcriptions of folk culture, poems and plays reached a wider audience and received more attention than the raw folklore texts gathered by the Lomaxes and the WPA. But works extolling such heroes as Paul Bunyan, Joe Magarac, and John Henry, Carl Sandburg's *The People, Yes,* modern dance projections of folk themes, and fine-art paintings of traditional subjects were exceedingly popular. Numerous academic collections of folklore materials were reviewed by the communist press in this period but were mostly ignored by the left-wing public. The Left should no more be criticized for this, however, than the greater American public. Then, as now, even highly educated people lack the aesthetic training and cultural perspective with which to appreciate the richness and diversity of our folk heritage in an undiluted form.

Of course, there were many in the communist movement during the Popular Front era who cared little for folklore in any context, ideological or entertainment. The Left's search for an indigenous working-class culture in folk traditions spread from the movement's center in New York to the West Coast, where it took root around 1938. But in many places, especially the Midwest, it never caught on quite so firmly.[67] Some left-wing individuals, seeing no relevance between folk arts and fine arts, simply ignored folklore and folk performances. Many more, especially those who were engaged in political or labor activity, failed to see what significance rural traditions had for urban industrial life, in particular the day-to-day mechanics of conducting the people's struggle. Recalling one two-hour speech at the 1936 New England District Convention stressing the importance of song to the movement, communist organizer George Charney remarked, "I always liked 'Bandiera Rossa,' but this was really stretching a point. A hootenanny revolutionist!"[68] Evidently the top party leaders also held this attitude, for during the Browder period (and afterward, as far as is known), they never directly committed the party to subsidize any folk singer or other traditional artist, folklorist, or folk music organization. On those occasions when performers of traditional materials were paid by the party for their services at communist functions, the district organizer or head of the local arrangements committee handled the details, including the monetary agreement, independently.[69]

It seems clear in retrospect that during the years prior to World War II most left-wing adherents, even where they personally favored the popularization of folk traditions within the movement, did not seriously regard this new cultural emphasis as any new concrete tactical weapon in the people's arsenal. Folklore might be entertaining, it described the roots and aspirations of the masses, yet for most radicals it bore little relation to the realities of daily living in the urban and progressive milieus. This outlook, however, was in sharp contrast to that of one group of performers in the Lomax tradition, the Almanac Singers, for whom the people's folk songs and folkways were central to their political ideology, attempts at agit-prop communication, and lifestyle. More than any other segment of the communist movement, they attempted to implement a proletarian culture based on American traditions, one that they and others might live as well as speculate about in the abstract. Though in the end they failed to reach a large audience, during their brief two-year existence at the beginning of the 1930s, the Almanacs laid down the practical foundations for the socially conscious use of traditional materials in an activist context that would later be enlarged on by the People's Songs and People's Artists organizations of the Old Left and by portions of the folk song revival in the succeeding generation.

NOTES

1. Dmitroff's remarks during the Congress were printed as *United Front against Fascism* (New York, 1935). For a review of the political history of the Popular Front, see Irving Howe and Lewis Coser, *The American Communist Party: A Critical History*, 2d ed. (New York: Da Capo, 1974).

2. Howe and Coser, *The American Communist Party*, 325.

3. For a thorough analysis of the impact of the Popular Front on American culture, see Theodore Draper, *The Roots of American Communism* (New York: Viking, 1957), Howe and Coser, *The American Communist Party;* and Michael Denning, *The Cultural Front: The Laboring of American Culture in the Twentieth Century* (New York: Verso, 1996).

4. A sketch of Bauman appears in John Sebastian, "Mordecai Bauman," *New Masses* (March 21, 1939), 31.

5. As evidenced by the contents of the AML and communist movement songbooks in the late 1930s. See, for example, *Songs of the People* (New York, January 1937); *March and Sing* (New York, 1937); and *Songs for America* (New York, 1939), the latter subtitled "American Ballads, Folk Songs, Marching Songs, Songs of Other Lands."

6. *Unison* 1, no. 1 (May 1936): 1.

7. Marc Blitzstein, Earl Robinson, and Lawrence Gellert, for example, all worked for the Federal Theater Project in the late 1930s, and Blitzstein's social musical "The Cradle Will Rock" and Robinson's cantata "Ballad for Americans" were first produced under its auspices.

8. "Viva La Quince Brigada" and "Los Cuatros Generales" are printed in *The People's Song Book,* ed. Waldemar Hille (New York, 1948), 42–43. "Si Me Quieres Escribir" may be found in *Sing Out!* 6, no. 3 (Summer 1956): 20–21.

9. Oscar Brand, *The Ballad Mongers: Rise of the Modern Folk Song* (New York, 1962), 77.

10. The texts for all these songs are available in the Labor History Archives, Wayne State University, Detroit, Michigan. "Spain Marches" and "No Pasaran" were published as sheet music by the American Music League. The Auville Spanish War songs include "The Story of Madrid: 1936" and "Salute to Madrid" and were distributed in mimeographed form.

11. Interview with Earl Browder, February 12, 1968.

12. *Daily Worker* (May 24, 1938), 7.

13. Information on the early history of these groups may be found in Irene Tannenbaum, "Mass Folk Music Aim of Workers Order Chorus," *Daily Worker* (May 27, 1938), 7; and Margaret Markham, "Folk Music Is One of America's Riches," *Daily Worker* (January 31, 1944), 5.

14. "New Collection of Folk Songs Out Soon," *Daily Worker* (October 28, 1941), 7; Donald Day, "John Lomax and His Ten Thousand Songs," *Saturday Review of Literature* (September 22, 1945), reprinted in *Reader's Digest* (October 1945).

15. John A. Lomax papers, University of Texas Historical Society Archives, Austin. Quoted by permission of Alan Lomax.

16. John A. Lomax papers. Quoted by permission of Alan Lomax.

17. Interview with Alan Lomax, May 28, 1968.

18. "Miserable but Exciting Songs," *Time* (November 26, 1945), 52.

19. See Ann Pescatello, *Last Cavalier: The Life and Times of John A. Lomax, 1867–1948* (Pittsburgh: University of Pittsburgh Press, 1992).

20. Interview, May 28, 1968.

21. Joe Klein, *Woody Guthrie: A Life* (New York: Knopf, 1980), 149.

22. Archie Green's unpublished bioblbliography is the best guide to the source material on Aunt Molly Jackson; see also the special Aunt Molly Jackson

memorial issue of the *Kentucky Folklore Record* 7, no. 4 (October–December 1961), and Shelly Romalis, *Pistol Packin' Mama: Aunt Molly Jackson and the Politics of Folksong* (Urbana: University of Illinois Press, 1999). Lead Belly's early life is chronicled in John A. and Alan Lomax, *Negro Folk Songs as Sung by Lead Belly* (New York: Macmillan, 1936), though with a paternalistic bias; it should be supplemented with Frederic Ramsey Jr.'s "Leadbelly: A Great Long Time," *Sing Out!* 15, no. 1 (March 1965): 7–24; and Charles Wolfe and Kip Lornell, *The Life and Legend of Leadbelly* (New York: HarperCollins, 1992). Burl Ives's background is sketched in his own autobiography *Wayfaring Stranger* (Indianapolis: Bobbs-Merrill, 1962), and that of Josh White by Robert Shelton in *The Josh White Song Book* (Chicago: Quadrangle, 1963). The published materials relating to Woody Guthrie are given in Richard Reuss, *A Woody Guthrie Bibliography* (New York: Woody Guthrie Foundation, 1968); see especially Guthrie's autobiography *Bound for Glory* (New York: Durron, 1943); Richard Reuss, "Woody Guthrie and His Folk Tradition," *Journal of American Folklore* 83 (January–March 1970): 21–32; and Joe Klein, *Woody Guthrie: A Life* (New York: Knopf, 1980). Lee Hays's biography is Doris Willens, *Lonesome Traveler: The Life of Lee Hays* (New York: Norton, 1988). Also, Hays's own columns in the *People's Songs* bulletin beginning with vol. 1, no. 12 (January 1947), contain autobiographical notes and references to Hays's early life.

23. David Dunaway, *How Can I Keep from Singing: Pete Seeger* (New York: McGraw-Hill, 1981).

24. Readers seeking a general guide to Pete Seeger's career and thought should begin with his splendid, partly autobiographical *The Incompleat Folksinger* (New York: Simon & Schuster, 1972), superbly edited from his many writings and new material by Jo Metcalf Schwartz. Other biographical sketches are numerous, though frequently stereotyped in content and character; the most thorough in spite of many minor errors of fact is Gene Marine's "Guerrilla Minstrel," *Rolling Stone* 106 (April 13, 1972): 40–48. Much of the material on Seeger's life and early political and music activity came from an interview with Seeger on April 9, 1968. See also Pete Seeger, *Where Have All the Flowers Gone: A Singer's Stories, Songs, Seeds, Robberies,* ed. Peter Blood (Bethlehem, Pa.: Sing Out!, 1993).

Few printed sources on Cisco Houston are available. (Lee Hays taped his reminiscences extensively before he died in 1961.) Introductory sketches by Lee Hays and Bill Wolff are provided in the Cisco Houston memorial issue of *Sing Out!* 11, no. 4 (October–November 1961): 4–13. Also see Ray M. Lawless, *Folksingers and Folksongs of North America,* rev. ed. (New York: Duell, Sloan & Pearce, 1965), 118–19. Material on Will Geer for this period can be found in Ben Burns, "Will Geer Laughs Last," *Daily Worker* (May 5, 1939), 7; and Ed Robbin, "Will Geer Comes Home," *People's World* (July 6, 1939), 5; and Sally Osborne Norton, "A Historical Study of Actor Will Geer, His Life and Work in the Context of Twentieth-Century American Social, Political, and Theatrical History," Ph.D. dissertation, University of Southern California, Los Angeles, 1980. Information on the American Square Dance Group was obtained from the late Margot Mayo in an interview on August 29, 1966, and from the group's press organ, *Promenade* (1940–1953).

25. Earl Robinson, *Ballad of an American: The Autobiography of Earl Robinson*, with Eric A. Gordon (Lanham, Md.: Rowman & Littlefield, 1997).

26. Dyer-Bennet sketches some of his early life in "Some Thoughts on the Folksong Revival," *Sing Out!* 12, no. 2 (April–May 1962): 17–22. The background of the Golden Gate Quartet is outlined in "Golden Gate in Washington" *Time* (January 27, 1941), 50. Earl Robinson's career is traced briefly in Lawless, *Folksongs and Folksingers*, 196–97; in Mickey Milton, "Ballad for Americans," *The Review* (formerly *Young Communist Review*) (June 24, 1940), 11; and most thoroughly in David Ewen, *All the Years of American Popular Music* (Upper Saddle River, N.J.: Prentice Hall, 1977).

27. "Preface," *Folksong U.S.A.* (New York, 1947), viii.

28. "Introduction," *Reprints from the People's Songs Bulletin, 1946–1949* (New York, 1961), 4.

29. Interview with Alan Lomax, May 28, 1968.

30. Interview with Irwin Silber, April 2, 1968.

31. Program numbers were copied down on the occasion by Margot Mayo who communicated them to the writer August 29, 1966.

32. Mike Gold, "One Columnist Who Fails to Cry in His Beer over 'Snow White'" ("Change the World" column), *Daily Worker* (April 7, 1938), 7.

33. Lee Stanley, "Folk Concert Brings New Vitality to Modern Dance," *Daily Worker* (May 14, 1941), 7. See also Ellen Graff, *Stepping Left: Dance and Politics, New York City, 1928–1942* (Durham, N.C.: Duke University Press, 1997).

34. Waldemar B. Hille, "Why All the Interest in American Folk and Worker's Songs?" *Elms* (Elmhurst College, Ill., student newspaper), 1939.

35. William Wolff, "Use Traditional Tunes for New Union Songs," *Daily Worker* (November 16, 1939), 7.

36. See Denning, *The Cultural Front.*

37. The dates for these reviews in *New Masses* are Hurston, February 25, 1936, 24; Scarborough, June 1, 1937, 26; Fowler, December 26, 1939, 25–26; Korson, February 7, 1939, 20–21; Gordon, April 25, 1939, 27; and Johnson, July 20, 1937.

38. Onah L. Spencer, "Stackalee" and Myra Page, "Ballad Woman" in *Direction* 4, no. 5 (Summer 1941): 14–17 and 29–31, respectively; Herbert Halpert, "The Piney Folk-Singers" *Direction* 2, no. 5 (September 1939): 4–6, 15.

39. Lee Hays, "Wants Communist Poetry" (letter to the editor), *New Masses* (January 11, 1938), 21.

40. Ralph Cheyney, "On New Program for Writers" (letter to Mike Gold), *New Masses* (February 1930): 21.

41. Robert Forsythe [Kyle Crichton], "Wanted: Great Songs," *New Masses* (January 25, 1938), 12.

42. *New Masses* (October 15, 1935), 24.

43. Martha Millet, "Is Poetry Dead?" (letter to the editor), *New Masses* (January 18, 1938), 20.

44. Hays, "Wants Communist Poetry." Also see Ira Benson, "Writers' and Readers' Writers" (letter to the editor), *New Masses* (February 1, 1938), 20.

45. For an account of the various congresses from a more general perspective, see Daniel Aaron, *Writers on the Left: Episodes in American Literary Communism* (New York: Harcourt, Brace & World, 1961).

46. Burke's paper and a résumé of the discussion it provoked are presented in Henry Hart, ed., *American Writers Congress* (New York: International, 1935), 87–94 and 167–71.

47. Published in Henry Hart, ed., *The Writer in a Changing World* (New York: Equinox Cooperative, 1937), 140–57.

48. See Donald Ogden Stewart, ed., *Fighting Words* (New York: Harcourt, Brace 1940), chaps. 2 and 5, for résumés of the proceedings of these sessions.

49. Interview with Lee Hays, August 16, 1965.

50. Interview with Moses Asch, April, 1964.

51. See Ronald D. Cohen and Dave Samuelson, *Songs for Political Action: Folk Music, Topical Songs and the American Left, 1926–1953* (Bear Family Records, BCD 15720-JL, 1996), for an extensive review of the recordings of this era.

52. Robert Shelton, "Folkways in Sound . . . ," *High Fidelity Magazine* (June 1960): 102.

53. See Victor Greene, *A Passion for Polka: Old-Time Ethnic Music in America* (Los Angeles: University of California Press, 1992).

54. See Israel Young, "Moe Asch: Twentieth-Century Man," *Sing Out!* 26, nos. 1 and 2 (1977), 2–6 and 25–29, respectively; and Peter Goldsmith, *Making People's Music: Moe Asch and Folkways Records* (Washington, D.C.: Smithsonian Institution Press, 1998).

55. *Mother Bloor 75th Birthday Souvenir Book,* July 18, 1937.

56. Brand, *The Ballad Mongers,* 124.

57. For example, see Alex Kolb, "Slave Songs of Protest," *Young Communist Review* (February 1939): 19–21; and an article by Harold Preece in *The New South* (March 1938).

58. See Denning, *The Cultural Front;* Lewis A. Erenberg, *Swingin' the Dream: Big Band Jazz and the Rebirth of American Culture* (Chicago: University of Chicago Press, 1998); and David Stowe, *Swing Changes: Big-Band Jazz in New Deal America* (Cambridge, Mass.: Harvard University Press, 1994). Also, John Hammond, *John Hammond on Record: An Autobiography* (New York: Ridge, 1977).

59. Donald Drew Egbert and Stow Persons, eds., *Socialism and American Life* (Princeton, N.J.: Princeton University Press, 1952), 738.

60. Gold, "One Columnist Who Fails to Cry in His Beer Over 'Snow White.'"

61. Harrison George, "Music and the People . . . ," *People's World* (March 18, 1941), 5.

62. Sidney Finkelstein, *Jazz: A People's Music* (New York: Da Capo, 1948). See also Finkelstein's article "What Is Jazz?" *New Masses* (November 5, 1946), 12–15; and "Jam Session: A New Masses Forum," *New Masses* (December 10, 1946), 14–18.

63. Earl Robinson, "The Greatest of the Folk Singers," *Our Times,* weekly magazine published by the *People's World* (March 3, 1950), 3. See also Earl Robinson, *Ballad of an American.*

64. Reuss, "Woody Guthrie and His Folk Tradition."

65. Mike Quin, "Double Check" column, *People's World* (April 25, 1940), 5.

66. "Woodie [sic] Guthrie: He Never Sold Out," *National Guardian* (October 14, 1967), 10.

67. R. Serge Denisoff, "The Proletarian Renascence: The Folkness of the Ideological Folk," *Journal of American Folklore* 82 (1969): 56.

68. George Charney, *A Long Journey* (Chicago: Quadrangle, 1968), 51.

69. Interview with Earl Browder, February 12, 1968. Charles Seeger reported to this author that the party did pay the rent on the room where the Pierre Degeyter Club held some of its early meetings.

7

The Almanac Singers:
Proletarian "Folk" Culture in Microcosm

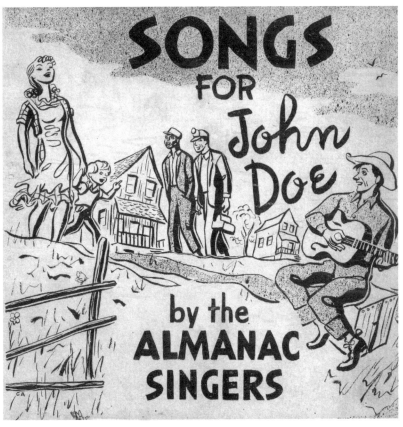

Reproduction of cover of Songs for John Doe *by the Almanac Singers*

On August 23, 1939, a startled world heard the German and Soviet governments announce the signing of a mutual nonaggression agreement. Thus began a so-called "peace" era, lasting for almost two years, during which Germany conquered and occupied much of Europe. Almost immediately the political coalitions forged in the Popular Front era collapsed, as the communists withdrew their support and adopted an extreme isolationist stance. Up until this time, the party had distinguished sharply between fascism and the more democratic varieties of Western capitalism; now it contended that these were merely different forms of the same socioeconomic evil. Consequently, communists and their sympathizers maintained a staunchly neutral and anti-involvement position when Germany launched World War II on September 1, 1939. The party turned savagely on Roosevelt's domestic policies at home, which it recently had supported with nearly equal fervor. Labor agitation within the CIO continued, but operatives made a sharper effort to dramatize the unionization struggle in class terms.

The attitudes and ideology of urban radical folk song writers and performers were a product of the cultural forces at work in the Popular Front era, as was the artistic and thematic content of their performances. It was from this group that the Almanac Singers coalesced into an identifiable entity, just when the Nazi–Soviet pact began to have its effects on the communist movement's members and supporters. The sudden reversal of the party's ideological position on world politics was not paralleled fully in the attitudes and activities of left-wing activists. Art and performances with topical themes made proper deference to the new party line. But, unlike the dramatic shifts that occurred when the Third Period gave way to the Popular Front, cultural expressions favored by the communists exhibited remarkably little fundamental change. The overriding communist concern for folk songs and other traditions of the American and world peoples—at least in an intellectual sense—continued unabated. The Almanac Singers built on and extended the work of the left-wing folklore popularizers of the Popular Front milieu, even though their initial political worldview, like that of the movement itself, now took an almost diametrically opposite turn from the former period.

ORIGINS AND EARLY ACTIVITIES OF THE ALMANACS

Much of the history of the Almanac Singers is obscure or contradictory because of the paucity of meaningful contemporary documentation and the diverse and sometimes carefully circumscribed accounts offered in interviews with former Almanacs. As one of their number accurately observed, "there are as many versions and interpretations as there were

Almanac Singers,"[1] and these totaled more than a dozen. Even their genesis and demise are surprisingly difficult to date precisely since few events at either end of the Almanacs' career can be characterized as decisive landmarks. What is clear is that the group's original personnel consisted of Pete Seeger, Lee Hays, Millard Lampell, John Peter Hawes, and later Woody Guthrie and that they were a functioning collective entity by February 1941.

Seeger came from middle-class origins and developed an early interest in folk music in response to his family's eclectic musical interests. Hays grew up in a traditional Arkansas setting and brought labor school experiences to the group. Lampell, the son of Jewish immigrants, was raised in New Jersey and attended the University of West Virginia on a scholarship. In his teens, like Seeger and Guthrie, he took to the road on occasional hitchhiking trips, working at assorted manual jobs en route to earn his keep. He also served for a time as a corresponding reporter for the *New Republic*[2] and later became a successful radio and television scriptwriter. Hawes, who grew up in Cambridge, Massachusetts, the son of an author of sea stories for boys, had a keen appreciation for New England lore and culture, especially sea chanteys. Though from a well-to-do family, he professed a staunch interest in working-class radical activities.[3] Just prior to the formation of the Almanacs, Guthrie returned to the West Coast, there to write his much acclaimed Columbia River songs before traveling to New York once more to join the group. Meanwhile, he maintained a steady correspondence with Seeger and Hays as the Almanacs moved through their formative stages.[4]

The Almanacs' genesis was gradual and unspectacular. Hays and Lampell began corresponding while both were still living in the South, and following their meeting in August 1940, they took an apartment together on New York's Lower East Side. Pete Seeger returned from one of his folk song trips the following November and was introduced to them by Peter Hawes, who had met all three within the year. The four quickly confirmed their mutual interests in American folk music and their strong radical political sympathies. Seeger and Hays began singing together at "cause" parties and other left-wing functions in December, their first booking being a luncheon at the Jade Mountain Restaurant in New York, for which they were paid $2.50.[5] The combination of Seeger's banjo playing and dedicated musical performance with Hays's fine bass voice, dry wit, and song-leading ability was a success, and demands for their services increased rapidly. All the while they sang endlessly in the apartment with Lampell, Hawes, and others who came by, talked current events, and composed their own topical songs in folk style.[6]

In February 1941, the Almanacs, now comprising Seeger (who used the name Pete Bowers to protect his father, then working for the U.S. government), Hays, and Lampell, sang at the national meeting of the American Youth Congress held at Turner's Arena in Washington, D.C. (A fourth singer presumably joined them, but who would fill the fourth position was not yet determined.) No two accounts completely agree on how this came about or what exactly transpired, but the date (February 7–9) is the most logical choice for an "official" beginning of the Almanacs' career. According to one report, the AYC leaders requested that the group sing a number of songs constructed around the political slogans of the meeting, including "Don't Lend or Lease Our Bases" and "Jim Crow Must Go." The Almanacs' peace songs were well received, but the AYC sponsors were less than satisfied by the trio's creation "Jim Crow" because the concluding refrain simply ended with the words "Jim Crow" instead of "Jim Crow Must Go!"[7]

At this point the Almanacs formalized themselves as a collective entity and developed a conscious rationale for their activities as agit-prop entertainers in a folk style. They chose the name "Almanac Singers" from a stray line of Woody Guthrie's, variously reported as coming from a letter written from the West Coast or from the manuscript of what later became *Hard Hitting Songs for Hard-Hit People*.[8] Asked what the name represented, the group explained:

> Well, if you want to know what the weather is going to be, you have to look in your Almanac. And if you want to know when to plant your spuds or what side of the moon to dig 'em in, or when to go on strike, and if you want to know what's good for the itch, or unemployment, or fascism, you have to look in your Almanac. And that's what Almanac stands for.[9]

The Almanacs' songs, in other words, were intended to serve as an all-purpose topical commentary, guideline, and reinforcement of political and social values for the left-wing movement. Identification with the working class or "people" came, among other ways, through the use of the folk song medium as the prime vehicle of agit-prop communication. "We think this is the first time there has ever been an organized attempt . . . to sing the folk songs of America," Lampell said. "We are trying to give back to the people the songs of the workers."[10] Accordingly, Almanac programs were made up of a mixture of traditional ballads and work songs and topical lyrics created by the group and others.

During the first months, most Almanac compositions exhibited "peace" themes with a strong anticapitalist flavor, reflecting the communist movement's claim that the Roosevelt administration would drag an unwilling nation into a European war fought mainly for the purposes of redistributing world markets and profits among the capitalist nations. The peace songs were the product of the entire group, but most were written initially by Millard Lampell and Lee Hays, with musical contributions from Pete Seeger. As events were to show, Lampell had a sharp wit and a natural way with a clever phrase, but sometimes he lacked a sense of tact. Nearly all Almanac songs were set to old folk tunes, such as "Billy Boy," "Jesse James," and "Liza Jane," and were sung with a verve and flair that helped offset the Almanacs' unpolished voices.

Eric Bernay's Keynote label recorded seven songs that were released in March 1941 as *Songs for John Doe.*[11] The songs were virulent and polemical, containing denunciations of war, the Roosevelt administration's cautious attempts at preparedness, and the chief figures of American government and capitalism. About war, for example:

> I'll sing you a song and it's not very long,
> It's about a young man who never did wrong.
> Suddenly, he died one day—the reason why no one could say.
> . . . Only one clue as to why he died—A bayonet sticking in his side!
> ("The Strange Death of John Doe")

With regard to the draft and preparedness:

> Remember when the AAA
> Killed a million hogs a day?
> Instead of hogs it's men today—
> Plow the fourth one under! ("Plow Under")

As for the war profiteers:

> Would you like to see the world, Billy Boy, Billy Boy,
> Would you like to see the world, charming Billy?
> No, it wouldn't be much thrill, to die for Dupont in Brazil;
> He's a young boy and cannot leave his mother. ("Billy Boy")

The most scathing attacks were saved for Roosevelt himself and were so vitriolic that they were to cause the Almanacs acute embarrassment once the Left swung back to a pro-administration stance during the war years. At once the most famous and infamous of these was "The Ballad of October 16th," which commemorated the date in 1940 initiating the first peacetime draft in the nation's history. The chorus (set to the tune of "Jesse James" refrain) said:

> Oh Franklin Roosevelt told the people how he felt.
> We damned near believed what he said;
> He said, "I hate war—and so does Eleanor,
> But we won't be safe till everybody's dead."

No other peace song of the Nazi–Soviet pact era proved more popular in the communist movement, and none would be cited more often in later histories of the party and anticommunist tracts aimed at folk singers in general and the Almanacs in particular.[12]

Indeed, the antiadministration lyrics were so polemical that reports circulated throughout the Left that the right-wing Roosevelt-hating America Firsters organization gleefully played the *John Doe* album at one of its meetings. Other lurid, unsubstantiated rumors gave accounts of the alleged reactions of the President and his wife when they heard the same songs. One rumor, for example, described FDR's remark to Supreme Court Justice Felix Frankfurter: "This [group] is the most dangerous voice in America," and Eleanor Roosevelt supposedly observed that the lyrics were "very clever but in extremely bad taste."[13]

The John Doe songs brought the Almanacs to the attention of the entire communist movement and generated considerable excitement about the group. After one performance before the League of American Writers, Theodore Dreiser jumped up, planted a kiss on the cheek of a startled Lee Hays, and declared, "If we had six more teams like these boys, we could save America!"[14] The *Daily Worker* publicized the group so much in its pages that a friend of Seeger's once suggested to him that the Almanacs themselves must own the paper. Communist front organizations, left-wing labor unions, and private party givers with progressive sympathies all vied for the appearance of the Almanacs at their various functions, and the American Peace Mobilization unsuccessfully tried to sponsor the group as its own official singers.[15] The *John Doe* album was widely praised in the radical press and its songs were reprinted frequently.

Several factors combined to produce the considerable impact that the Almanacs had on the communist Left in early 1941. The group itself was a novelty, being the first ensemble of its kind in an urban environment to sing folk and folk-styled songs in a nonformal or non–art song manner. The harmonies and arrangements, in other words, were unusual but appealing, notwithstanding the "rough" sound city audiences of that day were unused to hearing. The political content of Almanac lyrics reflected the party's line in specific and comparatively sophisticated terms, much more so than the topical creations of folk figures such as Aunt Molly Jackson or Lead Belly who sometimes entertained at communist functions. The words themselves often were humorous, usually very original and clever, carrying a "punch" that even their most bitter critics admired.

During this period, the movement itself was isolated from many of its former progressive allies and hard put to defend the sudden reversal of its antifascist policies of the Popular Front period. The Almanacs' songs provided a much needed positive, if polemical, reinforcement of the prevailing communist worldview and ideological position rather than another defensive apologia. To a lesser extent, the group also helped fill the partial entertainment void created when many progressive but noncommunist musicians temporarily ceased to perform before movement gatherings during the Nazi–Soviet pact era.

In the spring of 1941, the Almanacs moved to larger quarters on West 12th Street. "The Loft," as their apartment was appropriately nicknamed, soon became one of the more important cultural hubs of the movement in the early 1940s, as numerous "names" from the political, intellectual, and artistic spheres came by to sing, exchange ideas, and sometimes dine on the "erratic but interesting" cuisine; among them were Elizabeth Gurley Flynn, Mike Gold, Walter Lowenfels, Mother Bloor, Dashiell Hammett, Rockwell Kent, and Marc Blitzstein. Peter Hawes joined the group at this time and remained with the Almanacs in a performing capacity for the remainder of the peace period. The four sang in the annual communist-organized May Day parade, participated in an antiwar revue *Sign of the Times* with a progressive actors' troupe renamed the Almanac Players for the occasion,[16] and instituted weekend sings at the Loft that helped pay the rent. Almanac "sings" were the forerunners of the latter-day hootenanny gatherings.

The Almanacs recorded some militant union lyrics that included their own compositions "Get Thee Behind Me, Satan," "Talking Union," and Woody Guthrie's "Union Maid," as well as other contemporary labor songs; when released as *Talking Union* (Keynote 106), the album became their most successful recording venture. At the end of May, they were well received at a performance for nearly twenty thousand striking transport workers at Madison Square Garden. This favorable audience reaction led them to plan a summer tour across the country, with performances en route for as many labor and radical groups as possible.

With the help of Saul Mills of the left-leaning New York CIO Council, the Almanacs set up several informal bookings at union affairs and made additional contacts to obtain bookings. Through Alan Lomax and Commodore Records, they arranged to record two albums of traditional folk songs, one of sea chanties, the other of "sod-buster ballads," for which the Almanacs were paid $400. That gave them enough to buy a large second-hand Buick, vintage 1931, and sufficient gas for the first leg of their journey.[17]

As these preparations were being completed, word came on June 22, 1941, that German armies had invaded the Soviet Union. Several days of confusion followed in the communist movement as the implications of the "new situation" were debated, but the result was not long in coming. The "peace" period was abruptly terminated, and the party and its allies reverted to their former staunch antifascist position and now urged all-out participation in the war against Hitler. As this switch in outlook occurred, one communist functionary approached the Almanacs and demanded, "Do we have one war or two?"[18]—in other words, one battle with fascism or an isolated clash between European capitalist powers coinciding with the ongoing struggle between working and ruling classes. The answer, of course, was that there now was only one overriding concern: to defeat Hitler and the Nazis.

Amid conflicting party interpretations and arguments emanating from their independent assessments, the Almanacs struggled uncomfortably toward their personal decisions. Seeger, for example, summed up the progression of Almanac thinking:

> [I]t took over a period of about ten days. . . . Churchill really broke the ice, I think, for a lot of us by coming out the day after the invasion of Russia. He said "we must support the Soviet people with every ounce of our energy." And this really surprised the hell out of a lot of us.

Continuing in a philosophical vein, he said:

> I could hardly believe that these nations which had been so violently anti - Soviet were really going to support socialism, even under the press of war. But now it looked like they finally would. We realized that basically the United States establishment would get swung into this position, too. . . . And so we felt . . . that the historical situation had changed.

Seeger concluded that "perhaps we were fools not to have seen that it would change. But nevertheless when it did change we weren't going to stand on any foolish consistency. And so two days [after the invasion of Russia] we [stopped] singing 'Franklin D., You Ain't Going to Send Me across the Sea.'"[19] Having discarded the peace songs, the group henceforth limited its topical song repertoire to union and other subjects unrelated to the war until after Pearl Harbor.

Shortly before the Almanacs left on their summer tour in early July, Peter Hawes contracted pneumonia and was forced to withdraw from the trip. Woody Guthrie arrived in New York just in time to take his place and join the group for its recording session with Commodore and then to head West again as an Almanac inside of forty-eight hours. The four began their tour with an appearance at an American Youth Congress rally in Philadelphia on July 4, followed by performances for various CIO and left-wing labor audiences in Pittsburgh, Cleveland, Chicago, Milwaukee, Denver, and elsewhere en route to the West Coast. In California they sang for Harry Bridges's longshoremen's union but otherwise, as was the case in New York, entertained primarily at middle-class radical functions rather than at working-class gatherings. (Most genuine "workers" in the Old Left of this period were to be found in the factories and plants of the Midwest; the communist movement on the East and West Coasts had become heavily middle class.)

In San Francisco, the group temporarily began to come apart. Hays, who tended toward hypochondria, announced he was ill and returned home alone. The others journeyed on to Los Angeles, but there Lampell found romance with a woman who was traveling east and he too departed. Seeger and Guthrie made their way back to San Francisco and then to Portland and Washington, where they performed under the auspices of the progressively oriented Commonwealth Federation, before returning to New York in late September.

The tour and its attendant publicity did much to broaden the Almanacs' popularity in the labor–radical and communist movements outside of New York. But during the trip the group produced noticeably few important topical songs. In part this can be ascribed to the rigors of travel and the shunting of creative energy from songwriting to performance channels, but it is clear that the diminished creative output also reflected the group's uncertain sense of ideological direction, especially with regard to foreign affairs and the war in Europe. As one of the Almanacs observed afterward, "we knew we weren't singing the old peace songs, but still we didn't feel like singing '. . . let's go in and fight' either."[20] For a time, this lack of direction was so strongly felt that when the group reunited at the close of the tour, the Almanacs and several friends, including Mike Gold and the communist poet and newspaper editor Walter Lowenfels, discussed whether the group should change its name or even disband.[21]

The members soon changed their minds. In September, Pete Hawes found and rented a three-story building on West 10th Street in New York. They took up collective residence, promptly christening the place "Almanac House," and recharged their spirits with expanded personnel and renewed dedication. By the end of the month they once again were appearing at left-wing social and political functions. Peter Hawes, his younger brother Baldwin ("Butch"), Bess Lomax (Alan's younger sister), Agnes "Sis" Cunningham and her husband Gordon Friesen, Arthur Stern, and others all were enrolled on the membership roster during the fall. Other peripheral followers, admirers, and sometime participating performers, such as Jean Rogovin, Bernie Asbel, and Allan Sloane, were in attendance, and the comings and goings of individuals associated with the group soon turned Almanac House's entrance into a veritable revolving door. On a number of occasions, several teams of "Almanac Singers" were sent out to fill various bookings in a single evening, and sponsors were surprised if not irritated to find that the arriving entertainers were not necessarily those whose services they presumably had engaged. The

Sunday afternoon hootenannies (as they now were called) were revived, and they brought more people, intellectual ferment, and a limited amount of cash through the Almanac portals.[22]

Given the amorphous membership and the hectic pace created by the movements of so many people to and fro, the Almanacs' lifestyle was chaotic and a daily routine almost entirely absent. "Life," sighed Butch Hawes much later, "was one big organization meeting." Each individual went his way during the day and might or might not show up for appearances at bookings during the evenings. Only Bess Lomax held a steady outside job, and it was a scramble each week for the group to raise the additional funds needed to maintain even a minimum subsistence living standard. The constant "camping-out" atmosphere inevitably took its toll. On several occasions members moved out of Almanac House to find additional privacy and to escape the mayhem. Personality conflicts and petty jealousies plagued the Almanacs, perhaps an inevitable outgrowth of the close social as well as musical interaction of so many dynamic, strongly opinionated, and volatile individuals. Most accounts indicate that only Pete Seeger remained aloof from these feuds. Tensions reached such a point at the end of November that Lee Hays was expelled from Almanac membership by a vote of five or six to one, his own. Hays's departure temporarily eased some of the intragroup frictions but left a musical, performance, and songwriting void that the others thereafter found impossible to completely fill.

THE "PROLETARIAN" CULTURE OF THE ALMANAC SINGERS

The beginnings of the Almanacs' cooperative experiment were naive and idealistic—devoid of much theoretical superstructure. The decision to live together preceded their agreement to perform or create songs as a unit, and apparently was made without much thought; Seeger, for his part, recalled the original understanding to share the same dwelling and related expenses as no more unusual than a family's tacit agreement to reside in the same house cooperatively.[23] Hays took a much more consciously philosophical view; he was hardly a year removed from his experiences at Commonwealth Labor College in Mena, Arkansas, where communal living was both a necessary and deliberate lifestyle.[24] The other original members, Lampell and Hawes, never indicated their thinking with regard to the initial decision to live cooperatively, but it is doubtful that the rationales for their actions were as highly conceptualized as were Hays's.

Subsequently, and perhaps inevitably, guidelines governing the collective living experience were consciously developed, paralleling the principles of primitive communism familiar from time immemorial. All income was held in the group's name and disbursements for rent, food, and most individual needs were made from a common fund. Each Almanac was to receive a dollar a day as spending money, but their chronically bleak financial picture often mitigated against the actual implementation of this ideal. Cooking, cleaning, and house chores were divided among the members. At various times attempts were made to allocate the business management and musical affairs of the group on a similar basis.[25] Cooperative functioning broke down occasionally, usually in conjunction with financial and personality crises, but on the whole the communal way of life served the Almanacs' physical needs adequately if not sumptuously. In many respects it was a most pragmatic lifestyle, for communal living was cheaper than separate quarters and helped free the Almanacs from reliance on the capitalist system to make a living. Sharing food and shelter, in any event, was entirely consistent with the Almanacs' Marxist sociopolitical worldview, and it complemented the cooperative rationale behind the group's musical efforts.

By comparison, the rationale for the collective artistic endeavors of the Almanacs was far more concretely conceptualized. They believed that any creative effort was apt to be more socially meaningful and artistically satisfying if it was the product of a group experience rather than that of only one individual. As Hays noted later, "There was a critique in tossing verses back and forth which was much more than a mere trial and error, or 'thinking out loud' method. It was truly a matter of the sum being more than the total of the parts." He added, "A qualitative change took place which transcended individual abilities."[26]

In practice this meant communal songwriting sessions or group revisions of the works of particular members. Ironically, this creative process was a telescoped imitation of the traditional processes of community creation and recreation of folk song materials, although it is not clear to what degree the Almanacs themselves were consciously aware of this. Reporting for *People's World,* an observer described one such composing session:

How a Song Is Born

One night this week I happened to be at a home where the Almanac Singers were engaging in a sort of impromptu rehearsal. . . . They were organizing a new song. They all contributed—Woody a line, Pete a line, Lee a suggestion. Millard was at a portable typewriter, banging out the lines as they evolved. Occasionally they joined together to sing a completed verse or two. Then there were more rapid-fire suggestions, revisions. As they progressed the music evolved, too, beginning simply. New phrases came from the guitar or banjo, music phrases tossed in, very nonchalantly. Sometimes while Pete talked he strummed his banjo catching at a new line. . . . Woody, leaning back on a couch, suddenly broke out with a brand new verse. He jumped to his feet, sang the words, accompanied himself on the "geetar." The verse went down on the typewriter—and then it was revised. At the end of about an hour's work, four verses were completed. They got together and sang the completed song.[27]

Subsequent performances often suggested the need for revisions: ideas for additional lyrics, a new musical arrangement, or deletions of unsuccessful parts of the composition.

This kind of collective interaction lessened the importance of the individual composer or songwriter and shifted attention instead to the entire group, a trend that was actively encouraged by the Almanacs themselves. Seeger explained that "we tried in our publicity to get away from ourselves as individuals." He described an example: "A newspaper reporter would interview us and say 'Now let me find out something about your background and your background and your background,' and we would say 'Look, our individuals don't matter. The group is the important thing.'"[28]

In the same way, cooperative effort highlighted the musical products rather than the composers and performers, also consciously considered desirable by the group. The Almanacs' intentions were in part stimulated by the poets' Anonymous Movement (AM) organized by a close friend of Lee Hays, Walter Lowenfels, during his expatriate days in Paris in the late 1920s. In the Anonymous Movement emphasis was on "that which was written, and not upon the author's reputation."[29] As the AM never published the name of poets whose works it sponsored, so the Almanacs adopted the policy of not listing individual credit for a song produced from within the group. With few exceptions, the policy was observed initially. But later the collective songwriting spirit was somewhat subdued and individual efforts tended to stand out more. Group workshop sessions still took place, but frequently these were limited to offering critiques and polishing the musical ideas of particular members rather than developing new songs from whole cloth on the spot. The Almanacs sociopolitical philosophy and the lifestyle that had emerged were characterized by two principal touchstones: cooperative sharing on all levels of performance, songwriting, and daily living; and identification with "worker" art forms and values, especially as personified in the culture of the rural "folk."

The Almanacs' cooperative values were bound up hand and glove with the group's socioeconomic worldview, which sharply distinguished between capitalist and working-class society and the culture that each produced. In keeping with traditional Marxist theory of the pre–Popular Front era, the interests of the two classes were perceived as mutually conflicting and exclusive of one another. "There's the union people and the anti-union people," the Almanacs wrote in *The Clipper*. "Decide which side you're on."[30] Organizing the collective efforts of workers to build a union or create new cultural expression inevitably was regarded as a sign of the "people's" solidarity and identified with the progressive activity of the masses. So was the Almanacs' cooperative sharing, which was seen as a means to the same end.

With reference to the class conflict in the area of culture, the Almanacs and the communist movement at this time typically held that the bourgeois establishment controlled the media and all "legitimate" and commercial outlets for artistic expression. It fostered the public's exposure to only the most diluted class-conscious sentiments or else totally subverted the real workers' art in an ocean wash of "June-moon-croon" pop culture. Consequently, genuine "people's" aesthetic products could only be found beyond the pale of the American bourgeoisie's domain: in the folklore traditions of the rural lower classes; in the left-wing theaters, radical newspapers, and publishing houses; and, most important, in the union halls which the Almanacs viewed as the cornerstones of progressive working-class activity in the United States in 1941. "The Union hall," Woody Guthrie declared, "is the salvation of real honest-to-God American culture."[31]

Perceiving American cultural expression to be pluralistic and divided between that fostered by the capitalist establishment and that produced by working-class people and their sympathizers, the Almanacs accordingly rejected the former and dedicated themselves to the promulgation of the latter. They regarded their roles as twofold: (1) to create a portion of the needed people's art out of their personal experiences and (2) to stimulate the production and recognition of workers' cultural expression by workers themselves. "Songs of the people must belong to the people," Lee Hays remarked. "Unions have to preserve and extend this tradition of people's songs."[32] In proposing to service only labor and progressive organizations, the Almanacs foresaw that union and radical organizations of necessity would have to be willing to support artists and musicians so that they would not be forced to submerge or prostitute their talents to earn a living in American capitalist society. Consequently, the group followed a deliberate policy of accepting very few "benefit" bookings.[33]

Clearly the Almanacs advocated the development of a collective people's culture based on the already existing but scattered manifestations of workers' art in evidence around the country. The folk song idiom was ideal for their purposes. The form was not strongly identified with bourgeois music institutions, as was Tin Pan Alley or Broadway; folk music instead was a product of the American cultural experience associated with the rural lower classes. It conveyed straightforward, unpretentious, and sometimes class-conscious sentiments about every aspect of the "people's" life and struggles, and many songs were readily adaptable to a mass-singing context. Group pursuit of folk songs and folk singing supported both spiritual and agit-prop missions. "Folk singing is a form of battle and a frontal movement to preserve our own people's culture," Hays was quoted as saying.[34] Woody Guthrie observed, "The biggest parts of our song collection are aimed at restoring the right amount of people to the right amount of land and the right amount of houses and the right amount of groceries to the right amount of working folks."[35] An important by-product of such reasoning was the inevitable blurring of any distinction between the terms *folk* and *workers* (or *people*) and the largely interchangeable usage of these phrases and the concepts they represented.

This employment of rural traditional form and content in an urban context to initiate or further social, economic, or political goals has been defined by R. Serge Denisoff as "folk consciousness"; he notes that the Almanacs were the earliest formalized organization of this concept to appear in the American communist movement.[36] But, while the group utilized traditional songs and the folk idiom on behalf of workers' causes, it never considered that music of any kind in itself was a satisfactory substitute for direct action. As Hays insisted in his characteristic southern Methodist ministerial rhetoric, "Good singing won't do, good praying won't do, good preaching won't do, but if you get all of them together with a little organizing behind [them], you get a way of life and a way to do it."[37]

The "way of life" alluded to by Hays was a consciously sought-after goal for the Almanacs, for while the group allied itself philosophically with lower-class workers and "the people," in fact, most members were the offspring of middle-class parents. As young radicals in search of a revolutionary identity, the Almanacs attempted to flee their immediate pasts by submerging their bourgeois origins in a self-conscious bohemian lifestyle aptly characterized by one member as a world of "proletarian romanticism."[38]

Almanac's clothing typically consisted of blue jeans, denim shirts, and other garb associated with manual labor, partly for comfort and because of limited finances but also as a result of the conscious efforts of some members to "dress down" to the vaguely conceived "proletarian" level. Seeger, for example, later contrasted his attitude of that period to Lead Belly's: "There I was, trying my best to shed my Harvard upbringing, scorning to waste money on clothes other than blue jeans. But Lead Belly," he noted with embarrassing irony, "always had a clean white shirt and starched collar, well-pressed suit and shined shoes. He didn't need to affect that he was a workingman."[39]

Some of the Almanacs indeed have referred to themselves in retrospect as the "original beatniks." A friend once remarked to Arthur Stern, "Arthur, how is it I always see you with a two-day beard, never a one-day, or three, but always a two-day beard?"[40] The women in the group rarely wore makeup, and the Almanacs generally rejected any use of cosmetics to counteract the harsh effects of stage lighting. Speech tended toward the casual, even folksy, by those for whom "y'all" and "reckon" was ill befitting; occasional malapropisms and incongruous word usages were the result. Almanacs who hailed from suburban areas or cities in New England and New York sometimes consciously or unconsciously affected southern accents when singing; there was enough of a problem in this respect at one point that an inconclusive meeting was called to thrash the matter out.[41] Several in the group also were awed by Woody Guthrie's uninhibited sex life, mistakenly assuming in the process that liberation from Victorian morality ipso facto was a characteristic of working-class culture.

Woody, in fact, was admired for many reasons in addition to his obvious musical and songwriting talents. More than any of the other Almanacs, he embodied the prototype of the worker-poet to which the others aspired. He long since had proven his ability to become a successful entertainer in the commercial world, yet he remained totally committed to the people's cause; on several occasions he had walked out of well-paying jobs when faced with compromising his political and artistic integrity. Woody's knowledge of ballad and folk song forms was deeply ingrained; his refusal to depart very far from meaningful adaptations of these idioms served as a creative anchor and musical counterbalance to the clever but sometimes sophomoric and gimmicky lyrics of Mill Lampell and other Almanacs less well grounded in folk-styled expression. Above all, Woody had "been there;" he had spent most of his life among workers, dustbowlers, hoboes, and the rural peoples of America, and he was most suffused with their worldview and vernacular—or so most of the Almanacs believed. As a result, he was regarded by the others as a model to be emulated. He was, in effect, treated as someone unique and apart from the remaining members. For his part, Guthrie was sufficiently affected by the Almanac "proletarian" ethos to deliberately play down his early middle-class upbringing and stress his later years of poverty and cross-country ramblings.

In view of the Almanac tendency to adopt the presumed lifestyle of "the people," it is worth noting that working-class, even radical, audiences did not always appreciate the group's proletarian romanticism. Arthur Stern remembers one booking for a butchers' union local in Queens, Long Island, where a well-dressed audience threw crockery to drive the scruffy-looking Almanacs off the stage before the first number was over. Some Almanacs muttered about "getting back and singing for *real* working-class people again."[42] Other Almanacs tell of being surprised to learn from Detroit labor officials that union men and women shed their overalls and work clothes after hours and as a matter of course dressed up as neatly as possible when appearing in public. Even left-wing sympathizers were unimpressed with the Almanacs' cooperative philosophy when complete strangers and second-rate singers would show up at radical bookings as "the Almanac Singers" instead of Pete Seeger and Lee Hays. Incidents like these were infrequent, however, and didn't seem to influence the Almanac's lifestyle choices.

Blind romanticization of the real or imagined workers' lifestyle in some cases actually hampered the group's effective communication with the very people whom it sought to emulate. Folk singing was not an enormously popular idiom among union laborers, the urban "masses," or even many segments of the progressive movement itself in the early 1940s. The Almanacs had average voices and what for those days was a comparatively "rough" sound. In addition, their appeal was further diminished by the undisciplined character of much of their performance. Woody Guthrie was not far wrong when he facetiously remarked that the group was the only one to do its rehearsing onstage.[43]

Humorous but sometimes misplaced left-wing political cracks caused occasional embarrassment. By misreading and violating the expectations of their audiences in terms of appearance, idiosyncratic mannerisms, and erratic stage behavior, the Almanacs could only reduce the impact of their music and the frequent sociopolitical message it carried. After Pearl Harbor, when the group's base of appeal had broadened considerably, the liabilities of the members' casual "proletarian" lifestyle became even more apparent, and a number of "reorganization" meetings were held at sporadic intervals to try to realign the group with performance realities.[44]

SUCCESS AND CULTURE CONFLICT:
ALMANAC LATTER-DAY HISTORY

The Japanese attack on Pearl Harbor on December 7, 1941, clarified the Almanacs' political worldview considerably. Pearl Harbor assured American participation in World War II and once more firmly linked the goals of the communist movement with those of other progressive organizations and the greater American public. In doing so, it provided an all-encompassing, stable, and clearly identifiable ideological and cultural matrix within which the Almanacs could function. Between the invasion of Russia and the bombing of Pearl Harbor, the group had produced no songs of consequence on any topical subject relating to the European conflict, except Woody Guthrie's "Sinking of the Reuben James." Now, within ten weeks the Almanacs wrote most of their best-known antifascist compositions: "Round and Round Hitler's Grave," "Side by Side," Deliver the Goods," and "The Martins and the Coys." These new songs called for the complete commitment of the United States to all phases of the war effort and were in sharp contrast to the themes espoused in the earlier peace songs. Some lyrics emphasized the need for unity in the face of the Axis threat:

> It's gonna take everybody to win this war,
> The butcher, the baker, and the clerk in the store,
> The men who sail the ships and the men who run the trains,
> And the farmer raising wheat upon the Kansas plains. ("Deliver the Goods")

Others told of the sacrifices and additional efforts needed on the home front:

> Joe had gone to the fighting front and left his job behind.
> Now I must step into his place on the long assembly line.
> I said I'll learn to build a ship, I'll learn to build a plane.
> For the faster we speed our belt-line, girls, the quicker our boys return.
>   ("Belt-Line Girl")

A few miscellaneous verses hinted at past disagreements with U.S. government policies and personnel and self-consciously suggested a rapprochement:

> Now, Mr. President—
> We haven't always agreed in the past, I know,
> But that ain't at all important now.
> What is important is what we got to do,
> We got to lick Mr. Hitler, and until we do
> Other things can wait!
> In other words, first we got a skunk to skin! ("Dear Mr. President")

All of these war songs exhibited the enthusiasm, and certainly some the polemical tone, that had characterized the group's earlier work. "Round and Round Hitler's Grave," for example, was aptly described in an Almanac advertising brochure as a "gleeful dance of death."[45] Set to the tune of "Old Joe Clarke" and performed lustily with assorted whoops and yells and a great deal of spirit, it indeed sounded like the finale of the archetypal western with the cavalry rushing joyously in to the rescue, as it bragged:

> I wish I had a bushel, I wish I had a peck,
> I wish I had old Hitler with a rope around his neck.
> Round and round Hitler's grave, round and round we go.
> We're gonna lay that poor boy down, He won't get up no more.
> I'm a'going to Berlin, to Mr. Hitler's town;

I'm gonna take my forty-four and blow his playhouse down.
Mussolini won't last long; tell you the reason why.
We're gonna salt his beef and hang it up to dry.
I don't care which way we go, which way we go in
As long as the road we're traveling on leads into Berlin.

As before, many of these songs were composed collectively and subjected to group criticism; some verses and thematic concepts appeared
over and over again in different compositions in the manner of commonplace stanzas found in folk tradition. But on the whole, the hallmark of
the individual songwriter was stronger in the Almanac war lyrics than in
their earlier work, and the creative initiative less solidly grounded in the
rural folk song heritage of the past. One important reason for this was the
departure of Lee Hays. With Lee gone, the songwriting ideas of Lampell
and Seeger, who were less imbued with a profound knowledge of the folk
idiom, prevailed. As a result, later Almanac songs such as "The Martins
and the Coys" and "No More Business as Usual" tend to be either "cute"
or sloganeering.

From this point on, the story of the Almanac Singers is a narrative of
the contact and confrontation of the group's "proletarian" culture with
bourgeois society. For the war once again blurred the rigid lines separating capitalist and workers' culture as far as the communist movement was
concerned. Avenues previously closed to the Almanacs because of their
radical political outlook now opened up as establishment and far-left organizations made common cause in the struggle against fascism. It is no
wonder that the first few months after Pearl Harbor were the most successful in the group's history, not so much commercially but in the degree of media exposure. Besides the usual labor and progressive social
affairs, the Almanacs performed for numerous war effort causes, agencies,
and programs with more mainstream sponsorship. Examples include the
opening show in the *This Is War* radio series (carried by all four networks);
CBS's *We the People;* "The Treasury Hour," a U.S. Navy program; and various Office of War Information (OWI) broadcasts. The William Morris
booking agency expressed interest in representing the group, and Decca
Records offered a contract that was tentatively accepted. Bob Miller, Inc.,
a Tin Pan Alley music firm with sometime progressive sympathies, arranged to publish a folio of Almanac war songs,[46] and there even was talk
of a daily fifteen-minute CBS radio show featuring topical song compositions written by the group about the day's events. Friends in the commercial music world with left-wing views regularly hinted at ever-increas-
ing possibilities of bookings at large fees. Thus, by early 1942, the
Almanacs had won a limited entry into the bourgeois communications

media and seemed headed for success, if not stardom, in the ordinary capitalist music scene.

The Almanacs welcomed this sudden demand for their talents, but it posed serious ideological dilemmas that were never fully resolved. Cooperating with the media and commercial establishment in the entertainment and musical war efforts required an implicit curtailment of the expressions of the Almanacs' left-wing political worldview and bohemian lifestyle. The degree to which the group should permit censorship of its material, self-edit its own work, or otherwise compromise its values and songs for the sake of getting its antifascist and "win the war" messages to the people "through the System" was the subject of never-ending discussion among the members.

It manifested itself, for example, in the arguments about whether to change the name of the Almanac Singers, which took place at the beginning of 1942. At this time Alan Lomax, radio producer Nick Ray, and several Almanac members who were especially conscious of the expanding mass media opportunities urged the Almanacs to choose a new name. In the first place, they agreed, the Almanacs' name was bound up strongly with the *John Doe* album of polemical peace songs in the minds of many people, which, as time proved, was an embarrassing political liability. Second, the Almanac personnel, and to a lesser extent the sound, indeed had shifted drastically since the initial inception and early recordings of the group. Finally, Lomax in particular felt the need for a greater public identity of the Almanac membership with the native folk heritage. He wrote Woody Guthrie in January strongly encouraging the members to adopt a more "countrified" name and in the process to omit any immediate reference to the topicality of their songs. Lomax proposed, for instance, "The Headline Singers."[47] A concurrent debate was simmering about whether the group should form an overlapping musical organization incorporating the best-known and most popular progressive urban folk singers for the purpose of writing and performing topical compositions on current events for the mass media.

Both proposals came to naught. Several members felt a sentimental attachment to the Almanac name and, more important, regarded such ad hoc changes as subtle ideological sellouts to the capitalist socioeconomic world. Still, the refusal to make the practical concession of altering the group's nomenclature in the interests of political and commercial expediency, as encouraged by Lomax and others, cost the Almanacs dearly in the days to come. The debates continued all during the winter of 1942. Finally, a meeting of the Almanacs, the radio producer Nick Ray, and other prospective members of "The Headliners," including Richard Dyer-Bennet and Bart van der Schelling, a Spanish Civil War veteran, finally was held on May 12, 1942. For several reasons, not the least of which were inertia and unavailable radio outlets, the group never crystallized.[48]

This same ambivalence colored dealings with the bourgeois entertainment world. On the one hand, the Almanacs damned the show business idiom and establishment communications media. But they flirted with entertainment impresarios who beckoned with big-time bookings, suggestions of large fees, and promises to air the Almanacs' songs nationwide. Generally the Almanacs retained their distrust of bourgeois culture and were highly suspicious when well-meaning friends and colleagues talked glibly of commercial success on a grand scale. Mill Lampell, in particular, was the subject of much uneasiness, for he was just beginning a career as a radio scriptwriter and walked an exceedingly narrow tightrope between the Almanac proletarian and capitalist entertainment worlds. He had the most connections in the communications industry and secured nearly all of the few big commercial singing engagements the group got on its own. Yet he seemed apt to throw over the group and its "working-class" outlook at the least provocation. His fellow Almanacs admired and valued his talent, but they distrusted his loyalty to their ideological underpinnings.

The Almanacs' difficulty in reconciling their ideological roots and the capitalist "star" system is most clearly seen in the famous "Rainbow Room" episode, which took place in late winter 1942.[49] As a result of publicity the Almanacs received for appearing on the first *This Is War* radio show, they were invited to audition at this posh nightclub high above Rockefeller Center in New York. A successful audition guaranteed an opening into "the big time." The initial war songs performed were approved without incident, but trouble arose when some of the Radio City auditioners suggested the Almanacs don overalls, gunnysack dresses, farm hats, and sun bonnets to magnify the collective hillbilly yokel image. Feeling somewhat "put out" by this line of discussion, the members began improvising satiric new lines to Lead Belly's "New York City":

> At the Rainbow Room the soup's on to boil;
> They're stirring the salad with Standard Oil
> > In New York City, in New York City,
> > In New York City, boys, you really got to know your line.
> This Rainbow Room is up so high
> That John D.'s spirit comes drifting by
> It's sixty stories high, they say;
> It's a long way back to the U.S.A.
> > in New York City.

The agents representing the Rainbow Room and the William Morris organization thought the whole affair hilarious and were willing to hire the group, although they obviously still had some doubts about the long-range commercial feasibility of the Almanacs' material. The Almanacs were even more beset with indecision. Though the booking was theirs virtually for the asking, they hesitated. Ultimately, they declined.

At about this time, the first wave of anticommunist newspaper coverage attacking the group for its *John Doe* album and other alleged sins appeared in the New York press.[50] The attacks may have further influenced the decision of both parties not to consummate the arrangements; as it happened, soon afterward the William Morris Agency and Decca Records dropped their contract negotiations with the Almanacs. But as Pete Seeger, Bess Lomax Hawes, and others observed, neither side really thought seriously enough about the matter to try and work out the details of the booking. "We didn't think that we'd ever be allowed to sing the songs we wanted to sing," Seeger remembers.[51] For now anyway, in spite of occasional flirtations with the commercial entertainment world, the Almanacs clung to their "proletarian culture" existence and beliefs.

During these same months in early 1942 when the group was agonizing over whether and how much to collaborate with the bourgeois media, it continued as always to perform for labor and radical organizations, parties, and "cause" gatherings that hitherto had constituted the backbone of the Almanacs' audience. As a rule, there was no problem of compromising political expression for the sake of community censorship. But a minor crisis did arise soon after Pearl Harbor, when Earl Browder announced that the Communist Party henceforth would adhere to a "no-strike" pledge in the interests of fostering harmonious employer–employee relations during the war against fascism. For the second time in six months, a sizable portion of the Almanacs' repertoire had become politically obsolete; overtly militant class-conscious union songs like the following were now taboo:

Boss come up to me with a five-dollar bill,
Says "Get you some whiskey, boys, and drink your fill."
Get thee behind me, Satan, travel on down the line.
I am a union man, Gonna leave you behind. ("Get Thee Behind Me, Satan")

* * *

Suppose they're working you so hard it's just outrageous,
And they're paying you all starvation wages,
You go to the boss and the boss will yell
"Before I raise your pay I'll see you all in hell."
He's puffing a big cigar, looking mightly slick,
Thinks he's got your union licked,
Then he looks out the window and what does he see,
But a thousand pickets and they all agree—

> He's a bastard! Slavedriver!
> Unfair! Bet he beats his own wife! ("Talking Union")

The group had not yet written the bulk of its war songs and now was strapped for suitable material on labor themes. Ever attuned to the ridiculousness of blind adherence to the communist (or any political) line, Woody Guthrie jibed in a parody of his "Bad Reputation" song:

> I started out to sing a song
> To the entire population,
> But I ain't a-doing a thing tonight
> On account of this "new situation."[52]

In short order, however, the Almanacs composed new lyrics to complement the shifting war alignments, and subsequent labor songs deemphasized the class conflict and concentrated on the union contribution to the war effort and the recent cooperation with management:

> Me and my boss, we never could agree
> If a thing helped him then it didn't help me.
> But when a burglar tries to bust into your hourse,
> You stop fighting with the landlord and throw him out!

Some of these compositions, such as "UAW-CIO" and "Boomtown Bill," were especially good. They became familiar standards of the progressive labor movement or particular unions.

The group's topical lyrics met with widespread approval in the left-wing union and communist movements. Almanac war songs frequently were cited as models for "good" antifascist compositions that were needed to counteract or replace such superficial Tin Pan Alley products as "Slap That Jap," "This Is the Army, Mr. Jones," and "Rosie the Riveter."[53] The members' "Western Front" was well received when the demand for the opening of a second fighting theater became a staple cry of Russian sympathizers (and now there were many) after American entry into the war:

> I wrote a letter to Franklin D. (The time has come at last.)
> Said, ain't no sense waiting till '43! (The time has come at last.)
> Western Front! (Wait no longer!)
> The time has come at last!

Six of these various "win the war" efforts were released as *Dear Mr. President* (Keynote 111) in May 1942.

To be sure, some radicals still grumbled about the Almanacs' musical tastes or political positions. For example, the group's recent downplaying of the class conflict: "Most people are still singing 'Talking Union,'" one such person complained. "One would think you hadn't written anything since then. . . . Please don't slip to the point where your music will rank as mere entertainment like the Jack Benny program."[54] The Almanacs in truth were only following the trends of the communist movement and now were reaching a wider audience with their antifascist message than they ever had before. Even the Roosevelts indicated their approval of the Almanacs' war songs when Alan Lomax brought them to their attention.[55]

THE DECLINE OF THE ALMANAC SINGERS

At the UAW's huge "Conversion to War Production" rally held in Detroit's Cadillac Square in March 1942, the Almanacs (including Sis Cunningham and Charlie Polachek) performed to an enthusiastic audience and rousing success. Throughout spring 1942, a contingent of Almanacs had been touring several cities in the Midwest, performing for a variety of union and progressive organizations. Their success and the enthusiastic responses of some union officials prompted several of the Almanacs to consider moving to Detroit and starting another musical branch there, in yet another attempt to identify with the workers' culture that was so fundamental to the group's worldview. The largest number of union organizations in the country were concentrated in the Midwest in general and Detroit in particular, making the area especially attractive. Arthur Stern and other Almanacs regarded the Midwest as "the major domestic battlefront of the war."[56] At least one of the more left-leaning UAW officials, an education director, expressed some confidence that the members could be put on the union's payroll as morale-building and instructional entertainers. He and the Almanacs had optimistic visions of widespread dissemination of Almanac songs via songbooks, record albums, and union radio shows.

Coupled with these inducements were the problems the group faced in New York. Several periods of slack employment left the cooperative in a desperate financial position. In January, the Almanacs had been forced to move from their West 10th Street house to a smaller apartment complex on Sixth Avenue because they couldn't pay the rent. Only outside sources of funds such as Bess Lomax's library salary, Lampell's freelance journalism and scriptwriting, and Seeger and Guthrie's radio work kept the group going. Moreover, the Almanacs simply were becoming too unwieldy an aggregate. As many as ten or twelve members, part-time members, and hangers-on clamored to go on bookings and be included in the cooperative funding arrangements. Musically, it was difficult for so many people to blend well or interact suitably onstage. Creatively, the group was in the doldrums, having practically ceased to produce high-quality topical compositions. Petty frictions and personality squabbles again were taking their toll on the members' energy. Besides, the Almanacs were no longer a novelty in the New York area. By now they had appeared before virtually every radical, union, and "win the war" organization to which they had access. All things considered, a quartet consisting of Arthur Stern, Bess Lomax, Butch Hawes, and Charlie Polacheck decided to move to Detroit. In June 1942 they departed, leaving Sis Cunningham and Woody Guthrie behind to maintain the Almanac branch in New York.

Once in Detroit, the four encountered difficulties almost immediately. Bookings tentatively scheduled in advance with UAW administrative officials were not actually in place. Even more disconcerting was the news that under no circumstances could the Almanacs be put on the UAW payroll because of the vagaries of union politics and the more than faint smell of "red herring" associated with the group name. Yet once settled, the Detroit Almanacs had no trouble obtaining singing engagements from union and progressive gatherings on their own. Between June 10 and November 1, they fulfilled 107 different bookings, often several in one day; 68 of these were sponsored by labor organizations (37 by UAW locals), and the rest were divided between groups affiliated with the International Workers Order and various war relief, left-wing, and private social functions. They also appeared before audiences at the national conventions of the UAW in Chicago and the Rubber Workers in Akron. While money was never overflowing, the four at least were sufficiently well off to pay back debts owed by the Almanacs in New York.[57]

Musically, the Detroit Almanacs lacked the talents of the original Almanacs, but they worked hard to improve. Before long they developed an adequate performance savoir-faire; lengthy rehearsals and disciplined song arrangements became the rule rather than the exception. For their program, the Detroit Almanacs used the same types of material as their eastern brethren, except that at straight labor rallies or political meetings, the four rarely sang outright traditional folk material. They wrote a number of additional war songs, most with a union emphasis; the best was "UAW-CIO," composed by Butch Hawes.

Gradually a fundamental change took place in the songwriting philosophy of the Detroit Almanacs. Instead of creating lyrics preaching a "line" at workers, they tried to express the actual sentiments of workers themselves. The earlier Almanac worldview had never clearly distinguished between these two concepts; in fact, the agit-prop "message" song had dominated the group's compositions. Of the original Almanacs, only Woody Guthrie instinctively understood the difference, shaping his songs accordingly. Now the Detroit four turned from "what message must be given to workers" to "what are their needs, what are they complaining about, what are their wishes, what are the things they would like to see if they could." "Our highly politically-conscious ideas mean absolutely nothing unless they are cast in terms of these preceding questions," Arthur Stern wrote.[58]

The group thus sought to cast its "people's" songs in the context of human experience rather than propagandistic slogans. A well-known example of this new approach was "Slav Girl," composed in August 1942, about Ludmilla Pavilichenko, the famous Red Army woman sniper who reputedly killed three hundred Nazis by herself:

> "Slav girl, Slav girl, don't lie to me,
> Tell me where did you sleep last night?"
> "In the pines, in the pines where the sun never shines,
> I shivered the whole night through.
> My husband was a working man
> Killed a mile and a half from here.
> My bed is a pile of burnt black ash;
> My baby lay sleeping there.
> Last night in the woods I heard the roar
> Of soldiers marching by.
> The tree I'd cut fell across the road
> And I waited to watch three die."
> "Slav girl, Slav girl, where will you go?"
> "I'm going where the cold winds blow.
> In the pines, in the pines, where the sun never shines,
> I'll shiver the whole night through."[59]

As the dynamic initiative of the Almanac Singers passed to the Detroit branch, the collective activities of the eastern members declined. Pete Seeger entered the army in July, and with him went much of the musical soul of the Almanacs. Mill Lampell withdrew from all but sporadic work with the group as his radio script career took up more of his time; he, too, then went off to the army. Peter Hawes joined the Merchant Marine as a wireless operator soon after Pearl Harbor. Woody Guthrie began concentrating most of his efforts on finishing his autobiography, *Bound for Glory* (Dutton, 1943), and he no longer participated extensively. The others—Sis Cunningham and assorted folk singers on the Almanac periphery such as Cisco Houston, Sonny Terry and Brownie McGhee, a Russian folk song specialist named Harry Rhein, and now and then Guthrie and Lampell—struggled to keep the group's performing tradition alive, but the old spirit and most of the bookings were gone with the original personnel. In the late spring, the cooperative itself came to an end. Sis Cunningham and her husband Gordon Friesen handled remaining business affairs from their tiny apartment on Hudson Street. As it became apparent that the New York branch was all but moribund, the Detroit Almanacs pressed the Friesens ever more strongly to join them in the Midwest.

Eventually, though, the Detroit contingent experienced serious difficulties of its own. After the initial flush of activity, union bookings fell off markedly by the fall, again because the group was no longer a novelty. Left-wing sympathizers already had used the four in as many locals as they dared. Paradoxically, the radical press in Detroit gave the members almost no coverage. The Almanacs had to handle all of their own publicity—not their strong suit—in addition to booking performances. Butch Hawes and Bess Lomax fell in love at this point, and so went the group's "dialectical" activity.

Consequently, in the fall of 1942, the Detroit Almanacs ran into prolonged financial trouble. All four members took jobs in the war industries to supplement their incomes, for as Charlie Polacheck noted, work was extremely plentiful and there was no need to starve by singing.[60] Their plight reached the attention of the Communist Party in September, but like the UAW officials, party politicos were not willing to convert their applause into monetary support. A brief reprieve came when Mother Bloor, an old friend of Lee Hays and other original Almanacs, took the occasion of her birthday visit to Detroit to lecture local communist leaders on "how to handle people's artists of the republic." The result, as one of the Almanacs remarked, was that "for the next week every self-respecting goodguy [communist sympathizer] met us with a face redder than his politics."[61] A communist-backed hootenanny, held at one of the union halls, raised $120 to help offset the group's debt.

But bookings and earnings kept dropping. In late fall, Bess Lomax and Butch Hawes returned to New York to get married. Again, Arthur Stern, the group's leader, tried to persuade Sis Cunningham and Gordon Friesen to join the Detroit Almanacs. This time he succeeded, but not before the possibility arose that the Hawes arrival and the return of Lee Hays, coupled with Sis Cunningham's remaining in the East, might lead to the revival of the New York branch of the singers. Hays had smoothed out his differences with the remaining Almanacs some months before and taken over the negotiations of several bookings for the group after Mill Lampell entered the service. He and Sis Cunningham actually performed together on one occasion for CBS. With the Hawes' return, it seemed likely that similar engagements could be secured. Hays tried hard to dissuade the Friesens from moving to Detroit. He undoubtedly foresaw the end of the New York Almanacs, and he was right. The Friesens left New York in December 1942, effectively ending the career of the New York Almanacs.[62]

The Detroit Almanacs lasted scarcely much longer. Between November 1, 1942, and February 1, 1943, they performed only about twenty bookings, a far cry from their early days in the city when they would sing as many as five or six times a day. During this period, the group's extra energies were directed into war work. True to her own song, Sis Cunningham got a job as a "Belt-Line Girl," inspecting jackhammers as they came off the assembly line. One of the Detroit Almanacs' last appearances as a functioning unit was their second performance at Wayne State College (now University) on February 17, 1943, the only time they performed on a college campus.[63] By March, the Almanac Singers had ceased to exist.

Born in the cauldron of idealistic progressive ideology and social change prompted by extraordinary sociopolitical times—the heyday of the American communist movement, the rise of fascism, and the start of World War II—it is not surprising that the Almanac Singers' career was a brief roller-coaster ride of creativity, friction, and unstable financial status. Also not surprising is that their political values would develop, change, and be challenged and criticized throughout their existence. As performers, the Almanacs were subject to the same criticism as other outspoken commentators on public affairs, including attacks from the press in response to their left-wing and pro-union performances.

The first serious newspaper attacks occurred in the New York press during the last twelve months of the Almanacs' life.[64] One took place in February 1942, after the members had appeared on the opening *This Is War* radio show directed by Norman Corwin, condemning their prior peace stand. As a result the Almanacs were eliminated from further consideration in the scheduling of the remainder of the programs.[65] Early in January 1943, another wave of criticism was launched in the same newspapers because the Almanacs participated in a number of short-wave broadcasts for the Office of War Information. Nervous about any suggestion of communist connection, the OWI responded by destroying the recordings and dropping plans to use the Almanacs again. Ironically, the songs in question dealt only with innocuous union themes. These yellow-press attacks were supplemented in 1944, long after the group's demise, by the report of the House Un-American Activities Committee and thereafter by many conservative and right-wing organizations that repeatedly cited the group as communist entertainers.[66]

Polemics aside, that the Almanacs could be described as "communist entertainers" was pretty much the truth. But they did not consider their activities and messages rigidly bound by the limits of the communist movement. Nor did they engage in any kind of subversive activity or directly take orders from the Comintern, as implied by many of their reactionary critics. But the Almanacs' political ideology did complement the Stalinist worldview of the contemporary period, and the group itself contained actual party members as well as sympathizers and fellow travelers. Various of the singers sporadically met in a Marxist-Leninist discus-

sion group for the purpose of broadening their knowledge and clarifying
their thinking on political theory, current events, and left-wing culture.
Often these meetings focused on topics such as "How to Write a Good
Workers' Song" and were apt to degenerate into impromptu hootenannies as soon as one or two members picked up their instruments to illustrate their arguments. Party officials from the outside occasionally attended, but the communist leadership itself showed no particular interest
in assuming direct control of the group or its finances. "We were orphans,"
Pete Seeger recalls. "There was no [left-wing] organization that really
made themselves responsible for us."[67] In fact, the party's enthusiasm for
the Almanacs seemed to wane as the novelty of the group wore off.

One may raise the question to what extent the early "blacklist" articles
hurt the Almanacs or even caused the premature demise of the group.
Gordon Friesen later placed the blame for the decline of the singers almost entirely on the yellow-press attacks in 1942 and 1943.[68] With hindsight, the evidence suggests that the right-wing criticism only had the
effect of redirecting the Almanac Singers' activities back into the labor–
radical cultural channels from which they sprang and away from its war-
oriented performances. Otherwise, critical press attacks did not really affect the ability of the members to function and survive as a collective unit
with a progressive political agenda. Pete Seeger recognized as much when
he wrote Friesen from his Army base late in 1942:

> I felt a little disappointed, at first, to find that our album [*Dear Mr. President*]
> was spread here just by progressives. I'd like to feel that a portion of the rest
> of the country knew of us, too. But on second thought, it is only logical that
> our fame will be spread only by progressives, and I am proud to see how
> progressive influence reaches so many places.

Philosophical about the limits of left-wing groups to garner popular support, Seeger concluded, "The Almanacs will be known wherever there are
good union people, but not much farther, I guess."[69]

The anticommunist polemics of the New York newspapers may be considered an indirect reason for the decline of the group. For their eventual
demise, it is more accurate to blame the war (and coincidentally some
members' departure to join the armed services), the unwieldy size and
undisciplined character of the membership in New York beginning in the
fall of 1941, union political problems in Detroit, the never-ending series
of personality conflicts, and above all the communist movement's own
unwillingness to support the Almanacs in the pinch. This last was altogether typical of the party's attitude toward those folk singers who espoused its principles and spread the word with song.

What can be said about the Almanac Singers' attempts to forge a "proletarian" culture using the folk song idiom as the basis of its artistic ex-

pression? As far as its own members were concerned, the group actually did manage to create a semi-independent lifestyle and culture on a microcosmic scale. But the group lasted too short a time to have much effect on the labor–radical movement of the early 1940s, except those portions of it that already were predisposed to accept folk singers and the importance of the Lomax type of "people's" music. The war and the resulting collaboration of capitalist and communist worlds against Hitler sapped the "alternative" environment in which the Almanacs struggled to build their counterculture. It was no accident that the group coalesced during the Nazi–Soviet pact period when the political mood of the communist movement called for an independent aesthetic expression, and it was no coincidence that it folded during the war years when the artists of the Left were doing their utmost to cooperate with bourgeois society to defeat fascism.

Yet once the Axis powers had been smashed and the Grand Alliance of the fledgling United Nations fragmented in the cold war aftermath, the need for an "alternative" culture in the communist movement returned. At that time, a new organization came into being that attempted to revive and expand the prewar work of the Almanac Singers. That group was People's Songs, Inc.

NOTES

1. Lee Hays, untitled column on the Almanac Singers (Part I), *People's Songs* bulletin 3, no. 8 (September 1948): 9; R. Serge Denisoff "'Take It Easy, but Take It': The Almanac Singers," *Journal of American Folklore* 83 (1970): 21–32.

2. Interview with Millard Lampell, March 30, 1967.

3. David Dunaway, *How Can I Keep from Singing: Pete Seeger* (New York: McGraw-Hill, 1981), 82.

4. Millard Lampell, *Home before Morning* (unpublished autobiography).

5. Lee Hays, "On Almanacs" (Part II), *People's Songs* bulletin 3, no. 10 (November 1948): 9.

6. Lampell's *Home before Morning* contains a summary of the Almanacs' development.

7. Interview with Lee Hays, August 16, 1965.

8. Hays, "On Almanacs" (Part II); interview with Pete Seeger, April 9, 1968.

9. Hays, "On Almanacs" (Part II).

10. Don Russell, "They Sing the Hard Hitting Songs That Belong to America's Workers," *People's World* (August 8, 1941), 5.

11. Keynote 102. Because Bernay feared political repercussions, the labels of the records bore the imprint "Almanac Records." See Ronald D. Cohen and Dave Samuelson, *Songs for Political Action* (Bear Family Records, BCD 15720-JL, 1996), for a complete discography of Almanacs' recordings.

12. See, for example, Irving Howe and Lewis Coser, *The American Communist*

Party: A Critical History, 2d ed. (New York: Da Capo, 1974), 392; W. A. Swanberg, *Dreiser* (New York: Scribner, 1965), 470; and "OWI's Face Is Red as Its Own Hill Billies," New York *Daily News* (January 5, 1943); Robbie Lieberman, *"My Song Is My Weapon": People's Songs, American Communism, and the Politics of Culture, 1930–1950* (Urbana: Univesity of Illinois Press, 1989), 54; Maurice Isserman, *Which Side Were You On: The American Communist Party during the Second World War* (Middletown, Conn.: Wesleyan University Press, 1982), 55.

13. These accounts were described to me in interviews with former Almanac Singers. Archibald MacLeish, who supposedly was present, vehemently denied this comment ever took place in a letter to me, March1966.

14. Lee Hays, "Concludes Almanac History" (Part III), *People's Songs* 3, no. 11 (December 1948): 9; George Lewis, "America Is in Their Songs," *Daily Worker* (March 24, 1941), 7.

15. Data gathered from the Almanac papers of Millard Lampell, March 30, 1967. The group rejected the "paternalistic attitude" of the APM and preferred to maintain its independent left-wing existence as a matter of general principle.

16. See the review of this production by Ralph Warner entitled "'Sign of the Times' Spirited Labor Review" in the *Daily Worker* (May 17, 1941), 7. One of the Almanac Players was a young actress named Carol Channing.

17. Data on the various arrangements made in connection with the Almanacs' summer tour are from the Lampell interview and in part are corroborated by the Seeger interview.

18. Hays interview.

19. Seeger interview.

20. Seeger interview.

21. Interview with Walter Lowenfels, June 29, 1969.

22. For details of how the Almanacs acquired the word from the Washington Commonwealth Federation and introduced it into the vocabulary of the urban folk song revival, see Pete Seeger, "How Hootenanny Came to Be" ("Johnny Appleseed, Jr." column), *Sing Out!* 5, no. 4 (Autumn 1955): 32–33.

23. Seeger interview.

24. Hays interview. Lee remarked to this author that he had virtually "fanatic" ideas on the subject of cooperative living at this time.

25. Hays, "On Almanacs" (Part II); also Seeger interview. I have drawn from the typed minutes of the "Reorganization Meeting" of the Almanacs for April 12, 1942, in the possession of Pete Seeger, which provides a transcript of discussion by the group on the reallocation of Almanac business and music affairs to specific individuals in an attempt to improve efficient functioning.

26. Hays, untitled column (Part I).

27. Russell, "They Sing the Hard Hitting Songs."

28. Seeger interview.

29. Hays, untitled column (Part I).

30. "Hard Hitting Songs by Hard Hit People," *Clipper* 2, no. 7 (September 1941): 7.

31. "Hard Hitting Songs by Hard Hit People," 6.

32. Lillian Lowenfels, "One Million Americans Have Heard 'Almanacs,'" *Daily Worker* (September 2, 1941), 7.

33. Seeger interview.

34. Lowenfels, "One Million Americans Have Heard 'Almanacs.'"

35. Lewis, "America Is in Their Songs."

36. R. Serge Denisoff, *Great Day Coming; Folk Music and the American Left* (Urbana: University of Illinois Press, 1971).

37. Lowenfels, "One Million Americans Have Heard 'Almanacs.'"

38. Interview with Arthur Stern, December 28, 1965.

39. Pete Seeger, "Leadbelly" in *The Leadbelly Songbook: The Ballads, Blues, and Folksongs of Huddie Ledbetter,* ed. Moses Asch and Alan Lomax (New York: Oak, 1962), 7.

40. Stern interview, December 28, 1965.

41. Interview with Bess Lomax Hawes, December 4, 1967.

42. Stern interview; also interview with Gordon Friesen, July 28, 1965.

43. Seeger interview. Also see Pete's comment to this effect in the liner notes to his Columbia album *Waist Deep in the Big Muddy and Other Love Songs* (CL2705).

44. For a detailed account of one of these discussions, see notes for the "Reorganization Meeting" of April 12, 1942, previously cited.

45. Typed "List of Available Publications by the Almanac Singers" (Detroit, 1942), 3. Copy in the possession of Pete Seeger.

46. This was *Songs of the Almanac Singers* (New York, 1942).

47. Letter from Alan Lomax to Woody Guthrie, January 21, 1942; letter in the possession of Marjorie Guthrie estate.

48. This group should not be confused with another of the same name organized by Woody Guthrie in the fall of the same year. Members included himself, Sonny Terry, Brownie McGhee, and Lead Belly, but the four never performed together on a regular basis or "sang the headlines" in any conscious manner. Guthrie's intention apparently was to secure more work for all performers involved through collective booking efforts.

49. The account of what transpired as presented here is guided by the recollections of Pete Seeger and Bess Lomax Hawes in their respective interviews. Woody Guthrie presents a somewhat fanciful re-creation of the episode in *Bound for Glory* (New York: Dutton, 1943), 387–95, which omits the presence of the rest of the group. See Pete Seeger's explanatory note in his letter to the editor, *The Broadside* (Boston) 3, no. 11 (July 22, 1964), [15].

50. "Singers on New Morale Show Also Warbled for Communists," *New York World–Telegram* (February 17, 1942), 3; Robert J. Stephens, "'Peace' Choir Changes Tune," *New York Post* (February 17, 1942), 1.

51. Seeger interview.

52. Bess Lomax Hawes interview.

53. See, for example, the letters to the editor by Elie Siegmeister and Earl Robinson captioned "Two Composers on War Songs" in the *New Masses* (July 7, 1942), 22.

54. Undated letter [1942] in the possession of Pete Seeger.

55. In a letter dated January 21, 1942, to Woody Guthrie, Lomax states he played several of the Almanac war songs for Eleanor Roosevelt: "She thought they were swell, and asked for copies of the [acetate] records" (letter in the possession of Marjorie Guthrie estate). In a mimeographed form letter sent out to

prospective bookers of the Almanacs in Detroit, Arthur Stern wrote, "Mrs. Roosevelt, who owns our records, has written saying that both she and the President enjoy them."

56. Letter from the Detroit Almanacs to the New York Almanacs, n.d. [summer, 1942], in the possession of Pete Seeger.

57. The information in this paragraph and much of the data provided on the group's activities in the Midwest relies on an invaluable third-person report written by Arthur Stern in November 1942, primarily for Pete Seeger's benefit, entitled "The Almanac Singers in Detroit." This typed manuscript is thirty-eight pages long (pp. 1–12 and Sections I–III are missing) and contains a detailed account of the members' work, bookings, and philosophical thought (as seen by Stern) during the first six months after the group's removal to Detroit. The original manuscript is in the possession of Pete Seeger.

58. Stern, "The Almanac Singers in Detroit," 26.

59. Taken from an undated letter [early fall 1942] by Arthur Stern to Pete Seeger. The song is a reworking of the traditional "In the Pines."

60. Interview with Charles Polacheck, July 19, 1967.

61. Intra-Almanac correspondence, n.d. [late September or early October 1942]; names of correspondents are withheld. The hootenanny in question was held on September 19.

62. Data in this paragraph were provided by Sis Cunningham and Gordon Friesen in an interview, February 9, 1968.

63. For coverage of the group's appearances at Wayne State University, see "Almanac Singers Appear Today," *Detroit Collegian* (February 17, 1943), 1. The *Collegian* reported the Almanacs' earlier visit to WSU in its issues for April 29 and May 1, 1942.

64. The principal 1943 article was Jess Stearn, "OWI Singers Change Their Political Tune," *New York World-Telegram* (January 4, 1943), 1, 9. The story was picked up and carried by many other newspapers.

65. See Gordon Friesen, "The Almanac Singers—End of the Road," *Broadside* (New York) 15 (November, 1962), [8–9].

66. HUAC's citation is found in *Special Committee on Un-American Activities,* House Report 1311 on the CIO Political Action Committee (March 29, 1944), 97. For samples of later attacks on the Almanacs by right-wing writers, see David A. Noebel, *Rhythm, Riots and Revolution* (Tulsa: University of Oklahoma Press, 1966); and Jere Real, "Folk Music and Red Tub-Thumpers," *American Opinion* 7 (December 1964): 21–22.

67. Seeger interview.

68. Friesen, "The Almanac Singers—End of the Road."

69. No date [late summer 1942]. Letter in possession of Pete Seeger.

8

People's Songs, Inc.:
Proletarian "Folk" Culture in Microcosm

Pete Seeger and Henry Wallace (two people in back row unidentified)

179

Not long after the close of World War II, People's Songs, Inc., was formed, envisioned as a logical extension of the mission of the Almanac Singers. Between the Almanacs' dissolution and V-J day, the war finally came to a close, ending a worldwide conflict that had challenged many Americans' beliefs about Soviet-style communism, class struggles, and the future role of socialism and capitalism in a democracy.

On December 31, 1945, thirty-odd left-wing folk singers, choral directors, and union education personnel gathered at Pete Seeger's Greenwich Village apartment to found an organization that would take up the challenge of "disseminating the songs of [the] people [which] truly express their lives, their struggles and their highest aspirations.[1] Ultimately, People's Songs, Inc., proved to be a singularly ambitious attempt to consciously utilize traditional forms and material for political and social purposes.

INTERIM: THE WAR YEARS

The Almanac Singers were in fact defunct by the end of 1942. Just one year earlier, on December 8, 1941, America had officially gone to war with the Axis governments, and the all-pervasive character of the struggle soon made itself felt in all parts of society. Artists in every field were called on to contribute to the fight. Political persuasions notwithstanding, Americans were now united in the fight against fascism.

For left-wing musicians, the overriding concern soon became a need to create suitable war songs and music compositions for use at rallies in the fields of war as well as on the home front. Tin Pan Alley ground out a raft of typical productions on the order of "Let's Remember Pearl Harbor," "Don't Sit under the Apple Tree," and "There's a Star-Spangled Banner Waving Somewhere," but mainstream composers frequently admitted that World War II lyrics and music hardly matched such classics as "The Battle Hymn of the Republic" and "Over There" from former national conflicts.[2] The focus of discussion shifted to arguing why such songs weren't being created in the contemporary period or, if they were, why they weren't being distributed, and how to rectify both deficiencies.

In May 1942, Samuel Sillen, an important *New Masses* art critic, launched a major theoretical discussion of these issues in the communist movement with an article entitled "Battle in Search of a Hymn."[3] He reviewed the war songs produced by American fighting men from the Revolution to the Civil War, concluding his analysis with the query "Why has the current conflict generated no comparable music of a high quality?" He alluded to some of the recent superficial creations of Tin Pan Alley and demanded, "We want songs, not corn." He went on to define what he thought were the criteria for war songs: "Songs that make us burn and hate the Fascist enemy. Songs that make us cheer the heroism of our armed forces. Songs of dignity and hope and courage. Fighting songs that rouse and rally. Songs that celebrate our great fighting allies."

In the following weeks, radical songwriters, among them Elie Siegmeister, Earl Robinson, and Millard Lampell, responded to Sillen's challenging critique. Siegmeister wrote that there were too few good poetic lyrics available for composers like himself to utilize: "The poems I have seen are either too abstract, subjective, or too full of generalities to make successful songs." Lampell took Sillen to task for failing to recognize that the media was under the rigid control of the bourgeoisie, which was only interested in "hits" and the accruing profits. "The song market in this country is about as open as the editorial page of the *Chicago Tribune*," he wrote. For his part, Robinson observed that Tin Pan Alley in itself was unlikely to produce the war songs that were needed, "because its writers have still not discovered that this is a people's war and that a fundamentally new approach [from the pop music of the past] is necessary." He agreed with Lampell that the only real hope for the type of songs Sillen called for in his *New Masses* article lay with the songwriters of the labor–progressive movement.

In their replies, however, all three correspondents urged Sillen and *New Masses* readers to consider the virtues of the American folk idiom as a source for aesthetically and politically satisfying war songs. "I wish [some of our poets] could listen to the simplicity and naturalness of folk singers like Woody Guthrie and Josh White," Siegmeister declared. Robinson wrote:

> A significant thing about these [progressive war songs] is the fact they are almost entirely based on tried and true Americana, the old folk songs our common people have been singing ever since they arrived here. And they are sung not with the syrupy sweetness of radio crooners, but with the deep honesty and simplicity of people who know what they are singing about.

Lampell asked, "What makes good songs?" and then answered: "folk music. The Spanish Loyalists sing folk songs. The Red Army is singing folk songs and so are the Chinese. Folk songs, songs in the people's language and in the people's tradition. Songs made up yesterday and this morning." And then he laid down a challenge: "It's about time for somebody to slap down the idea that folk music means archaic ballads and hill tunes. Folk music is a living art of working people writing about their own lives." [4]

These and other left-wing composers continued to hammer at the same theme throughout the remainder of the war. They were abetted by still other radicals like Samuel Putnam, who identified the collective character of folk expression with the antifascist coalition of the United Nations. In a column written for the *Daily Worker* late in 1942, Putnam commented on the resurgence of popularity of the square dance in American society: "As for the revival of the square dance here in New York, . . . it just strikes me that there may be a connection between this and the times in which we are living." Drawing on a popular source of "folk" wisdom, Putnam reminded his readers, "At a time like the present, when we must all hang together or hang separately, as Benjamin Franklin said . . . well I'm not sure, but maybe it's a little of that old cooperative good neighbor spirit of the frontier coming back again."[5] Thus, while left-wing commentators encouraged artists in every cultural area to express the ideology of the movement's war outlook in appropriate terms for themselves, they went out of their way to praise individuals who created militant art within the framework of American traditional aesthetic forms.

For their part, the Lomax folk singers did what they could wherever they were to foster a national, even international, fighting spirit and goodwill through the use of the folk idiom. The Almanacs broke up by the end of 1942, but their work was continued informally by a similar group in Washington, D.C., known as the Priority Ramblers, featuring Tom Glazer, Bernie Asbel, and Jackie Gibson, and by individual members who continued to perform and record as their war commitments permitted. For example, Pete Seeger, Woody Guthrie, and Tom Glazer joined with Cisco Houston, Burl Ives, and Josh White, forming an ad hoc group, "The Union Boys," to produce *Songs for Victory,* an album of folk-styled war songs composed by the Almanacs and others; White and Glazer collaborated on *Citizen C.I.O.,* a compilation of ballads for the home front emphasizing labor union, antiprejudice, and solidarity themes; and Seeger, Glazer, and Bess and Butch Hawes recorded *Songs of the Lincoln Battalion.*[6] All of these efforts and many others were released by those left-wing recording companies, Keynote and Asch-Stinson, that managed to survive the war rationing of shellac.[7]

A number of the songs heard at this time were more overtly pro-Soviet than anything hitherto recorded by the Lomax folk singers. The Golden Gate Quartet, for instance, sang "Stalin Wasn't Stallin' Any More," and Josh White crooned:

> Now once there was a little man sitting on a fence
> Thinking and a-thinking about the current events,
> And helping to win the war with his chin on his fist
> Trying to tell a Nazi from a Communist.
> He was trying to see the war from every point of view,
> 'Cause after all a Nazi is a "person," too
> —While the Soviet Union goes rolling along.[8]

Such compositions were to prove a heavy liability in the postwar McCarthy period, but viewed in the context of a time that emphasized American–Soviet cooperation in all phases of political, military, and cultural life, they could be considered practically patriotic. Other folk song activity centered around the doings of the Roosevelt administration itself. In these years, Josh White and Earl Robinson were frequent visitors at the White House. Richard Dyer-Bennet, Woody Guthrie, and Sonny Terry, along with Will Geer in an actor's role, participated in a "people's bandwagon" revue, which toured in twenty-four states in support of the president's 1944 reelection.[9] When Roosevelt died several months later, Tom Glazer recorded a memorial cantata-like album *The Ballad of Franklin D.,* and Earl Robinson's "Lonesome Train" was widely played on radio stations during the mourning period, especially at the time Roosevelt's body was put on a train and brought to Hyde Park, where he was buried.[10]

As always, behind much of such urban socially conscious folk song was Alan Lomax. Lomax and his sister Bess both worked for the Office of War Information (OWI) during the war. At every opportunity, they pushed for the inclusion of the traditional music idiom, both original as well as adapted forms in OWI's programs. Perhaps as much as a hundred or more hours of the OWI's programming featured the antifascist folk singing of Burl Ives, Pete Seeger, Woody Guthrie, and other Lomax musicians in addition to much native traditional music in many languages.[11] Lomax also collaborated with Svatava Jakobson, the Czech musicologist and folklorist, in the production of the OWI mimeographed book *Freedom Songs of the United Nations* (Washington, D.C.: Office of War Information, 1943), a vast compendium of texts, background information, and bibliographical references to the more "progressive" historic and contemporary war songs of the Allied countries. Jakobson and Lomax's wife Elizabeth wrote the scripts and arranged for the broadcasts of "The Martins and the Coys" and "The Old Chisholm Trail," two "win the war" radio shows built around folk themes. The former, for example, was set in West Virginia and told how the Martins and the Coys, decimated in numbers by generations of feuding, resolved their differences and went off together to fight the Nazis. The performers included Pete Seeger, Woody Guthrie, Burl Ives, Will Geer, Sonny Terry, Cisco Houston, the Coon Creek Girls, and Arthur Smith (a traditional fiddler) singing a mixture of folk and topical antifascist material composed in a folk style. The show was an ideal exemplification of the Lomax folk singers' worldview on how to build a contemporary sociopolitical statement on a nexus of American folk traditions. Unfortunately, the production was recorded only for the British Broadcasting Corporation in the British Isles and was never broadcast in the United States.[12]

Left-wing young people organized several of their own ways to support the war effort. One, the Victory Dance Committee (VDC), was a modern dance conglomerate that entertained at war relief rallies, USO benefits, and similar affairs. The VDC spawned Folksay, which began about 1942 as a square dance adjunct. Before long Folksay outgrew the VDC, separated from the larger organization, and afterward maintained an independent existence as the New York State Folk Dance Group for one year. Around 1944, Folksay affiliated with the American Youth for Democracy, a more broadly based successor to the Young Communist League formed during the preceding twelve months.[13] At its peak, Folksay numbered almost eighty members and was the only AYD branch that actually had to limit its intake of new people because of size. It performed at numerous canteens, Red Cross meetings, and other functions connected with the war effort, and its "dance-arounds"—evenings of folk dancing and singing—and social activities became the focal points for much of the recreational life of many radical teenagers for the remainder of the 1940s. The organization itself continued to prosper until after the Henry Wallace campaign of 1948, when left-wing groups in general entered into a period of decline.

Folksay's purpose was the promulgation of the "people's" democratic heritage through traditional song and dance expression coupled with political action. During the war its slogan was "Folk Culture—A Weapon for Victory!"[14] Union and progressive sentiments were worked into all aspects of the group's cultural program; even its square dance calls sometimes preached the "message":

> Circle left along with me,
> We'll all go join the AYD.
> Swing that gal, you get the blues
> Unless you've paid your union dues.[15]

Besides swinging its union maids, the members also performed a number of "folk plays" over the years which developed the same themes. The most notable, Irwin Silber's "Circle Left," later retitled "Hallelujah Chorus," was based on the most class-conscious songs and traditions of American folklore combined with the more militant portions of Carl Sandburg's *The People, Yes*.[16] The show was produced more than fifty times in the New York vicinity to a total of perhaps a hundred thousand people. Not content to restrict its proseletyzing efforts to performances, the group worked hard at political action, circulating petitions, picketing in the streets, lobbying on specific issues in Washington, and donating blood for servicemen at the front.

Compared to earlier and later periods, though, innovative uses of folk traditions in behalf of progressive causes were relatively sparse. Following the defeat of Nazi Germany, Norman Corwin and Alan Lomax did bring together several of the old Almanac Singers for a final chorus or two of "Round and Round Hitler's Grave" on CBS's historic "On a Note of Triumph,"[17] but otherwise the end of the war found the Left preoccupied with more pressing ideological matters than the political uses of traditional music. And the Lomax singers themselves had scattered across the globe in the armed services or in war relief work.

Once in a while, a few individuals with radical sympathies and a love of American folk music met and managed to talk about what they might do to rekindle interest in the value of traditional music for recruiting war weary citizens to the cause. Stationed at Saipan in the South Pacific, Pete Seeger met USO entertainer Betty Sanders, another activist with musical talent who went by the name "Boots" (Mario Casetta), and Felix Landau. Together they considered the problem. Meanwhile, in Philadelphia, Lee Hays mused with his friend Walter Lowenfels on the possibility of getting out a postwar *Workers Almanac* magazine of labor verse, folk songs, and topical commentary. Out of their continued passion for folk music, people's music, and the need for a progressive political agenda came the birth of People's Songs, Inc.

THE BEGINNINGS OF PEOPLE'S SONGS, INC.

People's Songs, Inc., was founded in an uncertain period in the political history of the American communist movement. During the war, Earl Browder had led the party toward a democratic political stance in support of its efforts to cooperate with capitalist institutions against Hitler and to consolidate its newly won prestige as a respectable national organization. Mention of revolution and class conflict all but disappeared in official communist circles. Under Browder's leadership, communists supported indefinite extension of the "no-strike" pledge in the postwar era, universal military training, and other "conservative" policies and programs. Considered obsolete, the party itself was dissolved in 1944. The Communist Political Association was constituted in its place, charged with educating the masses in socialist political thought but not in such a way as to compete with the established two-party system. The less sectarian character of the new organization did attract more adherents. But William Z. Foster, a few other old party hard-liners, and a number of the more militant younger radicals believed the class nature of the movement itself was being sacrificed by Browder and his followers in the interests of national legitimacy and the international rescue of the Soviet Union from the Nazis.

As the war drew to a close, cracks appeared in the Grand Alliance, and it soon became obvious that the Soviet Union, the United States, and Great Britain were experiencing serious disagreements. In July 1945, at a signal from the international communist movement,[18] Browder was unceremoniously dumped as leader of the American party, a position he had held for nearly fifteen years. He was succeeded by his longtime colleague, William Z. Foster. This change foreshadowed the shift in the outlook of the world communist movement. Its implacable opposition to capitalist political and economic institutions was restored, and its class-conscious character was once again emphasized. The party quickly replaced the Communist Political Association. While the paths of the United States and the Soviet Union separated inexorably as the cold war deepened, new party leaders harped relentlessly that the United States was well on the road to fascism. The communist movement's new directions were already being implemented as People's Songs began its existence, but their full implications for the new music organization were not immediately apparent to its founding members, nor would they be for many months.

People's Songs founders wanted to broaden the scope of a "people's" culture begun by the Almanac Singers and other folk performers in the prewar years and only slightly developed during the war. The Almanacs had managed to fuse a folk-cum-proletarian worldview and song production to an unusual degree. But they were limited in their success for a variety of reasons, not the least of which was that the membership was circumscribed by the limits of the lifestyle they pursued. They were too few in number, too brief in their existence, and had too little access to the "worker" audiences they wanted to reach.

Woody Guthrie put it succinctly when he wrote the communist columnist Mike Quin: "We're full of ideas as a dog full of ticks, but somehow or other there comes a time when we feel like the old capitalist system itself—able to produce, but not able to distribute."[19] Thus, initially People's Songs conceived of itself as a service organization "to create, promote and distribute songs of labor and the American people."[20] The preamble of the first issue of the *People's Songs* bulletin in February 1946 read:

> The people are on the march and must have songs to sing. Now, in 1946, the truth must reassert itself in many singing voices.
>
> There are thousands of unions, people's organizations, singers, and choruses who would gladly use more songs. There are many songwriters, amateur and professional, who are writing these songs.
>
> It is clear that there must be an organization to make and send songs of labor and the American people through the land.

To do this job, we have formed PEOPLE'S SONGS, INC.
We invite you to join us.

As a clearinghouse for progressive song activity, People's Songs was designed to "circumvent . . . the music monopoly of Broadway and Hollywood." Its ultimate goal, as Pete Seeger stated in *New Masses,* was "A singing labor movement. Every meeting . . . should start and end with a song."[21]

The touchstone of all musical expression, as before, was to be the folk song idiom. Alan Lomax wrote a form letter designed to acquaint potential sponsors with the organization:

> We have based our program largely in the rich and democratic traditions of American folk music. We feel that the whole American folk tradition is a progressive people's tradition. For that reason our comments, our new songs, our activities are, in great measure, rooted in the fertile soil of American folk music.[22]

People's Songs contained many non–folk song–oriented musicians from all parts of the jazz and popular music milieus, among them Harold Rome, Morris Goodson and Sonny Vale, Bob Russell, and E. Y. "Yip" Harburg. For as Pete Seeger observed, "While . . . there is a preponderance of folk material [in the group] we aim eventually to have People's Songs cover every kind of musical expression which can be of use to musical organizations: folk, jazz, popular, or serious cantatas for union choruses."[23] Many of the Lomax-oriented People's Songsters were less tolerant of non-folk-styled performances than Seeger. But there were enough talented, diverse musicians and musical approaches actively represented in the group that this broader worldview gradually came to be at least partially accepted.

The founding meeting of People's Songs included the collection of donations from personal funds, yielding $135 to launch the new organization. The group rented a small office on West 42nd Street in New York in conjunction with Stage for Action, a radical drama group with similar political and performance goals. They drew up incorporation papers, started a monthly bulletin, and solicited membership subscriptions. A separate booking agency, People's Artists, handled arrangements surrounding the personal appearances of the professional musicians in People's Songs. Operating expenses initially came from fund-raising hootenannies, booking fees, subscriptions and advertising in the bulletin, and later sales of *The People's Song Book.*[24] A national board of directors was elected, consisting of Pete Seeger, Lee Hays, Alan Lomax, Earl Robinson, Bess Hawes, Woody Guthrie, Felix Landau, Millard Lampell, and Walter Lowenfels, soon supplemented by Benjamin A. Botkin, Tom Glazer, Bill

Wolff, Svatava Jakobson, Waldemar Hille, and John Hammond Jr., and later by Leo Christiansens "Boots" Casetta, Paul Robeson, Irwin Silber, Betty Sanders, and Sonny Vale. Pete Seeger served as national director during the organization's entire three-year existence.

People's Songs' first year was a resounding success. At the end of October 1946, memberships totaled 1,506 from thirty-two states, the District of Columbia, and five foreign countries.[25] Branches sprouted in Los Angeles, Chicago, and eventually more than a dozen cities and on several college campuses.[26] The organization was solvent, though barely; its hootenannies attracted such crowds that they were moved successively from various private apartments, to larger auditoriums such as the old Irving Plaza, and finally to Town Hall. During the same year Alan Lomax organized the "Midnight Special" concert series at Town Hall, featuring well-known jazz and folk artists and drawing rave notices from the *New York Herald-Tribune* as well as the left-wing periodicals. *Time, Fortune,* the *Christian Science Monitor,* and the *New York Times* all gave People's Songs favorable publicity. At its annual ball, the New York Newspaper Guild honored the organization for its "notable songfests in a democratic key."[27] Mike Gold and various writers for the *Daily Worker, People's World,* and other communist press organs heaped much laudatory publicity on the group.[28] Without a doubt, the early days of People's Songs reflected a vital and dynamic new force on the progressive music front. Its members' enthusiastic and novel approach to publicizing contemporary sociopolitical issues in song attracted admirers well beyond the fringes of the organized Left.

Meanwhile, People's Songs continued to build a broad-based education program. Members published a series of articles, mimeographed booklets, and printed pamphlets on how to run hootenannies, set up booking agencies, establish People's Songs branches, use audiovisual equipment, and lead mass singing. The group issued a *People's Songs Wordbook* and laid plans for a full-scale *People's Song Book* containing texts, tunes, and brief historical notes to more than one hundred folk, union, freedom, and topical political songs. Several members, including Pete Seeger, participated in a conference on "Folklore in the Metropolis" in New York on May 4, 1946, along with such academic folklorists as Harold Thompson, Benjamin Botkin, Herbert Halpert, Ruth Rubin, and Svatava Jakobson.[29] Later, an entire course on the writing of people's songs was taught at the Marxist-oriented Jefferson School of Social Science by Waldemar Hille. The organization also maintained a "library" of folk, union, and political songs, numbering some ten to fifteen thousand pages, from which it drew source material for its education, amusement, and agit-prop needs.

Political action rather than simply entertainment remained People's Songs' ultimate purpose. Members sang on the picket lines of striking

Westinghouse workers in Pittsburgh and performed at street corner rallies to save the Office of Price Administration after its termination by
Congress. They joined the California housing caravan that traveled to the
State House in Sacramento to demand progressive housing legislation and
marched in the annual communist-organized May Day parade. Others
produced a film strip for the National Maritime Union and recorded an
album of election songs for the CIO's Political Action Committee. They
took their talents to wherever they were needed to spread the ideology
of "people's" culture. The organization's most intensive and prolonged
period of political agitation came in 1948 when it assumed musical responsibility for the Henry Wallace campaign.

Wherever possible, People's Songs tried to root its agit-prop work in
the more progressive segments of the labor movement. "The . . . job,"
Seeger wrote, "is to get as members all union educational directors in the
country who want to use songs in building their unions, all ordinary union
people who like to sing, all leaders of union choruses, IWO choruses,
etc."[30] People's Songs in fact often viewed its work in the context of labor agitation rather than "progressive entertainment." Bob Claiborne told
People's World. "It's not that I'm not progressive. . . . And it's not that I
don't always try to be entertaining . . . but I feel that the kind of work I
and other People's Songs members are doing is a direct organizing job."[31]

Accordingly, People's Songs leaders consulted with several education
directors of the CIO on how the organization could best serve labor's interests. One or two, notably Palmer Weber, even participated in the founding meeting of People's Songs and some of its early activities. In spite of
these efforts, the group made little headway with its programs among
trade union workers.

People's Songs was an attempt by some of the more politically inclined
Lomax folk singers and their colleagues to build a macrocosmic workers'
culture along the lines envisioned but never fulfilled by the Almanac Singers in the prewar years. Many of the basic premises and functions of both
groups were identical. Folk traditions were posited as the basic touchstone
of American heritage and therefore as the foundation for the "singing labor movement's" developing aesthetic expression. Philosophical antagonism toward the art and society of established U.S. political and social
institutions remained the same. Both organizations served agit-prop and
entertainment purposes in the communist movement and wherever else
they could gain a hearing. Both were faced with making repeated choices
between upholding their alternative ideology in pure form and collaborating to some degree with the media and other bourgeois institutions in
order to achieve more limited ends.

Yet there were important differences, too. The Almanac Singers were a
microcosm of activists who lived their political philosophy deliberately

and as fully as possible. They lived together communally and pooled their songwriting efforts collectively on a scale that obviously was impossible for People's Songs to duplicate precisely because of its macrocosmic character. People's Songs was more amorphous in its musical composition since it included popular, even classical, artists as well as folk singers and lyricists who performed and created in a folk style. It occupied an intermediate position between that of the Almanacs and the old Workers Music League as it incorporated both the Lomax and workers' chorus orientations to folk music and culture, though in most cases the Almanacs style and substance predominated. For example, the Los Angeles branch of People's Songs claimed a far greater proportion of Hollywood and show business artists and popular songwriters than the performers and other members grouped around the New York main office, and it was considerably more commercial in outlook. The San Francisco postwar radical folk song scene in this period was largely dominated by the California Labor School Chorus; in comparison, its eastern counterpart, the Jefferson Chorus, had relatively little influence on the directions taken by Manhattan People's Songsters.[32] The net result was that People's Songs' programs, organization, and musical approaches were too diverse to have much more than a very general unified alternative cultural theory and philosophical worldview. The life of the group as a whole, moreover, was too hectic to allow for much extended debate on political and music theory. In essence, the mostly nonanalytic and spontaneous character of People's Songs' activities reflected the personality of its driving force and spiritual leader, Pete Seeger. Like the Almanacs, People's Songs' leaders were definitely concerned that the organization maintain a firm progressive stance. But Seeger and others in the national leadership invariably preferred to take direct action on specific political and social issues rather than engage in prolonged discussion of abstract questions of the nature of working-class art and culture.

People's Songs debates in the bulletin and behind the scenes revolved mostly around tactical considerations of composition and performance and the appropriateness of various types of people's music in given situations. One running debate, for instance, concerned the advisability of performing and publicizing agit-prop songs where they were deemed to be lyrically or musically deficient. Lee Hays, Bob Claiborne, Irwin Silber, and Waldemar Hille usually took the position that if a text dealt with a timely subject and had the proper progressive slant, it should be disseminated immediately by People's Songs, despite its structural weaknesses; perhaps it could be revised or edited thereafter where possible.

Pete Seeger and Alan Lomax, on the other hand, generally held that a politically sound but artistically poor composition was of comparatively little value in persuading the uncommitted of the justice in the particular cause being advanced, or even in entertaining or reinforcing the views of already sympathetic listeners.[33] The degree to which People's Songs ought to adhere to the folk idiom in its songwriting activities was another issue continuously discussed. Alan Lomax and Woody Guthrie had little interest in or enthusiasm for songs that wandered too far from rural American traditional music patterns. Pete Seeger and Lee Hays strongly favored folk song style and form themselves, but they were more tolerant of other kinds of musical expression. Hays wrote: "Who am I, or who is anyone, to say that the music of the juke-box, the beetle organ, which the millions of Americans listen to . . . is trash?" He drew a parallel between classical and folk artists that others did not share: "I believe in creativeness and experiment, in Picasso as in Woody Guthrie, in Bach as in Pete Johnson, in Verdi as in Blitzstein. I believe in a people's music that will come from us all . . . from all those of good faith who believe in the people."[34]

A third argument took place over whether songs in other languages ought to be translated into English for performance purposes. Ruth Rubin opened the discussion in the pages of the *People's Songs* bulletin by opposing such activity on the grounds that too much of the sound, structure, and intent of the original lyrics were lost in the transpoeticization process. Responses from members divided almost evenly, but Ernie Lieberman summed up the case of those who advocated translations when he wrote:

> It is [the performer's] job to create the widest possible audience for the particular song, at the same time keeping the essential message intact. . . . It is equally, if not more, important . . . to have his audience completely understand what he is saying if his work is to be successful. . . . Poetical translations may have faults. . . . But I believe they are far more interesting to an audience than a strange language and can say much more.[35]

THE COLD WAR AND PEOPLE'S SONGS: EBB AND DECLINE OF THE ORGANIZATION

The year 1947 was a time of stymied expansion and increasing financial difficulty for People's Songs. Membership totals leveled out after reaching two thousand by January.[36] Thereafter, the initial wave of enthusiasm that greeted the group's appearance subsided as their message saturated the "progressive" community. People's Songs faced the need to build a more solid institutional structure if its work was to continue. Accordingly, during their second winter, the leadership proactively sought to strengthen the organization's operation and efficiency.

Their initial approach was to reshuffle personnel who oversaw the day-to-day activities of People's Songs. During most of the first year, this leadership consisted of Pete Seeger, Lee Hays, and other volunteers and part-time assistants, notably Alan Lomax, Felix Landau, Bernie Asbel, Bob Claiborne, Waldemar Hille, and Butch Hawes. Seeger, however, was away on tour much of the time, Hays proved a creative but erratic bureaucrat, and Lomax was too involved with other projects to be able to maintain his intimate association with the group's doings on a daily basis. The others helped out where they could, deciding policy, screening songs, editing the *People's Songs* bulletin, and handling booking arrangements. Yet at best the organization's affairs were managed chaotically. At the close of 1946, a more streamlined leadership structure began to emerge. Seeger continued as national director, but Hays was expelled by the board of directors from his position as executive secretary after a series of personality disagreements with the other officers. His duties were briefly taken over by Felix Landau and then on a more permanent basis by Irwin Silber in May 1947. Leonard Jacobson, described by one member of People's Songs' as a "borscht-belt booking agent," was brought in to handle the organization's performance engagements, both commercial and progressive, and Waldemar Hille was given full-time responsibility for editing the bulletin.

Beginning in the spring of 1947, People's Songs leaders attempted to build a more viable national People's Songs organizational structure. Up until this time the organization's branches around the country were a confederation of local groups using the same name. The ability of each chapter to function efficiently and successfully depended almost wholly on what resources in personnel, creative ideas, and funds existed in each city or region. Ties between individual branches and the National Office ranged from extremely weak to nonexistent. The New York headquarters occasionally arranged visits to local chapters by singers or representatives who were headed for that particular area anyway. But the national office was simply too strapped for manpower and money to be able to guide effectively the activities of branches outside Manhattan. There never was any intention that People's Songs' local chapters take orders directly from New York.

Some large organizations, like those in Los Angeles and Chicago, functioned well on their own; others depended largely on the efforts of one or two individual members in each city, such as Barbara Dane and Rolf Cahn in Detroit or Bryant French in Cleveland; and a number of chapters, like those in San Francisco and Boston, existed for a long time more on paper than in fact.

To shore up this haphazard national edifice a three-day convention of forty-five People's Songs delegates from nine cities and states, with about as many more outside observers, met at Chicago's Hull House in October.[37] The group of People's Songs leaders developed a national constitution, outlined the steps for new membership and subscription drives, discussed bookings and techniques of songwriting, and held a spectacular hootenanny before two thousand people at nearby Orchestra Hall. Alan Lomax lectured on folk music as the democratic heritage of the American people, and several local labor leaders participated in a panel on "Music in the Trade Unions." While Pete Seeger and others in the national leadership originally viewed the affair as a combination nationwide organizing convention, get-together of People's Songs activists, and progressive trade show, they have agreed in retrospect that the most meaningful long-term result was the meeting and interaction of branch members from different parts of the country on a personal level.[38]

Such bureaucratic renovations in and of themselves were fairly successful and People's Songs did function somewhat more efficiently thereafter. Pete Seeger, as always, was the group's dynamic spark, lending an air of charisma and creative imagination to every task he pursued. Leonard Jacobson had many connections in the left-wing and nonpolitical summer camps in the New York area and for a time managed to bring in a fairly sizable number of bookings for the singers affiliated with People's Songs. Under Waldemar Hille's editorship, the bulletin's finest issues were produced, containing, among other things, a host of important labor, topical, and traditional songs; historical and biographical articles on "people's" singers and lore; brief news and notes; book and record reviews; and a memorable monthly column written from Philadelphia by Lee Hays in his "expatriate" status. After the Chicago convention, across-the-board communication between People's Songs branches and the national office improved considerably; subsequent issues of the bulletin were full of news briefs and sometimes whole articles on the doings of local chapters.

In spite of these achievements, persistent financial troubles began to close in on the organization the same year, slowing down and eventually reversing its momentum. The membership growth rate held steady but did not increase significantly during the year. Irwin Silber and others charged with managing People's Songs business affairs simply did not have the necessary practical experience to run the organization on a sound economic basis.[39] The hootenannies sponsored by the group in the preceding twelve months had drawn well and in some cases brought in hundreds of dollars, but a more ambitious full-scale concert series of folk performers at Town Hall in 1947–48 was poorly promoted and proved financially unsuccessful; the failure of two of these evenings in particular, in March 1947, may be pinpointed as the trigger that launched the long-term fiscal crisis People's Songs faced for most of the rest of its existence.[40] As outside income slacked off and debts piled up, staff members began skipping part or all of their paychecks in an effort to keep its financial machinery oiled adequately; these "loans" were supposed to be paid back later, but in most cases never were. Small but numerous bills owed to printers, photographers, advertising agencies, and other services accumulated rapidly. Multiplication of these "hard" debts is what finally brought down the flimsy People's Songs economic structure in 1949.

Through one means or another, though, the organization managed to stave off disaster for nearly two years. Lomax was able to secure some funds for the group now and then through his own connections. Requests for personal loans of $100 and $200 were sent out to many individuals in April 1947, resulting in some contributions. Boni and Gaer, the publishers of *The People's Song Book,* advanced the group $1,500 in royalty funds, most of which was used to pay Waldemar Hille's salary to continue editing both the book and the bulletin on a full-time basis. One or two songfests, notably a "High Cost of Living" hootenanny in December 1947, brought in badly needed cash at critical moments, and the Los Angeles branch of People's Songs, the only chapter consistently able to raise money, sometimes sent modest donations to the national office.[41] The biggest single financial reprieve came during the national election campaign of 1948. People's Songs members performed on behalf of the Progressive Party, and the demand for People's Songs performers generated by the Henry Wallace campaign sustained the organization economically for most of the year.

Beyond financial difficulties, though, ever more fundamental shifts in the postwar social and political patterns of American society were beginning to impair People's Songs' ability to function. In the little more than two years since World War II had ended, the spirit of cooperation between the great powers of the United Nations had dissipated. The United States and the Soviet Union had become locked in a cold war. The international communist movement under Stalin's leadership assumed a militant and aggressive position on foreign policy and class struggles, just as the government and a large proportion of Americans began exhibiting sharply increased suspicion and distrust of the Soviet Union. In 1947 and 1948, the Truman administration expanded its attempts to contain the spread of international communism by initiating the Marshall Plan, sending aid to Greece and Turkey to prevent partisan takeovers in those countries, and instituting the Berlin airlift to forestall a Russian appropriation of West Berlin. On the home front, the public worried about the increasingly hostile relationship between the United States and the Soviet Union, but still favored a progressive domestic agenda, as witnessed by the unexpected election of Truman in 1948 after a sharp shift to the Left on domestic issues. At the same time, a distinctly conservative mistrust of left-wing activity was developing and was reflected in congressional activity. The Taft–

Hartley Act, greatly curtailing labor union power and communist activities, was passed by the Republican-controlled Eightieth Congress over the protests of President Truman and the labor movement. The Democratic administration itself launched loyalty investigations of thousands of its employees. Across the land the ominous clouds of McCarthyism began to gather force.[42]

In this growing atmosphere of fear and repression, People's Songs found itself the target of increasing harassment from right-wing critics. More and more, the People's Songsters confined their activities to the narrow confines of the Left. Broad-based exposure gradually became a thing of the past, giving way to gatherings attended by a very circumscribed group of supporters. As early as 1946, articles attacking the group as a communist front appeared in the *New York World-Telegram, New York Sun,* and other press organs. *Life* ran an exposé on Communist Party doings and criticized Earl Robinson's "Ballad for Americans" and other forms of "people's music" as examples of Red degeneracy.[43] The House Un-American Activities Committee accelerated its endless series of hearings on radical subversion in the United States and among its investigations looked into the alleged misdeeds of Paul Robeson and Hanns Eisler. Later the notorious Tenney Committee of California (ultimately disbanded because of its political excesses) would cite People's Songs repeatedly as an agency of the great Communist conspiracy.[44] In June 1948, Montreal (Canada) city police confiscated copies of *The People's Song Book* during the course of a raid on a number of Marxist and progressive bookshops, citing the famous Hayes–Robinson composition of "Joe Hill" that was often found in the books for sale. After the Henry Wallace campaign of 1948, the Brooklyn College chapter of People's Songs was barred from campus activity by conservative administrators fearful of its radical, agitating activities.[45]

To these and other similar attacks People's Songsters reacted as best they could: they issued statements countering untrue claims; they participated in counterdemonstrations, urging repeal of conservative legislation and the abolition of the House Un-American Activities Committee; they promoted the progressive agenda every chance they got. "We're scared," the editors of the bulletin wrote in December 1947, "and every day's paper makes us a little bit more scared. . . . We're scared as citizens of a country proud of its democratic heritage and as cultural workers who know that the arts can only flourish in an atmosphere of freedom."[46] The editorial went on to encourage all subscribers to write their congressmen to oppose domestic fascist actions and to protest the growing right-wing incursion on American civil liberties through musical performance and the composing of new songs. Music and texts of songs also were published in the bulletin ridiculing the right-wing anticommunist agenda.[47] At the national convention in Chicago, People's Songs delegates passed a resolution de-

ploring the attempt of the U.S. government, eventually successful, to de-
port Hanns Eisler as an undesirable alien because of his pro-communist
sympathies.[48] And in a joint statement to Premier Duplessis of Quebec,
who ordered the raid confiscating *The People's Song Book,* Pete Seeger, Irwin
Silber, and Waldemar Hille wrote:

> We are proud that our organization of American and Canadian singers,
> songwriters, composers, etc., carries on in the tradition of Joe Hill, America's
> greatest labor-song writer. As Joe Hill, through his songs and his organiz-
> ing, carried on the fight against the copper bosses and company thugs of his
> day, People's Songs continues that struggle against the labor-haters and
> Fascists of today.[49]

As the cold war deepened in 1947–48, People's Songs' ties with progressive and nonpolitical institutions outside the communist movement continued to diminish. In the first year of the organization's existence, a small
but not insignificant number of calls for the group's services had come in
from other CIO, even AFL, unions, especially those in the New York area.
While the presence of People's Songsters as entertainers and agit-prop
musicians at these affairs hardly pressaged the arrival of the "singing labor movement" envisioned by Seeger and his colleagues, in the beginning
there was some reason to believe that these footholds might be expanded
ultimately to the construction of the idealized workers' culture.

By now, though, union leadership throughout the country was beset by
the same conservative pressures affecting the rest of American society.
Anticommunist rumblings in the CIO, substantially present in the organization during the war, grew louder and in 1949 finally resulted in the
expulsion of a dozen radical unions from CIO membership. As a result,
People's Songs' tenuous contacts with the greater American labor movement began to completely disappear. Even left-wing unions, as Seeger
remarked, "felt they had to concentrate on porkchops to the exclusion of
songbooks and choruses."[50] Seeger described one incident typical of this
whole process:

> I went down to Washington a couple of times and saw [a union official] who
> was working . . . in the CIO. And he was friendly but wasn't committing
> himself. He wasn't going to give any money. I wanted his support to put
> out a songbook. He said, "Well, no, we're working on our own songbook."

Seeger ruefully notes that

> in other words, they didn't want any left-wingers putting out a CIO song-
> book. And when their CIO songbook came out, it didn't have anything
> which would have offended anybody who was against the cold war. . . . And

finally [the official] himself had to get out of the CIO. . . . It just got too Establishment.[51]

Likewise, Palmer Weber and other education directors in the CIO quietly dropped their participation in People's Songs activities. By the end of 1949, radical unions which retained their communist-dominated leadership, such as the United Electrical Workers (UEW), the Fur and Leather Workers, and the Mine, Mill, and Smelters' Union were the only groups with which People's Songs had regular contact.

Quite aside from the increasing Red hysteria nationally and in the CIO, there was another more fundamental reason that People's Songs was unsuccessful in firmly rooting its work in the greater American labor movement. Prior to World War II, rights to collective bargaining and the very existence of the CIO itself were at issue in most disputes between workers and management. Public attention during strikes centered primarily on the picket lines and rallies sponsored by union supporters rather than the final negotiations with company executives which resolved the struggles. Protest-oriented folk music and dramatic performances conducted by the forerunners of People's Songs, Stage for Action, and other left-wing agit-prop cultural organizations often were welcome and necessary adjuncts to the unions' efforts to recruit, entertain, and maintain the morale of their members. In contrast, by the close of the war the right of workers in heavy industry to unionize and the CIO's de jure existence had been well established, and the main arena of conflict between labor and management accordingly shifted from the picket line to the conference table. Corporate boardrooms just don't lend themselves to songs, skits, filmstrips, and other union cultural activity. Thus, People's Songs found itself with no meaningful raison d'être in an agit-prop labor capacity.

Moreover, even during the CIO's most militant days, relatively few workers attended union meetings, much less sang labor or topical songs, except during strikes; Pete Seeger's optimistic estimate is 3 percent.[52] These few provided little basis for the foundation of an antiestablishment proletarian culture in the general American labor movement. Finally, People's Songs material was largely unfamiliar to the masses of northern workers who comprised the bulk of the CIO's membership. The folk idiom that left-wing Lomax singers postulated as the basis of a labor-orchestrated artistic expression was alien to them. In fact, rank-and-file union demonstrators were just as apt to prefer picket line jingles set to pop tunes, or takeoffs on current novelty lyrics such as Bing Crosby's "Swingin' on a Star" which became "Swingin' on a Scab,"[53] as they were the traditionally styled compositions of People's Songsters. Many People's Songs artists argued that this was simply because workers seldom had the chance to hear American folk songs on the bourgeois-controlled media. But in spite of the flurry of propagandizing in the name of traditional music carried on by Pete Seeger and company, many of their trade union listeners obviously continued to favor pop, rhythm and blues, or country western songs to folk music. People's Songs made little headway with its programs among the larger American labor movement in substantial part because its basic ideological premises about the feasibility, if not the need, of creating a workers' alternative culture based in the folk idiom were wrong. However, it was many years before this fact became clear to a number of the organization's members.[54]

PEOPLE'S SONGS AND THE HENRY WALLACE CAMPAIGN

With all of its difficulties, People's Songs might well have collapsed by the middle of 1948 had it not been for the renewed demands for its services during the Henry Wallace campaign. By the end of 1947, liberals, progressives, and radicals of many varieties were thoroughly disillusioned with the Truman administration's domestic and foreign policies. Some actually feared an imminent fascist takeover of the American government and sought a new leader in the Roosevelt tradition who by his influence would reverse the conservative domestic legislative tide. Activists were eager to promote civil rights and "brotherhood of man" programs at home, and abroad, to stimulate a new spirit of international cooperation among all nations, but especially with the Soviet Union and other socialist countries. They found, in the campaign of Henry A. Wallace, the former New Deal secretary of agriculture and vice president of the United States during Roosevelt's third term, a politician whose principles and goals they could rally around, and with whom they believed the formation of a viable third party was possible.

Wallace's campaign generated tremendous excitement among the more radical supporters of the old Roosevelt coalition, since it was presumed that their candidate's strong performance in the election would presage a return to the welfare-state liberalism and freewheeling intellectual climate permeating the halcyon days of the New Deal. As many observers have noted, the Progressive Party cause frequently was promoted with all of the enthusiasm and zeal of an old-fashioned religious revival.[55] To be sure, its theology was secular instead of sacred, harping as it did on the "Century of the Common Man" rather than the Kingdom of God, and its spiritual leader was the mortal Henry Wallace, not Jesus Christ (though critics were not always sure that the former vice president himself clearly understood the difference). But the similarities were there, nonetheless.

Even its music took on a semireligious character, at least for its practitioners, for the hymns of the third party movement were true "people's music," cleansed of all the trivial sentiments and banal platitudes of past election campaign lyrics and stemming ultimately from the deepest well-springs of the American heritage. As far as People's Songs and the more radical Lomax folk singers were concerned, this style meant folk music.

Early in 1948, as it became apparent that Wallace indeed would run for president on the Progressive Party ticket, People's Songsters and other Wallace enthusiasts around the country began to compose songs for the coming campaign. Some of the very first of these came from the pen of Bryant French, Cleveland People's Songs director, and included the stirring "Battle Hymn of '48," which became the movement's anthem:

> There's a fresh breeze a-blowing all across this mighty land,
> And it sings of peace and progress and prosperity at hand
> With security and plenty for the people to command,
> For the People's march is on.
> Glory, glory, hallelujah, glory, glory hallelujah,
> Glory, glory, hallelujah, for the People's march is on.
> From the Bay of Massachusetts out into the Golden Gate
> Henry Wallace leads his army 'gainst destruction, fear, and hate,
> We Americans will save the precious land that we create,
> For the People's march is on.

Other Third Party songwriters, amateurs and professionals, soon chimed in with their compositions, and before long People's Songs in New York and Wallace headquarters were inundated with campaign songs, a great many of them written in a folk style. It took the persuasive powers of Alan Lomax, however, to sell the Wallace political strategists on the value of turning the Progressive Party campaign into a nationwide singing movement.

Lomax himself was one of the earliest and most ardent supporters of Henry Wallace. He had many connections in the latter's entourage, among them Lew Frank, Wallace's principal speechwriter and a young radical. The details have never been fully clear, but apparently Frank called Lomax and asked him to assume responsibility for the music arrangements of the campaign.[56] Persuaded that the time was ripe for a dynamic use of the folk idiom in an election drive, Lomax agreed. After some difficulties with the more recalcitrant of Wallace's political advisers, who were unable to see any value in extensive musical—especially folk song oriented—activity, he eventually hammered out a multifaceted program with the Progressive Party strategists. Its major points, as Lomax recalled later, were as follows:

1. An agreement in principle that there should be a song sung for every speech made.
2. The topical songs promulgated by the Wallace movement should basically conform to the Almanac [folk-styled] genre.
3. The distribution of a national song booklet of the Progressive Party so that people everywhere would have a common musical point of reference.
4. A song leader at every meeting.
5. Pete Seeger to accompany Wallace on his national tours and perform at all rallies.
6. People's Songs, Inc., to be commissioned to handle all the music arrangements, song distributions, and performance details of singers for the Progressive Party.[57]

An undated People's Songs mimeographed report, prepared subsequently by Irwin Silber, similarly identified its Wallace campaign objectives as (1) to make the Wallace campaign a singing campaign, (2) to promote songs as a means of communication, (3) to deepen the mass understanding of issues through songs with appropriate content matter, and (4) to build a permanent singing movement.

Following a series of meetings between Alan Lomax and third party officials, Wallace himself presented Irwin Silber and People's Songs with a check for $2,500 in the name of the Progressive Party. Half went to People's Songs to pay general expenses in connection with the fulfillment of the Lomax music program, and the rest was reserved as salary funds for Mario "Boots" Casetta, former director of the Los Angeles People's Songs chapter, for his work at Progressive Party headquarters under Lomax's general supervision, maintaining a People's Songs music desk.[58] Casetta's functions were to provide singers at Wallace meetings as needed, distribute songsheets and music booklets at third party rallies, handle tour arrangements for the various musicians campaigning around the country on Wallace's behalf, and otherwise oversee the direction of all music activity carried on in the name of the Progressive Party. The Wallace politicos, in hiring People's Songs' services, were according music, specifically that which was folk styled, much greater importance in the overall organizational scheme of its campaign than any other major election effort in American history before or since, perhaps excepting the "hard cider and log cabin" campaign of 1840.

Until the election in November, People's Songs devoted most of its energies to furthering the Wallace cause through song. Besides fulfilling the booking needs of the Progressive Party funneled to it by Lomax and Casetta at the Wallace headquarters, the organization also found itself besieged with calls independently for its services and singers. Irwin Silber later estimated that 50 percent of all People's Songs bookings during 1948 were connected in some way with Progressive Party activity; for a time, People's Songs was forced to hire a second booking agent to work alongside Leonard Jacobson to handle the additional paperwork necessitated by the organization's campaign activities. Two editions of *Songs for Wallace,* edited by Alan Lomax and E. Y. "Yip" Harburg (composer of the score for the film *The Wizard of Oz*), were produced, containing words and music to some two dozen Progressive Party songs. Numerous smaller leaflets and song brochures were distributed, and as the result of another Lomax effort late in the campaign, two paper records of people's songs espousing the Wallace candidacy were released, but they were recorded without musical accompaniment because of a concurrent musician's union strike.

Pete Seeger, Paul Robeson, Michael Loring, Earl Robinson, and Bernie Asbel toured for the new party in various parts of the nation. Seeger accompanied Wallace and his entourage on his tour into the "egg and tomato" portions of the deep South; in Winston-Salem, North Carolina, Pete silenced a hostile crowd of hecklers by converting the old spiritual "Farther along, we'll know all about it" to "Farther along, *they'll* know all about it" which was taken up and sung heartily by black and white Wallace supporters.[59]

The single most important occasion at which People's Songs functioned was the Progressive Party's nominating convention in Philadelphia during late July. The usual brass band was dispensed with, replaced by Pete Seeger's banjo and guitars of several other left-wing folk singers and musicians, among them Michael Loring, Laura Duncan, and Jenny Wells. They shared the stage with Paul Robeson and a chorus directed by Waldemar Hille performing more formal choral music. The convention floor rang out with a collection of songs composed by Wallace supporters in the past six months, including "I've Got a Ballot," "Great Day, the People Marching," "The Battle Hymn of '48," "Friendly Henry Wallace," "Passing Through," and a clever piece written by Ray Glaser and Bill Wolff of Los Angeles People's Songs, "The Same Merry Go-Round," which quickly became the convention's favorite:

> The donkey is tired and thin,
> The elephant thinks he'll move in.
> They yell and they fuss, but they ain't foolin us,
> 'Cause they're brothers right under the skin.
> It's the same, same merry-go-round,
> Which one will you ride this year?
> The donkey and elephant bob up and down,
> It's the same merry-go-round. (toot, toot)

The singing was wholehearted and the response enthusiastic. As a result, the Progressive Party, to its surprise, found it had obtained considerably more favorable publicity in the mass media than expected. Nearly every major press and radio account of the proceedings mentioned the music of the delegates and People's Songsters, usually with a mixture of astonishment and admiration. Elmer Davis, the veteran columnist, approached Pete Seeger after one performance saying, "Young man, that you singing all those songs? Congratulations—other two conventions coulda used you."[60] It is perhaps not a coincidence that Wallace's running mate, Glen Taylor, was a western singer and guitarist.

Wallace enjoyed People's Songster's music. In later years he recalled that it had been a favorite part of the Progressive Party campaign.[61] His own interest in traditional folk songs had been stimulated years earlier by the native Mariachi bands he heard during a trip to Mexico as vice president–elect in December 1940, to attend the inauguration of President Avila Camacho. Upon returning to the United States, he was able to persuade CBS to feature a regular radio program of Latin American popular music. Later Wallace invited Burl Ives and friends to the Wallace family apartment in the Wardman Park Hotel to sing folk songs. Thereafter, Wallace displayed continuing enthusiasm for the traditional music of the United States and other cultures. Though he had little or no direct contact with the People's Songs organization during the 1948 campaign, he was immensely fond of the songs the musicians produced in his behalf. Favorites included "I've Got a Ballot" and "Passing Through," which was yet another variation on the "witness to the great moments in history" theme so popular in American folk and topical music. "Passing Through" was written to a mountain tune by Dick Blakeslee, then a young student at the University of Chicago:

> I saw Adam leave the garden with an apple in his hand.
> I said, "Now you're out, what are you gonna do?"
> "Plant my crops and pray for rain. Maybe raise a little Cain.
> I've so little time and I'm just passing through."
> Passing through, passing through,
> Sometimes happy, sometimes blue,
> Glad that I ran into you.
> Tell the people that you saw me passing through.
> I saw Jesus on the cross on that hill called Calvary.
> "Do you hate mankind for what they done to you?"
> He said, "Talk of love, not hate. Things to do, it's getting late.
> I've so little time and I'm just passing through."
> I shivered next to Washington one night at Valley Forge.
> "Why do the soldiers freeze here like they do?"
> He said, "Men will suffer, fight, even die for what is right,

Even though they know they're only passing through."
I was at Franklin Roosevelt's side just a while before he died.
He said, "One world must come out of World War II.
Yankee, Russian, white or tan, Lord a man is just a man,
We're all brothers and we're only passing through."[62]

Election night found many of the People's Songsters at Progressive Party headquarters, singing with Wallace and his supporters. One verse created for the occasion went as follows:

Poor old Truman, feeling so sad,
Didn't have the votes that he thought he had.

Around midnight there was a quick substitution—Dewey's name for Truman's.

Throughout the 1948 Wallace campaign, People's Songs participants experienced a sense of urgency reflecting some members' fear that the campaign might well represent the Left's last opportunity to prevent the nation from drowning its progressive worldview of the New Deal era in a postwar groundswell of neofascism. This was the main reason Alan Lomax, and several of his singers, urged People's Songs to commit virtually its entire energies and creative resources to the Third Party movement. Irwin Silber and other leaders, however, expressed concern that such a commitment made too casually might result in the loss of People's Songs' separate identity. Accordingly, while the organization in fact did devote the greater part of its efforts to the Progressive Party cause during the year, they took deliberate care to see that the lines of jurisdiction and responsibility for all Wallace music activity were delineated in advance. For example, Boots Casetta's salary for staffing the music desk in Third Party headquarters was paid to him directly by People's Songs, not the Progressive Party, even though the funds ultimately derived from the party.[63] Such arrangements had the desired effect of maintaining the structural independence of People's Songs during its extensive involvement with the Wallace campaign. Independence notwithstanding, People's Songsters experienced an emotional let-down when the final vote tabulations were in. Wallace received slightly in excess of one million popular votes and none in the Electoral College, far below the optimistic estimates of five to ten million popular votes anticipated by his supporters.

In retrospect, it is apparent that the conclusion of the Progressive Party campaign really was the end for People's Songs, too. For all its success in promulgating a singing election drive that attracted national attention, People's Songs was no more solvent than it had been previously; now, too, the extra money pumped into People's Songs by innumerable Wallace committees and local Third Party groups for its singers and services was gone. Besides being spiritually exhausted, People's Songs leaders had to endure a large share of criticism from some of its own membership for lining up with such partisanship behind one candidate. They also inherited much of the stigma attached to the Wallace movement in the last days of the campaign because of the Progressive Party's increasingly obvious pro-communist management; this was the parting of the road for such singers as Tom Glazer and Josh White, who thereafter stuck to performing for routinely commercial and otherwise politically "safe" audiences. And except for a few radical unions, the organization's few toeholds in the CIO labor movement were long gone; most of the CIO structure wound up endorsing Truman anyway.

In spite of these difficulties, People's Songs gave no thought whatever to folding up its own activities once the Wallace campaign drew to a close. Instead, it tried to regroup its forces and plan its future course of action. The lead story of the November 1948 edition of the bulletin editorialized:

> The votes have been counted and the machine politicians have put away the flags and bunting for another four years.
>
> But the issues which made 1948 a crucial year will not wait four years. Knowing that our songs and singing are not an end in themselves, we of People's Songs must ask ourselves WHERE TO? WHAT NEXT? What shall we be singing in the days to come?
>
> . . . We believe . . . that the American people need People's Songs more than ever before. Yes, the militant labor songs, and all good songs which tell the people's story: love songs, lonesome blues, square dance hollers, and hymns of brotherhood.[64]

At their national board meeting in December, People's Songs directors reviewed the status of the organization and outlined a varied program of activities for the coming year. A couple of examples illustrate the ambitious and optimistic tone of the meeting: (1) conduct a two-week summer workshop for People's Songs leaders, and (2) revamp the bulletin's format and reader appeal under the new editorship of Boots Casetta. The directors' hopeful conclusion: "People's Songs is today at a higher rate of productivity and exercises a greater influence in the country than ever before"[65]

As always, finances remained the chief problem and at this point assumed staggering proportions. At the close of 1948, People's Songs owed more than nine thousand dollars in back debts, about three thousand to printers and various commercial concerns, five thousand in salaries to its own former and present employees, and fifteen hundred in personal loans.[66] At critical points in the past, leaders had dealt with People's

Songs' shaky finances by holding special fund-raising projects; on one occasion, a small gathering of thirty people brought together to hear Paul Robeson and Earl Robinson at a wealthy Park Avenue residence in New York pledged two thousand dollars to People's Songs in less than a half-hour.[67] Yet these events never brought in enough money to stem the outwashing tide, and the "hard" debts owed to outside establishments continued to mount precariously. In early 1949, People's Songsters finally decided to go for broke on a lavish concert at Carnegie Hall, in a risky effort to raise enough money to clear away the accumulated debts of People's Songs once and for all. A host of comparatively well-known popular and folk artists, including Artie Shaw, Pee Wee Russell, Yma Sumac, Pete Seeger, and Oscar Brand agreed to appear on the program entitled "New York: A Musical Tapestry." William Gailmor, formerly a key Wallace aide, served as master of ceremonies. At the suggestion of Alan Lomax, several professional fund-raisers were brought in to help with the proceedings. The concert was held on March 4, a Monday night, and attracted an audience of over two thousand. Unfortunately, the last several hundred seats, which would have netted People's Songs their profit, were never sold and the attempts at securing additional pledges and cash donations for the organization in the middle of the show failed abysmally.[68] People's Songs did not even make expenses on the funds it took in, much less significantly reduce its outstanding debts.

A few days afterward, on March 11, 1949, the national board of directors met to consider the disastrous financial picture. Even though membership and subscription lists were at their peak, the organization's only prospect appeared to be to sink further into debt. The directors thus informally declared People's Songs, Inc., bankrupt, and disbanded the New York main office. Their official statement was published the same month in a truncated last issue of the *People's Songs* bulletin:

> This was to have been a gala Third Anniversary issue of the *People's Songs* bulletin, full of songs, articles, advertising, and big plans for the future. As it is, these plans have been filed away, and Volume 4, Number 1 is the final issue. The national office has been forced to close its doors for lack of funds.
>
> Obviously, the work begun by People's Songs will continue, for, more than ever, America needs the singers, musicians, and composers who have said that they know which side they are on. . . . The American people, along with the people of the world, have a fight on their hands for peace, democracy, and security, and the members of People's Songs, we know, will be in the thick of this fight.

Ironically, a flattering full page article on People's Songs published about the same time in the *Worker Sunday Magazine* as a third-birthday tribute instead became an unwitting obituary for the organization.[69]

As the national board of directors noted in their last proclamation, however, in the face of this momentary defeat the struggle to establish a people's culture was by no means over. Even as People's Songs was dissolving, plans were being laid for the creation of a new organization that would continue its work along similar lines. Taking its name from the organization's booking agency, the succeeding music group was entitled People's Artists, and its existence spanned the remaining years of the Old Left.

PEOPLE'S SONGS, INC., AND THE COMMUNIST PARTY

Was People Songs, Inc., really a subunit of the American Communist Party? At the risk of begging the question, it is fair to say no. But there is no doubt that the goals and even the identity of People's Songs, and later People's Artists, were substantially influenced by the worldview of the Communist Party in the postwar era. And there were many overlaps between the two organizations in personnel and policies. One of the party members was Irwin Silber, who provided most of the following descriptive information and whose willing candor about these matters is gratefully acknowledged.[70]

Perhaps the most salient point about the relationship between People's Songs and the Communist Party is that while there were folk singers and others deeply interested in folklore who were members of the Communist Party, the party generally did not take any direct organizational interest in folk traditions or in those members primarily concerned with them. Silber observes: "Now one would have the impression that the Communist Party sat around and figured what to do with folk music. Bullshit! The Communist Party didn't know what to do with folk music." On the contrary, Silber complains:

> Anything they [the leadership and most party members] did consisted of a series of reactions to it, to the extent that they even thought about it. "Yes, let's have a folk singer at our meeting. That's what those people over there do. And it's somehow peripheral, but they're interested in it and they're party members, so let them do it." And from time to time, they would say, "Well, OK, what are you up to?" And somebody would come around and we'd tell him, and that was the extent of it. There was practically no attempt at trying to give direction, particularly, in our field of work.

On the other hand, those few members of People's Songs and People's Artists who were especially concerned with the cultural implications of folk music and other "people's" traditions did organize among themselves and in time came to constitute an independent "club" within the Communist Party. (The term *cell* was not used in the American movement after the 1920s.) It was in this small unit at the lowest level in the party hierarchy that specific attention was given to the ideological direction of People's Songs and People's Artists. Silber explains how party influence filtered down:

> Although a number of us in the leadership of People's Songs and People's Artists were members of the Communist Party, the Party itself played almost no role in determining [PS/PA] policies and activities. We [in the] "folk music club" would frequently hold discussions about the overall direction of the developing folk revival and the role of People's Songs and People's Artists in it. But the decision-making process in both of these organizations was vested completely and solely with members, including both communists and noncommunists.[71]

The Party's Folk Music Club was formed in the late 1940s as one of several subdivisions of the Music Section of the Communist Party.[72] The Music Section, along with many other branches of the Party's Cultural Division, had existed as a special wing of the Industrial Division prior to World War II. Both were dissolved during Browder's Communist Political Association era, only to be reconstituted in 1947 after Browder's expulsion. At this time, musicians with common interests were grouped together as much as possible in "clubs" according to their interests. Among these were some individuals who were particularly interested in promoting their ideology through an identification with traditional music and the folk idiom.

The Folk Music Club numbered perhaps as many as twenty members during the People's Songs era (1946–49) and thereafter shrank to ten or twelve in the early years of People's Artists (1950–52).[73] In 1952, the Folk Music Club and most of the Cultural Division were dismantled when the Party sent some of the leadership underground at the height of the McCarthy era. The Cultural Division was restored in 1955, but the Folk Music Club never reappeared, principally because too few of its former members still remained in the party.

In theory, like other rank-and-file units of the Party, the Folk Music Club was supposed to meet once a week. At their meetings, the members debated Marxism, current events, political theory, racism, social trends, and art aesthetics, all of which had little to do with folk music directly. But in the process, as Silber observes, they tried to define their communist outlook as it related to People's Songster's music composition and performance. Nevertheless, as the following conversation makes clear, the Communist Party Folk Music Club did not directly plan the policies of either People's Songs or People's Artists, nor did it ever try to·

SILBER: The Communist Party club did not go into any great detail about how People's Artists or People's Songs should be run. That would not have been appropriate. And we made it very clear that if it was a matter of [the] specific policy of People's Songs, that was for People's Songs to decide. If we simply imposed our will because there might have been some key people in the organization responsive to Communist Party discipline . . . this would be a mistake. We should not get that specific. In other words, in the Communist Party club you should discuss the general [ideological] direction of the organization—a discussion which the organization itself might not even have. But . . . the Executive Committee of People's Artists would meet and decide what the Policy of People's Artists was. No Communist Party club would decide that.

REUSS: Well, for example, what about [when] People's Songs would come out strongly against the [anticommunist] regime in Greece or against the Marshall Plan?

SILBER: That was a People's Songs decision, not the Communist Party's. Now that might have been Communist Party policy and individual people would say, "yes, this is what we want," but it was never discussed in the Communist Party club—"Now we'll try to get People's Songs to do this." It just didn't work that way. . . . There was no need for it . . . because whether the other people involved were members of the party or not, there was a general mutuality of political outlook, . . . which is much more important than the fact that some of them were members of the party and some weren't. . . . I think if we had wanted to, we could have [arbitrarily decided People's Songs' policy]. There were enough of us in key positions to decide any way we wanted to. But its almost like wearing two hats. The very same people might call two different meetings and they would discuss [matters] two different ways. And it was not as if the party club or the party on any level really figured out [People's Songs'] problems.

In many cases, moreover, substantial disagreement persisted between members of the Communist Folk Music Club over the specifics of ideology and the directions certain programs should take; final conclusions often eluded them.

While those in the party club worked to shape a common radical sociopolitical outlook that they felt appropriate for their work in People's Songs and People's Artists, their efforts were mostly ignored by the rest of the communist superstructure. For one thing, the party itself never contributed any money to either folk song organization, nor was this for want of trying by some People's Songs individuals during one of the recurrent financial crises. Irwin Silber approached officials in the upper echelons of the communist hierarchy about securing funds for the group and was turned down flat.[74] In January 1946, Pete Seeger inundated a representative of the Party's Cultural Section with suggestions for building the new people's culture envisioned by the recently organized People's Songs founders; the startled and embarrassed response was "Sure, fine, great idea, put us on your mailing list."

Occasionally the party bureaucracy exhibited some interest in or concern about the work of People's Songs and People's Artists and the proselytizing activities of members and clubs. More often than not, these simply amounted to petty interference and "butting in." On one occasion during the People's Artists period, Betty Sanders, a member of the Party Folk Music Club, suggested that the songs chosen to appear in *Lift Every Voice* (*The Second People's Song Book*) be shown in advance to V. J. Jerome, the Communist Party's spokesman for cultural affairs on the National Committee. Jerome personally was a mild-mannered and likable individual, fond of folk songs and intimately familiar with the culture and traditions of East European Jews, of which he was a product; yet over the years in his role as the American party's ideological overseer on cultural matters, he proved as inflexible and rigidly dogmatic on questions of doctrine as anyone in the communist movement. When Silber showed him the musical selections for *Lift Every Voice,* his only comment was to inquire why the book contained two Israeli songs but only one Soviet song. The reason was pure coincidence, but Jerome indicated his displeasure, requesting that the balance be redressed. Silber and Sanders reluctantly reviewed space, topical considerations, and other factors, and they notified Jerome that to include a second Russian song, Woody Guthrie's "Roll On, Columbia" would have to be deleted. Jerome's reply was "It's not important. Take it out." It was.[75]

Incidents like this occurred frequently throughout the existence of the Old Left. As many historians and participants in the communist movement have observed, party politicos generally maintained minimal rapport with the writers, artists, and other cultural workers under their jurisdiction and often failed to comprehend their artistic problems and individualist natures. As a rule, there was an absolute minimum of bureaucratic concern with purely aesthetic matters. Silber remarks that most of the time it was a case of "The party stands for this. Now what can you do to influence other people in your field in relation to this political program."

Paradoxically, the top communist leadership exhibited an almost total lack of confidence in the ability of its cultural workers to express left-wing ideology in their work independent of strict regimentation. This was most clearly demonstrated in 1946 when *New Masses* published an article by

Albert Maltz entitled "What Shall We Ask of Writers." One of the better writers attached to the movement in the 1930s, Maltz mildly suggested that "a literary work must be judged on its artistic merits rather than on its ideology," and authors by "their work, *not* by the committees they join."[76] Such statements were too much for the party leadership. Maltz was subjected to an avalanche of hysterical criticism and forced to recant in the most humiliating terms.[77] Similarly, Silber recalls:

> I was a delegate to the National Convention of the Communist Party in 1957 after [the party had fragmented and divided bitterly following the famous Khrushchev de-Stalinization speech and the Soviet suppression of the Hungarian revolt]. And I served on a committee [that was] given the responsibility of drafting a resolution dealing with art and culture. And some guy from the National Committee was in charge of it.
>
> He was terrified when in the course of the discussion we talked about announcing the need [for] artists to experiment in new forms and new ideas, and so on. He said, "We don't want all this experimenting going on. . . . That's not discipline. That just opens the door to all kinds of crazy things. It's a very dangerous concept you're putting forward there." We had a big battle about it.

But perhaps Woody Guthrie best underlined the absurdity if not the dangers of such monolithic and dogmatic bureaucratic stances. Shortly after Browder's expulsion from the party in 1946, Guthrie was scheduled to appear before a communist gathering. As he got up to sing, a party functionary cautioned him, "Don't say anything about Browder. He's a diversionist!" "What's wrong with a little diversion?" Woody shot back.[78] It was because of such "political unreliability" that Guthrie's wartime application for membership in the Communist Party was never accepted.[79]

While leaders like William Z. Foster paid lip service to the people's historic art forms, including folklore, the Communist Party hierarchy generally was more concerned with upholding orthodoxy and discipline in its cultural ranks than debating artistic questions and programs with its members, party folk singers included. Accordingly, the prewar Almanac Singers and postwar People's Songs and People's Artists organizations at best commanded only the moral support of the official communist leadership and at worst (which was often) its disdainful neglect.[80]

Ironically, too, many radicals failed to take these organizations as seriously as they might have because of their own unconscious duality of mind with regard to their personal revolutionary commitments. For unlike most of the Old Left's cultural workers, the more politically conscious urban radical folk singers in fact occupied a fairly unique position within the movement after 1940 because of their relative lack of contact with capitalist artistic institutions, in substantial part through choice. Though there were some exceptions, most ardent left-wing performers and writers who were affiliated with the Almanac Singers, People's Songs, and People's Artists possessed an in-depth commitment to the projected working-class "folk" arts, which also carried with it an implicit refusal to participate extensively in the cultural activities of the aristocratic or commercial establishments. This ideal was waived to some degree during periods of comparative cooperation between communists and bourgeois governments, principally during World War II. In theory at least, it was generally believed that one either totally dedicated his energies to the workers, the unions, and "the people," or, by default, one sided with the class elitists who exploited the masses out of their own self-interests. On the whole, few of the more politically conscious folk singers of the Old Left believed that true "people's artists" could be both repeatedly successful commercially and simultaneously loyal to the class struggle. Those like Burl Ives and the Weavers, who on different occasions tried to maintain a foot in each camp, almost inevitably came to be viewed in the end as having "sold out" or otherwise compromised their personal integrity. Of this dilemma and his early days in the movement, Pete Seeger recalls:

> I remember being continually intrigued by the problem of how a person is going to be an artist and make a living at the same time. Do you teach and then be an artist on the side? Do you work in a factory and be an artist on the side? Do you prostitute your art to make a living by it as, say, an advertising man, or work for Hollywood or radio? Do you try and do both?

Somewhat wistfully, Seeger explains his resolution:

> And it seemed impossible to me at that time to do both. . . . I could meet a man like Theodore Dreiser and everybody could say this man is a great artist and he also makes a living. But it was such an unusual thing that for me the idea that I could do it was completely out of the question. And I assumed that if I was going to be an artist, and be an honest artist, that I would always be broke.[81]

Such a totality of commitment to the "people's" cause seldom was evident in the statements and activities of the vast majority of other cultural workers in the communist movement. Nearly all of the artists in adjacent fields—one estimate states 90 percent[82]—were employed in various areas of the commercial entertainment world, bourgeois fine-arts scene, or establishment media. Such individuals sometimes also held responsible or prestigious positions within capitalist art institutions, and most so placed were ready to bask in their acceptance and success. As a rule, they saw little or no contradiction between their cultural efforts for the bourgeoisie during the day and their left-wing political activities, ostensibly in the name of revolution, at night.

This dual existence occasionally led to paradoxical situations in the communist movement. One example: in the mid-1950s a party member who was an important radio director accepted the task of directing a vehemently anticommunist "documentary" program. Upon fulfilling his responsibilities, he was brought up for expulsion by the party. He and nearly all of his fellow communists in the mass media defended him by arguing that he was only carrying out the requirements of his job, that if he refused to direct the program he would lose his position, his senior status in the radio workers union (AFTRA), and his resulting influence as a communist. Since someone else would have been hired to direct the program anyway, there was no reason to throw away a career to make a hopeless stand on principle. After a long and bitter controversy, he was expelled anyway, justified by the belief that what he did was blatant heresy.

But as Silber observes:

> This was the problem. And you had people who were actors in anticommunist plays on Broadway, you had musicians who played in orchestras that provided music for anticommunist functions. You had communists who used to get hired as band musicians and march in parades on behalf of the American Legion.

Ruefully, Silber acknowledges their dilemma: "They said, 'Well, I'm a working musician'. . . and they saw no contradiction in it."

Many, it is true, postulated the development of an independent workers' culture, but most Old Left radicals psychologically were prepared to abandon their loyalty to the concept of a separate "proletarian" art as soon as Madison Avenue, Broadway, or Hollywood showed any interest in their work. "We were always fighting to get into the mass media," Silber recalls.

In short, the majority of communist movement cultural workers, nearly all middle-class in origins and income brackets, found it difficult to discount validation by the "System" as one of the prime measuring sticks by which to evaluate left-wing art. In the words of one critic, "The American mirror was too attractive to shatter, and they never got far beyond its glitter."[83] Making a full commitment to the class struggle as so many Marxist writers and theorists demanded in fact was far too threatening, for to most radicals employed in the arts it would have meant breaking with their comfortable, sometimes affluent, existence, their positions within the commercial establishment, and many of the nonrevolutionary middle-class values that unconsciously imbued their thinking. For example, when Silber assumed direction of the Music Section within the Cultural Division of the Communist Party, his first act was to assign Mao Tse-Tung's pamphlet *Art and Literature,* which outlines the revolutionary commitment of artists, to all section units for reading and discussion. "Everybody read it as an abstraction," Silber remembers, "but it didn't have anything to do with their lives. [But] the whole point that we in People's Songs had was that this *was* our lives."

Hence, the crucial difference between the radical folk singers in the Old Left and much of the rest of the communist movement lay in the underlying attitudes of each group toward the folk traditions and derivative styles, forms, and expression that each espoused. To the musicians, the folk idiom was of fundamental importance, a touchstone and guiding light for all, or nearly all, of their cultural activity. As with the Almanac Singers, the identification was often so compelling that left-wing lifestyles were reshaped to conform as nearly as possible to presumed folk/working-class habits. Folk culture provided not only new mediums for propagandizing the class struggle but also an entire avenue to a new art expression by and for the masses, separate from that controlled and sponsored by capitalism. As such, folklore, especially music, "represented a challenge to the established . . . system."[84] Its ideological importance to the radical folk singers and other musicians was enormous.

On the other hand, to the majority of urban intellectual members of the party, folk traditions were really window dressing, something with which to gild progressive art so as to provide another link, however tenuous, with "the people." From the 1930s on, communists and their sympathizers paid enormous lip service to the idea of folk-based working-class art. But most radicals paradoxically were too ingrained with old middle- and upper-class prejudices weighted in favor of "high art" to seriously contemplate actually participating in the formulation and propagation of such a different aesthetic expression. An anecdote recalled by Irwin Silber illustrates this tendency succinctly:

> I remember going to a [Communist Party Music Section] convention before I became section organizer, where people talked vaguely about developments in the field of music. [This was] in 1948 or '49, and maybe one hundred people were there. They talked how this or that was happening in music, about the symphony music field, serious composers, popular music. And I remember getting up in the middle of the discussion and saying, "You people don't know what's going on. You're talking about *their* culture. Nobody here has talked about the most incredible development of the last five years, that is what's happening with people like Pete Seeger, Earl Robinson, and the folk singers, and a new movement which is challenging the old accepted forms."

Silber didn't mince words in his exasperated response to his compatriots' myopia:

> "You people . . . are snobs. You don't think of this as a serious music or a serious cultural expression. To you this is some sort of side issue, a periphery that is not serious music to be thought about seriously. You think of it as maybe some kind of vague agit-prop which we need on occasion. But now, let's talk about serious music. Let's talk about Aaron Copland and what he's up to, and is John Cage real or abstract—is he really revolutionary or is he counterrevolutionary—and that's what you'll talk about. But you won't really deal with the things that have a chance to shape both musical ideas and general ideas in the form of music in this country." And this was the fact.

In many respects, the left-wing urban folk song milieu was too "radical"—or at least different—in its worldview to be profoundly comprehensible, much less acceptable, to most cultural workers in the communist movement. At the same time, one should not fault the majority of Old Leftists for failing to respond to traditional materials with an enthusiasm comparable to that of the Almanac Singers or People's Songs or to accord folklore an equivalent importance in the proletarian struggle. Most northern communists and their sympathizers had little or no firsthand contact with rural American aesthetic traditions, especially folk songs, and hardly could be expected to supplant their own urban art prejudices. Culturally and psychologically, the gap in values, modes of artistic expression, and sociopolitical worldview was too great to bridge.

The limited appeal of radical folk song organizations of the 1940s and early 1950s meant they were unable to command much tactical support from either the party leaders or most rank-and-filers when the chips were down. Had the party been willing to invest more than a token interest in the Almanac Singers and People's Songs by supplying concrete aid in the critical moments, it might have expanded their activities or at least prolonged the existence of both. Had more cultural workers in the organized Left been able to overcome their ingrained predispositions favoring "high art" and further contributed their talents to the aforementioned groups, the results might well have been the same. But such was not the case with People's Artists, however, for by the time it seriously began foundering, the communist movement itself was in its death throes as a viable political entity on the American scene.

NOTES

1. People's Songs International Constitution, *Preamble*, 1.
2. See, for example, Oscar Hammerstein II, "Report of the American Theatre

Wing Music War Committee" in *Writers' Congress* (The Proceedings of the Conference held in October 1943 under the sponsorship of the Hollywood Writers' Mobilization and the University of California) (Berkeley: University of California Press, 1944), 280.

3. Samuel Sillin, "Battle in Search of a Hymn," *New Masses* (May 19, 1942), 22–23. Sillen's call for suitable war songs was echoed repeatedly in the left-wing press during the war years.

4. The remarks of all three were published as letters to the editors. Siegmeister's and Robinson's responses appear as "Two Composers on War Songs" ("Readers Forum" column), *New Masses* (July 7, 1942), 22; and Lampell's observations as "More on War Songs" ("Readers Forum" column), *New Masses* (July 14, 1942), 22.

5. Samuel Putnam, "Collective Spirit Brings Back the Square Dance," *Daily Worker* (November 23, 1942), 7.

6. *Songs for Victory* (Stinson 346); *Citizen C.I.O.* (Stinson 349); *Songs of the Lincoln Battalion* (Asch Records; rereleased as Side I of *Songs of the Spanish Civil War*, Vol. I, Folkways Records FH5436), most of which are included in Ronald D. Cohen and Dave Samuelson, *Songs for Political Action: Folk Music, Topical Songs and the American American Left, 1926–1953*. Bear Family Records, BCD 15720-JL, 1996, with 212-page book of text and photographs.

7. See Peter Goldsmith, *Making People's Music: Moe Asch and Folkways Records* (Washington, D.C.: Smithsonian Institution Press, 1998), for a description of Asch's recording activities during this period.

8. "Little Man Sitting on a Fence" (anonymously recorded and issued) and included in Cohen and Samuelson, *Songs for Political Action*.

9. David Platt, "People's Bandwagon Rings Bell," *Daily Worker* (November 1, 1944), 11.

10. Irwin Silber, personal correspondence to author, December 1998.

11. Moses Asch had many of these recordings on the original electric transcription discs in his unreleased files of music accumulated over the years. They now reside in the Folkways Collection of the Smithsonian Institution.

12. It is reviewed by several people in "'The Martins and the Coys,'" *Radio Times* (London), June 23, 1944, 3. A tape of the show made from the cast copy album distributed to each of the participants is on deposit at the Archive of Traditional Music, Indiana University, Bloomington, Indiana. Rounder Records plans a reissue.

13. Interview with Irwin Silber, February 29, 1968.

14. Quoted in the program notes for Folksay's dramatic production "Circle Left" (mimeographed), n.d.; and "Swing Your Partner," *Spotlight* (AYD magazine) (March 1945): 12–13.

15. Printed in the group's mimeographed organ *Dancin' Round*, 2d series, 1, no. 3 (May 1947): 20.

16. Silber interview.

17. The script for the show, including the updated lyrics for "Round and Round Hitler's Grave," was printed by Simon and Schuster as *On a Note of Triumph* (New York, 1945). Corwin was the script's author.

18. The signal was the international publication of a letter written by Jacques Duclos, the French communist leader, in *Cahiers du Communisme,* April 1945, criticizing the Browderite wartime policies. For a detailed account of Browder's ouster with its political repercussions for the world communist movement, see Irving Howe and Lewis Coser, *The American Communist Party: A Critical History,* 2d ed. (New York: Da Capo, 1974).

19. Mike Quin, "Coast to Coast" column, *Sunday Worker* (January 4, 1942), Section II, 4.

20. Printed on the masthead of Vol. I, number 1 of *People's Songs* (February 1946): 1, and thereafter in much of the organization's publicity.

21. Pete Seeger, "People's Songs and Singers," *New Masses* (July 16, 1946), 9.

22. Unsigned mimeographed draft (n.d.) circulated among People's Songs executive board members

23. Seeger, "People's Songs and Singers," 8.

24. Silber interview. *The People's Song Book* was published in February 1948 by Boni and Gaer, and it since has gone through numerous editions.

25. Finance and membership report by Lee Hays, minutes of the National Board Meeting of People's Songs, Inc., October 27, 1946, 7–8.

26. In his "Report on Branches and Membership Activity" at the People's Songs national board of directors' meeting, December 18, 1948, Irwin Silber noted that branches of the organization then existed in Albuquerque, Chicago, Cleveland, Denver, Detroit, Los Angeles, New York, Philadelphia, Portland (Ore.), Rochester, San Francisco, Toronto, and on the campuses of Brooklyn College and Cornell University. The nuclei for People's Songs branches was present in Baltimore, Boston, Miami, Pittsburgh, Seattle, and Syracuse.

27. The citation by the New York Newspaper Guild is photographically reproduced in the *People's Songs* 2, nos. 1 and 2 (February and March 1947): 8.

28. Mike Gold columns on People's Songs include his remarks in "Change the World" *Daily Worker* (February 7 and 24, 1946), 5; other *Daily Worker* articles, among many, are Beth McHenry, "Lee Hays and His Buddies Hit the Picket Line Again" (May 15, 1946), 13; Marty Martin, "GI Folksay on the Political Front" (August 31, 1946), 11; "Workshop in Songs: A New Approach" (September 23, 1946), 11; Art Shields, "There's a Song in Their Hearts" (December 26, 1946), 4.

29. See the advertisement for the conference in *New Masses* (April 10, 1946), 27, and the same magazine's half-column on the forthcoming meeting in the next month's issue (May 7, 1946), 24. The previous year a similar conference had been held in New York, entitled "Folklore in a Democracy."

30. Seeger, "People's Songs and Singers," 9.

31. Bill Brownell, "Bob Claiborne Wants to 'Do a Job' for Unions," *People's World* (August 8, 1947), 5.

32. For information on the California Labor School Chorus, formed in 1945 and conducted by Leo Christensen, see Carl Williams, "Working and Singing in Unison," *People's World* (April 24, 1947), 5; and Louis Green, "Theirs Be the Music," *People's World* (March 13, 1948), section II, 2.

33. Interviews with Waldemar Hille, July 26, 1967; Pete Seeger, April 9, 1968; and Alan Lomax, May 25, 1968.

34. Lee Hays, "Let's Have More Common Sense about Folk Music," *People's Songs* 1, no. 9 (October 13, 1946), 4.

35. Rubin's remarks are printed as "Should Foreign Songs Be Translated," *People's Songs* 3, nos. 6 and 7 (July/August 1948): 16–17. Lieberman's reply appears in a letter to the editor of the same publication, vol. 3, no. 8 (September 1948), 11. Other comments by Norman Cazden, Joe Jaffe, and Waldemar Hille appear in vol. 3, nos. 8, 10, and 11 of the *People's Songs,* 11, 11, and 4, respectively.

36. "People's Songs—First Year," *People's Songs* 2, nos. 1 and 2 (February–March 1947), 2.

37. Irwin Silber provides a review of the proceedings in "United Songsters Make a Chain." *People's Songs* 2, no. 10 (November 1947): 2–3. See also Pete Seeger's letter to Silber on p. 10 of the same issue.

38. Seeger, Silber (March 14, 1968), and Hille interviews.

39. Silber interview, March 14, 1968.

40. A memo dated April 16, 1947, was issued by the People's Songs directors to its national board members outlining the financial crisis caused by the failure of the two March concerts and called for a series of personal loans and other fund-raising activities to make up the deficit.

41. Silber interview, March 14, 1968; Bill Wolff interview, July 23, 1967.

42. See Ellen Schrecker, *Many Are the Crimes: McCarthyism in America* (Boston: Little, Brown, 1998).

43. The attacks by the *New York World-Telegram* and New York *Sun,* written by Frederick Woltman and George Sokolsky, respectively, are mentioned in the publicity director's report by Felix Landau as part of the People's Songs national board meeting minutes for October 27, 1946, 3. The *Life* exposé is cited in *People's Songs* 1, no. 8 (September 1946): 2, in a news and notes column by Michael Scott entitled "Singing People."

44. The Tenney Committee's report on People's Songs appears in the *Fifth Report of the Senate Fact Finding Committee on Un-American Activities, California Legislature* (Sacramento: Senate Publications, 1949), 281–83.

45. Interview with Robert Black, June 1963.

46. "The Un-American Menace," *People's Songs* 2, no. 11 (December 1947): 2.

47. Among them were "Red Boogie," "Is There a Red under Your Bed?" and "Gol-Dern Red." The latter softened from "God-Damn Red" for publication purposes. Their words and music are found in *People's Songs* 3, nos. 1 and 2 (February–March 1948): 4.

48. For a review of the facts in the Eisler case, see Robert K. Carr, *The House Committee on Un-American Activities, 1945–1950* (Ithaca, N.Y.: Cornell University Press 1952), 42–47.

49. Mimeographed press release reprinted verbatim by the *Daily Worker* as "People's Songs Group Fights Canadian Book Seizure" (June 18, 1948), 11.

50. Pete Seeger, "Whatever Happened to Singing in the Unions?" *Sing Out!* 15, no. 2 (May 1965): 31.

51. Seeger interview.

52. Seeger, "Whatever Happened to Singing in the Unions?" 31.

53. Words printed in the *People's Songs* bulletin 4, no. 1 (March 1949): 3.

54. Josh Dunson notes in *Freedom in the Air: Song Movements of the '60s* (New

York, 1965), 57–58, that Pete Seeger expected unions and labor-song writers to be major contributors to the topical song magazine *Broadside,* founded in 1962. This expectation proved almost wholly unfounded.

55. The Wallace campaign is extensively treated by Curtis D. MacDougall in his three-volume work entitled *Gideon's Army* (New York, 1965) and less sympathetically by Karl M. Schmidt in *Henry A. Wallace: Quixotic Crusade* (New York, 1960). See also Robbie Lieberman, *"My Song Is My Weapon": People's Songs, American Communism, and the Politics of Culture, 1930–1950* (Urbana: University of Illinois, 1989).

56. Alan Lomax interview, May 28, 1968. Most of the other People's Songs leaders interviewed think Lomax approached the Wallace Party officials on his own initiative.

57. Lomax interview, May 28, 1968.

58. Silber interview, March 14, 1968.

59. This incident is described in *People's Songs* 3, no. 10 (November 1948): 10.

60. *People's Songs* 3, no. 8 (September 1948), 12.

61. Data on Wallace's own background interest in folk songs and the singing in the Progressive Party campaign are from letters to me, November 14 and 26, 1964.

62. In Vol. II of *Gideon's Army* (509), Curtis D. MacDougall notes that Wallace himself wrote another verse to this song, though it probably was never sung:

> When the phony liberals leave, let no Progressive grieve.
> One new Party must be made of two.
> When the Marshall Plan is dead and One World is just ahead
> We'll all be brothers and no longer passing through.

63. Silber interview, March 14, 1968.

64. *People's Songs* 3, no. 10 (November 1948): 1–2.

65. "National Board Meets in N.Y.C.," *People's Songs* 3, no. 12 (January 1949): 4.

66. Financial report submitted to the national board of directors at its December 1948 meeting by Jean Fox, the organization's last treasurer, especially the three pages entitled "Statement of Debts."

67. Silber interview, March 14, 1968.

68. Pete Seeger and Irwin Silber interviews, March 14, 1968. Both blame the overambitious nature of the project and the ineptness of the professional fundraisers for the concert's lack of financial success.

69. Sidney Finkelstein, "The Folk Song's Back to Stay," *Worker Magazine* (March 6, 1949), 2.

70. All material in quotes and set off from the text are from an interview with Silber on April 2, 1968.

71. Irwin Silber, personal correspondence to author, December 1998.

72. The Music Section was divided principally between those musicians who worked regularly in bands, orchestras, and shows on a day-to-day basis, and those variety artists, composers, songwriters, sheet music pluggers, music scholars and theorists, and other miscellaneous music-related personnel who functioned more on a craft basis. The former were almost exclusively concerned with

union problems and their activities as communist members of Local 802 (New York) of the noncommunist American Federation of Musicians union. The latter were more interested in the ideology of culture and other non-union-related problems and frequently complained that they could get no hearing for their own spokespeople in the Music Section, which was dominated by the working musicians. Consequently, in 1949 a second Communist Party Music Section was established for the craft musicians alone. Irwin Silber became its head a few months later. Silber estimates that in the late 1940s there were approximately 1,000 to 1,500 members of the Cultural Division of the Communist Party and 150 to 200 members of the Music Section.

For example, Silber notes with regard to the Music Section:

> In point of fact, it was never really that scientifically organized. While there was a folk music club for a while, and there were certain attempts to group people of common interests in other clubs, this was a very loose procedure; and aside from the folk music club, a member might be in one or another branch simply because the [meeting times were more convenient].

Also, the Cultural Division, while ostensibly national in scope, actually was limited in practical terms to the greater New York area and a small branch in Los Angeles, each under the jurisdiction of the Industrial Departments of their respective state Communist Party branches. Communist musicians, writers, and other artists who lived outside of these metropolitan areas belonged to neighborhood clubs rather than subsections of the party's Cultural Division.

73. Silber interview, April 2, 1968. Not wishing to inadvertently identify other members of the Communist Party, Silber is unwilling to state what percentage of the club's membership participated in both People's Songs and People's Artists. He does note that after 1949, the party began reducing the size of club units for organizational and security purposes.

74. Silber interview, February 29, 1968.

75. Silber interview, April 2, 1968.

76. Albert Maltz, "What Shall We Ask of Our Writers," *New Masses* (February 12, 1946), 19–20.

77. David A. Shannon, *The Decline of American Communism* (New York: Harcourt Brace, 1959), 56–57. Other accounts of this episode, no less damning, are found in Daniel Aaron's *Writers on the Left: Episodes in American Literary Communism* (New York: Harcourt, Brace & World, 1961), 398–401; and George Charney, *A Long Journey* (Chicago: Quadrangle, 1968), 182–84.

78. Lee Hays interview, August 16, 1965.

79. As told by Marjorie Guthrie, Woody's wife, printed in Dave Johnson, "'Just a Mile from the End of the Line,'" *Northwest Magazine* (Portland *Oregonian* Sunday Magazine) (February 2, 1969), 11.

80. William Z. Foster, "Elements of a People's Cultural Policy," *New Masses* (April 23, 1946), 6–9.

81. Pete Seeger interview, April 9, 1968.

82. Silber interview, April 2, 1968.

83. David Zanc Mairowitz, *The Radical Soap Opera: An Impression of the American Left from 1917 to the Present* (London: Wildwood House, 1974), 16.

84. Mairowitz, *The Radical Soap Opera,* 16.

9

People's Artists and the Decline of the American Communist Party

Reproduction of poster—People's Songs Hootenanny, Sunday, February 9, 1941

As the repressive cold war spirit of the late 1940s was giving way to the even more insidious McCarthyism of the early 1950s, People's Artists was born. The effects of the three-year struggle between the United States and the Soviet Union for control of the international balance of power now were everywhere on the domestic scene. Truman's election to the presidency in 1948 was due in part to the public's endorsement of his strong "containment" policy in the previous two years against the spread of communism. The fall of the Czech government to a Red-directed coup in February 1948 had precipitated a sharp decline in support for the Wallace campaign. The Alger Hiss trial and government loyalty investigations dragged on, punctured from time to time by spectacular "revelations" and lurid witness accounts that were exploited by the tabloid press. In June 1948, twelve of the ranking leaders of the American Communist Party were arrested by the federal government on conspiracy charges. Their subsequent trial generated more histrionics than insight from all concerned, including the presiding judge, Harold R. Medina.[1]

The news was no more encouraging the following year. Russia startled the world by detonating its first atomic bomb several years ahead of schedule. The Chinese communists under Mao Tse-Tung successfully completed their revolution by winning control of mainland China amid the charges by the right-wing "China Lobby" in the United States that the Truman administration had "sold out" the bankrupt Chiang Kai-Shek regime.

In the late summer of 1949, the Peekskill, New York, riots erupted, a clue to the degree of tension and fear that the cold war precipitated in ordinary people. Peekskill graphically illustrated how deeply the grass-roots identification with the liberalism of the 1930s had been eroded by the fear of communism. There local residents broke up one scheduled concert by Paul Robeson and stoned thousands of people who attended another a week later. Just around the corner were the first anticommunist attacks by Senator Joseph R. McCarthy of Wisconsin, in February 1950, and the outbreak of war in Korea four months later.[2]

Concurrently, although it might have been difficult to tell from articles in the popular press, the American communist movement was on the defensive. Its membership had slipped greatly in the twenty-four months since early 1947 when the party reached its peak enrollment of perhaps ninety thousand people.[3] Its top leaders were in jail awaiting trial and there were hints, not long unfulfilled, that more arrests of major communist figures would be forthcoming. In state, city, and municipal elections, voters were in the process of ousting the few remaining left-wing public officials—for instance, the New York City Councilman Benjamin Davis, a communist party leader, and American Labor Party Congressman Vito Marcantonio.

The movement's ties to other national progressive groups no longer existed, often less the result of outside political pressure than the party's intransigent dogmatism on issues where compromise might have preserved partial gains. In the summer of 1949, a dozen communist-dominated unions were expelled from the CIO. Labor leaders who had formerly been Red sympathizers—the National Maritime Union's Joe Curran and the Transport Workers Union's Michael Quill—had rid their ranks of party influence. The Americans for Democratic Action, an organization of anticommunist liberals, was formed to counteract communist agitation in progressive politics. The Progressive Party, which had inspired such enthusiasm for the "Century of the Common Man" dreamed of by Henry Wallace in 1948, now was a shell, possessing only a few adherents, mostly communists and fellow travelers. Radical institutions and press organs everywhere were forced to limit their scope or even disband in response to decreased interest. Along with People's Songs, some of the familiar names of the communist movement in the 1940s that disappeared at the end of the decade or in the first years of the next were *New Masses*, American Youth for Democracy (including Folksay), the Civil Rights Congress, and the American Labor Party. Given this situation, it is not surprising that People's Artists' activities and scope of operations were considerably less ambitious than its left-wing predecessors.

THE FORMATION OF PEOPLE'S ARTISTS, INC.

Like the reorganizations occurring throughout the communist movement, the year following the demise of People's Songs in March 1949 saw large-scale consolidation and change in the radical folk music milieu. The *People's Songs* bulletin had bound the progressive folk song enthusiasts together nationally. Without it, many individuals in local chapters went their own ways—some right out of the movement; others made no attempt to coordinate their activities with the former People's Songs leadership. Even in New York, several "name" performers no longer participated in radical folk song affairs. Popular performers such as Burl Ives, Josh White, Tom Glazer, and Oscar Brand became mostly inactive. On occasion, one or more of them might be coaxed to appear at some neutral meeting ground—for example, the Lead Belly memorial concert held at Town Hall, January 28, 1950, organized by Alan Lomax in tribute to the great African American bard who had died the previous month.

Other singers, songwriters, composers, and executive officials in the People's Songs movement drifted away, some to attend college, others to seek careers in the commercial world, and still others to return to the homes they'd forsaken for the excitement of New York City. Woody

Guthrie was in semiretirement as a performer, experiencing increasing health problems and concentrating his energies on writing. Alan Lomax departed for England in the latter half of 1950 and remained abroad doing fieldwork, research, and writing for more than eight years. Pete Seeger soon was involved in an unexpected big-time show business career with the Weavers; though he maintained an important voice in the deliberations of People's Artists, he thus was absent much of the time. Also in 1950, Boots Casetta returned to Los Angeles, and Waldemar Hille accepted a position as musical director of Union Seminary in St. Louis, there to organize his own progressive singing group, the Neighborhood Chorus.

As a result, the directors of People's Artists and many of its most noted performers were individuals who had formerly been in the second or peripheral ranks of the leadership. Some recently had been part of the Jefferson Chorus. They included Robert Wolfe, Ernie Lieberman, Laura Duncan, Herbert Haufrecht, Leon Bibb, Jerry Silverman, Sylvia Kahn, Fred Moore, Jackie Berman, and Elizabeth Knight. Aside from Pete Seeger, the major holdovers from the People's Songs leadership were Betty Sanders and Irwin Silber. Sanders was from New York, a multilingual folk singer of quite some popularity in the radical movement during the late 1940s and early 1950s, and very politically conscious. During People's Artists' entire existence, she was its chairwoman and took a leading role in policy decisions. Next to her close colleague, Irwin Silber, she was the key figure in the organization's day-to-day history.

Irwin Silber's career ranged from radical summer camp, to Folksay founder, to American Communist Party section leader, to director of People's Songs and its successor, People's Artists. Born of working-class Jewish parents, Silber grew up on the Lower East Side of Manhattan. A precocious youth, he skipped several grades, common in those days, and graduated from high school at the age of fifteen. From 1941 to 1945, he majored in English and American history at Brooklyn College. His exposure to American folk music came in the same years through the records and performances of Woody Guthrie and the Almanac Singers and the traditional and topical songs sung at the radical New Jersey Camp Wo-Chi-Ca (whose "Indian" name in fact derived from the first syllables in "Workers Children's Camp"), where he spent several summers both as a camper and counselor. With Hi Schwendinger, he was founder and codirector of Folksay for the first four years of its existence (1944–47), after which he became the executive director of People's Songs.

Of all the left-wing folk song enthusiasts active in the movement, Silber probably was the most political. His radical activities began in 1937 at the early age of twelve; he had been steered leftward by his mother, who herself had been active in neighborhood community affairs in the 1930s. Soon enough, he became absorbed with far-left political activities on his own. At fourteen he was president of the American Student Union chapter in his high school, one of the few branches of this predominantly college-based organization in the country. Subsequently he joined the Young Communist League and the American Youth for Democracy and became a member of the Communist Party in October 1943 on his eighteenth birthday. Though he held views that sometimes contradicted the official "line," he nevertheless rose rapidly in the lower echelons of the party hierarchy. In 1949, he became section organizer (chairman) of the Cultural Division's Music Section, occupying the fourth and sometimes third level of American communist leadership. Except for his ability to call square dances, he was a nonperformer in the music organizations to which he belonged; besides being an accomplished writer/journalist, his talents lay in the executive and promotional functions of such groups as Folksay, People's Songs, and People's Artists. Intellectual, shrewd, and politically astute, Silber served as an important counterbalance to the many left-wing folk singers who preferred action to theory, though he was every bit as activist oriented as they. His strong personality, opinionated worldview, and occasional arbitrary maneuvers in the interests of expediency and organizational survival regularly brought him into conflict with colleagues in both folk song and political circles. Nevertheless, his contributions as organizer and director were invaluable.

In the beginning, Silber had no intention of assuming the burden of leadership in People's Artists because his other political activities consumed so much of his time. When in the summer of 1949 it was decided to form a new music organization to succeed People's Songs, he and Pete Seeger persuaded a young formal composer from Oklahoma, Bob Wolfe, to accept the responsibilities of executive secretary and editor of the projected People's Artists publications. The old booking agency of People's Songs, which had been incorporated separately from the parent unit under the title of People's Artists, was still handling the performance arrangements for many radical folk singers and other performers while reserving some of its revenue for the start of a new organization. There seemed no reason not to retain the name of People's Artists.

The founding meeting of People's Artists took place on July 8, 1949, at the offices of the United Office and Professional Workers of America on East 29th Street in New York. Some 150 people attended and elected a steering committee consisting of Seeger, Silber, and Wolfe to oversee the mechanics of activating the group. Several people addressed the group urging active participation and expressing the need for such an organization. Paul Robeson spoke about the need for such a music organization, describing his observations of similar progressive groups in Europe.[4] The most striking part of the open discussion that followed was an impassioned plea by Alan Lomax that People's Artists concentrate its exclusive attention on traditional music and folk-based topical expression. He predicted the country was on the verge of a nationwide guitar boom and folk song craze, urging that the new organization be ready to further its own program by capitalizing on folk music's impending widespread popularity. To be sure, Lomax had never cared especially for the musical expression of many popular and formal composers and artists associated previously with People's Songs, but his comments in this case proved to be founded on more than bias; within a year and a half, "Goodnight Irene" and "On Top of Old Smokey" were at the top of the Hit Parade, and Lomax's prophecy of a general folk song vogue was borne out with remarkable accuracy. On the whole, though, People's Artists made little if any conscious attempt to adhere to the "all-folk" guidelines Lomax advocated.

Following the initial meeting, the People's Songs booking agency immediately was subsumed by People's Artists and its work expanded; for some time the agency provided almost the only source of income for People's Artists through concert fees and hootenannies. Later, People's Artists not only handled the bookings of performers but often produced entire programs that brought in still more funds. But, almost at once, the ill-fated first concert by Robeson at Peekskill brought People's Artists into the public eye.

Peekskill was a city of about ten thousand people in Westchester County, some fifty miles from Manhattan. Its conservative citizenry constituted much of the rockbed support for Governor Thomas E. Dewey's state Republican political machine. The surrounding countryside also was a summer resort area for many left-wing groups in the communist movement during this same period, a factor not calculated to bring out the most democratic sentiments of local residents as the cold war escalated. For several summers preceding 1949, Robeson had performed without incident for various radical gatherings in the area and now was scheduled to do a benefit for the communist-dominated Civil Rights Congress in the same vicinity. This time, however, local vigilantes broke up the planned concert of August 27 before it began and severely roughed up or terrorized a number of early arrivers.[5]

The communist Left and music fans in attendance were rightfully indignant; the civil rights and physical safety of the concert-goers clearly had been grossly violated (though Robeson himself was not hurt). Moreover, Robeson was currently the greatest cultural hero of the American progressive movement, not to mention the special patron symbol of People's Artists. He long since had proved his enormous talents in many areas (actor, singer, lawyer, athlete, public speaker), was lionized by the commercial world, yet remained totally dedicated to the cause of peace and the struggles for racial equality—for whose sake he had renounced the formal concert stage in March 1947.[6] He exhibited unsullied personal integrity, an unblemished moral character, and a spiritual charisma that impressed most everyone, from the dedicated activist to the casual listener. Numerous children of radical parents, both black and white, were named in his honor.[7] Like W. E. B. DuBois, his nearest counterpart in the political field, he became increasingly radical with age: in 1946 he testified before the House Un-American Activities Committee that he was not then a communist, which, while undoubtedly true, does not obscure the fact that he was, in Browder's words, "more loyal than the Pope."[8] Thus, his value as a left-wing symbol was incalculable.

Accordingly, both People's Artists and the larger communist movement felt it incumbent on themselves to vindicate Robeson's name with regard to the Peekskill incident and simultaneously to make a stand against what was perceived as incipient native fascism. People's Artists' directors issued a fiery denunciation of the unprovoked attack, written by Irwin Silber, Lee Hays, and Fran Dellorco, and readied its own supporting performers to return with Robeson himself to Peekskill for another concert as soon as the logistics for a mass demonstration could be worked out and the safety of its participants assured. On September 4, some twenty thousand radical, progressive, and "fair play" sympathizers, mostly from New York, held an emotion-charged concert at the same site of the riot on an abandoned privately owned golf course, surrounded by hundreds of World War II veterans recruited from several left-wing unions who literally stood shoulder to shoulder around the fifteen-acre perimeter of the gathering for hours in the hot sun. Pete Seeger, Hope Foye, Leonid Hambro, Sylvia Kahn, and other People's Artists shared the "stage" (the back of an old truck) with Robeson, thrilled by the chance to affirm their beliefs in song before so large a crowd at so epic a moment.[9] All went well until the spectators began to disperse. Police directed all the traffic down one prearranged two-mile gauntlet lined with stone-throwing protestors. More than 150 people were hospitalized, though miraculously nobody was killed.

Peekskill became a cause célèbre of the Left in the ensuing months, commemorated in song, poem, and hootenanny, as well as newspaper editorials and political polemics. Perhaps the most stirring and artistic account of the affair was the militant lyrics written by Lee Hays and recorded by the Weavers for Charter Records:

> Let me tell you the story of a line that was held,
> And many men and women whose courage we know well.
> As we held the line at Peekskill on that long September day,

We will hold the line forever till the people have their way!
Hold the line! Hold the line!
As we held the line at Peekskill we will hold it everywhere;
Hold the line! Hold the line!
We will hold the line forever till there's freedom everywhere.[10]
   ("Hold The Line")

    People's Artists' role in the Peekskill proceedings did nothing to win it any acclaim in the noncommunist commercial entertainment world. But in radical circles, the episode brought the organization an unusual amount of much-needed publicity. Bookings continued to be plentiful, paradoxically due to the increasing isolation of the Left from mainstream commercial entertainment. As the cold war deepened, the Left increasingly found its contacts with outside entertainers cut off. People's Artists was forced to rely more and more on its internal resources. Though the communist movement continued to shrink from its 1947 peak, a persistently sizable number of people remained in its ranks, particularly in New York, until after the dissolution of the McCarthy period.[11] Irwin Silber estimates that People's Artists handled performing arrangements for more than five hundred separate engagements per year for much of its existence, 75 percent of them for radical audiences. These were spread among as many as 150 to 200 entertainers, 50 percent of them for about 35 to 40 performers, most notably Betty Sanders, Ernie Lieberman, Laura Duncan, Osborne Smith, Leon Bibb, Pete Seeger when available, and a half dozen others.[12]

    For ten months, People's Artists had no press organ; indeed, there really had been no reporting on the left-wing folk song scene since the demise of People's Songs. Just prior to the dissolution of the bulletin, in February 1949, a number of anonymous Folksay members belonging to the Communist Party's "folk lore branch–youth cultural section" announced the birth of an ambitious monthly publication entitled *Singing Tomorrows*.[13] Its only issue, however, was a mere five pages, full of extreme Marxist cant atypical of both People's Songs and People's Artists publications, with apparently little connection with either organization. During the fourteen-month hiatus between the cessation of the *People's Songs* bulletin and the appearance of *Sing Out!* Pete Seeger sporadically issued a two- or three-paged mimeographed sheet inscribed "Interim Newsletter" that was mailed to various members of the defunct People's Songs leadership around the country. *Interim* was a purely personal effort on Seeger's part.

    Once People's Artists was established, the leaders delayed publication of a new magazine in the hope that sufficient funds could be raised to back the magazine from the outset, avoiding the printing cost difficulties that had plagued *People's Songs*. But when the funds never materialized, Seeger and his colleagues finally decided to begin publication anyway.[14]

In May 1950, *Sing Out!* made its debut as an ambitious sixteen-page monthly journal. Its title was taken from the cover feature of volume 1, number 1, which was "The Hammer Song," arguably the finest and most durable of all the songs composed by the People's Songs–People's Artists movement. Written by Lee Hays and Pete Seeger, it expressed in eloquently simple words and music the hopes, fears, and defiance of an entire generation of radicals:

> If I had a hammer, I'd hammer in the morning,
> I'd hammer in the evening—all over this land.
> I'd hammer out danger! I'd hammer out a warning!
> I'd hammer out love between all of my brothers—All over this land.
> If I had a bell, I'd ring it in the morning,
> I'd ring it in the evening—all over this land.
> I'd ring out danger! I'd ring out a warning!
> I'd ring out love between all of my brothers—All over this land.
> If I had a song, I'd sing it in the morning,
> I'd sing it in the evening—all over this land.
> I'd sing out danger! I'd sing out a warning!
> I'd sing out love between all of my brothers—All over this land.
> Well, I've got a hammer, and I've got a bell,
> And I've got a song to sing—all over this land.
> It's the hammer of justice! It's the bell of freedom!
> It's the song about love between all of my brothers—All over this land.

IF I HAD A HAMMER
(The Hammer Song)
Words and Music by Lee Hays and Pete Seeger
TRO –©– Copyright 1958 (Renewed) 1962
Used by Permission
(Renewed) Ludlow Music, Inc., New York, NY

In the years after the song's creation in 1949, it became a staple of the folk song revival and civil rights movement, a country western, rhythm and blues, and general pop hit, and a protest expression translated into and sung in many languages. Popular recordings by Peter, Paul and Mary, Trini Lopez, and others during the folk song revival of the 1960s obscured the militancy of the original arrangement. "We wrought better than we thought," Seeger wrote later. "The song has grown with time."[15] He spoke the truth.

Like the old *People's Songs* bulletin, *Sing Out!* continued to mix folk songs, topical music, historical articles, and political issues together in its pages, but in a more artistic format. Its worldview, though, became increasingly sectarian during the early 1950s. The magazine's editor, Bob Wolfe, became ill with tuberculosis after overseeing the production of several issues. Many members pitched in to help with editing *Sing Out!*

and performing the duties of People's Artists' executive secretary, but soon both jobs devolved on Irwin Silber.[16]

Although *Sing Out!* attempted to cover left-wing music activities of old and new people's songsters across the United States, especially folk song events, it lacked the national reader base that *People's Songs* had enjoyed since there were no organized branches of People's Artists outside New York. Consequently, the magazine's supporters were mostly Manhattan area residents, who had comparatively easy access to the singers and activities covered in *Sing Out!*'s pages. At first the editors tried to keep up a "news and notes" column from around the country, but the lack of response almost immediately forced Betty Sanders to publish a "Where Are You?" call to locate former People's Songsters who had left the area; among them were Earl Robinson, Jenny Wells Vincent, Bernie Asbel, and Michael Loring.[17] A number of musicians did respond to Sanders's efforts to reestablish communications between left-wing performers and People's Artists. But *Sing Out!* was not very successful in broadening its geographic base and maintained its overwhelming New York orientation to the end of the People's Artists period. Because of this and the corresponding shrinkage of the Old Left itself, the magazine boasted only a modest five hundred or so subscribers at the end of a year.

As People's Songs had faced continuing struggles with finances, so, too, did People's Artists, producing a continual strain on the new organization. The monthly hootenannies and other concerts, now run with considerably more efficiency than in the late 1940s, netted People's Artists between four and five thousand dollars a year, without which it could not have survived. *Sing Out!*, not surprisingly, lost money, but the booking agency provided steady but not sufficient revenues. Special fund-raising projects were an almost constant side activity; the most successful was the distribution of *Lift Every Voice* (*The Second People's Song Book*) in 1953, which sold out its entire press run of five thousand copies in six months and was a lifesaver for the organization. At forty-five dollars a week, Irwin Silber was the only full-time employee on a staff that was much reduced in size and salary compared to People's Songs. Even in the "flushest" periods, People's Artists barely was solvent; in leaner times the organization skipped occasional issues of *Sing Out!* (twice for the whole summer) and otherwise curtailed its activities.[18]

THE RADICAL "FOLK" WORLDVIEW OF PEOPLE'S ARTISTS

For several reasons, People's Artists was much more consciously theoretical in its approach to folk songs and topical problems than was People's Songs. First, the impetus for People's Songs came principally from performers like Pete Seeger—performers who placed progressive activism through music ahead of the formulation of abstract conceptions about their overall direction and behavior. Irwin Silber, Herbert Haufrecht, and Bob Wolfe were nonperformers and generally more overtly ideological in their outlook. They were much more apt to develop a conscious rationale for their activities before undertaking direct action. A second, related reason was the change in the position of the larger communist movement relative to the rest of American society. Through the Henry Wallace campaign of 1948, the party and its fellow travelers still belonged to an amorphous national coalition of left-wing groups surviving from the Popular Front era and war years. After 1948, communists and their allies were almost entirely isolated. Subjected to government harassment and social ostracism, those without a firm or clear commitment to the movement dropped by the wayside. Of necessity, those who remained were forced to intellectualize and interpret political convictions to justify to themselves and others the maintenance of an unpopular ideological position. Since the life spans of People's Songs and People's Artists fell on opposite sides of the political "divide," it is not surprising that the latter devoted considerably more time to formalizing and debating its overall worldview in theoretical terms.

The very first issue of *Sing Out!* provided ample evidence of this shift in orientation. In contrast to the tersely worded "call to action" of the People's Songs preamble, the opening editorial of People's Artists offered a clear formulation of the organization's goals and a concise definition of "people's music," which had never been outlined so precisely by the former group in spite of its de facto adherence to the same principles. The key paragraph read:

> We propose to devote ourselves to the creation, growth and distribution of something new, yet not so new, since its beginnings have been visible, or rather—audible, for some years now. We call it "People's Music." What is this "People's Music?" In the first place, like all folk music, it has to do with the hopes and fears and lives of common people—of the great majority. In the second place, like that other music of which we have spoken—call it "composed," "concert music," or whatever—it will grow on the base of folk music. We propose that these two hitherto divergent lines of music shall now join in common service to the common people and that is what we shall call "People's Music." No form—folk song, concert song, dance, symphony, jazz—is alien to it. By one thing above all else will we judge it: "How well does it serve the common cause of humanity?"[19]

These eloquent words, written anonymously, contained two notions basic to the history of song in American Marxist thought, one old and the other, in its vigorous expression, comparatively new. In the first place, the editorial confirmed the traditional socialist conception of the class nature of music and its corresponding development by stages in direct relationship to socioeconomic conditions. Then it offered a synthesizing framework through which the best music from each historical period might be incorporated into one unified "people's music," thereby blurring the traditional distinctions between art music and folk music prevalent in radical as well as general circles. In so doing, it provided a theoretical rationale long needed in the left-wing movement, enabling supporters of one idiom to accept the other on a basis of equality. This concept, to be sure, had been expressed in passing as far back as the mid-1930s by Charles Seeger, Elie Siegmeister, and those associated with the Workers Music League; in practice, however, they and most other musicians who identified with the radical chorus tradition of that decade seldom ventured very far from art music interpretations of folk songs—if they gave more than lip service to the cultural and aesthetic importance of folk music at all.

Conversely, in the early 1940s, the Almanac Singers and left-wing performers who were strongly influenced by the Lomax worldview paid only the most superficial attention to anything but the folk song idiom. Only in the People's Songs period was there an attempt to reconcile the two outlooks and only in the People's Artists era did a unifying theoretical synthesis receive a clear and forceful exposition.

People's Artists' overtly ideological tone was reflected in *Sing Out!*'s coverage of various radical choruses and other singing groups in the early 1950s. The Unity Chorus of New York, directed by Herbert Haufrecht, was portrayed not merely with regard to its musical activities but also in terms of the basic democratic character of its membership. A description of Waldemar Hille's Neighborhood Folk Chorus in St. Louis highlighted that body's interracial composition and its efforts to improve race relations between its members and within the larger community. The Jewish Folk Lab, which gave rise to the Jewish Young Folk singers led by Robert DeCormier, stressed its goal to preserve the Jewish folk heritage.[20]

In the increasingly sectarian atmosphere of the early People's Artists years, almost any kind of musical activity presented in too nonpolitical a framework was apt to be criticized, sometimes harshly, for its lack of ideology. As a case in point, when Ralph Ditchik departed from an opening theoretical exposition to a detailed account of the mechanics of "Forming a Chorus" in a long serialized essay for *Sing Out!* in 1951, the magazine's current music editor, James Hutchinson, inserted a polemical analysis taking Ditchik sharply to task. One can hear Hutchinson's dismay in the tenor of his remarks:

> It is because [the class nature of music] is not made clear that Ditchik neglects the background of the particular group of singers who know what to

sing and how, but are constantly being isolated from singing it because of the compromising effects of commercialism, political oppression, and the highly developed skills required to manipulate the modern symphony orchestra and the equally unsingable cantata. In a word, the impoverishment of the people culturally is forgotten [in Ditchik's presentation].[21]

Again, such theorizing was in contrast to the "activism first" worldview of the People's Songs milieu. When Pete Seeger organized the Good Neighbor Chorus in the spring of 1949, he envisioned an ensemble that would perform folk, union, and international songs in parks and on picket lines, using banjoes and guitars to accompany simple two- and three-part harmonies. His only other rationale for beginning the group, as stated in the *Daily Worker*, was "I feel that many fine songs can never be sung right by soloists, and also that most glee clubs and choruses overarrange the great people's songs which sound best when performed in a direct and straightforward manner."[22] Much the same explanation was offered some months earlier when Seeger, Lee Hays, Ronnie Gilbert, and Fred Hellerman combined to form the Weavers.

The Weavers were the most well-known and influential choral group produced from within the Old Left in these years. But to perform for more mainstream audiences, they were forced to forego some of their sociopolitical activism, creating ongoing ideological tension. The quartet was founded in November 1948 during the week following the conclusion of the Wallace campaign. Hays had returned from Philadelphia shortly before and with Seeger was eager to form a new ensemble modeled after the old Almanac Singers, but "with more discipline."[23] They recruited Fred Hellerman and Ronnie Gilbert, two young People's Songsters, who had met in 1944 as counselors at Camp Wo-Chi-Ca in New Jersey. As a teenager, Hellerman had hung around Almanac House frequently in the early 1940s, learned to play the guitar in the Coast Guard during the war, and afterward was a leading performer of Folksay. Gilbert studied music formally for ten years before discovering folk songs, sang for a time with the Priority Ramblers in Washington, D.C., then moved to New York and the People's Songs milieu.[24]

The group's first public performances were for Thanksgiving and Christmas hootenannies run by People's Songs in its waning days. In the following year, the members built up an increasingly enthusiastic left-wing following as they slowly matured musically. Eventually, their music acquired a driving style, an unusual blend of voices, and a polished yet still traditionally rooted sound. Aided by some excellent arrangements and a dramatic, infectious quality in their singing, the four soon had audiences everywhere calling for more. Presently their talent also led to an undreamed of commercial success.

Yet in the beginning, the Weavers thought of themselves strictly as another extension of the radical folk music scene. The group's name derived
from the title of Hauptmann's militant play, *The Weavers,* depicting the
English peasant revolt of 1381, which Hellerman had read at Brooklyn
College just as the quartet was forming. As he recalled:

> There is a scene in which the weavers, out on strike, are marching from vil-
> lage to village singing protest songs. Well, we wanted a name that didn't
> mean anything—that had no built-in connotations which would limit us to
> any particular kind of music. So I suggested "The Weavers." And we all
> liked the name right away. First, it didn't mean anything, but it seemed to
> have a sound of rhythm, and of work. It rang a kind of bell.[25]

All throughout 1949, the four sang together at radical gatherings. The
first major article to appear on the group in the *Daily Worker* stressed the
group's forthcoming appearance at a rally to "hail the new China," singing people's songs of Mao Tse-Tung's victorious armies.[26] With Howard
Fast narrating a script, they recorded a polemical but largely accurate account of the Peekskill riots. In this same period, Hays and Seeger collaborated on a series of superior topical songs with an explicit or implicit
left-wing slant, among them "The Hammer Song," "Hold the Line," "Tomorrow Is a Highway," and the nonpolitical "Kisses Sweeter Than Wine."
(Hays, who wrote most of the words, in many respects proved the finest
folk-styled songwriter of the Old Left other than Woody Guthrie; his compositions during the 1940s also included "Lonesome Traveler," "Wasn't
That a Time," "Pineville," "Get Thee Behind Me, Satan," and later, "Seven
Daffodils.")

Random bookings for the communist movement, however, yielded in-
sufficient income to support the Weavers financially. And so, after the
demise of People's Songs in 1949, they decided to turn professional. It was,
as Seeger remembers, easier and cheaper to hire himself alone.[27] Consequently, in spite of the enthusiastic acclaim by radical audiences, the group
for a time was on the verge of breaking up. Finally, Seeger forced the issue by refusing to accept any paid bookings other than with the Weavers. Still, the resulting increase in the quartet's engagements was not
enough. Reluctantly, the four turned to the commercial world. In late
December 1949, they secured a two-week tryout at the Village Vanguard,
a New York nightclub run by Max Gordon that periodically featured folk
music talent. Seeger had performed there as a soloist in the People's Songs
period on one or two occasions as a sideline activity, and his pay of two
hundred dollars a week now was divided evenly with the other Weavers. The four were now fully seasoned performers and a dynamic collective entity. They proved a sensation at the Vanguard and ultimately

stretched their original stay into six months. In the spring of 1950, they were signed by Decca Records and began a meteoric rise to fame with their hit renditions of Lead Belly's "Goodnight Irene" and the Israeli "Tzena, Tzena, Tzena," followed by Guthrie's "So Long, It's Been Good to Know You," and the traditional "On Top of Old Smokey." Over four million records by the group were distributed between 1950 and 1952; "Goodnight Irene" alone sold nearly half that total and remained at or near the top of the Hit Parade for some fifteen weeks. An enormously successful career of concerts and personal appearances followed, culminating in the quartet's signing for a national weekly half-hour television show. But at the height of their fame, the Weavers were cut down by the McCarthy-era blacklist blighting the entire entertainment industry.

Of the four members, Seeger and Hays especially had qualms about a commercial career. About their initial booking at the Village Vanguard, Seeger remarked to Irwin Silber, "It's one step up the ladder, [but] I don't want to get that far up the ladder that I can't ever step off . . . if that's what I want to do." For his part, Hays at first was even more opposed to singing in a nightclub; "This is where we're abandoning our main job," he told Seeger.[28] But aside from the lack of income from progressive sources, another consideration influenced the final decision of the Weavers to move into establishment entertainment circles, revealed most succinctly in an article written for *Sing Out!* years later by Seeger himself. In 1949, the American Labor Party of Brooklyn called People's Songs and requested Irwin Silber to secure the services of Richard Dyer-Bennet for a fundraising event. Silber agreed but suggested the organization accept Pete Seeger if the first artist was not available. "Oh we know Pete," the reply came. "He's sung on our soundtrucks and [at] our parties for years. But we need someone who can bring in a mass audience. We need to raise money." Comprehending the paradox, Seeger observed:

> When Irwin . . . told me [about] the conversation, I started doing some hard rethinking about my own work. Here I'd been knocking myself [out] all these years, congratulating myself on not "going commercial" and the result was that I was not as much use to the Brooklyn ALP as was my friend [Dyer-Bennet], a highly conscientious and hardworking artist, but one who also set out in a more conventional fashion to build a career.

Concluding with a comment on the irony of the situation, Seeger added, "He could bring in a big audience for them. I couldn't."[29]

Nevertheless, when the Weavers did turn commercial, they often found it difficult to back up their left-wing intellectual commitments with commensurate practical support. After securing their engagement at the Vanguard, they stopped coming to People's Artists' hootenannies and other public gatherings as announced performers and soon ceased to appear altogether. Though the group maintained a progressive tone in its repertoire throughout its career, it was forced to eliminate or temper its most outright militant songs and commentary for recording purposes and, to a lesser extent, for personal performances. When communist icon Mother Bloor died, the quartet was not permitted by its managers to sing at her funeral as the members wished to do. The rationale of the Weavers' agents on such occasions was that it was up to the group to become as commercially successful as possible because when they ultimately took a stance on national issues the impact of their opinions would be that much greater, but in the meantime no politically "questionable" activities must be allowed to interfere with the securing of a high position in the entertainment industry. From their acquiescence, it is clear that the members consciously or unconsciously accepted this explanation to some degree. Seeger said later of their dilemma:

> I was willing to [do almost anything] to make a dent in the wall that seemed to be between us and the American people. Here we were [left-wing] singers and songwriters . . . and we'd now gotten in such a box that we were just singing to our old friends in New York, which was all right, but we wanted to reach out beyond them.

But he lamented, "Of course then, in late 1950, our manager had us in a commercial box. Now [People's Artists] wanted me to sing for a hootenanny and I said 'I'm sorry, they won't let me do it.'"[30]

Nevertheless, Seeger was the only one of the Weavers who made a concerted effort to maintain close ties with People's Artists after the group began its commercial career. Inevitably, his actions took the form of private correspondence and office consultations with Irwin Silber and others; only on one occasion in these years, for example, did he contribute directly to *Sing Out!*, and this was a brief pseudonymous review of the Weavers' own recording of "When the Saints Go Marching In."[31]

People's Artists eyed the Weavers' commercial success with admiration, envy, and also not a little cynicism. The four were an eloquent testimony to the viability of the movement's music culture at its best and renewed proof that its outstanding left-wing talent easily could win high accolades in the "system" if it so chose. Yet simultaneously, there was considerable disappointment in the group's collective abandonment of the radical folk music milieu. Irwin Silber reluctantly concluded a review of one of its Town Hall concerts: "The Weavers would have sounded far better in the more vital and vibrant Hootenanny setting than they did in their formal attire on the Town Hall stage." But Silber also tempered his criticism with praise for their performance: "But if they are not able to be an integral part of the growing people's cultural movement, which is what I am sure they would prefer, they are still maintaining high standards of performance and artistic integrity in their work."[32]

Some recalled with annoyance the several Sunday afternoon sings the Weavers ran independently of People's Artists in late 1949 when both were hard pressed for living expenses; anticommunist critics carped at the quartet through parody ensembles such as "The Grievers" and "The Unravelers." The most subtle but meaningful criticism, however, consisted of the People's Artists "house group" of Betty Sanders, Ernie Lieberman, Laura Duncan, and Osborne Smith, founded in 1951 to sing at the organization's hootenannies and other functions. During its two-year existence, no one in People's Artists made any public attempt to portray the singers as the movement's answer to the Weavers. But the staunchly progressive character of their music and the balanced gender and racial composition of their membership were an ample reminder to many of the activist democratic song tradition the Weavers seemed to have forsaken. "If anybody had a meeting, we would push this group consciously," Silber remembers. "Because . . . if we could support these four people, make it possible for them to continue working as singers, we could prove that people dedicated to the 'cause' could live and make their contribution [at the same time]."[33]

Other critiques leveled at the Weavers in this period were byproducts of various ideological issues current in the People's Artists and communist milieus of the early 1950s. The first was the sometimes passionate tirade against "male chauvinism." Women traditionally have played an important role in radical American politics, the Old Left not excepted. Yet the charges of sex discrimination raised at this time and by the later women's movement frequently were justified within as well as without the progressive sector. But in its self-conscious efforts to be absolutely impartial in its treatment of men and women, the communist movement sometimes made a travesty of its cause. This had been demonstrated in the radical folk music scene as far back as 1947, when on one occasion at the California Labor School, Pete Seeger and Jenny Wells Vincent joined in an impromptu performance, exchanging humorous folk songs where first men, then women, secured the upper hand over the other. Some solemn left-wingers normally partisan to traditional and "people's" music were shocked at this breech of "good manners" if not "morality."[34]

By 1952 and 1953, the gender issue came to a head. Irwin Silber led the way with a major article in *Sing Out!* entitled "'Male Supremacy' and Folk Song,"[35] in which he postulated such ideas as follows:

All forms of mass entertainment are . . . dominated by the ideology of male supremacy—and we must conclude, therefore, that this is a deliberately

planned approach designed to help carry out the basic program of war, vio-
lence, and national chauvinism which are the cornerstones of monopoly-
controlled culture.

Arguing that sensitivity to underlying subtexts of songs must be considered, Silber concludes:

> The sharp weapon of satire, which in the hands of socially conscious cre-
> ative artists has been used to aid the people's struggles, has been deliber-
> ately blunted by directing it at women, love, and sexual relationships. For
> that reason, songs such as "The Farmer's Curst Wife," "The Fireship," "Dev-
> ilish Mary," "Wee Cooper of Fife" and others can only do great injury to the
> developing struggle for peace and human rights.

"Little Phoebe" and other folk songs in which women triumphed over
men were seen as "obvious barbs at 'male supremacy.'" John Jacob Niles's
"chauvinistic" composition "Venezuela" carefully was noted as not being
a product of oral tradition. Fortunately, Silber concluded, male chauvinist songs represented only a small proportion of the American folk song
heritage. Silber himself later characterized his more sectarian statements
in this essay as "masterpieces of inanity, Victorianism and bigotry."[36] In
fairness to Silber's motives, most of his arguments, though polemical, read
more reasonably with the hindsight of the consciousness-raising era initiated by the women's movement in the 1980s.

Though Silber, among others, warned against the dangers of overreac-
tion and "militancy," "male chauvinist" excesses sporadically dotted the
People's Artists milieu for some time. A number of performers gave up
singing all traditional and topical songs having to do with relationships
between the sexes for fear of committing some impropriety. One group
dropped from its repertoire the chorale "Because All Men Are Brothers,"
written by Tom Glazer to a Bach chorale, because it lacked explicit reference to women in the all-embracing generalization of the title.[37] Much of
Sing Out!'s criticism of the Weavers, especially that by Irwin Silber, came
as a result of the quartet's alleged catering in their music and stage humor to "Tin Pan Alley" female stereotypes.[38] And in the most influential
incident, a number of young people in People's Artists strongly opposed
to male supremacy on any level sharply took issue with "The Hammer
Song" for its repetition of the phrase "all of my brothers" in each verse
without a corresponding reference to the word "sisters." Lee Hays, the
author of the lyrics and never one to take sectarian ideology too seriously,
ruminated at some length about the Weavers only wanting to sing about
the brotherhood of man, then sarcastically inquired if "all of my siblings"
wouldn't resolve the controversy.[39] Pete Seeger was finally persuaded of
the validity of the male chauvinist argument, and he later sang the song

with the line in question altered to "my brothers and my sisters." When young Bernie Krause joined the long-since rejuvenated Weavers in 1963, he was genuinely shocked when Hays jokingly informed him that his audition tape contained the "Communist Party version" of "The Hammer Song."[40]

Far more important than the issue of male supremacy, however, was the movement's preoccupation with African American social equality and civil rights, especially within its own ranks. This had been a communist concern from the very beginning, and, like the matter of women's freedom, it was an area in which radicals had made many legitimate efforts and contributions. But in the early 1950s, discussions of problems of African Americans and black–white relationships took on a particularly intense and introspective character and often a rigidly sectarian tone. Numerous party members were expelled on grounds of "white chauvinism" in these years and, among other things, the United States government repeatedly was charged with the pursuit of a genocidal policy toward blacks. Only after several years of near-hysteria did the extremism end in 1953 with the publication of articles in major communist periodicals by William Z. Foster and Eslande Goode Robeson urging moderation on racial issues.[41]

On the positive side, *Sing Out!* instituted an African American history and folk song issue each year and devoted many of its pages to recounting the doings and, where possible, promoting the careers of black artists such as Paul Robeson, Hope Foye, Leon Bibb, Laura Duncan, and Osborne Smith. *Sing Out!* published a series of polemical articles against the commercial exploitation and general debasement of African American culture by the entertainment industry. The most important was Irwin Silber's two-installment essay, "Racism, Chauvinism Keynote U.S. Music,"[42] which in spite of its partisan tone accurately outlined many of the historic problems faced by blacks concerning the co-opting of their material by whites. Silber developed one aspect of his critique further in a subsequent review of a Weavers' folk song folio that credited several Lead Belly pieces and other African American–derived music to the pseudonymous "Paul Campbell" and "Joel Newman" (representing the Weavers and Lomax–Ledbetter copyright interests, respectively). "At a time when an increasing number of white musicians are aligning themselves with the struggle for Negro liberation," Silber wrote, "the Weavers render a grave disservice to the cause of Negro-white unity by this callous approach to the musical heritage of the Negro people."[43]

Another controversy involving the Weavers and black folk music was touched off in October 1951, when Fred Moore reviewed the quartet's recent Decca album. Regarding "Easy Rider Blues," Moore said:

It is my opinion that such a group may study and present fairly accurately many of the songs of the American Negro, but they will lack the ability to get across the content, intention and deep feeling of the songs precisely because they have no direct connection with Negroes in a performance capacity.[44]

Moore's remarks touched off an explosive debate among *Sing Out!* readers, though his stand presently was reaffirmed by the People's Artists executive board in a brief editorial statement. The disagreement, however, was sharp enough that the magazine followed up Moore's article the next month with an open discussion entitled "Can an All-White Group Sing Songs from Negro Culture?" which ran for several issues.[45] Most of the published sentiment sympathized with Moore. One writer, identified only by his initials H.J.L., observed, "In spite of their fine contribution to America's culture, The Weavers are limited by being an all white group." Pronouncing the value of assembling performers from diverse backgrounds, Moore suggests that diversity should come even before musical compatibility:

If they would be true to the democratic sentiments of many of the songs they sing, they must correct this weakness. It should be an easy matter to find one or more Negro artists to integrate into their group, and by the heightened quality of their future work they could set a splendid example for many lesser-known groups.[46]

The Weavers themselves took no formal cognizance of these arguments, though they in fact had worked briefly with black artists, particularly Hope Foye, in their precommercial days and regarded such proposed "solutions" as narrow and mechanical, though, as Seeger noted later, they recognized that the group perforce sang African American folk songs as whites rather than blacks, albeit as tastefully as possible.[47]

People's Artists successfully revamped its hootenanny formats in this period to attract more African American youth to its functions. In the 1940s, with the proliferation of square dance groups in urban centers, left-wing folk sings usually had concluded with a period of American and European folk dances, with all present participating. But by 1950, the American Square Dance Group, Folksay, and similar dance organizations were all but defunct, and the marriage of folk song and dance hitherto characteristic of the city folk song revival ended in divorce. More observant radicals likewise noted about this time that most African American teenagers cared little for Anglo-European-derived music, and so postconcert entertainment was switched to several hours of social dancing. For some years afterward, People's Artists drew as much as a fourth

of its hootenanny audiences from the New York African American community, with the total sometimes rising to half on occasions when blacks
arrived late just for the dance floor socializing.[48] While most blacks who
came were not politically committed in a partisan sense, the generally
friendly racial interactions were regarded as an encouraging sign by
People's Artists promoters.

Yet many of the organization's efforts in the name of black freedom
bordered on the absurd, indicative of the Left's general isolation from the
mainstream of American and African-American life in this period. At each
executive board meeting of People's Artists, for example, Irwin Silber was
obliged to report the number of bookings obtained for African Americans
as opposed to those secured for whites. Any function utilizing the services
of three or more singers almost ipso facto required the presence of a black
artist or charges of "white chauvinism" were apt to be raised by critics in
the sponsoring organization or within People's Artists itself.[49] *Sing Out!*'s
topical songs and magazine articles on race issues, though containing
many essential truths about black–white relationships in the United States,
were often too extreme to be taken seriously. Albert Wood's powerful
composition "Genocide," for instance, said:

> Young woman bleeding in a cotton field;
> Her head's been broken, her privates revealed.
> The rapists laughed and they strolled away,
> What a terrible price the black women pay.
> It's genocide, genocide,
> Genocide we charge
> [It's] genocide, genocide,
> And the criminal's still at large.[50]

An anonymously written critique of the St. Louis Neighborhood Folk
Chorus began with the statement "One of the first prerequisites for a
people's chorus in the United States today is that its composition must
basically reflect the inter-racial character of the people's movement for
peace and civil rights." The essay then proceeded to examine the group's
activities in this light, with a stern eye and noticeably sectarian language.
In one case, the chorus elected a full slate of white officers until it was
pointed out: "This type of occurrence is a . . . subtle form of white chauvinism . . . since it means that there is not an equal sharing of leadership
responsibility." Expressing a clear bias, the author continues, "Certainly,
an all-white executive committee is not going to be as alert on the questions of white chauvinism or on the positive program of the chorus for
[the] struggle for civil rights as an inter-racial committee." "It is encouraging to know," *Sing Out!*'s editors added, "that this kind of frank criticism

and self-criticism is taking place. . . . [We] believe that this type of discussion will prove most valuable to people's choruses throughout the country."[51]

Consistently intertwined with issues of racial inequity in these years was the question of commercial exploitation of workers' cultural products, particularly folk songs, in part reflected in a series of repeated attacks on Tin Pan Alley. There was little originality in these charges; they dated back at least to the 1930s and in more generalized form could be found in much of the earliest socialist literature. But they were advanced anew with some considerable force in the People's Artists period, notably by Irwin Silber and Sidney Finkelstein, the latter a former newspaper writer turned Marxist arts critic. In a polemic entitled "Song Pirates Fly Skull-and-Bones over Tin Pan Alley," Silber wrote:

> As the already sterile creative processes of the music monopoly become completely barren, these same [Tin Pan Alley] hacks have seized upon the rich creative fruit of the past, primarily from folk song and the classics, and run it through the profit mill. The fact that the end product usually represents a complete prostitution of the original does not discourage the pirates, nor should it surprise us—since along with the corruption of all moral principles goes a degeneration of artistic standards.[52]

Finkelstein, whose best works represent a major contribution to socialist cultural thought, in 1952 published a brief and politically narrow volume, *How Music Expresses Ideas.*[53] He described the Metropolitan Opera House in New York as "a typically feudal structure, built by the 'robber barons' as a 'society' toy," and commercial pop music was characterized as a "formalistic factory-manufactured" art expression that had to "borrow, steal, [and] plagiarize" its material from everywhere: "Grieg and Tchaikovsky, Mexican tangos and songs from every national group, cowboy and mountain song."[54] Most of his one chapter on the American music scene is devoted to the commercial exploitation of black culture. Likewise, Tin Pan Alley products repeatedly were claimed to reflect U.S. imperialist ambitions. On this point, Silber expostulated, "Not only do Chopin, Verdi, Brahms, etc., suffer from the piracy of their music [*sic*], but the musical heritage of the Polish, Italian, and German peoples is destroyed and debased by the music profiteers." Admittedly provocative in tone, Silber observed:

> Along with the bayonets, warships, bombs, and Coca-Cola which the Marshall Plan provides, comes the "Americanized" version of the national cultures of the various peoples . . . [the] racist, stereotyped-filled, degenerate picture of the rich culture of the peoples of the world.[55]

Most of the best and worst in People's Artists' critiques of bourgeois commercial music efforts also were encapsulated in Silber's *Sing Out!* review of the *Fireside Book of Favorite American Songs,* published by Simon and Schuster in 1952. The illustrations, he noted, particularly of blacks, were full of white supremacist stereotypes; the lyrics included "the foul words of racism"; the worst song material included "Under the Bamboo Tree," described as a "Tin Pan Alley writer's vile nightmare about Africa," and "The Bonnie Blue Flag," the official anthem of the southern Confederacy. The translation of the Mexican revolutionary song "La Cucaracha" depicted the people of that nation as only interested in smoking marijuana; in several cases, no references were made at the appropriate junctures to the origins of songs among African Americans of the United States and elsewhere. "Despite the inclusion of some basically democratic material," Silber concluded, ". . . the book is so dominated by a combination of crass white chauvinism and a patronizing air of condescension . . . that whatever positive elements are contained in it are completely overshadowed."[56]

Like so many expositions by Old Left spokespeople in the early 1950s, these remarks blended valid observations with astigmatic distortions of complex realities and commisar-like language. Cut off from the American public and harassed at every turn by anticommunist legislators and superpatriots, the movement in its agony vented its frustrations in semanticist extremes and frequently accompanied the latter with the flimsiest of charges and outright purges of suspect members. People's Artists was no more extreme in its sectarianism than the rest of the Old Left, in some instances less so, yet its sporadic polemics in *Sing Out!,* behind the scenes, and at its public functions amply reflected the narrowness and unhappy puritanism of the larger movement in those years.

PEOPLE'S ARTISTS AND MCCARTHY ERA POLITICS

The American communist movement, never much more than a "radical fringe" of mainstream politics, gradually became almost totally isolated during the McCarthy years. The movement still possessed a sizable number of adherents, though membership had dwindled to perhaps a third of the ninety thousand members of the early postwar years. The lifeblood of any cultural organization is the flow of information to and from the greater society. Isolation resulted in very few communication outlets for the Left to channel its voices. The Left was forced to rely exclusively on its own resources and personnel to maintain its limited political perimeter and internal activities. People's Artists was one of the movement's primary cultural organizations in this period, providing many basic services otherwise unavailable principally, but by no means entirely, in the area of music. It produced most of the hootenannies run by "progressives" in New York; supplied innumerable singers and other performers for every imaginable kind of radical function; began its own record company, published *Lift Every Voice,* the only major left-wing songbook of the McCarthy years; and otherwise had a hand in directing many programs associated with the arts in the communist movement in the early and mid-1950s.

Though proportionately reduced in size and influence, the component features of the Old Left's musical landscape were much the same as during the movement's heyday in the Popular Front era of the late 1930s. The workers choral tradition, long since nativized in membership and repertoire, remained very much in evidence. A host of new ensembles replaced the Freiheit Gesang Ferein, Jefferson Chorus, and other familiar names. Among the new groups which came and went in the Left's declining years were the Unity Chorus, North Star Singers, Neighborhood Folk Chorus, and the best-known if not artistically superior Jewish Young Folk singers. Even collectively, though, these newer choruses never were as influential on communist music culture as their predecessors had been.

The prewar Lomax tradition, of course, was represented by a great variety of individual performers and small groups within People's Artists. Accompanying themselves with banjoes and guitars or other traditional instruments, they persistently tried to adhere to the original style and free arrangements of American folk music. But as before World War II, many art interpreters of folk songs were in their midst, not a few of them black singers heavily oriented to the Paul Robeson/Marian Anderson musical tradition.[57]

Similarly, the radically oriented small record companies of the 1930s and early 1940s had disappeared, succeeded by new ventures attempting to fill the resulting void in left-wing recorded music. Keynote Records sold out to Mercury in 1947, which immediately discontinued the former's partisan topical offerings; two years later, the Disc Company, owned and operated by Moses Asch, was forced to declare bankruptcy. Stinson continued to exist but did so partly at the expense of its ardently radical material, which was dropped in favor of exclusive concentration on folk and jazz listings. To take the place of these companies, Charter Records was begun by Mario "Boots" Casetta of People's Songs in 1946. After issuing one album and eleven single releases, it folded a year later, and was followed by Hootenanny Records which managed to exist on a skeletal basis for the duration of the McCarthy period. Hootenanny technically was owned by Irwin Silber and Ernie Lieberman, but it actually was run by and for the benefit of People's Artists; over the years it pressed some eight single records and a long-play album of left-wing topical music and folk songs.[58]

Not directly connected to People's Artists but sharing its progressive worldview and that of its predecessor, People's Songs, was Folkways Records, founded in 1950 by Moses Asch with the help of Marian Distler after the collapse of the Disc Company. Though frequently sympathetic to much of the Old Left's outlook, Asch stubbornly maintained his political and artistic independence. He refused to compromise his mission, which was to produce albums of music and cultural documentation from whatever points of view interested him, regardless of political expediency. Accordingly, in the late 1940s, Asch caused his name to be removed from the list of People's Songs board of sponsors and never again allowed it to be used publicly by either People's Songs or People's Artists. While Folkways Records eventually issued a wide range of new topical material, and rereleased a number of older partisan recordings,[59] unlike the Charter and Hootenanny companies' works, its products reflected no narrow political orientation. The great bulk of Folkways's offerings comprised an astonishing variety of traditional, jazz, ethnic, and other material ultimately running into thousands of items. It is no overstatement to say that Asch's work, especially with Folkways, constitutes one of the greatest single contributions in American history toward the preservation of native and world culture.[60]

Peace, international goodwill (especially vis-à-vis the socialist countries), and civil rights were the dominant themes of the Old Left's sociopolitical activities of the early 1950s. These themes were reflected amply in the activities of People's Artists. For instance, *Lift Every Voice*, published in 1953, differed from *The People's Song Book* of five years earlier precisely on these points. The earlier collection stressed trade unionism, the native folk song heritage, economic security, and antifascism, in contrast to the newer emphases on peace and the dignity of all people.

The peace and goodwill motifs were enunciated by People's Artists on numerous occasions and venues: in an early "Sing Now for Peace" contest for songwriters sponsored in 1949 by Pete Seeger and several left-wing folk singers; at various hootenannies and in many new song creations; through an album *Goodbye, Mr. War* recorded by Ernie Lieberman; in *Sing Out!* reports of overseas youth and cultural congresses attended by Betty Sanders and Hope Foye; and in the organization's endorsement of the Stockholm Peace Petition of 1950, which was intended to secure the signatures of millions of antiwar sympathizers around the globe. The most widely sung peace song of the period grew out of this latter campaign. "Put My Name Down," by Irwin Silber, recast an earlier Tom Glazer war effort composition set to the tune of Woody Guthrie's "Hard Travelin'":

I've got a brother in the infantry,
I thought you'd know.
I've got a brother in the infantry,
Way down the road.
He's got a home and a wife and baby,
He don't like war and he don't mean maybe,
And he's gonna put his name down.
Put my name down, brother,
Where do I sign?
I'm gonna join the fight for peace
Right down the line.
Ashes to ashes and dust to dust,
If you don't sign up the world goes bust,
So I'm gonna put my name down.[61]

People's Artists' agitation for civil rights fell into two main areas: discrimination against African Americans and the harassment of left-wing activists by anticommunist panegyrics. Befitting its ideological position with regard to black justice and equality, People's Artists supplied various singers and topical compositions for demonstrations to rally support for several legal cases in which African Americans were accused unjustly of major crimes or convicted under biased circumstances. These demonstrations began in 1949 with the Trenton Six affair and continued into the early 1950s with the separate sentencings of Willie McGhee, Rosa Lee Ingram, and the Martinsville Seven. Similarly, throughout the McCarthy era, People's Artists's topical song creations in the folk idiom appeared—in support of the defense of political prisoners, beginning with the trial of eleven top Communist Party leaders in 1949. Even before People's Artists itself was formally organized, radical musicians were dedicating their efforts to securing their acquittal; "Wasn't That a Time" and "The Hammer Song," two of the movement's finest topical songs of the late 1940s, were both composed against the background of the Foley Square trial.[62]

A May Day revue the same year, entitled "Now Is the Time," sponsored by the Music Section of the Cultural Division of the Communist Party and featuring a number of well-known left-wing folk singers, was performed in honor of the indicted leaders.[63] *Sing Out!* carried regular reports and editorials on succeeding violations of "progressive" civil rights, from the Peekskill riots to the government proceedings against V. J. Jerome and Walter Lowenfels and the many investigations of radical entertainers by the House Un-American Activities Committee. Hootenannies were organized under the auspices of the radical Labor Youth League for proclaimed champions of American civil liberties, one in tribute to Gus Hall.

In 1952, People's Artists also undertook the support of the Progressive Party election ticket. The third party movement by now was a pale shadow of 1948; Henry Wallace himself had resigned after the outbreak of war in Korea when the ranking leadership of the party voted to condemn Truman's intervention with troops in an attempt to push back the North Korean advance. The departure of Wallace and most of the few remaining liberals only further underscored the preeminence of communists and their sympathizers among the third party remnants. Its candidates in 1952 were left-wing lawyer Vincent Hallinan and black newspaperwoman Charlotta Bass, both from California.

In contrast to People's Songs' enormous efforts during the 1948 campaign, People's Artists conducted a lackluster effort on behalf of the futile Hallinan–Bass cause. Paul Robeson, Betty Sanders, Ernie Lieberman, and Laura Duncan performed at the Progressive Party nominating convention in Chicago, and several songsheets were run off and singers provided for succeeding rallies and demonstrations. *Sing Out!* published a few new election parodies and an article encouraging the use of songs in the campaign, but otherwise People's Artists contented itself with cheering from the sidelines.[64] Unlike 1948, the organization received no money to maintain a music desk at third party headquarters, nor was it in any position to commit commensurate resources to the election drive. Four years earlier, there had been real hope of building a grass-roots alternative political movement in the United States; in 1952, the Old Left was going through the motions, and everybody, including People's Artists, knew it.

People's Artists' most important and wholehearted commitment of time and energy to a political or civil rights affair came in late 1952 and early 1953 as the campaign to save Julius and Ethel Rosenberg, convicted atomic spies, reached its climax. Complex and emotionally charged, the Rosenberg case was the last major cause for which the movement was able to rally considerable noncommunist support. Though the presiding trial judge, Irving R. Kaufman, was Jewish, as were the prosecutor and other principals, a large segment of the Old Left believed that the couple was being sentenced to death partly on the basis of anti-Semitic sentiment. During the last year prior to the Rosenbergs' execution in June 1953, People's Artists devoted part of each hootenanny to their cause and published two booklets of poems by Edith Segal in their name.[65] *Sing Out!* printed several songs, editorials, and one cover story concerning the Rosenbergs, and its parent organization supplied numerous performers, especially of Jewish descent, to the many save-the-Rosenberg demonstrations held in the New York area. Several People's Artists were on hand at Union Square the night of the death watch and helped lead an impromptu memorial service when word came that the couple's executions had been carried out.[66]

In these years, members of People's Songs and People's Artists often were forced to defend themselves from the McCarthy hysteria as conservatives. Many left-wing folk singers found themselves prime targets for such harassment, beginning in 1950 with the red-baiting of the Weavers. That year, *Counterattack,* an anticommunist magazine founded by three former FBI agents, published several articles over a twelve-month period accusing the group of pro-communist activities. In June 1950, *Red Channels* appeared, a veritable who's who of reputed left-wing artists in sympathy with Soviet causes. It became the unofficial blacklisting "bible" of the entertainment industry for the duration of the McCarthy era (and indeed long afterward). Pete Seeger alone was cited thirteen times in the book, and numerous other onetime People's Songsters found their names listed. Those who had built up successful commercial careers in the meantime, or who otherwise relied on the bourgeois media for all or part of their livelihood, suddenly faced almost total unemployment. Peripheral People's Songs member John Henry Faulk, for example, found himself without work soon after both *Counterattack* and *Red Channels* listed him in their publications. Faulk had been a radio personality on CBS and married to Hally Wood, and he was a folklore student of J. Frank Dobie. Much time and attorney's fees later, he was awarded three million dollars in damages as a result of the allegations made against him.[67]

Of the regular singing performers from the Old Left, the Weavers were the hardest hit. At the crest of their popularity on the strength of several recordings in the summer of 1951, they were scheduled to appear at the Ohio State Fair in Columbus and on the NBC Dave Garroway program, when publicity about their reported communist sympathies, based on the *Counterattack* articles, caused officials of both shows to cancel the group's performances. Thereafter, the group found its bookings and income steadily drying up as the anticommunist polemics snowballed. A most damaging bit of "testimony" on this score came late the same year from Harvey M. Matusow, a former Communist Party member who became a paid professional witness for the House Un-American Activities Committee and similar investigative bodies. Matusow joined the party in the late 1940s and worked for People's Songs. He contacted the FBI himself, insisting he wanted to testify. Matusow recalled of his first meeting with one of the editors of *Counterattack:*

> [We] discussed my forthcoming role as witness before the House committee . . . [and] the careers of a well-known quartet who, at the time, had the top-selling phonograph record in the United States. One of its members was listed in *Red Channels,* but there was nothing that could be pinned on the group specifically—they could not be placed in the Communist Party. Having known all four of them, not as Communists, but as friends, I triumphantly said, "I know them, and they are Communists."[68]

During the early 1950s, the validity of such irresponsible charges was questioned by few Americans, least of all by the commercial entertainment industry. Because of the success of the red-baiting attacks, the Weavers became virtually unemployable, and at the beginning of 1953, they broke up, not to reunite again until the end of 1955. [69]

Those whose political loyalties and professional activities fell under suspicion in these years really had only two choices if they wished to maintain their careers: they could cooperate with congressional and self-appointed investigating bodies by providing details about their own activities and the names of past and present associates, or they might refuse to cooperate and ride out the ensuing social criticism and economic ostracism as best they could, possibly facing a prison sentence. Of the urban folk singers who took the former course, only Burl Ives implicated others; Josh White confessed details about his own left-wing activities but insisted he was no longer a participant in the movement. Among those who elected to ride it out were Pete Seeger, Lee Hays, Irwin Silber, and Earl Robinson. A very few, such as Alan Lomax, left the country.

Of the few performers who cooperated with anticommunist agencies, Ives's case is worth considering in some detail since it was typical of the dilemma of the cooperative witness who, reluctant to testify, nevertheless did so to protect his own privileged present position from a past that currently was viewed as hostile and threatening by much of American society. Before and during World War II, Ives, as a musician with left-wing sympathies, was often to be found in the company of the radical Lomax performers. His work with them ranged from joint appearances at Spanish Civil War rallies and other progressive functions to radio shows and several anonymous recordings with Pete Seeger and others as "The Union Boys," singing such union classics and win-the-war efforts as "Solidarity Forever," "We Shall Not Be Moved," and "Sally, Don't You Grieve."[70] But in 1945 Ives secured a starring role in Alfred Drake's Broadway musical "Sing Out, Sweet Land," and he coterminously began to disassociate himself from his former colleagues. Though his name subsequently was listed on the People's Songs board of sponsors, he in fact had almost no contact with the organization and quite early was regarded by some of its key members as having "sold out" his progressive principles. In 1950, however, Ives's name was cited in *Red Channels,* and as successive pro-communist allegations piled up in right-wing propaganda, he agreed to testify before the Senate McCarran Committee in 1952 as a friendly witness in an effort to clear himself. He named a few names, including Richard Dyer-Bennett, and generally excused most of his past actions and associations on the basis of ignorance or the misappropriation of his name for various causes by left-wing groups. There was much truth in his words when he added, "Outside of politics, there has been a sort of group which has some sort of cohesiveness, you might say, of all the ballad singers, and there are quite a number of them." Reflecting on the special connection among folk singers, Ives continued, "Just by the nature of what we do, there is some kind of a relationship, a sentimental thinking about the songs and everybody interested in singing folk songs."[71]

Ives could not re-create another historical period accurately without further acknowledging the highly political and partisan character of that era and his own comparatively conscious alliance with those now come to be considered "enemies." His only recourse in testifying was to plead lack of information, collective "sentimental thinking" about folk songs by both "good guys" and "bad guys," and a purely monetary interest in the cash paid folk singers at left-wing bookings.

For being listed in *Red Channels,* Oscar Brand found his long-standing WNYC radio folk song show and other professional activities in jeopardy. According to Irwin Silber, Brand issued a polemical statement at Cooper Union in New York late in the fall of 1951, referring to the "pernicious influence upon the American folk music field" of left-wingers and observing that "the presentation of traditional material is impossible where the Communist wield their influential censorship."[72]

The case of Josh White followed much the same line as Ives's in terms of the philosophical rationales he used to justify his former progressive endeavors. While he did not disclose names as Ives did, nor was he so painfully self-righteous in his remarks, he subjected himself to the McCarthy hearings to prove his anticommunist position. White "voluntarily" appeared before the House Un-American Activities Committee to read a statement affirming his belief in the American way of life, and he claimed total ignorance of the "subversive" forces behind the labor and civil rights causes he had supported as an entertainer and citizen in previous years.[73] White was trying to walk a fine line between cooperation under intense pressure from the FBI and not implicating his colleagues, particularly Paul Robeson, which he did not do. Perhaps because as an African American his groveling before the anticommunist sentiment in the land smacked of Uncle Tom–ism, his behavior appeared particularly pathetic; one subsequent "purification" rite, for instance, consisted of an article written for *Negro Digest* entitled "I Was a Sucker for the Communists."[74]

Less publicized, though equally unenviable, was the testimony before HUAC of Allan Sloane, onetime peripheral member of the Almanac Singers, who in later years had bitterly turned on his old associates, especially his roommate Millard Lampell. His remarks, like those of Harvey Matusow, presented a highly slanted, almost ghoulish, portrait of the radical milieu of the 1940s.[75]

Radical folk singers remaining in the Old Left not surprisingly deeply resented such anticommunist confessions. The names of "turncoat" performers immediately became anathema to those in the People's Artists movement, and on several occasions *Sing Out!* published fiery editorials harshly denouncing their perfidy. "The future of Burl Ives should be interesting," wrote an editor on one occasion. "We've never seen anyone sing while crawling on his belly before. But maybe Burl Ives will be able to figure it out. . . . Nothing's too hard for a stoolpigeon—except keeping his integrity."[76]

Much backbiting also went on behind the scenes between those who chose to maintain their left-wing commitments openly and others who preferred to be more discreet in expressing their beliefs or who had modified their former radical opinions. One important composer, whose membership in the communist movement dated back to the Workers Music League, repeatedly attacked another musician with progressive sympathies dating from the same period for seemingly having compromised his social beliefs in the interest of political and economic expediency. Tom Glazer was openly criticized for having recorded "Old Soldiers Never Die" in honor of General Douglas MacArthur in 1951 and for otherwise deserting the Old Left camp. Pete Seeger later reviewed Burl Ives's paperback collection of *Sea Songs* in glowing terms for *Sing Out!* but could not resist the temptation to discuss Ives's political sins for most of the second half of his essay.[77]

People's Artists lavished scorn and satire on the anticommunist inquisitors. Replying to attacks on the Weavers for having sung at the funeral of Bob Reed, a New York communist leader, Lee Hays commented sharply:

> I read a eulogy at Reed's funeral. . . . Bob Reed was a known Communist. He was known and loved by more nonCommunists than any Communist I've ever known. He was my neighbor and life-long friend. If any more of my friends die, I don't care whether they're Republicans or Communists, I'll be at their funeral to speak if I am asked.[78]

Pete Seeger, Irwin Silber, and Woody Guthrie issued equally defiant statements on various occasions. When Irwin Silber and Betty Sanders were subpoenaed by the House Un-American Activities Committee in February 1952 (the hearings were subsequently canceled), the People's Artists executive board exclaimed in print:

> The summoning of two leaders of one of the most outspoken people's cultural organizations in the United States by the Un-American Committee represents a further attempt on the part of the "Un-Americans" to impose a deadly censorship on all forms of free cultural expression.

Expressing outrage at the tactics of HUAC, their statement warned, "The censorship of an artist is likewise a censorship on the right of the artist's audience to hear ideas freely expressed. We therefore call on all of the people of this country to take part in a campaign to stop this creeping fascism."[79]

People's Artists also manifested hostility to the superpatriotic attacks in numerous songs and parodies spoofing or sardonically needling McCarthyite excesses. These ranged from the anonymous *South Pacific* parody, "Some Subversive Evening," to Harold Rome's hilarious "The Investigator Song" ("Who's gonna investigate the man who investigates the man who investigates me"), and Betty Sanders's and Irwin Silber's "Talking Un-American Blues."[80] One of the most popular efforts in this vein was Walter Lowenfels' poem written to the old broadside "No Irish Need Apply":

> O my name is Joe McCarthy but I'm not the man you think,
> I dig ditches for a living and I never was a fink;
> I dig ditches for a living, I'm dirty as can be,
> But I never smeared a person like that Senator smeared me.
> Sure, McCarthy is my monicker, McCarthy is my name,
> But me and the Senator are surely not the same.
> I am proud of the McCarthys, but we are not to blame.
> It's that feller down in Washington that's brought us all to shame.[81]

Pete Seeger, Lee Hays, Earl Robinson, Irwin Silber, and Tony Kraber refused to cooperate. Seeger declined to answer questions based on the First rather than the Fifth Amendment to the U.S. Constitution. For this he was formally censured for contempt of Congress by the House of Representatives in July 1956. The court case dragged on seven years, ending only in 1962 with the reversal of his initial conviction and the cancellation of the accompanying one-year jail sentence.

Such confrontations produced eloquent statements on civil rights and in some cases moments of high drama; at other times clashes between radical folk singers and right-wing critics gave rise to scenes of low comedy. During Irwin Silber's 1958 interrogation by HUAC, for example, he was asked if he had formerly taught at the communist-sponsored Jefferson School of Social Science in New York. Silber acknowledged that he had. "What did you instruct?" was the next query, obviously asked with the intent to elicit "The State and Revolution" or a similar response. "Square dancing" came the reply.[82]

In spite of such brief episodes of levity, these were dark years for People's Artists and indeed all performers of folk songs, radical or not. For a time, the taint of such a number of folk musicians under suspicion for their left-wing proclivities was so great that it affected much of the public's attitude toward all of traditional music sung in a folk song revival context. Accordingly, nonpolitical performers or those not wishing to be stigmatized by the red brush sometimes found it expedient to change the name of the musical genre in which they worked. Country and western singer Tex Ritter, for example, later remarked:

> At one time I called myself a folk singer. [But] it got to the point there for a few years where it was very difficult to tell where folk music ended and Communism began. So that's when I quit calling myself a folk singer. It was the sting of death if you were trying to make a living.[83]

Moreover, the impact of the repressive McCarthy-era spirit on the creative sensibilities of left-wing artists was devastating. People's Artists did not go "underground" (in a literal sense) as did some of the communist leadership. But it may be said that uncensored aesthetic expression suffered a knockout in the McCarthy era.

Only a few good topical songs were written between 1951 and 1957, and they scarcely could find a hearing other than at left-wing rallies or hootenannies. Traditional music, as noted earlier, was utilized or interpreted in impossibly doctrinaire and sectarian ways. Like the Far Left of which it was a part, People's Artists was isolated, hemmed in, stultified in its atmosphere, and largely lacking in both imaginative concepts welding art and politics together and the means to introduce them into American society. The insularity of the movement, to be sure, soon would be broken as internal and external forces combined to dismantle the barriers separating the communist milieu from a realistic perception of world events and life in the United States. But it was too late; within four years the Old Left and People's Artists were all but moribund.

THE DECLINE OF THE COMMUNIST MOVEMENT AND PEOPLE'S ARTISTS

Even as the cold war reached its zenith in 1952 and 1953, the seeds of disintegration were being planted. Joseph Stalin died on March 4, 1953, and the new Russian leaders soon proved more amenable to negotiating disputes with the United States. An armistice agreement ended hostilities in Korea in July 1953; many fires of confrontation between the two superpowers were reduced to embers. In 1955, Austria was reunited as one country when the Allies and Russians withdrew their occupation forces. Later the same year, President Eisenhower met with Soviet officials at Geneva, Switzerland, in an atmosphere of cordiality subsequently dubbed "the spirit of Geneva." The East European socialist countries and the United States upgraded their diplomatic legations to the ambassadorial level. Simultaneously, the USSR began its first tentative steps toward de-Stalinization.

The McCarthy "era of night" began to fade as Americans came to their political senses. Social Studies replaced the improvised "Citizenship Education" as the familiar title for one part of New York's high school curriculum. The Cincinnati Redlegs baseball club reverted to its old nickname, the "Reds," which prior to the McCarthy years the team had enjoyed since 1869. The trials of second and third-string communist leaders gradually ended with defendants initially receiving shorter sentences and eventually outright acquittals or reversals of previous convictions. In 1954, Senator McCarthy himself finally committed political hara-kiri in the course of a tumultuous conflict with the U.S. Army, which wound up on television. McCarthy emerged from the battle largely shorn of his power, influence, and much of his following. These developments relieved the pressure and allowed the communist movement and People's Artists to function more normally. The party's underground apparatus was disbanded in 1955, and those members who had been sent into hiding or otherwise dropped from sight returned to their homes and open political activity.

Even at the nadir of the political repression, there were those in People's Artists who objected to the tenor of much that was written in *Sing Out!* and discussed behind the scenes. Waldemar Hille and Earl Robinson wrote repeated letters taking issue with the tactics of Irwin Silber and those who handled the affairs of the magazine and organization. Others recognized the need to modify many of People's Artists' practices and public statements. This was especially true concerning *Sing Out!* In the fall of 1954, the magazine shifted from monthly to quarterly publication. With barely one thousand subscribers, and unable to keep up with payroll demands of a labor-intensive product, the magazine reluctantly sought a more modest publication schedule. More important, though, were the concurrent alterations in the magazine's format, temper, and political tone. Folk songs gradually assumed a more prominent place. Well-researched articles and thoughtful book reviews containing contents of substance began to appear with increasing frequency. The editorial page was curtailed sharply and in 1957 eliminated altogether. *Sing Out!*'s previous polemical character was tempered and sometimes even obliterated. To be sure, the magazine never gave up its left-wing worldview, but its ethos now tended to become "progressive" rather than radical.

In 1955 and 1956, *Sing Out!*'s staff attempted to shift to a more broadly based cooperative effort. After the appearance of each issue, *Sing Out!*'s editors hosted public meetings at which several songs from the previous edition were sung, the contents of the magazine discussed and criticized, and suggestions put forth for future issues. As many as forty to sixty people might attend these sessions, and many of the ideas generated on such occasions were subsequently incorporated into the magazine.

The drift away from the sectarian practices of the past also was reflected in other ways. For one thing, the hootenannies acquired a new dynamism, full of hope and enthusiasm, which was not missed by outsiders who happened to witness them. Under the caption "The Songs of the Hootenanny Are Still Ringing in My Ears," Joseph Starobin of the *Daily Worker* observed of one such occasion:

> I was struck by the wholesomeness of the Hoot. . . . The Hootenanny is an institution by now. It answers the deep needs of our time, of solidarity. It does so in a language that makes sense to many millions whom progressives are not at the moment reaching in other ways, the language of dance and song.

Suggesting the value of "entertainment" as a means to provoke political awareness, Starobin was clearly impressed: "The Hootenanny is not just something to enjoy, but something to think about."[84]

Other evenings sponsored by People's Artists featured the folk and formal art music of other nations, especially East European, along with the more familiar traditional and topical music of the United States. Such programs were perceived by People's Artists as building "a bridge of friendship and cultural exchange between peoples of different lands." This idea was hardly new, but the atmosphere generated by these concerts was indeed refreshing. So was the mood of the *National Guardian* album *The Unforgotten Man*, (1955), a dramatic reconstruction of governmental reform in the interests of the people during the Roosevelt years. Its unidentified cast, featuring in part the singing of Pete Seeger and Fred Hellerman, concluded its prose and song narration with the optimistic theme "these times shall come again." Such thoughts no longer just seemed like wishful thinking.

The extent to which the air had cleared by the end of 1955 was confirmed by the return of the Weavers, who reunited for a historic and fabulously successful concert at Carnegie Hall that Christmas, followed by a busy touring schedule unimpeded by serious blacklisting attacks. "It is hardly coincidental," Irwin Silber remarked,

> that the Weavers chose the close of 1955 for their public reunion. The recent easing of international tension as a result of the Geneva Conference, together with the growing repudiation of McCarthyism by the American people, has created a new and favorable atmosphere for groups like The Weavers.

Assessing current developments, Silber admitted that mainstream voices inevitably carried more weight in society than all the efforts of radical activists:

> One great advantage to hearing The Weavers after three years of silence is the gain in historical perspective. Looking back now to a different period from the vantage point of 1955, it is possible to see how many of us (and this writer not the least) seriously underestimated both the artistic achievement and overall cultural impact of The Weavers from 1949 to 1952 when their songs were on the lips of tens of millions of Americans. The isolation (all too often self-imposed) of the cultural left from the mainstream of American cultural expression was the cause of many such errors in judgement.[85]

As the thaw in the international cold war and the diminishing domestic political repression continued, People's Artists began losing ground. While the Old Left was almost completely cut off from the rest of American society, People's Artists became a major source of left-wing cultural activity and entertainment. Consequently, the group secured almost as much work as it could handle. But with the ebb of the McCarthy period, communications with outside talent and artistic programs once again became possible, and People's Artists experienced increasing competition for bookings.

The Communist Party experienced a steady decline of membership that accelerated in the mid-1950s as the need for leftists to band together in self-defense waned. The loss of rank-and-filers occurred for many reasons: defections by the tired and politically faint of heart; intragroup purges by the party itself; disillusionment with the Old Left's policies, programs, and polemics. The work of People's Artists in turn was affected by the attrition of the greater movement of which it was a part. Many of the more important figures in the organization were a younger, impatient breed of radicals who long since had become dissatisfied with the W. Z. Foster regime, which had dominated the Communist Party since 1945. Most members consequently now dropped out. Not infrequently, they disassociated from People's Artists as well.

Meanwhile, People's Artists suffered internally from increasingly divisive tensions, most commonly concerning bookings. Performers exhibited considerable jealousy, most notably some who took an active role in the decision-making process of People's Artists but who otherwise were blessed with only mediocre artistic talent. (There was no machinery established by which those wishing to book through People's Artists might be screened for their performing abilities.) Irwin Silber, in particular, was the target for much of the backbiting and hotheaded criticism because of his dominant position within the group, long-term associations with the organization's booking agency, and aggressive personality. While arguments on who was getting what bookings persisted for more than five years prior to the final dissolution of People's Artists in 1957, the period between 1953 and 1955 was especially contentious.[86]

The seeds for the breakup of both the Old Left and People's Artists thus were germinating by 1956, when Nikita Khrushchev gave his famous de-Stalinization speech. When the Soviets crushed the Hungarian revolt by force, the American communist movement was dealt its death blow. Khrushchev's address, as Silber has observed, marked the advent of communist protestantism, and as such it had a tremendous impact on the already-shaken Old Left blocs in the United States and abroad. Huge reservoirs of anxieties, doubts, and tensions dammed up for years in the service of party discipline and solidarity burst forth with the publication of the Russian leader's secret remarks to the USSR Twentieth Congress. Thousands in the movement simply quit; others rallied behind *Daily Worker* editor John Gates and much of his staff in a prolonged struggle with the remainder of the Foster bureaucracy for control of the party. All usual lines of authority and normal activity within the communist movement ceased for more than a year while warring factions battled for ideological supremacy and political domination amid a rapidly shrinking membership. In the fall of 1956, the conflict became even more acrimonious when the Soviet Union forcibly put down what was obviously a popular revolt against communist repression in Hungary. Many American communists identified strongly with the insurgents, and their brutal suppression by Russian tanks and troops was the final straw for many hundreds if not thousands. The reformist Gates faction was so weakened by defections that it was easily defeated by the Foster Old Guard at the party's national convention in New York in February 1957. Foster and his cohorts won a hollow victory, however, since the party now numbered only between five and ten thousand, mostly in their middle and upper years, and was all but dead as a viable political, social, and intellectual force on the American scene. During the next decade a new generation of radicals would ignore its ideology and shun its structural corpse.[87]

These international developments provoked only a limited amount of public comment from People's Artists, most notably at one or two hootenannies. Behind the scenes, though, the Khrushchev speech had a profound impact on the organization, contributing to the end of many of its sectarian practices. *Sing Out!* published two songs by executed Jewish poets and a brief note honoring them and that of their "fellow victims" after Khrushchev's revelation of anti-Semitic persecution in Russia under Stalin. (At first, however, the magazine omitted the ironic stanza in one of the compositions that lauded the Soviet leader).[88] Another issue in passing remarked favorably on the growing demands of East European students for academic freedom, and a third printed a pointed anecdote about recent censorship in Hungarian opera. This last drew at least one hostile reply from a disgruntled reader:

> I get enough baloney like that in the whorehouse press from day to day without paying an additional fee to reread it in a magazine which should know better. When renewal time comes around, just remember the song— So long, it's been good to know you.[89]

But otherwise, the magazine adhered closely to its new policy of restricting its nonmusical editorial politicizing.

People's Artists was at the end of its rope. The organization was in financial difficulty, owing three thousand dollars, mostly in the form of personal loans. The Old Left itself was fragmented, disillusioned, and decimated in number; the group could not survive on the meager income still accruing to the organization. *Sing Out!*'s subscription roster boasted only a very modest fifteen hundred names. But there were indications that the numbers of subscribers might be expanded if more money and better publicity were available: the popular interest in folk song was once again on the rise after its setback during the McCarthy years. Moreover, the collapse of the Old Left and the fresh intellectual currents sweeping through the communist world seemed to indicate that the time was ripe for fundamental change.

Consequently, in the fall of 1956, after some months' discussion, the executive board voted to disband People's Artists and channel all future energy into the production of *Sing Out!* As was the case with the demise of People's Songs, the remaining assets of the organization were turned over to Irwin Silber, who with Pete Seeger and Jerry Silverman constituted the interim committee charged with forming a new organization to run the magazine. On February 28, 1957, the new company emerged as Sing Out Incorporated. It assumed the residue of back debts owed by People's Artists and struggled along for more than a year—indeed, it almost went under on one occasion—before Moses Asch of Folkways Records was persuaded to invest in the magazine's stock. Now financially stabilized and beginning to ride the burgeoning nationwide enthusiasm for folk music sparked anew by the Kingston Trio and other popular folk song groups after the fall of 1958, *Sing Out!* soon enjoyed considerable success as a folk song–cum–progressive periodical. As such it was almost the only Old Left publication to both survive the 1956 debacle and prosper during succeeding years in its new, more mainstream, format.

Few of the former People's Artists activists participated in the magazine's post-1956 rebuilding. Of those individuals still present in the organization's leadership at the time of its dissolution and reconstitution (sans booking agency) as Sing Out Inc., only Irwin Silber remained in the Communist Party. But he, too, departed in January 1958, when the *Daily Worker,* longtime opponent of Foster's conservative ruling party clique, ceased operations. John Gates resigned, and the last of the reformers associated with the Party upheavals of 1956–57 drifted away.[90] The Old Left's leading role in the popularization of American folk music was dead.

People's Artists, in sum, was conceived by its founders as a musical and ideological extension of People's Songs. Yet for most of its existence it was in no real position to actually expand the work of its predecessor beyond the borders of the communist movement. The cold war, the Old Left's internal weaknesses, and the organization's own resource limitations meant that People's Artists' primary function would be to supply artistic talent and cultural leadership within the communist movement itself. The group was not actually called on to convince or persuade outsiders through its rhetoric. As a result, there was a stronger ideological tone to the work of People's Artists, a greater organizational agitation within the framework of accepted basic principles, than ever was the case with People's Songs. Combined internal and external pressures caused many of the group's precepts to be enunciated through doctrinaire polemics and sectarian language; these same pressures were eased only by the winds of sociopolitical change which were to destroy the communist movement and with it People's Artists in the middle years of the 1950s. Nevertheless, People's Artists was an important catalytic force in holding together the progressive popular folk music tradition during the years of domestic civil repression and international cold war. A decade hence many of the causes espoused by People's Artists would be taken up again by others with new names and often new songs. The American heritage of making music with a mission persisted, though the continuity would not be apparent to many of the latter-day militants.

NOTES

1. See Ellen Schrecker, *Many Are the Crimes: McCarthyism in America* (Boston: Little, Brown, 1998).

2. For a review of these events in their cold war context, see Eric F. Goldman, *The Crucial Decade and After: America, 1945–1960* (New York: Knopf, 1965).

3. In August, 1948, the party reported its membership as slightly more than sixty thousand. See David A. Shannon, *The Decline of American Communism* (Chatham, N.J.: Chatham Bookseller, 1959), 97.

4. "Robeson to Address New Music Group," *Daily Worker* (July 7, 1949), 11.

5. See, for example, Howard Fast's partisan *Peekskill USA* (New York, 1951).

6. See "Robeson Quits Concert Field," *New York Times* (March 16, 1947), section II, 1.

7. Irwin Silber interview, April 2, 1968.

8. Earl Browder interview, February 12, 1968.

9. Fast, *Peekskill USA*, 81.

10. Printed in *Sing Out!* 1, no. 1 (May 1950): 3.

11. Silber interview, April 2, 1968; see also George Charney, *A Long Journey* (Chicago: Quadrangle, 1968), 252.

12. Silber interview, April 2, 1968.

13. Mimeographed in New York. The reference to the "folk lore branch–youth cultural section" of the Communist Party is obscure; there is no evidence for any such structural arrangement.

14. Pete Seeger interview, April 9, 1968.

15. Pete Seeger, *American Favorite Ballads* (New York, 1961), 19.

16. Silber officially was listed as editor of *Sing Out!* in vol. 2, no. 4 (October 1951) but in fact had assumed production responsibility four or five issues previously when several interim editors proved unable to devote the necessary time to its publication (interview, April 2, 1968).

17. *Sing Out!* 1, no. 5 (September 1950): 13.

18. Details on People's Artists finances are from the Silber interview, April 2, 1968.

19. *Sing Out!* 1, no. 1 (May 1950): 2.

20. "The Unity Chorus—Democracy at Work," *Sing Out!* 2, no. 6 (December 1951), 4; "St. Louis Builds an Inter-Racial People's Chorus," *Sing Out!* 2, no. 7 (January 1952): 6–7; "Jewish Folk Lab Gets Yiddish Songs," *Sing Out!* 1, no. 9 (February 1951): 4.

21. "A Reply to Ralph Ditchik," *Sing Out!* 1, no. 10 (March 1951): 10.

22. Barnard Rubin, "On the Line" ("Broadway Beat" column), *Daily Worker* (May 20, 1949), 13.

23. Oscar Brand, *The Ballad Mongers* (New York, 1962), 107; Seeger interview.

24. Seeger interview; see also Brand, *The Ballad Mongers,* 108.

25. Joseph Haas, "The Weavers: They Were America Singing," *Chicago Daily News Panorama Magazine* (December 29, 1963), 5.

26. "From Kentucky Mountain Ballads to Chinese People's Songs," *Daily Worker* (June 14, 1949), 23.

27. Seeger interview.

28. Silber interview, April 2, 1968; Seeger interview.

29. Pete Seeger, "Johnny Appleseed, Jr.," *Sing Out!* 15, no. 5 (November 1965): 105.

30. Seeger interview.

31. Nathan Charlieres, "Record Review," *Sing Out!* 2, no. 3 (September 1951): 16.

32. Irwin Silber, "The Weavers—New 'Find' of the Hit Parade," *Sing Out!* 1, no. 9 (February 1951): 12.

33. Silber interview, April 2, 1968.

34. Interview with Irving and Kathleen Fromer, July 12, 1967.

35. Irwin Silber, "'Male Supremacy' and Folk Song," *Sing Out!* 3, no. 7 (March 1953): 4.

36. Letter to Archie Green, November 26, 1957.

37. Silber, "'Male Supremacy' and Folk Song."

38. Silber's criticism of the Weavers on male chauvinist grounds are included in his "The Weavers—New 'Find' of the Hit Parade," cited earlier, and in his review "The Weavers Sing at Town Hall," *Sing Out!* 3, no. 5 (January 1953): 16. See also Jenny Wells Vincent's letter to the editor in the same magazine, vol. 2, no. 11 (May 1952): 14.

39. Pete Seeger, "Johnny Appleseed, Jr.," *Sing Out!* 15, no. 5 (November 1965): 105.

40. Interview with Lee Hays, August 16, 1965.

41. The party's campaign against white chauvinism is traced in some detail in Shannon, *The Decline of American Communism,* 242–48. Foster's article on "Left-Sectarianism" appeared in *Political Affairs;* Robeson's in *Masses and Mainstream.*

42. *Sing Out!* 2, nos. 5 and 6 (November and December 1951).

43. Irwin Silber, "Weavers Issue Folk-Song Folio," *Sing Out!* 2, no. 8 (February 1952): 5.

44. Fred Moore, "Decca Issues Folk Song Album with the Weavers," *Sing Out!* 2, no. 4 (October 1951): 6.

45. *Sing Out!* 2, no. 7 (January 1952): 2, 14.

46. Letter to the editor, *Sing Out!* 2, no. 8 (February 1952): 14.

47. Seeger interview.

48. Silber interview, April 2, 1965.

49. Silber interview, May 3, 1968.

50. *Sing Out!* 2, no. 8 (February 1952): 3.

51. "St. Louis Builds an Inter-Racial People's Chorus," *Sing Out!* 2, no. 10 (April 1952): 7.

52. *Sing Out!* 2, no. 12 (June 1952): 6.

53. Sidney Finkelstein, *How Music Expresses Ideas,* rev. ed. (New York: International, 1970). See his additional works: *Jazz: A People's Music,* rev. ed. (New York: Da Capo, 1975) and *Composer and Nation,* 2d ed. (New York: International, 1989).

54. Finkelstein, *How Music Expresses Ideas,* 112, 108.

55. Irwin Silber, "Song Pirates Fly Skull-and-Bones over Tin Pan Alley," *Sing Out!* 12 (June 1952): 7.

56. Irwin Silber, "New Fireside Songbook an Insult to America," *Sing Out!* 3, no. 5 (January 1953).

57. Silber interview, April 2, 1965.

58. These included recordings by the Weavers, Hope Foye, the People's Artists Quartet (Ernie Lieberman, Laura Duncan, Betty Sanders, Osborne Smith), Martha Schlamme, the Jewish Young Folk Singers, and others. The LP later was reissued on Folkways Records as *Hootenanny Tonight* (Folkways FN 2511) and was the first live recording of folk song concerts to be issued on commercial records. See Ronald D. Cohen and Dave Samuelson, *Songs for Political Action: Folk Music, Topical Songs and the American Left, 1926–1953* (Bear Family Records, BCD 15720-

JL, 1996, with 212-page book of text and photographs), for an extensive discussion of the issue.

59. The latter included *Six Songs for Democracy* (FH5436) and *Talking Union* (FH5285), both formerly issued on Keynote.

60. Peter Goldsmith, *Making People's Music: Moe Asch and Folkways Records* (Washington, D.C.: Smithsonian Institution Press, 1998).

61. Printed in *Sing Out!* 1, no. 3 (July 1950): 3.

62. See "Walter Lowenfels," *Sing Out!* 3, no. 11 (October 1953): 2; and "Town Talk," *Daily Worker* (June 1, 1949), 11.

64. Bob Reed, "May Day Smash Review Put on by Communist Cultural Division, On Stage," *Daily Worker* (May 4, 1949), 11.

64. Songs include "H-A-L-L-I-N-A-N," "The People's Polka," and several election parodies published in *Sing Out!* 2, no. 10 (April 1952), and vol. 3, no. 1 (September 1952), respectively. The one article is "Get Ballots with Ballads," vol. 3, no. 1, 4–5.

65. *Give Us Your Hand* and *I Call to You Across the Continent,* the latter published after the Rosenbergs were executed.

66. Silber interview, May 2, 1968.

67. Both John Henry Faulk and his attorney, Louis Nizer, have described this case in detail. See John Henry Faulk, *Fear on Trial* (Austin: University of Texas Press, 1983), and Louis Nizer, *The Jury Returns* (Garden City, N.Y., 1966).

68. Matusow provides a brief sketch of his early life in his autobiography *False Witness* (New York: Cameron & Kahn, 1955), from which this quote is taken (51). He served as an office employee of People's Songs in its latter days under the name of Harvey Matt. For his public testimony on the Weavers, see "Singing Group Called 'Reds' by FBI Agent," *Santa Ana Register* (February 26, 1952), 2.

69. Their only commercial work was done anonymously. Fred Hellerman and Lee Hays, for example, recorded "Good Night, Sweet Dreams, Mary Lou" for X Records, a Decca subsidiary, about 1954, along with Gordon Jenkins's orchestra, chorus, and an unidentified female singer. The record was an obvious attempt to reproduce "Goodnight Irene" in format and commercial success, in both cases to no avail.

70. See Mel Steele, "Songster Burl Ives: Folk Singer with a Conscience," *People's World* (April 19, 1946), 5. *Songs for Victory* was recorded by the Union Boys (Asch 346). "Solidarity Forever" was released as Stinson 622, a single record.

71. "Subversive Infiltration of Radio Television and Entertainment Industry— 'Testimony of Burl Icle Ives,'" in U.S. Congress, Senate Committee on the Judiciary, Subcommittee on Internal Security, *Hearings* (Washington, D.C.: U.S. Government Printing Office, 1952), 217.

72. "Folk-Singer Oscar Brand Joins Witch-Hunt Hysteria," *Sing Out!* 2, no. 5 (September 1951): 2.

73. "Hearings Regarding Communist Infiltration of Minority Groups— 'Testimony of Josh White,'" in U.S. Congress, House Committee on Un-American Activities, *Hearings* (Washington, D.C.: U.S. Government Printing Office, 1950), 2835–41. White's testimony is reprinted in its entirety in Robert Shelton, ed., *The Josh White Song Book* (Chicago: Quadrangle, 1963), 32–38.

74. Josh White, "I Was a Sucker for the Communists," *Negro Digest* (December 1950): 27–31.

75. "Communist Methods of Infiltration—'Testimony of Allan E. Sloane,'" in U.S. Congress, House Committee on Un-American Activities, *Hearings* (Washington, D.C.: U.S. Government Printing Office, 1954), 3851–77.

76. "Burl Ives Sings a Different Song," *Sing Out!* 3, no. 2 (October 1952): 2.

77. Pete Seeger, "Sea Song Paperback," *Sing Out!* 6, no. 4 (Winter 1957): 21.

78. "Columbus and Americanism" (editorial), *Sing Out!* 2, no. 3 (September 1951): 2.

79. "People's Artists Leaders Subpoenaed," *Sing Out!* 2, no. 8 (February 1952): 2, 11.

80. "Some Subversive Evening" is in the People's Songs Library; Rome's "The Investigator Song," written earlier, appears in *The People's Song Book* (New York, 1948), 102–04; "Talking Un-American Blues" is printed in *Sing Out!* 2, no. 10 (April 1952): 10–11.

81. "McCarthy vs. McCarthy," *Sing Out!* 3, no. 12 (November 1953): 2.

82. Silber interview, February 29, 1968.

83. Reese Cleghorn, "High Noon for Tex Ritter," *New York Times Magazine* (July 12, 1970), 14.

84. Joseph Starobin, "The Songs of the Hootenanny Are Still Ringing in My Ears," *Daily Worker* (July 1953), 11.

85. Irwin Silber, "Carnegie Hall Rocks as the Weavers Return," *Sing Out!* 6, no. 1 (Winter 1956): 31–32.

86. Silber interview, May 3, 1968.

87. David A. Shannon traces these developments in some detail in *The Decline of American Communism* (Chatham, 1959). An excellent shorter sketch is provided by Robert Claiborne in "Twilight on the Left," *The Nation* (May 11, 1957), 414–18. See also Schrecker, *Many Are the Crimes,* and Irving Howe and Lewis Coser, *The American Communist Party: A Critical History,* 2d ed. (New York: Da Capo, 1974).

88. The two songs were "Birobidjan Lullaby" and "Ch'bin a Bocher a Hultay" by Itzik Feffer and Moyshe Kulbak, respectively, printed in *Sing Out!* 6, no. 3 (Summer 1956): 30–31. The former contained the laudatory reference to Stalin. See the letter to the editor by Morris U. Schappes in *Sing Out!* 6, no. 4 (Winter 1957): 31, accompanied by the complete text.

89. Frank Collier, letter to the editor, *Sing Out!* 8, no. 1 (Spring 1958): 36. The anecdote drawing his fire is given in vol. 7, no. 4 (Winter 1958): 24. The reference to East European student demands for academic freedom appears in vol. 6, no. 4 (Winter 1957): 24.

90. Silber interview, June 26, 1969.

10

The Folk Music Legacy of the American Communist Movement

On November 2, 1956, as Soviet tanks rolled through the streets of Budapest, Pete Seeger addressed an open letter to People's Artists members and supporters announcing the organization's decision to disband. "As you can imagine," he wrote, "this was not easy to decide.

Alan Lomax (Library of Congress Collections)

However, we came to the conclusion that the important function originally served by People's Artists since its inception in 1949 could best be carried forward in new ways." He added accurately—probably missing the irony of his words—"It is a tribute to the ground-breaking work of People's Artists, and its predecessor, People's Songs, that there are today, many groups and individuals carrying forward the job of promoting and popularizing folk music."[1] How different an ending to the four decades of Old Left interest in folk songs and people's culture than that envisioned by the enthusiastic, optimistic radical musicians who participated in the early years of the movement! The Workers Music League, the Almanac Singers, and People's Songs, not to mention People's Artists, defined as their chief task not the popularization of American folk song but the reconstruction of society along classless lines with the help of workers' music rooted in national traditions. "The people are on the march and must have songs to sing," the *People's Songs* bulletin preamble bravely began, while People's Songs dedicated itself to promoting "songs of labor and the American people." In his valedictory statement on behalf of People's Artists, Seeger did not suggest that the latter was People's Artists' chief purpose, either, but he did imply correctly (if unwittingly) that helping stimulate the American folk song revival was a proud result, if not the only result, of the Old Left's interaction with native traditions. Quite a few radical singers went on to successful popular careers in the 1950s and 1960s, including Seeger himself along with the Weavers, Burl Ives, Josh White, Oscar Brand, and Richard Dyer-Bennet. Woody Guthrie and Cisco Houston fared less well in their personal careers, but their recordings became staple listening fare for neophyte folk song fans.

Sing Out! became the major press organ of the folk song revival, soon claiming as many as ten thousand subscribers and many times that number in actual readers. During the heyday of the folk song revival through the mid-1960s, *Sing Out!*'s circulation reached upward of twenty-five thousand readers. In the late 1960s, partly in response to the Vietnam War, Irwin Silber once again attempted to turn *Sing Out!* into a partisan musical journal. A sharp split developed between Silber and most of the editorial board, and a business realignment in 1967 enabled Silber to leave the magazine for other projects. The management of *Sing Out!*'s business affairs by several interim editors proved unsuccessful and the magazine plunged into deep financial trouble along with the collapse of the folk song revival boom market. Like so many cultural institutions, antiwar politics during the Vietnam era eroded *Sing Out!*'s economic and editorial stability.

Besides boosting the popular interest in folk song, the communist movement also left in its wake a tradition of using rural folk materials for agit-prop and political purposes. Not apparent immediately because the declining years of the Old Left—the late 1950s—were notably devoid of much folk-styled topical song activity, the tradition only became clear as the 1960s progressed. During most of the previous decade the great majority of new folk song aficionados, few of whom had any prior affiliations with the radical causes of the 1940s and early 1950s, tended to eschew the "message" lyrics which had comprised the largest single portion of the repertoires of Old Left music groups. Instead, they focused their attention on traditional music content, singing styles, and instrumental accompaniments. Performances were applauded, or not, on the basis of their own intrinsic merits rather than because they represented "people's songs" in any partisan sense.

In at least one instance audience reaction to the politicization of the folk idiom by the Communist movement and its adherents was couched in specific terms. *The Bosses' Songbook* (subtitled "Songs to Stifle the Flames of Discontent," parodying the Wobbly "Little Red Songbook" motto) first appeared in 1958 and was a composite production of several socialist, Trotskyist, and nonpolitically affiliated satirists. Its contents were a mixture of sardonic antiprogressive spoofs, on the order of "Fink's Song," "Bosses Lifeguard," and "Talking Management Blues," and songs lampooning the historic foibles of the Old Left.[2] One pokes fun at the tradition of musical rabble-rousing with particular wickedness: "Ballad of a Party Folk-Singer," was set to the tune of the traditional "Wreck of the Old '97":

> Well, they gave him his orders, up at Party headquarters,
> Saying, "Pete, you're way behind the times.
> This is not '38; this is 1947; there's been a change in that old Party line."
> Well, it's a long, long haul from "Greensleeves" to "Freiheit,"
> And the distance is more than long,
> But that wonderful outfit they call People's Artists
> Is on hand with those good old People's Songs.
> Their material is corny, but their motives are the purest,
> And their spirits will never be broke,
> As they go right on with their great noble crusade
> Of teaching folk songs to the folk.[3]

In the face of such satire and apathy toward topical songs during this period, *Sing Out!*, Pete Seeger, and a few others nourished a weak tradition of making contemporary social comments via the use of rural music mediums. *Sing Out!* instituted a "Folk Process" column beginning with its first quarterly issue,[4] which carried much of the topical verse written in folk style during the next seven years. The topical song output of the late 1950s also was documented in large part by Pete Seeger on Folkways Records, notably in the albums *Love Songs for Friends and Foes* and *Gazette*.[5]

Beginning in the early 1960s, though, the folk-styled message song was once again being revived on the urban scene as the progressive tide of the Kennedy era began to roll forward. Bob Dylan, Phil Ochs, Tom Paxton, Len Chandler, Gil Turner, and a host of other songwriters in northern cities began to compose topical lyrics in the tradition of People's Songs and People's Artists before them. Of the singers emerging as important in the new generation of socially-conscious musicians, only Pete Seeger and Malvina Reynolds had a history of extensive contact with the Old Left. The 1964 presidential election campaign saw popular folk singers publicly endorsing or singing on behalf of Lyndon Johnson, on a scale which had not been seen since the Progressive Party's music-making efforts for Henry Wallace in 1948.[6] The tradition persisted, though on a lesser scale, during the Eugene McCarthy (1968) and George McGovern (1972) campaigns.

In the South, meanwhile, the African American freedom movement quickly produced a host of songs adapting traditional words and melodies, many of them spirituals, reflecting the black struggle for civil rights and economic and social equality. Included in their number were a few old standards taken directly from the left-wing movement of a generation earlier, notably "The Hammer Song," "We Shall Not Be Moved," and "Which Side Are You On," though in some cases the words were revised to fit the new circumstances. And again, the Vietnam War, and even Watergate, spawned their own sets of songs reminiscent of Old Left standards.

There is no doubt that collective efforts to change the status quo—strikes, rallies, demonstrations—typically engender a natural impulse to translate verbal protests into music and song. Although the folk song revival has fragmented since the mid-1960s, and the topical song trend within its context diminished somewhat, the tradition of social commentary in urban music espoused by the communist movement and nurtured thereafter in popular folk song circles persists. Bob Dylan and his followers expanded the focus into rock music beginning in 1965, where it revolutionized popular music's direction and tone. Though the Old Left's political ideology was not apparent in the folk and rock-styled topical music of the 1960s, its sociocultural themes of democratic fair play and the sovereignty of the people were carried through to the newer generations of musicians and their songs.

And what was the communist movement's legacy regarding traditional music and folklore on scholars? What was the impact of the radical ethos of the Depression era and subsequent left-wing thought on the professional work of academic folklorists? In the early years, the 1930s and

1940s, few academics were directly involved in the communist movement. One, Harold Preece, newspaperman and Western folklore specialist, published a letter in *New Masses,* emphatically stating, "As one of the few left-wing folklorists in the country, I am especially interested in any effort to use the folklore tradition for the advancement, rather than the regression, of human culture."[7] Even though few academics were actively involved in the communist movement between 1935 and 1955, there is no doubt that the later publications of John and Alan Lomax,[8] the promotion of folk songs in various social and governmental contexts by Charles Seeger, the folklore treasuries and selected other writings by Benjamin A. Botkin, and John Greenway's *American Folksongs of Protest* all reflect the influence of the Old Left's activities and ideology in the area of native American tradition. Greenway's definition of "folk" in economic terms ("He is the CIO worker, not the AFL worker, who is labor's aristocrat"), though historically, if unintentionally, the best American academic defense of Marxist notions on the class character of folk tradition ironically was met with only lukewarm enthusiasm by People's Artists' partisans.[9]

The work of certain radical writers, especially Lawrence Gellert, Sidney Finkelstein, and Russell Ames, have scholarly value even though they were not spawned in a strictly academic environment. Gellert's collections of African American traditional music have proved invaluable to folklorists and historians; Finkelstein, a newspaperman turned Marxist arts critic, wrote several books stressing the folk roots of fine art; and Ames authored a widely accepted popular history, *The Story of American Folk Song* (New York: Grosset Dunlap, 1960).

In conclusion, what can be said about the American communist experience with folklore? First, the movement's discovery of native traditions by and large was accidental and at first evoked no great positive response from most of its members. Only the shift in the worldview of international communism to an emphasis on collective unity, nationalist spirit, and antifascism in the mid-1930s, coupled with a concurrent domestic interest in regional Americana fostered by the New Deal environment, created the conditions leading to the Old Left's subsequent glorification of folk materials.

Once these developments had occurred, radical intellectuals tended to equate rural folk culture with both the most progressive features and best aesthetic products of the entire American working class. In many cases, folk traditions assumed an ideological significance far beyond anything intrinsically present in the actual lore itself. Folklore now symbolized democracy, equality, social justice, and the class struggle, as did other material created in imitation of folk tradition. Mason Roberson, *People's World* columnist, rhapsodized:

To Lead Belly, folk songs are more than just music. He preaches sermons and makes political speeches in song. "Folk songs," he said, "are democracy. Folk songs are freedom. Folk songs make people come together in unity and peace." During the last several presidential election campaigns he sang some political songs for President Roosevelt—"because Mr. Hoover was going to give Dewey some ideas."

Preempting any challenge to the truth of his assertions, he concluded, "If you've any doubt as to their effect, look at the returns."[10]

Woody Guthrie observed in the *Daily Worker,* "Our best folk song & ballad players and singers are like ball players, the very top crop step up sometimes and fan out." Emphasizing his strong conviction of the power of "people's" music, he added, "The ones that stay closest to the troubles, fights, and ups and downs of the trade union worker are most apt to turn out the best stuff and to have the finest, highest type of an audience. The mother lode of the folk vein is the battle of the trade union worker."[11] Without enunciating their views in so many words, urban left-wingers sought to identify rural folk materials with the long-envisioned American workers' cultural tradition that derived from the national experience yet was neither the product of the native aristocracy nor bourgeois capitalists, and not subject to their crass socioeconomic manipulations.

Almost inevitably the attempt to construct a dynamic "people's" culture based on traditional rural expression sometimes led to the radical romanticization of folklore in the noble savage tradition, which in one form or another dated back to Herder and the Grimms. "There was a feeling," Waldemar Hille commented,

> that everyone had to get to sources—grassroots. The point wasn't to read books or even emulate performances of some like Earl [Robinson] so much as to see, hear, and feel the real beginnings: Negroes on a chain-gang doing a work song . . . , Aunt Molly with her direct participation in songs, strikes, hunger.

Emphasizing the focus on rural rather than urban sources, Hille explained, "Of course we had the . . . industrial labor songs, but . . . we looked to the rural cultural honesty as real examples—call it 'inspiration'—for what could be worked out for the urban rallies [and] meetings."[12] Presaging the folklorists' conclusions, though, Hille remarked, "Of course once some [urban pop-styled] songs were sung and proved successful at union or topical affairs they in turn gained their own validity." He refers primarily to the music of singers belonging to the Lomax tradition, but Hille's comments also typify the character if not the content of many of the broader movement's statements on folklore.

Over time, increasingly divergent styles found their places in the communist movement, chiefly those associated with the European revolutionary chorus and fine-art milieus, on the one hand, and the radical citybilly environment nurtured by the Lomax singers, on the other. In time, though, an umbrella rationale of "people's" art based on folk expression developed, encouraging all varieties of progressive folk-styled expression, and some strains of nontraditional left-wing art, to coexist reasonably well under one philosophical roof.

But aside from questions of style and content, there were other differences separating the Lomax performers and their adherents from other exponents of folk traditions in the Old Left. First, many individuals associated with the Almanac Singers, People's Songs and, to a considerably lesser degree, People's Artists, were essentially unconcerned with theoretical issues. While a broad worldview for their activities indeed was evident, most left-wing musicians concentrated on creative productivity, albeit within a framework of sociopolitical action, rather than on formulating carefully structured programs and theories. Most simply avoided the ideological controversies, ambiguities, and destructive orgies of self-criticism that plagued the movement from time to time. For example, in the entire literature of the radical folk singers of the 1940s and early 1950s, there is hardly a reference to such topics as socialist realism or the Andrei Zhdanov critiques of formalism in postwar Soviet music. Irwin Silber states that People's Songs, taken as a whole, had little or no consciousness of theoretical debates on culture in the international communist movement. Those, for example, who read the speeches of Zhdanov failed to clearly comprehend their arguments or to meaningfully relate them to their own work in People's Songs.[13] It appears, as a matter of fact, that People's Songs was entirely untouched by the turmoil caused in the Soviet Union by the purges and public self-criticism of cultural workers, especially in music, during the late 1940s when Zhdanov was the chief minister of the arts in the USSR.[14]

Instead, as Silber has commented, the activist orientation of People's Songs and similar groups reflected a negative reaction to the bureaucratic strictures of European Marxism. As such, it also exercised a major influence on the direction of subsequent left-wing music movements in England, Australia, Italy, Germany, and elsewhere. Most of these movements borrowed heavily from the song stock, folk style, and agit-prop character of the American radical folk music scene of the postwar period. The English *Sing* and Australian *Singabout,* begun in 1954 and 1956, both were patterned loosely after *Sing Out!* with which they shared a common Old Left ideological orientation.

Similarly, the radical folk singers of the 1940s and early 1950s diverged from a mainstream trend of the Old Left in their relatively firm commitment to a workers' culture that was distinctly separate from bourgeois society and capitalism. Unlike the middle-class movement adherents, who found it difficult if not impossible to resolve the duality of their lifestyles and sociopolitical ideology, such groups as the Almanac Singers, People's Songs, and People's Artists by choice and through historical circumstance managed to isolate themselves from establishment cultural organizations and activities for brief periods. In doing so, they were able to practice as well as preach their "alternative" proletarian existence to a much greater degree than most other contemporary radical artists.

But in the long run, the socially conscious radical singers were unsuccessful in reaching the outside masses with their "songs will help save the world" message. American workers, as it turned out, by and large were uninterested in left-wing ideology once the worst abuses in labor-management relations were eliminated in the course of the CIO's organizing drives. The idiom chosen by the politically committed folk singers in the communist movement proved unfamiliar to the urban proletariat, which, contrary to expectations, made no immediate or strong move to adapt American folk art expression for its aesthetic or agit-prop purposes. Finally, a separate "proletarian" culture based on traditional forms and styles had no practical foundation in reality since workers in the United States on the whole had no strong sense of class identity except during moments of crisis, such as strikes, and then usually only within a given occupational context. Marxist propaganda notwithstanding, ethnic, regional, religious, and bourgeois media influences remained the chief factors shaping most of the cultural expression in the United States. It was not the laboring masses but another generation of young middle-class Americans searching for their sociohistoric roots and spiritual raison d'être who once again took up the Old Left theme that rural traditions had significant philosophical importance for the aesthetic life of urban society.

Walter Lowenfels once observed that defining the relationship between art and politics is an ongoing and never-ending struggle.[15] The unfolding sequence of human events constantly alters society's structural relationships and the variables of its component parts, so that repeated adjustments are necessary, and certain ideas, forms, and styles of expression reflecting their interactions become more apropos of one period than another. In this light, some may view the idealism, naivete, and unrealistic manner with which individuals in the American communist movement sought to promulgate folklore and derivative topical expression for social and political purposes as quaint or curious. Others may perceive their actions as a dangerous and threatening phenomena, or an unwarranted exploitation of the nation's cultural heritage. Still others may regard their attempts as a noble experiment or undertaking. But certainly to see the utilization of folk tradition as an exclusively communist, or a wholly detrimental occurrence, is myopic and ultimately harmful. Irwin Silber's retrospective observation in 1958 captures this truth: "To the extent that Communists at any given point were in tune with mass sentiment on vital issues, they too utilized the political folk song to win popular support." But, Silber cautions,

> to make it appear that the political folk song, even in recent times, is largely a Communist invention is to cast into the shadows one of the most important parts of our folk song heritage. The tradition of the topical song—from Mother Goose to Calypso and from "Yankee Doodle" to "Solidarity Forever" is far too precious to be made the property of any one political trend.

Silber concludes that "the political folk song belongs to all of us—and maybe if more of us exercised our rights in using it and developing it, we would be helping to make America a better place to live."[16]

NOTES

1. Pete Seeger, letter to People's Songs members, November 1956 (mimeographed).

2. Dick Ellington, Dave Van Ronk, et al., eds., *The Bosses Songbook: Songs to Stifle the Flames of Discontent* (New York: Rickard Ellington, 1959). A somewhat similar collection of songs specifically satirizing Communist Party excesses entitled *Ballads for Sectarians* was recorded by Joe Glazer and Bill Friedland for Labor Arts about 1954 and was rereleased in Ronald D. Cohen and Dave Samuelson, *Songs for Political Action: Folk Music, Topical Songs and the American Left, 1926–1953.* Bear Family Records, BCD 15720-JL, 1996, with 212-page book of text and photographs.

3. *The Bosses Songbook,* 2d ed., 12. In the first edition, this was entitled "The Ballad of Pete Seeger."

4. "Folk Process," *Sing Out!* 4, no. 7 (Fall 1954).

5. FA2453 and FN2501 and FN2502, respectively.

6. See the ad in the *New York World-Telegram* and *Sun* for October 18, 1964, promoting a three-hour Johnson/Humphrey Folk Concert featuring Peter, Paul, and Mary, Odetta, Judy Collins, Leon Bibb, Carolyn Hester, and the Clancy Brothers and Tommy Makem.

7. *New Masses* (September 1, 1936), 22.

8. John Lomax, *Our Singing Country* (New York: Macmillan, 1941), and John Lomax, *Folk Songs U.S.A.: The 111 Best American Ballads* (New York: Duell, Sloan & Pearce, 1947) reflect the increasing influences of Alan Lomax.

9. See Irwin Silber's review in *Sing Out!* 3, no. 10 (June 1953): 10–11.

10. *People's World* (March 30, 1945), 5.

11. *Daily Worker* (September 29, 1949), 13.

12. Letter from Waldemar Hille to me, August 1, 1967.

13. Silber interview, June 26, 1969.

14. For material bearing on the "confessions" by Soviet composers of "formalist" trends in their work, see *On Soviet Music* (New York: American Russian Institute, 1948). For Zhdanov's own ideas, see Andrei Aleksandrovich Zhdanov, *Essays on Literature, Philosophy, and Music* (New York: International, 1950).

15. Interview with Walter Lowenfels, June 29, 1969.

16. Irwin Silber, "Politics and Folk Music," *Caravan* 10 (May 1958): 10–11.

Sources

INTERVIEWS

Moses Asch	April 1964
Mordecai Bauman	March 10, 1968
Robert Black	June 1963
Benjamin A. Botkin	March 7, 1968; June, 1969
Earl Browder	February 12, 1968
Leo Christensen	(interviewed by Archie Green) September 1, 1958
Gordon Friesen	April 6 and July 28, 1965; with Agnes (Sis Cunningham) Friesen: September 7 and December 28, 1965; February 9, 1968
Irving and Kathleen Fromer	July 12, 1967
Will Geer	December 28, 1966
Lawrence Gellert:	August 31, 1966 (taped); March 27 and May 7, 1968 (both taped); June 25 and September 11, 1969 (both taped)
Ralph J. Gleason	July 2, 1967
Kenneth S. Goldstein	July 20, 1970 (phone)
Sarah Ogan Gunning	September, 1968
Wayland D. Hand	July 18, 1967
Baldwin Hawes	July 21, 1967; with Bess Lomax Hawes: December 4, 1967
Lee Hays	August 16, 1965
Waldemar Hille	July 21 and 25, 1967
Sam Hinton	July 2, 1967
Helen Hosmer	July 10, 1967
Millard Lampell	March 30, 1967

Alan Lomax	August 29, 1966; May 28, 1968; January 28, 1971 (phone)
Walter Lowenfels	June 29, 1969 (taped)
Albert Maltz	July 17, 1967
Max Margulis	March 12 and 15, 1968
Margot Mayo	August 29, 1966
Norman Pierce	July 8, 1967
Charles Polacheck	July 19, 1967
Malvina and Bud Reynolds	July 11, 1967
Al Richmond	July 10, 1967
Edward Robbin	July 5 and 11, 1967
Earl Robinson	December, 1967
Charles Seeger	June 8 (taped); November 3 and 6, 1967
Peter Seeger	April 9, 1968 (taped)
Elie Siegmeister	February 24 and March 16, 1968
Irwin Silber	November 19, 1966; February 29, March (taped), April 2 (taped), and May 3 (taped), 1968; June 26, 1969 (taped)
Arthur Stern	December 28, 1965
D. K. Wilgus	July 18, 1967
William Wolff	July 23 and November (n.d.), 1967

BIBLIOGRAPHY

Aaron, Daniel. *Writers on the Left*: *Episodes in American Literary Communism.* New York: Harcourt, Brace & World, 1961.

Adler, Selig. *The Isolationist Impulse: Its Twentieth-Century Reaction.* New York: Free Press, 1966.

Ames, Russell. *The Story of American Folk Song.* New York: Grosset & Dunlap, 1960.

Beck, Horace P., ed. *Folklore in Action: Essays for Discussion in Honor of MacEdward Leach.* New York: Kaaus Reprint, 1970.

Belfrage, Cedric. *A Faith to Free the People.* New York: Dryden, 1944.

Benedict, Ruth. *Race: Science and Politics.* New York: Viking, 1959.

Bernstein, Irving. *The Lean Years: A History of the American Worker.* Boston: Houghton Mifflin, 1960.

Bluestein, Gene. *The Voice of the Folk: Folklore and American Literary Theory.* Amherst: University of Massachusetts Press, 1972.

Botkin, B. A., ed. *Folk-Say: A Regional Miscellany.* Norman: Oklahoma Folk-lore Society, 1932.

———, ed. *Lay My Burden Down: A Folk History of Slavery.* Chicago: University of Chicago Press, 1968.

———, ed. *Treasury of American Folklore: Stories, Ballads, and Traditions of the People.* New York: Crown, 1944.

Brand, Oscar. *The Ballad Mongers: Rise of the Modern Folk Song.* New York: Funk & Wagnalls, 1962.

Brown, Michael E., et al. *New Studies in the Politics and Culture of U.S. Communism.* New York: Monthly Review Press, 1993.

Burkhart, James. *Writers and Partisans: A History of Literary Radicalism in America.* New York: Wiley, 1968.

Cantwell, Robert. *When We Were Good: The Folk Revival.* Cambridge, Mass.: Harvard University Press, 1996.

Chaplin, Ralph. *Wobbly: The Rough and Tumble Story of an American Radical.* Chicago: University of Chicago Press, 1948.

Charney, George. *A Long Journey.* Chicago: Quadrangle, 1968.

Coffin, Tristram P., ed. *Our Living Traditions: An Introduction to American Folklore.* New York: Basic Books, 1968.

Cohen, Robby. *When the Old Left Was Young: Student Radicals and America's First Mass Student Movement, 1929–1941.* New York: Oxford University Press, 1993.

Cohen, Ronald D. *Rainbow Quest: Folk Music and American Society, 1940–1970* (forthcoming).

———, ed. *"Wasn't That a Time!" Firsthand Accounts of the Folk Music Revival.* Metuchen, N.J.: Scarecrow, 1995.

Cohen, Ronald D., and Dave Samuelson. *Songs for Political Action: Folk Music, Topical Songs and the American Left, 1926–1953.* Bear Family Records, BCD 15720-JL, 1996, with 212-page book of text and photographs.

Conforth, Bruce Harrah. "Laughing Just to Keep from Crying: Afro-American Folksong and the Field Recordings of Lawrence Gellert." Unpublished master's thesis, Indiana University, Bloomington, 1984.

Cross, Wilbur L. *The Development of the English Novel.* New York: Macmillan, 1942.

Cunard, Nancy, ed. *Negro: An Anthology.* New York: Negro Universities Press, 1969. Reprint.

Cunningham, Agnes "Sis," and Gordon Freisen. *Red Dust and Broadsides: A Joint Autobiography,* ed. Ronald D. Cohen. Amherst: University of Massachusetts Press, 1999.

Darling, Charles. *The New American Songster.* Lanham, Md.: University Press of America, 1983.

Denisoff, R. Serge. *Great Day Coming: Folk Music and the American Left.* Urbana: University of Illinois Press, 1971.

Denning, Michael. *The Cultural Front: The Laboring of American Culture in the Twentieth Century* New York: Verso, 1996.

Dennis, Peggy. *Autobiography of an American Communist: A Personal View of a Political Life, 1925–1975.* Westport, Conn.: Hill, 1977.

DeTurk, David A., and A. Poulin Jr., eds. *The American Folk Scene: Dimensions of the Folksong Revival.* New York: Dell, 1967.

Deutscher, Isaac. *The Prophet Armed: Trotsky, 1879–1921.* New York: Oxford University Press, 1970.

———. *The Prophet Outcast: Trotsky, 1929–1940.* New York: Oxford University Press, 1963.

———. *The Prophet Unarmed: Trotsky, 1921–1929.* New York: Oxford University Press, 1980.

Dorson, Richard M. *American Folklore.* Chicago: University of Chicago Press, 1977.

———. *Buying the Wind.* Chicago: University of Chicago Press, 1964.

Draper, Theodore. *American Communism and Soviet Russia*. New York: Viking, 1960.

———. *The Roots of American Communism.* New York: Viking, 1957.

Dreiser, Theodore, ed. *Harlan Miners Speak.* New York: Da Capo, 1970.

Duberman, Martin B. *Paul Robeson.* New York: Knopf, 1988.

Dunaway, David K. *How Can I Keep From Singing: Pete Seeger.* New York: McGraw-Hill, 1981.

Dundes, Alan. *The Study of Folklore.* Upper Saddle River, N.J.: Prentice Hall, 1965.

Dunson, Josh. *Freedom in the Air: Song Movements of the Sixties.* New York: International, 1965.

Eastman, Max. *Artists in Uniform: A Study of Literature and Bureaucratism.* New York: Knopf, 1934.

Egbert, Donald, and Stow Persons, eds. *Socialism and American Life.* Princeton, N.J.: Princeton University Press, 1952.

Erenberg, Lewis, and Susan E. Hirsch, *The War in American Culture: Society and Consciousness during World War II.* Chicago: University of Chicago Press, 1996.

Ewen, David. *All the Years of American Popular Music.* Upper Saddle River, N.J.: Prentice Hall, 1977.

Fast, Howard. *Peekskill USA: A Personal Experience.* New York: Civil Rights Congress, 1951.

Faulk, John Henry. *Fear on Trial.* Austin: University of Texas Press, 1983.

Finkelstein, Sidney W. *Art and Society.* New York: International, 1947.

———. *Composer and Nation: The Folk Heritage in Music.* 2d ed. New York: International, 1989.

———. *How Music Expresses Ideas.* Rev. ed. New York: International, 1970.

———. *Jazz: A People's Music.* New York: Da Capo, 1975.

Fischer, Louis. *The Life of Lenin.* New York: Harper & Row, 1964.

Flynn, Elizabeth Gurley. *I Speak My Own Piece: Autobiography of the "Rebel Girl."* New York: Masses & Mainstream, 1955.

Foner, Philip S. *American Labor Songs of the Nineteenth Century.* Urbana: University of Illinois Press, 1975.

Foner, Philip S., and Herbert Shapiro, eds. *American Communism and Black Americans: A Documentary History, 1930–1934.* Philadelphia: Temple University Press, 1991.

Ford, Hugh E. comp. *Nancy Cunard: Brave Poet, Indomitable Rebel, 1896–1965.* Philadelphia: Chilton, 1968.

Garland, Jim. *Welcome the Traveler Home: Jim Garland's Story of the Kentucky Mountains,* ed. Julia Ardery. Lexington: University Press of Kentucky, 1983.

Gates, John. *The Story of an American Communist.* New York: Nelson, 1958.

Glazer, Nathan. *The Social Basis of American Communism.* New York: Harcourt, Brace, 1961.

Glen, John. *Highlander, No Ordinary School, 1932–1962.* Lexington: University of Kentucky Press, 1988; updated and reissued: Knoxville: University of Tennessee Press, 1996.

Gold, Michael. *The Hollow Men.* New York: International, 1941.

Goldman, Eric F. *The Crucial Decade—and After: America, 1945–1960.* New York: Knopf, 1960.

Goldsmith, Peter D. *Making People's Music: Moe Asch and Folkways Records.* Washington, D.C.: Smithsonian Institution Press, 1998.

Gordon, Eric. *Mark the Music: The Life and Work of Marc Blitzstein.* New York: St. Martin's, 1989.

Gornick, Vivian. *The Romance of American Communism.* New York: Basic Books, 1977.

Graff, Ellen. *Stepping Left: Dance and Politics, New York City, 1928–1942.* Durham, N.C.: Duke University Press, 1997.

Green, Archie. *Only a Miner: Studies in Recorded Coal-Mining Songs.* Urbana: University of Illinois Press, 1972.

———, ed. *Songs about Work: Essays in Occupational Culture.* Bloomington, Ind.: Folklore Institute, 1993.

———. *Wobblies, Pile Butts, and Other Heroes: Laborlore Explorations.* Urbana: University of Illinois Press, 1993.

Green, James. *Grass-Roots Socialism: Radical Movements in the Southwest, 1895–1943.* Baton Rouge: Louisiana State University Press, 1978.

Greene, Victor. *A Passion for Polka: Old-Time Ethnic Music in America.* Berkeley: University of California Press, 1992.

Greenway, John. *American Folksongs of Protest.* New York: Barnes, 1960.

Guthrie, Woody. *Born to Win.* New York: Macmillan, 1965.

———. *Bound for Glory.* New York: Dutton, 1943.

———. *Pastures of Plenty: A Self-Portrait,* ed. Dave March and Harold Levanthal. New York: HarperCollins, 1990.

Hammond, John. *John Hammond on Record: An Autobiography.* New York: Ridge, 1977.

Hart, Henry, ed. *American Writers' Congress.* New York: International, 1935.

———. *The Writer in a Changing World.* New York: Equinox Cooperative, 1937.

Haywood, Harry. *Black Bolshevik: Autobiography of an Afro-American Communist.* Chicago: Liberator, 1978.

Herskovits, Melville J. *The Myth of the Negro Past.* Boston: Beacon, 1990.

Hicks, Granville, et al., eds. *Proletarian Literature in the United States.* New York: International, 1936.

Hicks, John D. *The Populist Revolt: A History of the Farmers' Alliance and the People's Party.* Lincoln: University of Nebraska Press, 1961.

Himmelstein, Morgan Y. *Drama Was a Weapon.* New Brunswick, N.J.: Rutgers University Press, 1963.

Howe, Irving. *Echoes of Revolt.* Chicago: Quadrangle, 1966.

Howe, Irving, and Lewis Coser. *The American Communist Party: A Critical History.* 2d ed. New York: Da Capo, 1974.

Isserman, Maurice. *Which Side Were You On? The American Communist Party during the Second World War.* Middletown, Conn.: Wesleyan University Press, 1982.

Ives, Burl. *Wayfaring Stranger.* Indianapolis: Bobbs-Merrill, 1962.

Jackson, Bruce, ed. *Folklore and Society: Essays in Honor of Benj. A. Botkin.* Hatboro, Pa.: Folklore Associates, 1966.

Katulas, Judy. *The Long War: The Intellectual People's Front and Anti-Stalinism, 1930–1940.* Durham, N.C.: Duke University Press, 1995.

Klehr, Harvey. *The Heyday of American Communism: The Depression Decade.* New York: Basic Books, 1984.

Klehr, Harvey, and John Earl Haynes. *American Communist Movement: Storming Heaven Itself.* New York: Twayne, 1992.

Klehr, Harvey, John E. Haynes, and Kyrill M. Anderson. *The Soviet World of American Communism.* New Haven, Conn.: Yale University Press, 1998.

Klein, Joe. *Woody Guthrie: A Life.* New York: Knopf, 1980.

Kornbluh, Joyce L., ed. *Rebel Voices: An I.W.W. Anthology.* Chicago: Kerr, 1998.

Korson, George. *Coal Dust on the Fiddle: Songs and Stories of the Bituminous Industry.* Hatboro, Pa.: Folkore Associates, 1965.

———. *Minstrels of the Mine Patch: Songs and Stories of the Anthracite Miners.* Philadelphia: University of Pennsylvania Press, 1938.

Lasswell, Harold D., and Dorothy Blumenstock. *World Revolutionary Propaganda.* New York: Knopf, 1939.

Lawless, Ray M. *Folksongs and Folksingers of North America.* Rev. ed. New York: Duell, Sloan & Pearce, 1965.

Leach, MacEdward, and Tristram P. Coffin, eds. *The Critics and the Ballad.* Carbondale: Southern Illinois University Press, 1961.

Lenin, Vladimir I. *On Culture and Cultural Revolution.* Moscow: Progress, 1970.

Leuchtenburg, William E. *Franklin D. Roosevelt and the New Deal, 1932–1940.* New York Harper & Row, 1963.

———. *The Perils of Prosperity: 1914–32.* 2d ed. Chicago: University of Chicago Press, 1993.

Levin, Dan. *Stormy Petrel: The Life and Work of Maxim Gorky.* New York: Schocken, 1986.

Lewy, Guenther. *The Cause That Failed: Communism in American Political Life.* New York: Oxford University Press, 1990.

Lieberman, Robbie. *"My Song Is My Weapon": People's Songs, American Communism, and the Politics of Culture, 1930–1950.* Urbana: University of Illinois Press, 1989.

Lomax, Alan, Pete Seeger, and Woody Guthrie, comps. *Hard Hitting Songs for Hard-Hit People: American Folk Songs of the Depression and the Labor Movement of the 1930s.* New York: Oak, 1967.

Lomax, John A. *Adventures of a Ballad Hunter.* New York: Macmillan, 1947 .

Lumpkin, Grace. *To Make My Bread.* Urbana: University of Illinois Press, 1995.

MacDougall, Curtis D. *Gideon's Army.* New York: Marzani & Munsell, 1965.

Mao, Tse-Tung. *Art and Literature.* New York: Naeoruam Khru Kaona, 1975.

Marx , Karl, and Friedrich Engels. *Literature and Art: Selections from Their Writings.* New York: International, 1947.

Matusow, Harvey. *False Witness.* New York: Cameron & Kahn, 1955 .

Murray, Robert K. *Red Scare: A Study in National Hysteria, 1919–1920.* New York: McGraw-Hill, 1955.

Naison, Mark. *Communists in Harlem during the Depression.* Urbana: University of Illinois Press, 1983.

Nettl, Bruno. *Folk Music in the United States: An Introduction.* 3d ed. Detroit, Mich.: Wayne State University Press, 1976.

Noebel, David A. *Communism, Hypnotism and the Beatles.* Tulsa, Okla.: Christian Crusade Publications, 1965.

———. *The Marxist Minstrels: A Handbook on Communist Subversion of Music.* Tulsa, Okla.: American Christian College Press, 1974.

———. *Rhythm, Riots and Revolution.* Tulsa, Okla.: Christian Crusade Publications, 1966.

Norton, Sally Osborne. "A Historical Study of Actor Will Geer, His Life and Work in the Context of Twentieth-Century American Social, Political, and Theatrical History." Unpublished doctoral dissertation, 2 vols., University of Southern California, Los Angeles, 1980.

Noyes, John Humphrey. *History of American Socialisms.* Philadelphia: Lippincott, 1870.

Ofari, Earl (Hutchinson). *Blacks and Reds: Race and Class Conflict, 1919–1990.* East Lansing: Michigan State University Press, 1995.

Ottanelli, Fraser M. *The Communist Party of the United States: From the Depression to World War II.* New Brunswick, N.J.: Rutgers University Press, 1991.

Pescatello, Ann M. *Charles Seeger: A Life in American Music.* Pittsburgh: University of Pittsburgh Press, 1992.

Plekhanov, George V. *Art and Society.* New York: Critics Group, 1936.

Pope, Liston. *Millhands and Preachers: A Study of Gastonia.* New Haven, Conn.: Yale University Press, 1965.

Porterfield, Nolan. *Last Cavalier: The Life and Times of John A. Lomax, 1867–1948.* Urbana: University of Illinois Press, 1996.

Rabkin, Gerald. *Drama and Commitment: Politics in the American Theatre of the Thirties.* Bloomington: Indiana University Press, 1964.

Renshaw, Patrick. *The Wobblies: The Story of Syndicalism in the United States.* Garden City, N.Y.: Doubleday, 1967.

Reuss, Richard A. *A Woody Guthrie Bibliography.* New York: Woody Guthrie Foundation, 1968.

Rideout, Walter B. *The Radical Novel In the United States, 1900–1954.* Cambridge, Mass.: Harvard University Press, 1956.

Robeson, Paul. *Here I Stand.* Boston: Beacon, 1988.

Robinson, Earl, with Eric A. Gordon. *Ballad of an American: The Autobiography of Earl Robinson.* Lanham, Md.: Scarecrow, 1997.

Romalis, Shelly. *Pistol Packin' Mama: The Cultural Politics of Aunt Molly Jackson.* Urbana: University of Illinois Press, 1998.

Roszak, Theodore. *The Making of a Counter Culture.* Garden City, N.Y.: Doubleday, 1969.

Schrecker, Ellen. *Many Are the Crimes: McCarthyism in America.* Boston: Little, Brown, 1998.

Seeger, Pete. *The Incompleat Folksinger.* New York: Simon & Schuster, 1972.

———. *Where Have All the Flowers Gone: A Singer's Stories, Songs, Seeds, Robberies,* ed. Peter Blood. Bethlehem, Pa.: Sing Out!, 1993.

Seeger, Pete, and Bob Reiser, comps. *Carry It On! A History in Song and Picture of the Working Men and Women of America.* New York: Simon & Schuster, 1985.

Shannon, David. *The Decline of American Communism.* Chatham, N.J.: Chatham Bookseller, 1971.

Shelton, Robert. *The Josh White Song Book*. Chicago: Quadrangle, 1963 .

Siegel, Dorothy S. *The Glory Road: The Story of Josh White*. White Hall, Va.: Shoe Tree, 1991.

Siegmeister, Elie. *Music and Society*. New York: Haskell House, 1974.

Slonimsky, Nicholas. *Music since 1900*. 5th ed. New York: Schirmer, 1994.

Sokolov, Y. M.. *Russian Folklore*. Hatboro, Pa.: Folklore Associates, 1966.

Solomon, Mark. *Red and Black: Communism and Afro-Americans, 1929–1935*. New York: Garland, 1988.

Stambler, Irwin, and Grelun Landon. *Encyclopedia of Folk, Country, and Western Music*. 2d ed. New York: St. Martin's, 1969.

Starobin, Joseph R. *American Communism in Crisis 1943–1957*. Cambridge, Mass.: Harvard University Press, 1972.

Stavis, Barrie. *The Man Who Never Died: A Play about Joe Hill*. New York: Haven, 1954.

Stewart, Donald Ogden, ed. *Fighting Words*. New York: Harcourt, Brace, 1940.

Stowe, David. *Swing Changes: Big-Band Jazz in New Deal America*. Cambridge, Mass.: Harvard University Press, 1994.

Swanberg, W. A. *Dreiser*. New York: Scribner, 1965.

Thomas, Hugh. *The Spanish Civil War*. New York: Harper 1961.

Thompson, Fred. *The I.W.W.: Its First Seventy Years, 1905–1975*. Chicago: Industrial Workers of the World, 1955.

Tick, Judith. *Ruth Crawford Seeger: A Composer's Search for American Music*. New York: Oxford University Press, 1997.

Tippett, Tom W. *Southern Labor Stirs*. New York: Cape & Smith, 1931.

Weinstein, James. *Ambiguous Legacy: The Left in American Politics*. New York: New Viewpoints, 1975.

Weinstein, James, and David Eakins, comps. *For a New America: Essays in History and Politics from Studies on the Left, 1959–1967*. New York: Random House, 1970.

———. *The Grand Illusion: The Communist Party and Trade Unionism*. Somerville, Mass.: New England Free Press, 1975.

Wilgus, D. K. *Anglo-American Folksong Scholarship since 1898*. New Brunswick, N.J.: Rutgers University Press, 1959.

Willens, Doris. *Lonesome Traveler: The Life of Lee Hays*. New York: Norton, 1988.

Williams, Henry. *Black Response to the American Left, 1917–1929*. Princeton, N.J.: Princeton University Press, 1973.

Williams, Jay. *Stage Left*. New York: Scribners, 1974.

Williams, Raymond. *Marxism and Literature*. New York: Oxford University Press, 1977.

Wish, Harvey. *Contemporary America*. 4th ed. New York: Harper & Row, 1966.

Wolfe, Charles, and Kip Lornell. *The Life and Legend of Leadbelly*. New York: HarperCollins, 1992.

Yurchenco, Henrietta. *A Mighty Hard Road*. New York: McGraw-Hill, 1970.

Zuck, Barbara. *A History of Musical Americanism*. Ann Arbor, Mich.: UMI Research Press, 1980.

Index

283

Flynn, Elizabeth Gurley, 34, 71, 153
folk culture: government interest in, 16–17; idealization of, 19; propaganda value, 16, 21, 30–31, 140; widespread interest in, 70, 75–76
folk idiom: and American communist movement, 36, 40, 43–44, 53, 57, 66–77, 116, 130–40; idealization by Old Left, 269–70; in Popular Front ideology, 116, 117; in proletarian music, 31–32; Soviet attitude toward, 59, 62; as tactical weapon, 16, 21, 30–31, 140; urban proletariat reaction, 52–53, 64, 70, 74, 89–90, 93, 107, 109, 197–98, 272; for war songs, 180–83; widespread interest in, 70, 75–76
folklore: and American communist movement, 36, 40, 43–44, 53, 57, 66–77, 116, 130–40; in American culture, 34–35; communist theories of, 62–64; defined, 19–20; Marxism on, 25–36; as propaganda vehicle, 16, 21, 30–31, 140
Folk Music Club, 207–9
folk music *versus* art music, 5–6, 59, 121, 213–14, 232, 244
Folksay (American Youth for Democracy), 25, 184, 223, 228, 240
folk song revival (1960s), 5, 38n24, 99, 140, 229, 258, 266
folk songs: in American culture, 34–35; commercial exploitation, 242; defined, 20; gender discrimination in, 238; in Popular Front ideology, 116, 117; as proletarian music, 40, 47–49, 52–53; as a propaganda tool, 20–23; singability, 82
Folkways Records, 4, 135, 245, 258, 268
Foner, Philip, 8, 20
Food and Tobacco Workers, 103
Ford, Henry, 35

Ford, James, 98
Forsythe, Robert, 132
Foster, William Z.: leads Communist Party (USA), 185–86, 210, 256–57, 259; urges racial moderation, 239
Fowler, Gene, 131
Foye, Hope, 227, 239, 240, 245, 261n58
Frank, Lew, 199
Frank, Richard, 93, 94, 110
Frankfurter, Felix, 152
Freiheit Gesang Ferein, 41, 42, 67
French, Bryant, 192, 199
Friesen, Gordon, 100, 155, 171, 172, 174
Fulbright, J. William, 18
Fur and Leather Workers, 197

Gailmor, William, 205
Garland, Jim, 89–91, 125
Gastonia textile strike, 71, 83–86, 111n8
Gates, John, 256, 259
Geer, Will, 76, 107, 126, 129, 183
Gellert, Hugo, 96
Gellert, Lawrence: background, 96; collects African American music, 52, 96, 269; *Negro Songs of Protest*, 72, 95–98, 118, 134, 136; relationship to International Music Buro, 65–67
gender discrimination: and American communist movement, 237; in folk songs, 238
George, Harrison, 137
Gibson, Jackie, 182
Gilbert, Ronnie, 233
Glaser, Ray, 201
Glassie, Henry, 10
Glazer, Joe, 7
Glazer, Tom: in McCarthy era, 251; People's Songs involvement, 187, 204; popularity, 223; in Priority Rambers, 182; recordings, 119, 183; song writing, 238, 245–46

About the Authors

Richard A. Reuss came to folklore studies by way of his interest in music. He led a folk-singing group while a counselor at summer camp and as an undergraduate student at Ohio Wesleyan University. He pursued his interest in history and folklore throughout his academic career, earning a Ph.D. from Indiana University in 1971 and publishing several articles in the following ten years. He studied the roots of American folk music and left-wing politics by interviewing dozens of people who had been participants in the movement and by immersing himself in institutions, including a stint working at *Sing Out!* He taught at Wayne State University in Detroit, where his research interests broadened to include labor lore and music. Even when his career focus changed from academia to social work, he continued to teach and publish and was exceptionally pleased to accept a position as shop steward when the staff of his social services agency unionized. He was almost finished preparing this book for publication at his untimely death in 1986.

Joanne C. Reuss studied folklore with Ellen Steckert as an undergraduate student at Wayne State University. From Steckert she learned much about the field of folklore as her student assistant for three years. She pursued a career in public health and social work, concentrating her efforts on technical writing and clinical practice. She is currently a research administrator at the University of Michigan and a freelance writer.